KEY CONCEPTS IN RENAISSANCE LITE...

University Centre at

Palgrave Key Concepts

Palgrave Key Concepts provide an accessible and comprehensive range of subject glossaries at undergraduate level. They are the ideal companion to a standard textbook making them invaluable reading to students throughout their course of study and especially useful as a revision aid.

Accounting and Finance
Business and Management
  Research Methods
Business Practice
Criminology and Criminal Justice
Cultural Studies
Drama and Performance (2nd edn)
e-Commerce
Human Resource Management
Information and Communication
  Technology
Innovation
International Business

Law (2nd edn)
Leisure
Management
Marketing
Operations Management
Philosophy
Politics
Psychology
Public Relations
Social Research Methods
Sociology
Strategic Management
Tourism

Palgrave Key Concepts: Literature
General Editor: Martin Coyle

Contemporary Literature
Creative Writing
Crime Fiction
Literary Terms and Criticism (3rd edn)
Medieval Literature
Modernist Literature
Postcolonial Literature
Renaissance Literature
Romantic Literature
Victorian Literature

Palgrave Key Concepts: Language and Linguistics

Bilingualism
Language and Linguistics (2nd edn)
Phonetics and Phonology
Second Language Acquisition

Further titles are in preparation
www.palgravekeyconcepts.com

Palgrave Key Concepts
Series Standing Order
ISBN 1–4039–3210–7

(outside North America only)

You can receive future titles in this series as they are published by placing a standing order. Please contact your bookseller or, in the case of difficulty, write to us at the address below with your name and address, the title of the series and the ISBN quoted above.

Customer Services Department, Macmillan Distribution Ltd
Houndmills, Basingstoke, Hampshire RG21 6XS, England

Key Concepts in
Renaissance Literature

Malcolm Hebron

First published 2008 by
PALGRAVE MACMILLAN
Houndmills, Basingstoke, Hampshire RG21 6XS and
175 Fifth Avenue, New York, N.Y. 10010
Companies and representatives throughout the world

PALGRAVE MACMILLAN is the global academic imprint of the Palgrave
Macmillan division of St. Martin's Press, LLC and of Palgrave Macmillan Ltd.
Macmillan® is a registered trademark in the United States, United Kingdom
and other countries. Palgrave is a registered trademark in the European
Union and other countries.

ISBN-13: 978–0–230–50767–8
ISBN-10: 0–230–50767–0

This book is printed on paper suitable for recycling and made from fully
managed and sustained forest sources. Logging, pulping and manufacturing
processes are expected to conform to the environmental regulations of the
country of origin.

A catalogue record for this book is available from the British Library.

A catalog record for this book is available from the Library of Congress.

Contents

Acknowledgements

I am grateful to the Headmaster of Winchester College for granting me a period of reduced teaching to work on this book and to my English Department colleagues for making this leave possible by generously taking on extra classes. The Vacation Programme for Teachers run by Jesus College, Oxford, greatly assisted the early stages of research. At Palgrave Macmillan, Suzannah Burywood and Karen Griffiths have smoothly shepherded the book through the production process, while the series editors and an anonymous reader have provided helpful reports on the work at various stages. Needless to say, any errors that remain are my own responsibility.

General Editors' Preface

The purpose of Palgrave Key Concepts in Literature is to provide students with key critical and historical ideas about the texts they are studying as part of their literature courses. These ideas include information about the historical and cultural contexts of literature as well as the theoretical approaches in the subject today. Behind the series lies a recognition of the need nowadays for students to be familiar with a range of concepts and contextual material to inform their reading and writing about literature.

But behind the series there also lies a recognition of the changes that have transformed degree courses in Literature in recent years. Central to these changes has been the impact of critical theory together with a renewed interest in the way in which texts intersect with their immediate context and historical circumstances. The result has been an opening up of new ways of reading texts and a new understanding of what the study of literature involves together with the introduction of a wide set of new critical issues that demand our attention. An important aim of Palgrave Key Concepts in Literature is to provide brief, accessible introductions to these new ways of reading and new issues.

Each volume in Palgrave Key Concepts in Literature follows the same structure. An initial overview essay is followed by three sections – Contexts, Texts and Criticism – each containing a sequence of brief alphabetically arranged entries on a sequence of topics. Contexts essays provide an impression of the historical, social and cultural environment in which literary texts were produced. Texts essays, as might be expected, focus more directly on the works themselves. Criticism essays then outline the manner in which changes and developments in criticism have affected the ways in which we discuss the texts featured in the volume. The informing intention throughout is to help the reader create something new in the process of combining context, text and criticism.

John Peck
Martin Coyle

General Introduction

'Renaissance' means rebirth. In history books, the term usually denotes the four centuries between about 1300 and 1700: over this period, classical ideas were revived in scholarship and culture, and a number of momentous events in the spheres of religion and politics profoundly affected European consciousness. This period is in turn divided into two broad phases: in the first two centuries (the Early and High Renaissance) the movement was mainly contained within Italy; and from about 1500, Renaissance ideas crossed the Alps, bringing about 'The Northern Renaissance' including in England.

Books on the English Renaissance usually cover nearly two centuries of writing (1500–1660). A flourishing of Renaissance ideas occurred especially in the Elizabethan (1558–1603) and Jacobean periods (1603–1625). For some, it is the last phase, covering the Caroline Age (1625–1649) and the Commonwealth (1649–1660), which sees the fulfilment of the Renaissance movement, particularly in the writings of John Milton.

The validity of the term 'Renaissance', used to describe both a cultural movement and a time period, has been much debated. Some distinguished writers have declined to use the word at all, seeing it as too broad in its application to have any usefully specific meaning. But before we discuss this subject, let us look at a particular text and see what it can tell us about the time we label 'The Renaissance'.

The following lines come from the nineteenth elegy of John Donne (1572–1631), 'To His Mistress Going to Bed', probably written in the 1590s. In it, a lascivious male speaker describes his mistress undressing for bed, and then joins her there himself:

Licence my roaving hands, and let them go, [roving
Before, behind, between, above, below,
O my America! My new-found land,
My kingdome, safeliest when with one man man'd. [ruled
My myne of precious stones: My Emperie, [emperor's land
How blest am I in thus discovering thee?
To enter in these bonds, is to be free;
Then where my hand is set, my seal shall be.

(lines 25–32)

In these lines we can immediately find much to engage us. To begin with, we can admire the poet's skilful use of language: his deft handling of iambic metre and rhyming couplets (with the concluding quadruple rhyme); the witty wordplay ('My myne'), and the modulation of tone from rapturous adoration ('O my America') to decisive affirmation ('my seal shall be'). We also note that the poet draws on language from several fields to express the speaker's thoughts: besides the extended imagery (a conceit) of colonial discovery there is an approving reference to government by a single ruler ('with one man man'd'); and in the last two lines, the poet employs legal terminology in allusions to the bonds, rituals ('where my hand is set') and seal of the contract of marriage. The exclamatory language, the colourful and varied images and shifting rhythms all evoke the man's excitement at taking sexual possession of his mistress. She, by contrast, is silent. The man is a conqueror, and the woman is a newfound continent, existing – in the mind of the speaker – in order to be ruled, exploited (like a goldmine) and owned (signified by 'my seal') by the male; yet at the same time she is rather forbidding, a whole perilous continent, a hard mine of stones.

This use of language introduces us to some key elements of Renaissance culture. One of these is Rhetoric – the mastery of patterns in language for persuasive effect. Here the rhetoric seems ostentatious: the poet shows off his virtuosic handling of ideas, his clever puns and use of rhetorical figures. We recognise the paradox of line 31; and trained Renaissance readers would have seen in 'man man'd' an example of the figure *traductio*, in which a word is played on in different parts of speech (here, noun and verb). Through such skilful manipulation, the speaker's sexual triumph is mirrored in the poet's triumph over language.

Rhetoric in turn suggests something about the wider taste of the age. The word 'artificial' for us usually has a pejorative sense. But in the Elizabethan and Jacobean periods it was a term of praise: it was used to applaud artistic skill, the craftsman's mastery of techniques and materials. We can see this quality of artful contrivance – equivalents to literary rhetoric – in many Renaissance artefacts, from miniature paintings to intricate polyphonic music. In the late sixteenth and early seventeenth century, this cleverness often involves startling mental pictures. An example in our poem is the use of surprising analogy. Small is compared with big: the woman's body is like a continent, the husband is like a King. Another pleasant surprise is the way that unlike things are yoked together in unexpected comparisons: the woman's soft body, as we have noted, is like a mine of hard stones.

The poem's imagery is thus an illustration of Renaissance rhetoric and virtuosity. It also leads us into some major themes of Renaissance history. The lines we are investigating allude to the discovery of the New World, following Columbus's voyage in 1492, and the subsequent colonisation by European powers of these new-found lands. In Donne's lines we can see some of the reactions to this episode: a sense of the marvellous ('O my America!') with a strong possessiveness ('O *my* America!'). The 'manning' of the woman reflects the brutal European exploitation of resources and enslavement of native populations, then just beginning. In this context, though, we need to remind ourselves that England at this time had no colonies to speak of: the lines express the *hope* for conquest – of territory and the woman's body – rather than the gloating voice of an established imperial power.

Colonialism led to competition between the European powers, or rather envy of the leading power, Spain. There is perhaps a more subtle reference to this here. 'Licence', the first word in our passage, means 'Allow'. But it could also refer to the licence, or permission, which Queen Elizabeth I (*r.*1558–1603) gave to men like Sir Francis Drake (*c.*1540–1596) and Sir Walter Raleigh (1552–1618) to plunder Spanish ships. If we follow this sense, then the lover's roving hands suggest the predatory ships of English privateers, roaming the ocean 'Before, behind, between, above, below'. Conquest of new lands is thus mixed with conflict between the powers of the old world, and there is an undertone of violent conquest in the lines of the poem. More straightforwardly, beneath the erotic energy of the text, we have a reminder that during much of the Renaissance period, England was a nation at war.

Next, there is the praise of monarchy in the line 'My kingdome, safeliest when with one man man'd' (possibly 'woman' hovers around the sound of 'one man', a sly reference perhaps to England's *female* monarch, Elizabeth). This line points us to the interest in different forms of government which plays such an important part in Renaissance culture and history, from Shakespeare's study of republicanism in the Roman plays to the actual establishment of a Republic in England after the execution of Charles I in 1649. We usually find in Renaissance writing that the public, political sphere and the sphere of private experience are inseparable, integrated at the level of normal thinking. More usually, one is described in terms of the other: the analogy drawn by Donne in these lines between the government of a state and the government of a woman by a man is typical of the way Renaissance writing reflects large-scale issues in depictions of private and domestic experience. Indeed, thinking through analogy – describing one thing in terms of another thing – is a characteristic of Renaissance writing generally.

Through these few lines, then, we can enter the flow of history and ideas, as they played on the feelings and imagination of one particular mind. It is not only the mind depicted in the poetry that is at issue here, though, but our own mind, too. A text brings us some of the cultural baggage of one age, but in turn we bring our own assumptions and opinions to the text when we read. As inhabitants of a particular time in history, we most quickly recognise themes – such as gender relations and imperialism – which remain live issues for us. In the light of feminism, and post-imperial guilt, these are aspects of the poem that we will soonest respond to. We may well deplore the attitudes expressed by Donne's speaker, who apparently approves of the exploitation of colonised countries and regards the woman merely as a passive object to be appropriated and enjoyed. In this way, the poem can speak to us about topics which are central to our own age and move us to strong feelings of approval or disagreement.

Yet as well as being relevant to our own concerns, this text, like all writings from previous centuries, also challenges us to enter a different world and see through the eyes of people remote from us in their outlook and beliefs. How would an educated sixteenth-century gentleman – Donne's first audience – have responded to this text? Possibly he would have shared the ideas about women and colonies set out here, but it is equally likely that he would not have taken them very seriously to begin with. Our hypothetical reader would very probably have seen this text as first and foremost an ingenious literary exercise. He – and I stress 'he' since it is historically likely to have been a male reader, and a male reader is arguably implied by the text – would probably have read it intertextually, that is by mentally placing the poem against other texts, to appreciate how Donne was playing with certain traditional formulae. He would see, for example, that Donne is writing a *blazon*, a specific kind of text which specialises in describing a woman's beauties. Read against other blazons, the poem becomes a sophisticated literary exercise, playing with inherited conventions. Our hypothetical reader might also have considered the poem as variations on a source text, frequently of great importance in Renaissance writing. Where we might prize novelty and originality, Renaissance readers were interested in seeing what an artist could do with older materials – whether these were stories, literary forms or intellectual concepts. The most important text 'behind' Donne's poem is the *Amores* by the Roman poet Ovid (43 BC–17 AD). The *Amores* describe, with sensuous eroticism, the psychology of a lustful male: because of their sexual content, they were not taught in schools and could freely circulate only in Latin – thus they were safely restricted to the educated elite. Donne's sequence of elegies (so-called because they describe the sufferings of love) starts with some close imitation of his Roman model and then moves into freer variations on the basic theme of a man desiring a woman. Its first readers must have relished their 'forbidden fruit' quality, and have listened out for the poet's own witty play on the voice of the Ovidian male.

Donne thus looks back to Ovid, but at the same time he is clearly alive to the experience of colonialism, a key issue of his own day. This is the quintessential feature of much Renaissance culture: it looks back to the classics, but in order to shape and examine the modern. Renaissance art uses the materials of the past to make new things in the present. Just as Donne uses Ovid's verse to present the mind and voice of a sixteenth-century lover, with sixteenth-century preoccupations, the architects Inigo Jones (1573–1652) and Christopher Wren (1632–1723) used elements of classical buildings to make modern palaces and churches. The Renaissance is, we might say, both a 'rebirth' of the classical and a reshaping of classical elements to make a new world.

Having acknowledged that Donne is working within a tradition, we might still ask questions like 'Does the poet mean what he is saying? Does he want us to sympathise with the speaker and share in his expressions of delight?' Inevitably, we are going to have assumptions about the relation between text and writer, but these assumptions change from age to age. We are still influenced today by the Romantic movement, which conceived of poetry as the intense expression of a powerfully felt experience. At some level we still expect a poem to have some clearly traceable link with the psyche and biography of the poet. Yet Renaissance poems very often work differently. They are not usually a direct record of the inner experiences of the poet; rather, they are more like miniature theatres, in which different personae play out psychological dramas. We can see in Shakespeare's plays this fascination with the possibilities of 'trying on' another character in the many instances of disguise and pretence in his plots. In the same way, Donne in this poem may be 'trying on' the voice of a particular kind of lover, exaggerating his triumphant boastfulness to the point of comedy. Both poems and prose texts of the Renaissance often have this quality of performance: authors use writing to explore ideas by acting out parts, and the voices we hear may all be fictive, existing at an ironic distance from the thoughts and feelings of the writer. This still raises the question of a writer's responsibility for the words he puts down; and to say that Renaissance writers knew nothing of sincerity would be going too far. However, when reading a Renaissance text, we should be wary of assuming that it represents an attempt by the writer to present a truthful record of a real experience.

Still another challenge to the modern reader lies in the circumstances in which we meet a text. We are likely to come across a poem like Donne's in print, in a book, annotated by an expert editor, and possibly as part of a taught course. It is thus on several levels an 'authorised' text. We have already seen how Donne's readers would have regarded these quasi-pornographic pieces as something *anti-official*, with the pleasure of contraband goods (a printing of Marlowe's English versions of Ovid was actually burned by order of the bishops in 1599). And while we may see Donne's poems as a book, the first readers saw it only in private handwritten papers. One hundred and fifty years after the invention of movable type, gentlemen like Donne still preferred to circulate their works in manuscript among friends. Consequently, the poem we have been discussing was not printed until some 70 years after it was written. It was passed around Donne's circle, rather as we might circulate an email or digital image to friends today. This 'coterie culture' creates a particular community of interpretation: there may be in-jokes, private understandings and coded references which outsiders struggle to understand. When the poem passed into print – itself a key Renaissance invention – its conditions of reception, and consequently its potential meanings, also changed.

It is time to summarise our findings. We have seen how some lines by Donne have led us to some key themes of Renaissance history of society: colonialism, war, attitudes to women, forms of government. They have also illustrated some aspects of literature and culture: rhetoric, artifice, the imitation and adaptation of classical models, the fictive persona, manuscript and print, the educated reader, coterie culture. These closely interrelated matters are among the topics we shall be exploring in this book. In studying them, we shall also take notice of the methods and insights offered by modern literary criticism and theory: Feminist criticism helps us to examine the depiction of women in texts; Rhetorical criticism trains us to perform detailed close readings, in Renaissance terms, while textual and bibliographical scholarship can help us to understand the forms in which texts were encountered. Literary theory can further assist us in exploring the kinds of questions which our brief discussion has raised: Is it legitimate to read a Renaissance poem out of its context and look for issues relevant to our own time? Or should we be thinking ourselves back into the age when a work was written and interpreting it in its own context? When we read, should we bring our own moral convictions to bear and make judgements on how a poem depicts women or people of other races? Or should we leave moral reactions to one side and accept that different ages have different values to our own?

There are, of course, other important Renaissance literary topics and themes, other critical approaches and other important theoretical issues. In this book, we shall be describing some of these, but inevitably leaving out many others. Part One explores the wider contextual world: political, religious and historical processes which flow through and around the writings of the age. In Part Two, we look at topics in literature, such as genres, modes and Renaissance theories of what literature was for. Finally, in Part Three, we shall consider some of the critical approaches taken to studying the Renaissance today and the theoretical questions they raise.

Such is the structure of the present book. How it is used depends very much on the nature of the project being undertaken. We have seen how a few lines of one poem can take us into many themes and issues. Equally, one subject can cross many texts and involve material from history, literature and modern criticism: the study of a female Renaissance author, for example, would involve researching the situation of the Renaissance woman, the writings of women in the period and the approaches offered by modern feminist analysis. These are the kinds of tasks which this book is designed to assist. Neither the book nor its individual entries can hope to be comprehensive. But I hope that they are at any rate useful as a starting point, and above all suggestive of ways in which Renaissance literature may be studied. As well as helping with particular assignments, I also hope that the material in this book might encourage you to pursue fresh lines of enquiry, which in turn will enlarge our understanding of this rich and fascinating field.

1 Contexts: History, Politics, Culture

Historical Introduction

The English Renaissance has no clear beginning, but the date of 1485 will serve as a starting point. In this year, Henry Tudor defeated Richard III at the Battle of Bosworth and so initiated the rule of the House of Tudor that was to last through five monarchs until the death of Elizabeth I in 1603. The date of 1485 is a useful vantage point from which to look at a wider panorama. In Italy, especially in the Republic of Florence, humanists were engaging with the language and ideas of the Greeks and Romans, and artists and poets were similarly energising their work with classical ideas. In 1453, the city of Constantinople (modern-day Istanbul) had fallen to the Turks. Greek scholars continued their emigration westwards at a faster rate, and the resulting spread of knowledge of Greek contributed to the detailed study of ancient Greek philosophy and re-examination of the scriptures and the early Christian Church: the latter avenue of enquiry would contribute to the upheaval of the Reformation. The fall of Constantinople also meant that the overland trade routes between Europe and Asia were effectively lost, and explorers were forced to search for alternative means of reaching the Indies (the source of luxury goods and essential spices for preserving food). The first voyage of Columbus, in 1492, was only a few years off, and the consequent discovery of a new continent (America) and a new ocean (the Pacific) was about to transform ideas about the size and nature of the globe and its human inhabitants. Printing in movable type had been invented about a generation ago, and Caxton had already set up his press in Westminster (1476). By selecting these elements, we can portray the age as one of revolutionary change.

Yet when Henry Tudor was crowned Henry VII, probably no one in England would have heralded the dawn of a new era. Bosworth could have been seen as just the latest in a series of conflicts between two branches of the royal family, the Houses of York and Lancaster. This conflict, known as the Wars of the Roses, had lasted 30 years (1455–1485), causing destabilising fragmentations of power and largely sealing English cultural life off from continental developments. On becoming King (and his claim to the crown was decidedly weak), the Welshman Henry Tudor first had to consolidate his power in the realm. This he did by eliminating rivals, reducing the power of local lords and strengthening both royal finances and the national economy. By marrying the Yorkist Elizabeth, daughter of Edward IV, Henry symbolised a union between the two Houses; the Earl of Warwick, who had a stronger claim to the throne, was imprisoned and later executed. Two colourful episodes in Henry's reign were provided by pretenders to the throne: Lambert Simnel pretended to be Warwick and, having been easily defeated at Stoke (1487), was employed in the royal kitchens. Perkin Warbeck, who pretended to be the younger of the princes in the tower (allegedly murdered on the orders of Richard III), was executed (1497). A more insidious threat to central power came from overmighty local lords, who commanded bands of retainers amounting to small private armies. These were reduced through statutes which prohibited liveried servants in great households. Justice was enforced through the King's Council, the Star Chamber (so called because of the ceiling decoration), and by local justices of the peace. In all of these, gentry and lesser nobility loyal to the King supplanted the great magnates: the rise of these 'new men' is an important social theme in the period. Royal income was increased through the ruthless taxation methods pursued by the churchmen Morton and Fox and the 'ravening wolves' Empson and Dudley. England's principal export was wool, and important treaties were made with the Flemish, who imported this for their cloth industry.

Henry's chief aim was to unify the nation around the central power of the crown. Marriages were arranged with the aim of consolidating relations at home and abroad. Henry's eldest son Arthur was married to Catherine of Aragon (1501) – binding England to the great power of Spain – and his daughter Margaret was married to James IV of Scotland (1502): the kings of the House of Stuart in the next century spring from this marriage. Slowly the intellectual currents of the continent found their way to England: Henry's reign saw the first generation of English humanist scholars, such as Thomas Linacre (c.1460–1524), who studied in Italy, and William Grocyn (c.1446–1519), teacher to Erasmus, More and Colet. The climate for the 'new learning', based on the study of ancient Latin and Greek texts, was such that Erasmus, who came to Oxford in 1498, said that England could provide a first-rate classical education. The foundation of St Paul's School (1509) marks the spread of such education. In the same year, Henry VII died, leaving an England more united around the throne and with a full treasury.

National cohesion and financial security provided a strong foundation for Henry VIII on his accession. At the outset, Henry's popularity was consolidated by both his personal attributes and policies. His skill at courtly pursuits, from martial exercises to music, was generally admired, and his intellectual interests in astronomy, literature, theology and other disciplines led Erasmus and other humanists to look to him as a great patron of learning. Henry sought an imperial image and presented himself as a Renaissance prince, the equal of the emperor Charles V and Francis I of France. To this end, a massive building programme was undertaken, and many new palaces, including Whitehall, were constructed in his reign. Henry's marriage (by papal dispensation) to Catherine of Aragon, his brother Arthur's widow, was also well received, as was the calculated execution of the hated Empson and Dudley. Early in Henry's reign, Scotland was defeated at the battle of Flodden (1513); this saw the death of James IV and the massacre of the Scottish nobility and thus severely damaged Scotland's own Renaissance fortunes. Abroad, the great powers were France and the Holy Roman Empire: English policy, run by the brilliant Thomas Wolsey (Chancellor 1515), was to maintain the balance of power between them. One particularly colourful event as part of this policy was the spectacular meeting between Henry and Francis I at the Field of Cloth of Gold (1520). France and the Empire had a protracted conflict as they fought over possession of the weak Italian states, and Charles V's sack of Rome in 1527 marked a significant gain for the empire and had momentous consequences for future English history.

Henry needed a male heir to continue the Tudor Dynasty, but the marriage with Catherine had produced only a daughter (Mary). Frustrated, and in love with Anne Boleyn, Henry sought papal permission for the annulment of his marriage on the grounds that marrying his brother's widow was sinful. However, the Pope was now prisoner of Charles V, who happened to be nephew to the Queen, and hence was in no position to grant a divorce. Wolsey was dismissed for his failure to resolve 'The King's Great Matter' satisfactorily and died shortly before facing trial for high treason (1530). Wolsey's position as Henry's right-hand man was taken by Thomas Cromwell (c.1485–1540), whose two main objectives were the establishment of the absolute power of the Crown and the separation of the English Church from Rome. With Cromwell's assistance, Henry proceeded to marry Anne Boleyn and break allegiance with Rome in a series of Acts passed by the 'Reformation Parliament' (1529–1536); in the 1534 Act of Supremacy, he was declared 'Supreme Head of the Church of England'. Parliament was itself a totally compliant body whose business was to enact the royal will: any voicing of independent views was liable to be construed as treasonous. England was now a self-governing 'empire'; in the contemporary sense of owing no fealty of any kind to any outside body. Henry was aware of the new Protestant ideas but was himself strongly Catholic: indeed, he had been acclaimed defender of the Faith (*Fidei Defensor*) by the Pope for a book refuting Luther. England was technically still part of the Catholic Church, only with Henry rather than the Pope in charge in England: the 'Henrician Reformation' was thus based on establishing non-papal Catholicism. However, Henry was also ready to exploit resentment at the Catholic establishment which the new ideas had stirred up and was insistent that obedience to the crown superseded loyalty to Rome. His rule was as absolute as any of his continental counterparts, and arguably more so, since he was ruler in both realms, Church and State. Thomas More was executed for his refusal to accept this new supreme status (1535): failure to conform to the King's ruling on religious matters was tantamount to treason. The individual had no freedom of conscience whatever.

Henry next raised funds and grateful clients by raiding the vast holdings of the Church. Through the dissolution of the monasteries (1536, 1539), Church wealth passed to the crown, and the support of the new gentry was bought with massive transference of land. Many buildings fell into decay, while others were adapted as country houses. The welfare and educational services provided by abbeys and monasteries were utterly destroyed. A northern rebellion against these policies, the Pilgrimage of Grace (1536), was crushed, but it indicated the affection many people felt for the old religion, especially in the northern counties. English Church doctrine, enshrined in the Six Articles (1539), incorporated elements of both the new protestantism and traditional practices. Religious observance was a set of practices prescribed by the state and enforced by law; Church teaching was intrinsically connected to state power. The quest for a male heir claimed another victim in Anne Boleyn, who had given Henry another daughter (Elizabeth, the future queen), a crime for which she was punished by execution for alleged infidelity (1536). Henry's third wife Jane Seymour (m. 1536) eventually gave birth to Edward, who succeeded as Edward VI when Henry died an obese physical wreck in 1547.

Edward VI was only nine years old when he came to the throne, and his reign (1547–1553) is dominated by the two protectors, first the Duke of Somerset (1547–1549) and then the Duke of Northumberland (1549–1553). How much policy was owing to the clever and sickly boy king is a matter of debate. Somerset continued Henry's plan of marrying Edward to Mary Stuart (the infant Mary, Queen of Scots), but after the 'rough wooing', which consisted in invasion and the sacking of Edinburgh, Mary was instead married to the French prince, later Francis II. A moderate protestant, Somerset relaxed Henry's laws against heresy, and more continental reformers entered the country. In line with Reformation thinking, the Chantry Chapels (dedicated to saying masses for the dead) were deemed superstitious and dissolved in 1547; Cranmer's first Prayer Book in English of 1549 gave liturgical form to this blend of Protestant belief and inherited custom and was reinforced by an Act of Uniformity which imposed it on the whole country (angering Cornishmen, who resented having to say prayers in English rather than Latin). Somerset's years of control were also marked by severe economic hardship, a situation worsened by the policy of enclosures: this refers to the enclosing (with hedges) of public land, which was sold to private landlords for sheep farming, causing unemployment and misery in rural areas (sheep farming requires far less human labour than the cultivation of crops). The uprisings which followed, such as Robert Ket's rebellion in 1549, led to Somerset's downfall and replacement by the rapacious Northumberland. Under him, England turned towards a more extreme form of Protestantism: churches were ransacked, and a huge number of ecclesiastical artworks were destroyed on the puritanical principle that they promoted idolatry (the worshipping of images). The second version of the Prayer Book (1552) and the accompanying Act of Uniformity were much more protestant in content. When it became clear that Edward was dying, Northumberland tried to avoid the passing of the crown to Edward's Catholic half-sister Mary (the daughter of Catherine of Aragon) and persuaded Edward to designate his (Northumberland's) own daughter-in-law Lady Jane Grey as heir. Yet when Edward died, Mary succeeded in escaping arrest and it soon became clear that it was she who commanded popular allegiance. The unfortunate Lady Jane Grey was 'Queen for nine days' before being executed. Mary duly took the crown in 1553.

Mary Tudor is still known as 'Bloody Mary' for her persecution of English Protestants as part of her policy of returning England to the Church of Rome. Yet she was initially welcomed after Northumberland's extreme brand of Protestantism had offended traditional sensibilities. Early in her reign, Mary dismissed several protestant bishops, and Parliament repealed religious legislation passed under Edward. However, Mary's plan to marry King Philip II of Spain caused apprehension: alliance with Spain would, it was feared, bring the loss of independence, and the introduction of the Inquisition, the most notorious of the tools of the Counter-Reformation, the Catholic Church's strategy of defending and reinforcing itself in the face of Protestant attacks. Sir Thomas Wyatt led a rebellion against this marriage in 1554; on its failure, he was executed, and Mary's half-sister Elizabeth (daughter of Anne Boleyn) was arrested and, initially, imprisoned in the Tower of London. Mary and Philip were married at Winchester in 1554, and the nation was pardoned by Cardinal Pole for the sin of schism (division of the Church). In 1555, the Marian persecutions began: the most famous victims were Cranmer, Latimer and Ridley. The tribulations of the Protestant martyrs under 'Bloody Mary' were recorded in Foxe's 'Book of Martyrs' and caused such revulsion that the cause of returning to the Catholic Church lost public support (though it might be said they were mild compared to state atrocities elsewhere). The last years of Mary's reign saw the loss of England's last possession in France, Calais (1558). Mary died the same year, probably of a cancer which she took to be a pregnancy, the marriage with Philip having produced no heir. The next in succession was thus Elizabeth, whose long reign (1558–1603) produced the 'Elizabethan Age', which is at the centre of our general notion of the English Renaissance.

Under previous monarchs, the English Church had broken with Rome and moved from Catholicism to moderate, then extreme Protestantism and back again. Popular religious sensibility was probably a mixture of these various strands, while separate groups adhered rigorously to different confessions and positions. An important part of domestic policy was the 'Elizabethan Settlement' (1559), an attempt to forge a Church under which most English could unite. This so-called *via media* (middle way) combined elements of Catholic discipline (such as church ceremony) with protestant teaching. The Settlement excluded, as non-conformists, committed Catholics at one end and Calvinist Puritans and Presbyterians at the other (Presbyterians believe in a church governed by elders rather than a hierarchy of bishops): a degree of national unity was achieved, and enforced through compulsory church attendance and fines for absenteeism, though dissent continued throughout Elizabeth's reign. Elizabeth I herself seemed to wish for obedience rather than compelling inner adherence to certain articles of faith by making 'windows into men's souls'. Nobles and others with Catholic affiliations could be tolerated provided they paid their fines and did not make trouble. Nonetheless, persecution of heretics, including torture and execution, continued to be a routine method of state policing. Another unifying strategy, which also served to distract from such matters, was the cultivation of Elizabeth's image as the Virgin Queen, effectively portrayed through various media from portraits to tournaments. Under Elizabeth, the court flourished and was largely responsible for the flourishing of the arts: the age saw remarkable creations in art (Hilliard), music (Gibbons, Tallis, Byrd), architecture (grand country houses like Hardwick Hall) and of course literature. A frequent characteristic of artistic creation was rich pattern and ornament, partly to advertise the wealth of the new rich who paid for it. Next to artistic achievement, the age is also famous for its statesman (Cecil, Walsingham) and sailors and explorers (Hawkins, Raleigh, Drake). Such achievement did not take place against a background of national contentment, however. Rising prices, agrarian depression and unemployment continued throughout Elizabeth's reign, driving the desperate poor into London and other growing cities which were unable to manage them. State attempts to manage the hardship and threat of civil disorder ranged from stern rules against vagabonds to the beginnings of state-provided welfare with the Poor Law of 1601.

Religious conflict was also a key feature on the European stage. The Counter-Reformation Catholic Church acted aggressively against Protestant countries: in 1570, Pius V excommunicated Elizabeth, inviting princes to overthrow her. Jesuits preached secretly in England and ministered to the Catholic faithful, and numerous plots against the crown were uncovered: hence to be Catholic was potentially to be regarded as a traitor. This situation lies behind the tragic story of Mary, Queen of Scots who fled her own kingdom after a series of misadventures and threw herself on the mercy of her cousin Elizabeth (in 1568). While under home arrest in England, however, Mary was the natural focus for Catholic hopes to depose Elizabeth, and when she was eventually implicated in a plot, Elizabeth had to authorise her execution (1587). Added to England's material assistance of the Protestant Netherlands who were rebelling against the rule of imperial Spain, this led to open war between England and Spain, something Elizabeth had been at pains to avoid. The most celebrated event in this conflict was the defeat of the Spanish Armada in 1588, though the war continued until the end of the reign. Other problems facing Elizabeth included serious uprisings against Tudor colonial rule in Ireland, the lack of a direct heir to the throne and a House of Commons increasingly aware of its own power as a body voting in new taxes. The emerging independence of Parliament was a problem passed on to succeeding monarchs and led eventually to Civil War. Elizabeth died in 1603.

Elizabeth I reportedly approved as her successor James VI of Scotland, the son of Mary Queen of Scots and great-great-grandson of Henry VII. With his accession, the English crown passed to the Scottish dynasty of the House of Stuart. As James I of England (r.1603–1625), the new King ruled over two kingdoms, though Scotland and England were not constitutionally united for another century (the Act of Union of 1707). With Ireland now brought under English control, the idea of the British Isles as one political entity was beginning to take shape. At the same time, the British Empire also grew under the Stuarts; under James, Elizabethan adventures turned to serious colonisation of the East coast of North America and the West Indies and the establishment of trading stations from Africa to India. This imperial expansion, eased by the peace with Spain which James signed in 1604, had several consequences: the growth of the slave trade, in which many great towns and families were involved; the importing of goods from tobacco to tea, together with the influx of precious metals which drove up prices and caused serious economic problems; and the enrichment of the middle classes who profited from the new commercial situation.

Money was a crucial factor in the greatest domestic problem of James's reign, the tension between the crown and Parliament. The King needed Parliament to pass money bills, to maintain the country's economy and also to fund his court's expensive lifestyle. But the newly rich Parliament increasingly flexed its muscles and resisted new taxation. James turned to unpopular money-raising policies, including the sale of peerages. Parliament found much to be offended at in James: the vulgar and profligate habits of a court packed with Scottish hangers-on; lectures on the divine right of kings and the handing of ministerial office to handsome and incompetent favourites, most notoriously George Villiers, the first Duke of Buckingham (1592–1628). James meanwhile was offended at the refusal of the House of Commons and the country's judges to offer their complete subservience to the crown, which he believed was an office held by divine right and thus surpassing national law and custom. James's mixture of genuine erudition and total inability to understand or manage the country's institutions led to him being called (by the French King Henry IV) the 'wisest fool in Christendom'.

King and Parliament were equally at odds over religion. On his accession, both Protestants and Catholics invested hopes in James: he came from a Scottish Presbyterian background and his mother (Mary, Queen of Scots) was a Catholic. But at the Hampton Court Conference (1604) – the most signal achievement of which was the instigation of the Authorized Version or 'King James Bible' eventually published in 1611 – James made his dislike of Puritanism clear. Consequently, the English Church adopted Catholic ceremonial aspects, particularly under William Laud (1573–1645), who became Archbishop of Canterbury under Charles I, while Parliament had a Puritan majority. Under the direction of their bishops, priests preached the doctrine of total obedience to the divinely appointed monarch. Thus Catholicism became associated with tyrannical monarchy and Calvinist Protestantism with Parliamentary freedom. This meant freedom for Protestants only, of course. Disappointed by the persistence of laws penalising their faith, some disappointed Catholics turned to plots, culminating in the attempt to blow up Parliament in the Gunpowder Plot of 1605, an act of attempted terrorism which discredited the old faith in England for generations (we note in passing there is a serious argument that this plot was actually the work of the State). Parliament took the opportunity to pass various savagely repressive laws against all Catholics, restricting them to second-class citizens until the emancipation acts of the nineteenth century. Meanwhile, James was totally at odds with the sensibilities of his subjects, pursuing the scheme of marrying his son Charles to the Spanish infanta (largely to secure a colossal dowry) and allowing the Spanish ambassador Gondomar to dictate England's foreign policy. It was largely to please

Gondomar that the old Elizabethan hero Sir Walter Raleigh was sent on an impossible mission to find the gold of El Dorado (in Guyana) and then executed after a staged trial for treason in 1618. The planned marriage alliance failed: an idiotic visit in disguise to the Spanish court by Charles and Buckingham (1623) did not help, the conditions demanded by Spain – amounting to a complete repeal of anti-Catholic laws – could not be met, and popular sentiment was fiercely against Spain and for the restoration of the Protestant Palatinate, from which James's son-in-law Frederick had been deposed by invading Spanish forces in 1618 (at the outset of the Thirty Years War). When James died, he bequeathed religious, financial, parliamentary and foreign policy problems which Charles I was unable to resolve, leading to the Civil War of 1642.

Charles I's reign lasted technically from 1625 to 1649, but his authority effectively ended in 1642, on the outbreak of Civil War. In terms of cultural history, Charles is associated with a high point of courtly arts: under him, and particularly owing to the enthusiasm of his French wife Henrietta Maria, the court masque was brought to a pinnacle of sophistication; he increased greatly the magnificent royal collection of paintings, by masters such as Rubens and Van Dyck; and the architect Inigo Jones introduced the austerely classical Palladian style to England. Politically, however, Charles's reign was dominated by conflict between the monarchy and Parliament, a crisis which led with the seeming inexorability of tragedy to civil war. In the first four years, a largely Puritan House of Commons was suspicious of Charles's marriage to an openly practising Catholic (the French princess Henrietta Maria), fearing the introduction of despotic Catholic rule in England, on the continental model. It was aggrieved also by the domination of the incompetent Buckingham (assassinated in 1628).

Parliament was reluctant to grant Charles the money bills required to pursue wars with Spain and France. Like James, Charles turned to other, frequently ingenious, ways of raising money. While Charles inherited his father's belief in divine right, Parliament, led by formidable men such as John Pym, Henry Coke and John Eliot, adamantly defended English freedoms. The Petition of Right (1628), attacking Charles's use of arbitrary imprisonment, forced loans and other offences against the people, is an important milestone in English constitutional history. Charles's response to this situation was to dismiss Parliament and govern without it until 1640 (referred to as the period of personal rule). During this period, hostility was increased by the actions of two of Charles's ministers: Thomas Wentworth, later Earl of Strafford (1593–1641), enforced the royal will through what he called 'thorough' government, first in northern England, then in Ireland, where he managed to alienate the whole population. These years are marked by some iconic moments in English history, in which the Parliamentary cause found popular 'martyrs' to advance its cause: William Prynne lost his ears for publishing a pamphlet attacking episcopacy and allegedly besmirching the virtue of the Queen (1634); John Hampden was imprisoned (1637) for refusing to pay Ship Money (a contribution to naval defence that Charles effectively turned into a tax) and Sir John Eliot died in the Tower (1632). Puritan emigration to America, which had started under James, increased dramatically. Wentworth's aggressive attack on dissent through the courts was accompanied by the church reforms of William Laud (Archbishop of Canterbury in 1633), who enforced ceremony and the preaching of divine right, and thus associated the Anglican Church entirely with Charles, and raised fears that the Church of England was to be returned to Rome. The tension led to military confrontation when Charles and Laud attempted to impose the English Prayer Book on the Presbyterian Scots. Another iconic moment duly occurred when Jenny Geddes (1637) threw a stool at the Dean of St Giles in Edinburgh, and the so-called 'Bishops' Wars' (1639, 1640) followed, with a Scottish army occupying much of the north of England.

The need to deal with the Scots forced Charles to recall Parliament in 1640 (this was the so-called 'Short Parliament', April to May 1640, followed by the Long Parliament, beginning in November 1640 and lasting until 1660). Parliament duly took the opportunity to force a number of concessions: Laud was imprisoned (1640), and Strafford was imprisoned and executed (1641), with Charles feeling unable to exercise a royal pardon. Parliament was to meet every three years (the Triennial Act) and was not to be dissolved without its own consent. A list of 210 objections to Charles's government (the Grand Remonstrance) was passed (1641), and the Courts of Star Chamber and High Commission were abolished. Fears of Catholic powers were fanned by the Catholic Irish rebellion and the massacre of Ulster Protestants (1641). At the same time, fissures were opening within Parliament between those who sought a resolution through compromise with the monarchy and a revolutionary party who looked for wholesale constitutional change. The King's attempt to arrest five MPs in 1642 precipitated the slide into Civil War which officially began when Charles unfurled the royal banner outside the Castle of Nottingham.

The English Civil War of 1642–1646 was won by Parliament, who had the support of the navy, the rich merchant class and the City of London. The 'New Model Army' led by Oliver Cromwell (1599–1658) also came to be superior to the royal army, which was supported by forces from Ireland and Scotland. However, the image of two coherent sides – Court and Parliament, the Cavaliers and the Roundheads – is simplistic. Parliament divided into two parties: the Presbyterians, who favoured rule through the existing Church of England; and the Independents, who were more radical Protestants. It was from the Independents that the army was chiefly formed. In 1646, Charles surrendered to the Scots, hoping to exploit these divisions within the English Parliament, and he continued intrigues to that end even after the Scots handed him to Parliament in 1647. There followed a second civil war between the Presbyterians – allied to the King and the Scots – and the Independents. This was effectively a war between the army, who were unpaid and refused to disband, and those who wished for rule through Parliament. Key events in this second war were Cromwell's capture of Charles (1647), Charles's escape, the defeat of the royalist army at Preston (1648) and 'Pride's Purge', in which Colonel Pride expelled Presbyterian members from the Commons, leaving a 'rump' of 100 Independents. Thus, while the King lost the war, so did Parliament, as parliamentary democracy was dismantled by a military coup. Charles I was tried by an unconstitutional commission, whose authority he refused to recognise, and condemned by a minority of that commission, itself constituting a minority of an illegally manipulated Parliament, acting without the House of Lords. The general unpopularity of the execution of the King was manifested in the groan which greeted his execution at Whitehall (30 January 1649) and the popularity of the texts which were purportedly his prayers and meditations in *Eikon Basilike*. John Milton's learned attempts to counter this text and justify regicide had little persuasive effect on the people at large. For the next 11 years, England was ruled by a republican dictatorship.

Between 1649 and 1660, England was a Commonwealth, ruled by a Council of State and the rump Parliament. Its initial business was war. The execution of Charles I caused widespread revulsion abroad, including in other Protestant countries, and stirred royalist sympathies across the British Isles. Oliver Cromwell, who initially served purely as a military leader, put down royalist uprisings in Scotland (Edinburgh and the Lowlands were subsequently occupied by the English) and Ireland. In Ireland, Cromwell successfully besieged the strongholds of Drogheda and Wexford and then slaughtered the entire garrison (1649); English garrisons were then installed and the southern Irish given the choice between renouncing their Catholicism or being resettled in inhospitable marshland, an early modern instance of ethnic cleansing. Cromwell called this a 'marvellous great mercy', arguing that initial severity would deter future bloodshed, but to others it was 'the curse of Cromwell', and ensured lasting infamy for the English Commonwealth in Ireland itself. A Scots army in support of Charles's son, the future Charles II, was defeated at Worcester (1651), and Charles eventually escaped to France after famously hiding in an oak tree. There was war against the Dutch over trade: the background to the First Dutch War (1652–1654) was competition over the East Indies, and the immediate cause was England's Navigation Act, which had the effect of banning imports carried by Dutch vessels. England won thanks largely to the skill of Admiral Robert Blake.

Domestically the new Republic also faced much turbulence. The army were resentful of the rule of the complacent Rump of MPs, who had not had to face re-election, and who moreover proposed to give themselves the right of veto over future members. Cromwell and a band of soldiers duly dismissed the Rump: Cromwell's terse statement 'You are no parliament' and reference to the mace as 'a bauble' have passed into popular history, and suggest the contempt of the self-appointed righteous few for Parliamentary rule. However, the righteous failed to come up with a workable alternative to the Commons: the rule of 129 sufficiently godly 'saints', the so-called 'Barebones' Parliament (1653), was hopelessly unworkable; the 'Instrument of Government', in which Cromwell as Lord Protector oversaw a unicameral Parliament of 400, was dissolved by Cromwell when some MPs presumed to criticise his king-like powers. Cromwell then divided England into eleven regions, each ruled over by a Puritanical major-general: fines for gambling, swearing, drunkenness and various other acts of puritanical legislation were deeply unpopular and served only to intensify the yearning for a return to some kind of monarchy.

Cromwell himself was a complex figure. Against his brutality on the battlefield and impatience with parliamentary debate can be set more sympathetic characteristics: like other Puritans, he was undoubtedly sincere and believed that godly government was best for the country; foreign policy in these years was notably successful; as a passionate bible-reader and philosemite, he invited the Jews to return and practise their religion (1656); and, provided they had no taint of Catholicism, protestants of all sorts could hold livings in the Church of England. Nonetheless, Cromwell's personal rule did not yield any lasting legacy. Like any monarch, he passed his office of Protector on to his son, Richard Cromwell (1626–1712), a country gentleman who was quite unready to resolve the problems facing the country. Richard Cromwell's Protectorate lasted only eight months (1658–1659). Government was virtually non-existent and Parliament and the army quarrelled. In January 1660, General George Monck led a march on London. He summoned a free parliament, which included a majority of Presbyterians (formerly expelled in Pride's Purge). Events moved swiftly towards a return to the monarchy. In the Declaration of Breda (1660), Prince Charles promised a pardon to those who had acted against the crown, and 'liberty to tender consciences' in matters of religion, provided that the kingdom was not subverted. A free Parliament of Lords and Commons was called and voted to invite

Charles Stuart to return to England as King. In 1660, the restoration of the monarchy brought an end to the English Commonwealth.

Further Reading

Introductory

George Chamier, *When It Happened* (London: Constable, 2006).
Robert Lacey, *Great Tales from English History: Chaucer to the Glorious Revolution* (London: Little, Brown, 2004).

General narrative

Rebecca Fraser, *A People's History of Britain* (London: Chatto and Windus, 2003).
Simon Schama, *A History of Britain*, 3 vols (London: BBC, 2000–2002), vols 1 and 2.

The Tudors

Susan Brigden, *New Worlds, Lost Worlds: The Rule of the Tudors 1485–1603* (London: Allen Lane, 2000).
Richard Rex, *The Tudors* (Stroud: Tempus, 2002).
James Shapiro, *1599: A Year in the Life of William Shakespeare* (London: Faber, 2005).

Stuarts, Civil War, Republic

Barry Coward, *The Stuart Age: England 1603–1714*, 3rd edn (Harlow, Essex: Longman, 2003).
Stevie Davies, *A Century of Troubles: 1600–1700* (London: Channel 4 Books, 2001).
Diane Purkiss, *The English Civil War* (London: Harper Collins, 2006).

Cultural History

John Buxton, *Elizabethan Taste* (London: Macmillan, 1963).
F. E. Halliday, *An Illustrated Cultural History of England* (London: Thames and Hudson, 1967).
Roy Strong, *The Spirit of Britain: A Narrative History of the Arts* (London: Hutchinson, 1999).

Biographies

There are countless biographies covering the period. The following are personal recommendations:
Peter Ackroyd, *The Life of Thomas More* (London: Chatto and Windus, 1998).
Stephen Greenblatt, *Will in the World: How Shakespeare Became Shakespeare* (London: Jonathan Cape, 2004).
David Starkey, *Elizabeth: Apprenticeship* (London: Chatto and Windus, 2000) [see also TV series *Elizabeth*, on DVD].
John Stubbs, *Donne: The Reformed Soul* (London: Viking, 2006).
Michael Wood, *In Search of Shakespeare* (London: BBC, 2003) [see accompanying TV series, on DVD].

The Book Trade

Printing was a key invention of the Renaissance and unlike manuscripts, printed books were published – that is, put into the public domain, not handed around between private owners. *Publisher* is a potentially misleading word. Some Renaissance title pages refer to the publisher as 'The Printer', meaning the person who caused the book to be printed. In others, the publisher is also the bookseller. A publisher was in fact anyone who acquired the rights to a text, paid for copies to be made and then sold them wholesale to booksellers. Most publishers were stationers: their main trade was selling books, and so they were in a good position to judge the market for a new title. 'Publishing' was a commercially speculative activity rather than a profession in its own right.

Publication of a book came under the control of The Stationers' Company. This was founded as a guild in 1403 and given a royal charter by Mary Tudor in 1557. The Company was based in Stationers' Hall, south west of St Paul's Cathedral. Consequently, the area around St Paul's, particularly to the west, became the hub of the London book market. Just outside the Cathedral, sermons were preached to large open-air audiences at Paul's Cross. The cluster of stationers, combined with the fierce oratory of the preachers, and discussion among their listeners, meant that this small part of the city must have become to some extent a forum for the circulation of ideas. Outside London, licences for printing were restricted to the university towns of Oxford and Cambridge, leaving most of the country without any regular access to printed material.

The Stationers' Company was responsible for regulating the trade in books. Regulation was intended primarily to protect the livelihoods of those in the trade rather than as a system of censorship. Publishers paid a fee (usually sixpence to a shilling) for the right to enter a title in the Stationers' Register (such entries are the primary source of evidence for our dating of books). By doing this, they acquired exclusive rights to print that title. The licence to print a particular text would also be recorded on the author's manuscript, which was not usually returned and generally stayed with the printers, who turned it into printed text. Copyright for a work lay with the publisher rather than the author, who would usually have his work purchased from him in one transaction for a flat fee. This arrangement maximised the chances for a publisher to recoup his investment, and possibly make a profit. Besides rights for individual works, publishers could also secure lucrative patents for producing all books of a similar type: in 1575, Queen Elizabeth granted the English composers William Byrd and Thomas Tallis a monopoly on music publishing, giving them sole rights to print any kind of music.

The fact that copyright lay with the publisher put the author at the bottom of the publishing food chain. Indeed, it need not even be the author who sold a work to the publisher: an acting company might sell a copy of a play, or a manuscript might simply be sold on by someone who found it. But even if the author did sell his own work, in so doing he resigned any claim to ownership of the text as his intellectual property. The new owner, the publisher, could then anthologise, excerpt, arrange or revise the text as he pleased. While authors had only very limited control over the form in which their work reached the public, however, they did at least have a new kind of patron in the form of hard-headed entrepreneurs who could commission books. The speed of book production was also accelerated: writers and their publisher-patrons could respond swiftly to changes in fashion; and 'pamphlet wars', in which debates were fought out with furious polemic, became a part of the literary landscape. These conditions favoured the emergence of identifiable authorial voices. Print might thus generate some kind of 'brand recognition' for an author's name in the minds of the reading public. The publication of Jonson's *Works* in folio in 1616 is an important moment in the emergence of professional authorship in the period. Usually, though, writing was an extremely precarious occupation from a cash point of view: publishers would evidently want to drive down the fee, and even if a book was successful enough to go through more than one printing, the author would not enjoy any of the profits of its success. Writers reacted in different ways to the printing revolution: some, like Michael Drayton (1563–1631) and George Wither (1588–1667), saw it as a means for a poet to establish himself as a public voice. For varying reasons, other writers preferred to stick to manuscript.

Once rights were acquired, the next stage was to turn the manuscript text into a printed book. To do this, the publisher would take the manuscript to a printer, who would manufacture the stipulated number of copies. A printing house was simply the equipment and employees needed to work it. Printers were not publishers, and though some printing houses also engaged in publication, most were the equivalent of businesses today which offer photocopying services for a fee. To lessen risk, print runs were usually limited, a fact which should warn us against overestimating the impact of individual works. The printed books would then be sold to booksellers, who (provided they belonged to the Stationers' Company) could purchase at wholesale rates. The booksellers then tried to sell the volumes at retail price to the public. Through printing, books thus became consumer objects in a competitive commercial market.

Books were printed in standard formats, depending on the times a sheet was folded. A sheet of paper measured about 35×29 cm, roughly similar to a sheet of A3 today. In a Folio, the sheet is folded once in the middle, giving four sides which can be printed on (each side measuring approximately 17 × 29 cm). The next size down is a Quarto. Here the same sheet is folded in the middle, and then again, giving four leaves (hence 'Quarto'), making eight sides, each approximately 12 × 18 cm. In today's terms, this is something like a side of A5, though early modern paper sizes were not as standardised as modern ones. Other kinds of book are referred to by the number of sheets made from folding the original: Octavo (eight leaves), Duodecimo (12). Book sizes suggest the status of the work and its social function. The larger the book, the more expensive it is. The First Folio of Shakespeare's works (1623) said something in its size about the importance of its contents. The smaller quartos were cheaper and aimed at a larger public. Book sizes are also related to function: a small prayer book might be designed to be portable, a grand Bible intended to remain in a Church, clearly visible to the whole congregation.

For the student of Renaissance literature, the context of the book trade raises various issues. The collaboration of publisher and printer in the production of a text challenges traditional notions of authorship, while text layout (for example type in black letter, bold, italic or different sizes) and illustration generate new interpretive possibilities hidden in modern editions. It is always a sensual pleasure to read a Renaissance book in facsimile, and attention to such matters as chapter headings, capitalisation and glosses at the side of the page can soon prompt questions about the meanings generated by these visual aspects of a work. When we see statistics of the different kinds of work in the early modern book market, we notice that these bear little relation to the impression created by modern courses in Renaissance literature, which privilege certain genres over others. Renaissance plays, for example, rarely went into a second edition and were generally comfortably outsold by popular verse and homiletic writings. The mass of printed books were on religious subjects, and almanacs, school-books and law-books, as reliable sellers, were far more prominent in a Renaissance bookshop than the poetry which receives our attention today: how far does our own principle of selection distort the picture of actual Renaissance intellectual life as it was lived by the people of the time? We might also ask how the medium affects the message: as a text moves from manuscript to the homogenising medium of print, how are meanings lost, gained or altered? Details about the print runs, ownership, commercial success and patronage of books take us beyond the text as verbal icon to considering it as physical object, with specific functions in the intellectual economy of the time.

See also *Contexts*: City, English Reformation, Humanism, Manuscripts, Printing; *Texts*: The Bible; *Criticism*: Language Criticism, Textualism

Further Reading

Martin Elsky, *Authorizing Words: Speech, Writing, and Print in the English Renaissance* (Ithaca and London: Cornell University Press, 1989).

Zachary Lesser, *Renaissance Drama and the Politics of Publication: Readings in the English Book Trade* (Cambridge: CUP, 2004).

James Raven, *The Business of Books: Booksellers and the English Book Trade, 1450–1850* (New Haven and London: Yale UP, 2007).

Jason Scott-Warren, *Early Modern English Literature* (Cambridge: Polity Press, 2005), ch.3 'Print in the Marketplace', 75–101.

Catholicism

The Catholic Church underwent significant self-examination in the sixteenth and seventeenth centuries. This process is divided into two phases, known today as the Catholic Reformation and the Counter-Reformation. The Catholic Reformation, which predated Protestantism, was an attempt to address the most serious problems in the Church: a poor and ill-educated clergy in the parishes, a wealthy higher clergy in the cathedrals distracted by secular matters and a lack of discipline among the monastic orders. An important figure in the Catholic Reformation was Desiderius Erasmus (1466–1536), who sought to serve the Church by drawing attention to its weaknesses. Erasmus's works, such as his famous *Praise of Folly* (1511), satirising ignorance and corruption among churchmen and others, were designed to renew the Church from within, not attack it from without.

The Catholic Church was compelled to take a more aggressive line by Luther's Protestant Reformation, starting in 1517. Lutheranism threatened the Catholic Church with disintegration, both on the material level, as states rebelled against Rome's authority, and on the theological level, as its doctrines were challenged by the new theology. In the face of this threat, the Church energetically defended itself and attacked its opponents: the Counter-Reformation is the name given to this belligerent self-assertion. Spiritual discipline was stressed, and new monastic orders like the Capuchins (1525) were formed, dedicated to countering the propaganda of the Protestants through preaching. A key figure was the Spaniard Ignatius Loyola (1491–1556), who founded the Jesuit Order (the Society of Jesus, 1534, recognised by the Papacy in 1540). Jesuits were an intellectual fighting force: highly educated and organised, they advised and confessed great churchmen and statesmen, founded schools and seminaries, answered Protestant claims through their own publications, and served as missionaries in countries where Catholicism was outlawed, seeing martyrdom in the cause as an honour.

At a different level, state governments, including France and the Holy Roman Empire, became actively involved in the strengthening of the

Catholic Church in their own countries. In the three sessions of the Council of Trent (1545–1547, 1551–1552, 1562–1563), the basic tenets of Catholic belief were reaffirmed: salvation is won through faith and works (not, as Luther insisted, by faith alone); the Church cares for the soul through the seven sacraments (baptism, confirmation, penance, Eucharist (communion), marriage, holy orders and extreme unction); the Eucharist is not symbolic but the miraculous transformation of the body and blood of Christ into bread and wine (the doctrine of transubstantiation, also known as the Real Presence) and the Catholic Church is the sole authority for interpreting God's word. Adherence to these teachings was required of all Christians in Catholic states, and enforced through the Inquisition (a medieval institution reinforced from 1542), and the Index of prohibited books (first published 1574), which banned Catholics from reading seditious authors such as Luther and Machiavelli without special licence. There was a close connection between the Counter-Reformation and the Baroque movement in art and literature. Baroque art – illustrated by the works of Bellini (c.1530–1616) and Bernini (1598–1680) – tends to be expressive and theatrical, asserting the power of the Church. Yet at the same time, writings stressed the illusory nature of earthly glory next to the heavenly kingdom: the violence of the Inquisition went hand in hand with a deep spirituality and piety.

In England, separation from the Catholic Church effectively began in 1533, when England declared itself an 'empire', free from any foreign rule, as part of the legislation making Henry VIII Supreme Head of the Church in England. Though at this stage the doctrines of Rome were still accepted, it meant that loyalties could be divided: loyal subjects were to submit to the King, not the Pope, in religious as in other matters. After England had swung towards radical Protestantism under Edward VI (1547–1553), then back to Catholicism under Mary (1553–58), Elizabeth I found some middle ground in her early legislation (Act of Uniformity, 1559), though the Church in England was essentially Protestant, retaining some aspects of Catholic ceremonial (such as vestments and the status of the communion). Religion and politics were indivisible: the Head of State (the monarch) was also Head of the Church, and thus anyone obeying the Pope was open to accusations of disloyalty and of being in league with the Catholic countries who were enemies of England. Catholics tended to be accused of treachery more than heresy. This situation was reinforced in 1570, when the Pope excommunicated Elizabeth I, consigning her to damnation and effectively legitimising her assassination. There were certainly serious threats made by more extreme Catholics, such as the plots (Ridolfi (1572), Throckmorton (1582) and Babington (1586)) to replace her with the Catholic Mary Queen of Scots (imprisoned in 1568, executed 1587). Jesuit missions, and priests trained in the English seminary at Douai, ministered to the Catholic faithful, in the great Catholic families of the north and elsewhere. Meanwhile the Irish, an ancient Catholic people, fought against the Protestant English colonial power with Spanish assistance.

As England moved to open warfare with Spain, it became still more difficult for Catholics to profess their faith and at the same time be regarded as loyal subjects of the Crown. The perception of Catholic dangers was increased by the rhetoric of Protestant preachers. As a result, Catholics everywhere were controlled through several measures: the Oath of Allegiance to the crown had to be sworn as a condition of graduation from the universities; and fines were imposed for non-attendance at church (in 1581 increased from 12d a week to an astronomical £20 a month). Jesuits and seminary priests were regarded as traitors and subjected to imprisonment, torture and death: about 120 clergy and 60 lay persons were executed under Elizabeth (extreme Puritans who also threatened the stability of the state were similarly dealt with). From about 1600, the threat posed by Catholics to the state receded, though the legislation remained and was pursued or relaxed according to the political situation of the day: in 1605, for example, James I renewed the Oath of Allegiance in a strongly worded form, as part of the reaction to the Gunpowder Plot of that year. In the Stuart period, the Court was generally associated with Catholic tendencies, exacerbated whenever peace treaties with Catholic countries were discussed, while Parliament retained a strongly Puritan element.

This is the historical background to Renaissance texts which touch on religion. But political events tell us little about the inner, imaginative life of people. 'What happened to Catholic England?' is an important question to ask of the period. Nearly a thousand years of religious tradition, with all the culture and outlook that went with it, could not disappear overnight. Scholars like Eamon Duffy have shown the survival of many Catholic elements well into the sixteenth century; for many people, their spiritual and imaginative world must have been a confused mixture of what they remembered their parents saying and what they were told to think by the powers of the day. In literature, Catholic belief systems could persist at the level of imagery, or be transferred: the classical gods, for example, were in some sense substitutes for the Catholic saints, and the emotional world of the love lyric explores similar psychological territory to devotional literature. A figure produced by the period was the recusant, who changes his religion. A famous example is John Donne (1572–1631), who was born of a Catholic family but as a youth accepted Anglicanism, probably from a mixture of motives, and later rose to be Dean of St Paul's, one of the highest positions in the English Church. Other Catholics refused to abjure their faith, often choosing a life of hardship and exile.

Among these were Robert Southwell (c.1561–1595), an English Jesuit poet and priest who wrote much of his poetry in prison before being hanged at Tyburn and becoming a Catholic martyr. Richard Crashaw (1612/13–1649) was an Anglican priest who was progressively moved by ceremony and the spiritual life before converting to Catholicism (c.1644). The work of both Southwell and Crashaw corresponds to Counter-Reformation baroque conventions of expressing ardent religious feelings through elaborate rhetorical tropes and intensive imagery. However, many of these aspects can be found in metaphysical writers such as Donne, and there is a risk of identifying the English Catholic writers too much in terms of their faith (as we have here) rather than considering the stylistic affinities they may have with writers of different confessions.

Indeed, we may still not have left behind altogether the complex notions of Catholicism which were constructed in this period. The legacy of continued anti-Catholicism in English history has brought with it a Protestant bias in much historiography, and this has left its mark on anthologies and choices of texts for teaching, leaving Southwell and Crashaw on the margins of the canon, known only through such individual pieces as Southwell's superbly intense 'The Burning Babe'. Four centuries on, it has been argued, these great exponents of baroque sensibility are still in need of reclamation as central figures in the story of English literature.

See also   *Contexts:* Historical Introduction, English Reformation, Protestant Theology; *Texts:* The Bible, Non-fictional Prose

Further Reading

A. D. Cousins, *The Catholic Religious Poets from Southwell to Crashaw: A Critical History* (London: Sheed and Ward, 1991).

Eamon Duffy, *The Stripping of the Altars: Traditional Religion in England, 1400–1580* (New Haven and London: Yale UP, 1992).

Alison Shell, *Catholicism, Controversy and the English Literary Imagination, 1558–1660* (Cambridge: CUP, 1999).

A. C. Southern, *Elizabethan Recusant Prose, 1559–1582* (London: Sands & Co., c.1950).

Chain of Being

The Renaissance inherited the concept of the *scala naturae* – the ladder of Nature, or Chain of Being. According to this, all things in Creation, from highest to lowest, are linked in a continuous series. In the divinely ordered universe, everything has its proper place and its proper relations to other things. The different parts of the whole are also related to each other by a system of correspondences: artistic creation corresponds to divine Creation; the proportions of a classical column correspond to the essence of the human form, and the mathematics of these proportions is held to be at the foundation of the created universe. The Chain of Being involves various features which, for ease of reference, we treat separately in this book: the elements, the humours and the model of the cosmos. In the wider scheme, these are indivisible: the parts of the universe gain their meaning from each other. Whether everyone in the Renaissance agreed on these meanings, according to a unitary world picture, may be doubted. Nonetheless, familiarity with the Chain of Being can certainly help us to understand much of the imagery that we find in the literature of the period.

At the head of the Chain of Being comes God, the first Mover and Maker of all things. Everything descends from God in a hierarchical chain. Angels make up an order of being between God and man and are themselves subdivided by rank: Seraphins, Cherubim, Thrones, Dominations, Virtues, Powers, Archangels and Angels. Each kind of angel has its proper function: in Milton's *Paradise Lost* (1667), Satan, as an archangel, has natural superiority over the other fallen angels in Hell. Angels exist in the ether, which extends over space as far as the superlunary sphere (above the moon). As with all things in the Chain of Being, angels are defined according to their relations to what comes immediately above them (God) and below them (man). In his poem 'Aire and Angels' Donne imagines an angel assuming a physical 'body' of face and wings to become visible to man in the polluted sublunary sphere.

> Then as an Angell, face, and wings
> Of aire, not pure as it, yet pure doth weare,
> So thy love may be my loves spheare;
> Just such disparitie
> As is twixt Aire and Angells puritie,
> 'Twixt womens love, and mens will ever be.

Just as angels are midway between God and man, so man is midway between angel and beast. Man is a microcosm of the greater macrocosm: like the universe, he is hierarchically composed. His higher, Rational Soul, allows him to perceive divine perfection. But in his fallen state, man cannot always govern his passions with the Rational Soul, and so he equally has much in common with the beasts. His soul aspires to the heavens, while his earthly body draws him down. This is the duality of human nature expressed by Hamlet:

> What a piece of work is a man, how noble in reason, how infinite in faculty, in form and moving how express and admirable, in action how

like an angel, in apprehension how like a god – the beauty of the world, the paragon of animals! And yet to me, what is this quintessence of dust?

(2.2)

Man's lower nature makes him akin to animals. Bestial imagery is typically used by writers to describe human behaviour according to ungoverned, irrational instincts. Beneath the bestial layer lies an even lower, demoniac nature, the result of corruption by the devil. When this is in the ascendant, as it is in the character of Macbeth, man works actively to destroy the natural order. The tragedy of such a figure lies in the fact that a higher nature is patently being usurped by a lower one: Macbeth throughout remains rational enough to know that he is damned, an abject form of existence he later shares with Milton's Satan.

Below man come beasts, plants and inanimate objects. These in turn are subdivided into categories: the lion, the dolphin and the eagle are the princes of animals, fish and birds, respectively. The oak is supreme among trees, and gold is at the top of the scale of minerals. Everywhere the material world indicates a cosmos ordered by rank. By the Chain of Being, hierarchy is confirmed as a part of nature. In acting against its nature, something can have effects reaching right up the chain: Macbeth's murder of Duncan disrupts the equilibrium of the world and is followed by other unnatural events. The storm in *King Lear* suggests the primeval chaos that has been released now that the bonds of family and the state have been sundered.

As with other aspects of the 'world view' such as humours and the elements, we may well ask how literally Renaissance people believed in the Chain of Being. This is perhaps not quite the right question. The Chain of Being is not a scientific hypothesis to be tested against evidence. Its value lies in the vision of being which it makes possible. It would probably be fair to say that many Renaissance writers and readers did not 'believe' in it literally. But that does not mean that they disbelieved in it, rather that they did not make the modern distinction between literal and metaphorical. In the inherited medieval view, the material and literal world is by its very nature metaphorical. The world is a book of symbols, expressing the divine intelligence. In Renaissance paintings of the Annunciation, for example, the Virgin is commonly depicted in a contemporary Renaissance interior, a visual union of the ideal and the real. Every part of that interior can be read symbolically: the domestic is religious and the religious is domestic; at the highest level, the god being conceived at the moment of the Annunciation is both godhead and earthly man. Metaphor and symbol are not devices for poetic or artistic ornamentation, but tools for understanding; and what is understood is a series of natural, hierarchical relations.

The Chain of Being, then, is a kind of generator of infinite metaphor, as different elements correspond to each other by describing the same set of relations. In the lines from Donne cited above, angels and air correspond to the heavenly and the earthly, the soul and the body, the pure sphere of the sun orbiting the impure earth, perfect and earthly love. Fire (the superior element), the sun, the lion, the dolphin, the eagle and the oak are all natural images for majesty. The following lines from Shakespeare's *Richard II* use three of these:

> Be he the fire, I'll be the yielding water.
> The rage be his, while on the earth I rain
> My waters; on the earth and not on him.
> March on, and mark King Richard how he looks.
>
> [*Richard appears on the walls of the castle*]
>
> See, see, King Richard doth himself appear
> As doth the blushing discontented sun
> From out the fiery portal of the east
> When he perceives the envious clouds are bent
> To dim his glory and to stain the track
> Of his bright passage to the occident.
>
> YORK: Yet looks he like a king. Behold, his eye,
> As bright as is the eagle's, lightens forth
> Controlling majesty.
>
> > (*RII*, 3.3.58–70)

Fire, sun, king and eagle all correspond, having the same function in the *scala naturae*. Richard's eye 'lightens' the earth with the bolts of lightning which are the instruments of justice wielded by Jove, King of the gods. The 'envious clouds' are the sublunar air, dividing the earthly realm from the ethereal sun. The lines above also show that this system of metaphors was able to integrate the classical (Jove's lightning) with more Christian symbolism, as in the God-King moving from the East to the West. Fresh meanings are added when we consider the context of these speeches in the play: the first speech is spoken by Bullingbrook, who deposes Richard, while we have earlier seen Richard as distinctly undivine in his conduct. The language preserves the idea of the Chain of Being, while the drama itself explores the ambiguities and ironic distance between that system in theory and the real conduct of majesty on earth.

The Chain of Being also provides an idea of Creation. God's Creation, manifested in the design of the cosmos, is a complex pattern: it represents order imposed on chaos, love dominant over strife. Human creation was frequently seen as analogous to this divine act. From woodcarving to music and the visual arts, Renaissance artworks are characteristically ornate and highly wrought. They represent a triumph of skill over recalcitrant raw material: 'ingenious', 'curious' (meaning 'made with care') and 'artificial' are common terms of praise. Artistic creation is a counter to the corrupted state of the world as man has made it and an image of the golden age of perfect harmony. For Sidney, the poet is a God-like figure, creating a world in the microcosm of art:

> The poet . . . doth grow in effect another nature, in making things either better than nature bringeth forth, or, quite anew, forms such as never were in nature.
>
> (Sir Philip Sidney, *An Apologie for Poetrie*, 1595)

The Chain of Being represents a universe arranged according to a logical, ordered system. Literary artifice, like other arts, had a natural aim of emulating this pattern, pointing the reader towards a perfection only possible to the trained inner world of the imagination.

We have considered the question of whether Renaissance man 'believed in' the Chain of Being. A further question is whether there was any such thing as a Renaissance 'model' of the cosmos and its inner workings, shared by the generality of people in the period. Today critics are sceptical of the idea of a unitary Elizabethan 'world picture' and look for evidence of marginalised, eccentric or dissenting voices. Critical fashion has changed from the search for collective beliefs to explorations of fractured and dissonant patterns of thought. The Chain of Being is certainly not a straitjacket of beliefs, but more a general framework of metaphor, within which writers could express ideas. As we have seen, it could be approached subversively and ironically, and with a wide tonal range: in the lines we have read, Shakespeare gives a speech hailing the cosmic role of majesty to the person in the process of disrupting that order by usurping the throne; Donne gives the impression of playing with available ideas rather than solemnly subscribing to them. Art which simply restates an overarching model of ideas soon becomes static; literary texts can be seen as dynamically exploring the tensions, ambiguities and uncertainties of meaning which imaginative engagement with the model can yield.

The model of the Chain of Being can also be read politically, as a means of legitimising the distribution of power by claiming it was 'natural'. Spenser's celebration of the divine pattern in his epic poem *The Faerie*

Queene has as its corollary the approving allegorical description of the brutal imposition of order on Ireland in Book V, where dissidence is crushed by the machine Talus. The reinforcement of order is more or less beautiful, depending on which side of power you find yourself.

See also   *Contexts*: Cosmos 1, Cosmos 2, Elements, Humours, Magic, Medicine, Platonism Science; *Texts*: Pastoral, Theory of Poetry; *Criticism*: Ecocriticism

Further Reading

G. Holderness, *Shakespeare: The Histories* (Basingstoke: Macmillan, 2000).
Arthur O. Lovejoy, *The Great Chain of Being* (Harvard University Press, 1972).
E. M. W. Tillyard, *The Elizabethan World Picture* (London: Penguin, 1943).

The City

London grew rapidly over the early modern period, from an estimated 50,000 in 1530 to 120,000 in 1550, 200,000 in 1600 and nearly 300,000 in 1660 (this is against an English population of about 3 million in 1550, rising to 4 million in 1600). Before the Reformation, about half of the area within the city walls was occupied by church buildings: the seizure of these in the Dissolution released huge amounts of money and estate, which mostly went to private hands (hence the sharp increase from 1530 to 1550). New building programmes were started, and the city was visually transformed. As the mercantile economy increased, there was a steady influx of young men from the country looking to get on (Shakespeare, from Warwickshire, was one of these). Another attraction of London was the guilds, bringing hordes of apprentices to the capital, an ongoing source of civil disorder. Rogues, vagabonds and thieves naturally gravitated towards the rich pickings of the capital. Maimed veterans of the wars in Ireland were driven to London in an attempt to survive, while Protestant refugees from the continent added to the growing human mass. The city could not adapt physically to the growing demands of its population, and there were constant problems with sanitation. Curfew and the locking of the gates were part of the attempt to keep some order, in the absence of any regular police force.

London had three distinct sites: the City, Westminster and Southwark. The first of these was the ancient City of London, still largely bounded by the city walls, and divided into 26 wards. The City was the economic centre of the kingdom, home to the monopoly trading companies. Rich merchants, in turn, helped to found important schools such as the Merchant Taylors' and Mercers' Schools. The principal buildings of the City included the Tower of London and St Paul's Cathedral: 'Paul's

Walk', the cathedral nave, was in Tudor and Stuart times a meeting place, where merchants traded, lawyers received clients, the unemployed sought work and cutpurses stole from everyone. Public sermons were given at St Paul's Cross outside, and St Paul's Churchyard was the home of the book trade. Lawyers studied at the Inns of Court, throughout the period a centre for witty discussion and literary creation. The City was also home to the capital's prisons: Newgate, Bread Street and Poultry Counters, Ludgate, Fleet and the Clink, all of them run for private profit. To these may be added Bridewell, which, although it was designed as a means of addressing poverty, was in practice run as a correctional facility, whipping masterless men out of their presumed idleness. To the south, the Strand was a wide street, where great aristocratic houses looked over the Thames; but most other streets were narrow and unpaved.

To the West, Westminster was the seat of government at Whitehall; the Archbishop of Canterbury had his palace on the other side of the river, at Lambeth. The Court in Westminster was the arbiter of fashion and the apex of the patronage system. The third main part of London was the Borough of Southwark, or Bankside: this lay across the river from the City, connected by London Bridge, and outside the jurisdiction of the City authorities. This was the site of the public theatres (The Swan, The Rose, The Globe) and other popular entertainments such as bear-baiting and cock-fighting. It was also the area for prostitution: the 'stews' or brothels concentrated there were usually legal and brought in a useful income for the landlord of Southwark, the Bishop of Winchester. The City, Westminster and Southwark were all connected by the River Thames, which served as harbour and channel for people and goods (the cries of 'Eastward Ho!' and suchlike come from the cries of the rivermen plying for trade). The Thames was wider then than now, since the embankment had not yet been built.

London is represented in multifarious ways in the literature of the period. The great *Survey of London* (first ed. 1598) by the antiquarian John Stow (1525–1605) provides much of our information. This work, suffused with nostalgia, is an attempt to record the past history and present changes of the city, drawing on oral sources, documents and observation of buildings, customs and people. A different kind of picture is painted by the cony-catching pamphlets, closely associated with the name of Robert Greene (1558–1592), an author who is himself so surrounded by fiction that little is known about him: an example of the genre is his pamphlet *A Notable Discovery of Coosnage* (1591). Cony-catchers were tricksters who tricked their gulls or 'conies' in a variety of ingenious methods. The pamphlets described the practices of these conmen and advised Londoners how to avoid being robbed, cheated at dice and so forth. A useful source for social historians, these writings have also interested literary critics. One issue is veracity. Though purportedly factual, it is not clear how truthful the cony-catching pamphlets are: anecdotes might be exaggerated or invented, as they seek to create the alarm which they then offer to remedy; the author can appear as a character in the work (as, in one famous instance, does the printer). Thus the genre of cony-catching literature both offers insight into the London underworld and presents a kind of underworld of the imagination, marked by a blurring of the borderline between fact and fiction, a fantastical literary and linguistic invention (the texts are thick with the jargon of criminals) and a register of the fearful psychosis of city life.

London is also the setting for the City Comedies, plays written especially between 1600 and 1640 which depict the types of the London middle classes in urban settings like ordinaries, taverns and prisons. Examples of this genre are Ben Jonson (1572–1637), *Bartholemew Fair* (1614), *The Devil Is an Ass* (1616); Thomas Middleton (1580–1627), *A Chaste Maid in Cheapside* (1611); Philip Massinger, *The City Madam* (1632). Pithy portraits of city types are presented in collections of characters, such as the *Microcosmographie* (1628) by John Earle (*c.*1601–1665). Our image today of such city types as constables and Puritans is filtered through the satire of such works. The type of the city person – shrewd, sharp, streetwise, defined against the innocent rustic – is given powerful force in literature and became a stock topic in the later Restoration Comedy.

See also   *Contexts*: Book Trade; *Texts*: Theatres

Further Reading

Lawrence Manley, *Literature and Culture in Early Modern London* (Cambridge: CUP, 1995).

Dieter Mehl and others, *Plotting Early Modern London: New Essays in Jacobean City Comedy* (Aldershot: Ashgate, 2004).

Liza Picard, *Elizabeth's London: Everyday Life in Elizabethan London* (London: Weidenfeld and Nicolson, 2003).

Gāmini Salgādo, *The Elizabethan Underworld* (London: J M Dent, 1977).

Cosmos (1): The Old Cosmology (geocentric)

The sixteenth and seventeenth centuries saw a transformation in the representation of the universe. Gradually, the ancient and medieval views of a geocentric universe, with the earth at the centre, gave way to a modern model of a heliocentric cosmos, centred on the sun. This change in understanding was a slow process. It began as an elite intellectual project, and only very slowly filtered into the general imagination: for our period, it is the 'old cosmos' which dominates as a source of literary imagery, but in the latter part we can see writers like Donne and Milton exploring the new science at a poetic level.

The Old Cosmology

The Renaissance inherited a model of the cosmos which had its roots in the ancient world. Key figures in its development were the Greek philosopher Aristotle (384–322 BC) and the Egyptian astronomer and geographer Ptolemy (c.90–168). Aristotle was in turn modified by Christian theology, particularly in the work of St Thomas of Aquinas (1225–1274), and subsequently the system also incorporated neoplatonic ideas. Thus the picture of the universe which reached the Renaissance represented a complicated mix of ideas, fusing ancient and Christian accounts of the human condition.

The picture which reaches the Renaissance is that of the cosmos as an ordered whole. The universe is a vast but finite totality: temporally its limits are the Creation and the end of time, and spatially it is enclosed within a sphere. The centre point of the sphere is the earth, making it geocentric (sometimes hell is placed at the centre of the earth, making it the very lowest point of the universe). Moving outwards from the earth are a series of concentric spheres. The first seven of these are defined by the trajectories of the planets:

1. The Moon
2. Mercury
3. Venus
4. The Sun
5. Mars
6. Jupiter
7. Saturn

Beyond the planets we come to (8): The Fixed stars, (9): A Crystalline Sphere, and (10): The Primum Mobile, or First Mover, which sets the whole system in motion. The First Mover easily translated into Christian thinking as God. God, as a transcendent being, is not bounded by his creation but exists in the empyrean Heaven; this is outside space and beyond human comprehension. In Dante's description, the Empyrean is 'pure light, intellectual light, full of love; love of true good, full of joy; joy that transcends all sweetness' (*Paradiso* 30.39–42).

This Old Cosmology unites Philosophy and Science: indeed, Science was only separated as a distinct discipline from Philosophy in the course of the seventeenth century. The 'book of nature' was the outward revelation of the divine, and learning to read it was part of the process of understanding God's will for man. The meanings drawn from this particular model of the universe inform much Renaissance writing, though we cannot be sure how much creative use of these ideas represents the actual inner convictions of the writer. Two important interrelated themes are dualism and hierarchy.

Dualism

The Old Cosmology is a system containing dual natures: although it has a powerful internal logic, its elements are heterogeneous. The earthly and the celestial components do not follow the same physical laws: they represent different kinds of existence and are hence ontologically distinct. The earth is the habitat of fallen and mortal man and is consequently everywhere marked by his imperfection. It is a place where life is generated and instantly corrupted; bodily, social and moral life are characterised by flux, inconstancy and mutability, and man's corrupted nature always threatens to drag his world back into primordial chaos. Situated at the centre of the spherical cosmos, the earth also represents the lowest point of the universe and is as far away from the Empyrean as it is possible to be. It is also physically tiny: according to the popular medieval *South English Legendary*, a journey upwards from the earth at a rate of 40 miles a day would not have reached the fixed stars after 8000 years. Earth's sphere is composed of the four elements, and the material world of the senses obscures the vision of the soul: this changeable earthly space is fit for 'Dull sublunary lovers love / (Whose soul is sense)', as Donne puts it in 'A Valediction forbidding mourning'. The superlunary, heavenly realm presents a contrast: it is vast, orderly, constant, eternal, and its element is pure ether. Where earth is dark, the rest of the universe is a place of light, constantly illuminated by the sun (night was understood as the conical shadow cast by the earth as it moved around).

This earthly/heavenly duality of being provides a frame of reference for many Renaissance texts. *King Lear* illustrates the tragic themes of transience, instability and corruption, while other works, like the religious poetry of George Herbert (1593–1633) and Henry Vaughan (1622–1695), reflect on human perfectibility and the unchanging world of the divine. Donne's poetry moves constantly between the two. The earth/heaven pair corresponds to the dual nature of man himself, who is formed of flesh and spirit, body and soul. A play like Shakespeare's *The Tempest* (performed 1611) seems to explore the possibilities for resolution of the physical and spiritual aspects of man, personified in the characters of Caliban and Ariel. Spenser's *The Faerie Queene* (1590, 1596) depicts through allegory the struggle between man's baser and higher instincts. Renaissance painters take an intense interest in the accurate representation of the objects and textures of physical reality; but at the same time their works present forms of idealised beauty: the material and the ethereal inform each other. Theology and Philosophy can be understood within the same terms of reference. A pessimistic sense of damnation focuses on man's distorted nature and remoteness from the divine, while a more hopeful vision stresses the opportunity for man to exercise his divinely bestowed faculties and aspire towards salvation: Calvinism and Neoplatonism, Machiavellian and utopian conceptions of the political, exist within the same imaginative space. Renaissance culture looks upwards and downwards, giving a 'world picture' that is dialogic and dynamic rather than unitary and orthodox.

Hierarchy

The hierarchical universe of the Chain of Being becomes the model and metaphor for other arrangements. One of these is the ordering of human society: in the frontispiece to a Latin treatise *Sphaera Civitatis* (1588), by the Elizabethan scholar John Case, the monarch Elizabeth is placed in the position of the First Mover. Under her, the fixed stars are the Council, and the spheres are the virtues which govern the body politic: *Maiestas, Prudentia, Fortitudo, Religio, Clementia, Facundia, Ubertas Rerum*. The subject occupies the lowest place, his interests being best served by this benign and wise governance. In Shakespeare's *Troilus and Cressida* (c.1602), Ulysses famously praises hierarchy as the best means of establishing an ordered society: 'Take but degree away, untune that string / And hark what discord follows'. Jonson's comedies are predicated on the notion that disruptions of this order – through wanton thought and behaviour – are ultimately a threat and need to be resolved and rectified. Art is a microcosm of the universe – an internally ordered whole. Musical and architectural works similarly give form to the idea that separate parts should be integrated into a unified whole, each part performing its proper function in the overall scheme of things. We could see a poetic form like the sonnet as an ordered frame in which diverse elements – the fluctuating emotions of the lover, for example – work together to make up a unified composition. Works of art were in turn categorised by kind and rank in the theory of genres. And art itself was a picture of the art of life: by living harmoniously, in concord with his God, his society and the natural dispositions of his soul, man could aspire to the *musica mundana*, the harmony of the spheres which intimated the perfect meeting of loving beings in the divine design.

This perception of finite and perfect order inspired much beautiful art; we might also see it as a convenient legitimation of the distribution of power in society as it was, providing 'natural' reasons against any desire to rise in station. Yet just as the Renaissance 'world picture' looks upwards and downwards, so it provides pictures of disorder as well as order. Indeed, the urge towards harmony is suggestive of an underlying concern with the possibilities of disorder. This is a governing notion in *The Faerie Queene*. Aesthetic unity and spiritual harmony, the theory went, are found through variety: *discors concordia, discordia concors* (discord in concord, concord in discord). Metaphysical poetry yokes together unlike elements to make a greater whole, drawing on the endlessly complex series of analogies and correspondences within the universe. The dynamic of the human spiritual narrative is generated by the continual tension and controlled resolution of contending elements: this dynamic is represented through art, which in turn is an approximation towards the *concinnitas* (unity through variety) of the divinely ordered cosmos.

The image of political life as the *sphaera civitatis* (1588) is in tension with the picture painted by Machiavelli's *The Prince* (written 1513): here arrangements in politics do not correspond to the divine scheme but simply express the brute realities of power, fear and cunning. We find the same tension in the speech from *Troilus and Cressida* referred to above: in its dramatic context, Ulysses' persuasive eloquence is ironically undercut by the fact that he and his fellow generals are openly admitting in this scene that pursuit of war is a cynical exercise, serving no moral principle whatever, and passing their time in self-indulgent displays of oratory. Shakespeare's plays constantly explore the dangers of misrule when order slips, but at the same time are conscious of the weaknesses of prevailing schemes: *King Lear* (*c*.1603) shows the calamities when the structure collapses, yet it shows severe weaknesses in the parental and monarchical figures whose power derives from that structure. A play like *Coriolanus* (first pub. 1623) seems to explore critically every possible location of power, from the fickle and cowardly mob to a complacent aristocracy and an emerging political class of tribunes, who are motivated more by envy than by love of the public good. Jonson's plays, too, lend themselves to similar readings: in *The Alchemist* (performed 1610), society has been so viciously deconstructed through satire that it hardly seems worth saving, and it is far from clear at the end that vice has been punished, as the master of the house colludes in his servants' trickery. Meanwhile, Puritan and other Reformist schools of thought challenged the hierarchical system of church government, though often to replace it with a comparably strict scheme.

See also *Contexts*: Chain of Being, Corruption, Cosmos (2), Elements, Humours, Science; *Texts*: Mimesis, Theory of Poetry; *Criticism*: Ecocriticism

Further Reading

See entry for Cosmos (2).

Cosmos (2): The New Cosmology (heliocentric)

A geocentric universe is intuitively correct: it really does seem as if the moon and other planets travel round the earth from East to West. We still refer to sunrise and sunset, indicating that the geocentric universe still survives in our habits of speech. Nevertheless, as Renaissance scientists found, certain features are hard to accommodate within the old system. The orbits of Mars and Jupiter in particular pose problems, since they appear to go backwards at certain points. In order to 'save the appearances' and maintain the geocentric model, complex epicycles were postulated to account for this eccentric movement (an epicycle is one circle revolving around, or within, another, like a hoop spinning around the hips).

The heliocentric model, in which the earth and other planets revolve around the sun, is a neater hypothesis to account for the observable behaviour of the stars and planets. It does not depend on a telescope and was proposed as early as 250 BC by the Greek astronomer Aristarchus (310–230 BC). It was subsequently displaced by the Ptolomeic cosmos and did not return to Western imaginings until the Renaissance revolution in cosmology, which began with the Polish astronomer Copernicus (1473–1543), and his work *De Revolutionibus Orbium Coelestium* (*On the Revolutions of the Heavenly Spheres*). The conclusions of this book were recognised as dangerous to established ideology: though completed in 1530, it was not published until near the time of the author's death and dedicated to Pope Paul III, presumably as a pacifying gesture. Copernicus postulated the heliocentric universe which, like the geocentric one, is conceived as a sphere, whose outer boundary is the fixed stars, and which is composed of a series of concentric inner spheres. Night and day are explained by the earth spinning on its axis (in the geocentric cosmos the earth is stationary). Mars and Jupiter orbit around the sun, but the earth orbits faster and thus catches up with them: against the background of the fixed stars this makes them appear to go backward.

The century 1550–1650 saw the workings out of the Copernican revolution, initially restricted to the learned elite but gradually superseding the old model. Kepler (1571–1630) used applied mathematics to conclude that the planets' orbits are elliptical and that they do not move with uniform movement and speed – a blow to the spherical cosmos.

The Danish astronomer Tycho Brahe observed in 1572 what he took to be a new star in the constellation of Cassiopeia: this was in fact a supernova (an exploding star) but its significance was that it was an inexplicably new event in a supposedly unchanging cosmos. In 1577, Brahe observed a comet coming from beyond the Moon: its trajectory cut through the spheres, but this would be impossible according to the fixed model, in which the spheres are solid. The work was continued by Galileo Galilei (1564–1642) in works such as *Starry Messenger* (1610) and *Dialogue . . . Concerning the Two Chief World Systems* (1632). In these, Galileo demolishes the distinction between the lunar and the sublunar spheres. Using a telescope, he discovered irregularities in the Moon, proving it to be imperfect. Similarly, his observations of solar spots showed that the Sun was not a perfect sphere either and was subject to change. Galileo also observed the satellites of Jupiter, which demonstrated that not everything orbited the earth. The concept of the dual nature of the earth and the heavens was effectively destroyed by such observations.

The findings of the new astronomy conflicted with Church teaching. Galileo was forced to recant his science by the Roman Catholic Church, which formally condemned the heliocentric theory in 1616. Luther, too, condemned Copernicus on the grounds that he contrasted with the truths of scripture: did not Joshua command the sun to stand still? As well as contradicting the letter of scripture, the heliocentric cosmos also disturbed some deeply rooted notions: it presented a universe as homogenous, all parts subject to the same physical laws, a finding which destroyed the idea of man's special position. The old hierarchy is dissolved, and the earth becomes a planet like any other. The implications of the new model were imaginatively explored in the work of Giordano Bruno (1548–1600), the free-thinking Dominican friar whose heretical writings led to his imprisonment (1592) and eventual execution by fire. Bruno was not a scientist and was sceptical about the reliability of human sense-based observation. In *De l'infinito universo e mondi* (1584), written for a wider audience in popular Italian rather than Latin, he posited an infinite universe, without any privileged centre. This infinite universe contains a plurality of worlds (*mondi*): infinity and plurality are attributes of a God who, Bruno writes, is not a transcendent *primum mobile* on the outside of the cosmos, but an immanent presence within it, a kind of essential energy or organising force. Bruno was also anti-dualist, that is to say he denied any distinction between matter and spirit: thus all things are material, and anything material embodies the divine spark.

Bruno's writings indicate some of the vast potential for new thinking generated by radical revisions of the received model of the cosmos. In particular, perhaps, it suggests that a cosmos which is not earth-centred could actually magnify the power and mystery of God, who becomes a less anthropomorphic and a more mystical presence. English literature of the period, however, remains largely rooted in the Ptolomeic cosmos. This is not a matter of stubborn adhesion to the older system. Poetic imagery does not shift in obedience to Science, and at the level of images – from standard topics such as the rising sun to the developed astrological patterns of *The Faerie Queene* – it is the inherited model which predominates. At the same time, employment of metaphor does not prove intellectual subscription to its underlying idea. Donne draws on imagery from the new cosmology in 'Ignatius his Conclave', and Milton enthuses about Galileo's use of the telescope (see *Paradise Lost*, V. 262 ff.) while developing from the available models his own particular picture of the universe.

See also   *Contexts*: Chain of Being, Cosmos (1), Elements, Humours, Science, Travel and Colonialism; *Criticism*: Ecocriticism

Further Reading

Introductory

C. S. Lewis, *The Discarded Image: An Introduction to Medieval and Renaissance Literature* (Cambridge: CUP, 1964), ch 5, 'The Heavens', 92–121.

Isabel Rivers, *Classical and Christian Ideas in English Renaissance Poetry*, 2nd edn (London: Routledge, 1994), ch. 6 'Cosmology', 68–87.

Full Length

Ernst Cassirer, *The Individual and the Cosmos in Renaissance Philosophy* (New York: Barnes and Noble, 1963).

Stephen L. Collins, *From Divine Cosmos to Sovereign State: An Intellectual History of Consciousness and the Idea of Order in Renaissance England* (Oxford: OUP, 1989).

S. K. Heninger, Jr., *Touches of Sweet Harmony: Pythagorean Cosmology and Renaissance Poetics* (San Marino, California: Huntington Library, 1974).

S. K. Heninger, Jr., *The Renaissance Glass: Renaissance Diagrams of the Universe* (San Marino, California: Huntington Library, 1977).

The Court

The court was a central institution of Renaissance states, linking the worlds of politics and culture. Much of the art and literature of the period is concerned with the court and courtliness. Some 400 treatises for knights, and 800 for ladies, are recorded from the fifteenth and sixteenth centuries; Castiglione's *The Courtier* (written 1508–1516, translated into English in 1561) is the best known of these, and was read across Europe. The Renaissance court was an object of fascination and emulation and a principal site for the commission and consumption of art.

'The court' has various senses. It can denote a physical space, such as a palace. Like any noble house, this will be staffed by guards, secretaries, falconers, ostlers and so forth. Palaces denoted the power and importance of their lords: Wolsey's Hampton Court presented him as a regal figure; and Henry VIII constructed numerous palaces as part of his desire to be one of the great figures of Europe. It will also have a specific architecture with such typical elements as courtyard, chambers, chapel, royal chamber and antechamber. The use of these spaces distanced the Prince from his subjects, creating a sense of sacrality: at Hampton Court, for example, Henry VIII clearly distinguished the gentlemen allowed to enter his privy chamber from those only permitted to attend him in the audience chamber. Other monarchs followed this practice: when the Earl of Essex (1566–1601) returned without leave from his disastrous expedition to Ireland (1599), he is supposed to have entered the Queen's private chambers while she was still being prepared for the day – a terrible offence. Through the symbolic use of space, the court creates an aura around the monarch.

A second sense of 'court' is an institution. The body of people around the Prince constituted a unique social configuration, with its own complex pattern of rituals. The court is also simply wherever the Prince, attended by this tribe, happens to be. The Renaissance initially continued from the Middle Ages the practice of an itinerant court. This provided the sovereign with a means of receiving the produce of the land and of overseeing his subjects and dominions. The great Renaissance princes Henry VIII, Charles V and Francis I all had multiple residences and the court moved around with them. This entourage could number hundreds and even thousands of people. Such a mobile mass provided opportunities for grand royal entries, ceremonial displays and other lavish entertainments; and it was a stimulus for local lords to build grand country houses suitable for monarchs and their locust-like retinue. Sir Christopher Hatton (1540–1591) ruined himself building the vast house of Holdenby chiefly in the hope that Elizabeth I would visit it. She never did. Over the year, a court may alter in size: Henry VII's court was bigger in winter, when he stayed in London at the palaces of Richmond, Greenwich, Hampton Court, Whitehall and Nonesuch; when he travelled in the summer, numbers declined. Nonetheless, throughout our period, the court involved large numbers of people and represented a serious drain on finances.

Nobles

Members of the Renaissance court fall into various groups. At the top of the scale were the nobles, who were honoured by serving the monarch and were expected to bring magnificence to the court through gorgeous dress and refined manners. Court life was a theatrical spectacle, glorified by painters and poets as a gathering of the terrestrial gods. The splendours and sophistication of the court and its quasi-divine prince were also a source of patriotic pride. Sir Thomas Smith, Elizabeth I's ambassador in Paris, boasts of the English love of ceremony in his study of government *De Republica Anglorum* (1565):

> No man speaketh to the Prince nor serveth at the table but in adoration and kneeling, all persons of the realm be bareheaded before him, insomuch that in the chamber of presence where the cloth of estate is set, no man dare walk; yea though the Prince be not there, no man dare tarry there but bareheaded.

(Smith's discomfort at having a female monarch might be sensed in his reference to a masculine Prince.) The Renaissance saw a marked increase in the splendour and intricacy of such ceremony, and an important function for noble courtiers was the enactment of these codes, through which the cult of the monarch was established. A nobleman's own position in turn could be dignified by prestigious offices such as Chamberlain and Marshall: Robert Dudley, the Earl of Leicester (1533–1588), was Master of the Queen's Horse. Such posts were titular only, and the actual work was of course done by someone else. Peers could get the monarch's ear, receive graces and favours, be personal witness to the cult figure of the sovereign and in turn enhance their status as part of the inner circle. Peers would also take the fashions they had seen back with them to their regions, making the court a primary vehicle for the transmission of culture between and within countries. The monarch in turn could keep an eye on the nobles, reduce the power of individuals by keeping them in competition with each other and keep them away from their local power bases. In the court setting, everything was highly visible: insults, slights and rebuffs entered the rumour factory immediately, and expulsion from the court was a serious disgrace. Henry Howard, Earl of Surrey (1517–1547), wrote much of his poetry when he was dismissed to Windsor by Henry VIII, after striking someone in an argument.

Favourites

Sometimes a young nobleman, commended by personal attractions, occupied the special position of favourite and become a companion in the sovereign's private chambers. Examples of favourites from England are Sir Christopher Hatton, the Earls of Leicester and Essex and Sir Walter Raleigh at the court of Elizabeth I and the Duke of Buckingham at the court of James I. Sumptuously dressed favourites could provide a relief from the business of court and a counter to the tediousness of ceremony and over-formality. Inevitably, they caused resentment among other courtiers, sometimes leading to open hostility. Romantic or erotic resonances could surround the unclear nature of this companionship: Christopher Marlowe's *Edward II* (1594) dramatically explores Edward II's intimate relationship with his favourite Piers Gaveston. Favouritism is also a theme of Shakespeare's *Richard II* (c.1595), in which the 'caterpillars of the commonwealth' are seen as having too much influence over the King. Elizabeth's fondness for Leicester, Raleigh and Essex continues to provide lively material for popular treatments of her reign today. Around the figure of Elizabeth I there arose a complex code involving the courtier as suitor and would-be favourite.

Bureaucracy

Beneath the nobles came a middle group of courtiers who handled day-to-day bureaucracy: this class of administrators, lawyers and diplomats expanded as the centralisation of state power increased the amount of business that had to be done. Court bureaucracy was a professionalised activity and offered an opportunity for educated men of a lower rank to rise through the court: Thomas Wolsey (1475–1530) was an example of one of these new men, resented by the traditional aristocracy, whose status was further threatened by the new wealth that followed the dissolution of the monasteries. Once established, the new men could found dynasties of their own, and some of these families, such as the Cecils and the Russells, have continued to occupy positions of power and influence in public service from that time. As in Wolsey's case, a senior position in the secretariat could also bring with it real executive power: the bureaucrats of court were officially there to execute the orders of the sovereign but could in practice become autonomous agents. A humanist education followed by legal studies at university and service in the household of a great man would be a conventional route to the court bureaucracy: 'civic humanism', or the emphasis on the practical benefits to the state of a good classical education, was an accompanying philosophy, marrying the worlds of learning and worldly accomplishment. Thomas Elyot's *The Book Named The Governor* (1531) advocates the classical education of a young gentleman to prepare him for the responsibilities of government. At the outset of Henry VIII's reign, humanists like Elyot had high hopes for his court as a centre of the new learning: Erasmus, who himself wrote a book *The Education of a Christian Prince* (1516), praised the young king, who took his studies seriously and tried to learn Greek. Catherine of Aragon and Anne Boleyn also patronised intellectual endeavour. Literature was regarded as of practical value, not simply a recreational refinement. But as the court became more absolutist, and disconnected from Italy through the Reformation, such early hopes were dashed.

Culture

The court was a natural centre of culture, as both producer and consumer: leisure was an important part of its business, as the prince and his entourage would relax in the evenings with poetry, music, chess and other sophisticated activities such as courting, witty conversation and dancing, all with an eye on keeping up with the latest fashions. This intensely social field is reflected in the art of the court itself: poems and songs are often addressed to an implied audience with an intimated dialogue between speaker and listener; even when interior feelings are treated, as in the sonnet, the effect is one of a speaker displaying and adorning his material, communicating to others with the rhetorical aims of persuading, delighting and moving an audience. As in dances today, a participant can be performer one minute and spectator the next, or both at the same time. This lack of distinction between being in the act or out of it is reflected in the quintessential art form to be created in the world of the court, the masque, which would end with spectators and performers dancing together.

It was not only leisure but the nature of politics which made the Renaissance court a centre of cultural production. The historian Jacob Burckhardt argued that in this period the state became 'a work of art' (*The Civilization of the Renaissance in Italy*, Part I). Through a range of symbols, the Prince and his court needed to demonstrate to an increasingly educated populace its right to govern. The medieval customs of splendid banquets, tournaments and hunts were insufficient for this purpose, and so princes became patrons of projects which provided a complex and subtle iconography supporting those in power. Palaces, emblems, histories, paintings and poetry all served this end. Burckhardt's examples are taken from the small Italian states, but the thesis can also be applied to England. Sophisticated propagandistic art reached a high point in the manufacture of the public image of Elizabeth I. As scholars have shown, the cult of Elizabeth as Cynthia, Astraea and the Virgin Queen was a project spanning all the arts; through solemn entries and other public ceremonies, the Queen herself became a work of art, a living symbol of the people.

Conclusion

There are various ways in which the Renaissance court might enter into the study of the literature of the period. There is the substantial body of work by courtiers such as Surrey, Raleigh and Sidney, which expresses courtly preoccupations and values. These are also espoused in the many texts praising either sovereigns or nobles: Ben Jonson's epigrams lauding King James (number 4), Lucy Countess of Bedford (76), Elizabeth Countess of Rutland (79) and William Earl of Pembroke (102) provide succinct formulations of the virtues which dignitaries were supposed to embody; while 'An Epigram on William, Lord Burleigh, Lord High Treasurer of England', praising Elizabeth's advisor William Cecil (1521–98) articulates the values of good governance in the figure of courtier as guardian of the state. Representations of the court also reward study: Shakespeare's *Richard II* presents a picture of the court as a place of ceremony and formality, but also of greed, corruption and intrigue. Satire of the court often had an anti-Italian flavour. Plays such as Webster's *Duchess of Malfi* (performed 1614, printed 1623) depict Italian courts as places of Machiavellian intrigue and every kind of depravity. Where Castiglione's Urbino (as depicted in *The Courtier*) had initially provided the model of the Renaissance court, in post-Reformation England the Catholic courts of Italy were places onto which every fear and suspicion of the realities of courtly behaviour could be projected.

This perception of the court as a cesspit of vice is visible in *Hamlet* (*c.*1599) and grew in strength in the Jacobean period. The court and the country came to symbolise different political factions, and from a country perspective the cavaliers of the court were not models to emulate but examples of decadence. *Memoirs of the Life of Colonel Hutchinson* (first published 1664) by Lucy Hutchinson (1620–1681) provides an interesting Puritan perspective, depicting the court as a centre of luxury and excess, whose rotten influence contaminates the life of country houses. Even where the court is not explicitly mentioned, as in pastoral idylls, it may be present as an implied contrast to the subject matter being celebrated. The Renaissance court was an integral part of the establishment of the modern state, combining administration with the enactment of the noble life. But the state was increasingly run by a separate bureaucracy, and the mystique of the court was removed by the growing power of parliament and the dissolute behaviour of monarchs and their entourage; meanwhile the Puritan movement encouraged people to look to plainer, more scriptural models of behaviour. The court was left with little to do but pursue ostentatious consumption and flamboyance as ends in themselves. This narrative can be traced in the literature, from the earnest civic humanism at the court of Henry VIII to the cavalier poetry of the later seventeenth century.

See also *Contexts*: Courtier, Patronage, Women; *Texts*: Masque, Prose Style, Rhetoric

Further Reading

Peter Burke, 'The Courtier': in Garin, Eugenio, ed., *Renaissance Characters* (University of Chicago Press, 1991), 98–122.

Mary Hill Cole, *The Portable Queen: Elizabeth I and the Politics of Ceremony* (Amherst, MA: University of Massachusetts Press, 1999).

R. Malcolm Smuts, *Court Culture and the Origins of a Royalist Tradition in Early Stuart England* (Philadelphia, PA: University of Pennsylvania Press, 1987).

David Starkey: *Henry VIII: A European Court in England* (London: Collins and Brown, 1991);

David Starkey, *Elizabeth I: The Exhibition Catalogue* (London: Chatto and Windus, 2003).

Roy Strong, *The Tudor and Stuart Monarchy: Pageantry, Painting, Iconography*, 3 vols (Cambridge: Boydell Press, 1997–1999).

The Courtier

If the knight in armour is the iconic figure of the Middle Ages, then the courtier is that of the Renaissance. We find the two together in Chaucer's *Canterbury Tales*, where the valiant crusading knight is accompanied by his son, the Squire, who reflects the court of Richard II (*r*.1377–99), a century before our period begins. In all essentials, though, Chaucer's portrait presents the model of the Renaissance courtier. Skilled in the arts of war (the Squire has fought in France) and horsemanship, the Squire also cultivates the arts of refined leisure: he dresses well, and exercises his talents in music, singing, jousting, dancing, drawing and writing. He is modest in demeanour and given to falling in love. We see that the court provides the model for courtesy, or proper conduct: 'Curteis he was'. With his all-round abilities, the Squire is a 'Renaissance man' on the lines of Hamlet, as Ophelia remembers him in his prime:

> Oh what a noble mind is here o'erthrown!
> The courtier's, soldier's, scholar's, eye, tongue, sword,
> Th'expectancy and rose of the fair state,
> The glass of fashion and the mould of form,
> Th'observed of all observers...
>
> (3.1.144–148)

Hamlet was born into the court, and Chaucer's Squire would have been sent there as a page to learn through practice the various accomplishments expected of a nobleman and courtier: how to talk, dance, make jokes and laugh in the accepted manner, exercise the martial arts, compose and appreciate music and poetry. Spenser called the court 'the great school mistress of all curtesy', and the lessons of this mistress were given expression in writings such as popular Arthurian romances, in which the courtier is held up as a model: 'the mould of form, / Th'observed of all observers'. From at least the tenth century, the royal court had been held up as a model for courteous conduct, with Ciceronian terms such as *urbanitas* and *decorum* adopted to describe the virtues to which knights should aspire. In the world of drama, actors were measured by their ability to reproduce the mannerisms and occupations of courtiers and nobility.

Spenser's great mistress was also portrayed in the particular genre known as the courtesy book, or conduct manual. This kind of book gives direct prescriptions on courtly accomplishments. *Il Cortegiano*, or *The Book of the Courtier*, by the Italian Baldesar Castiglione (1478–1529) was the best known of these. Castiglione's book was finished in 1516, published in 1528 and read across Europe: an English translation by Sir Thomas Hoby was published in 1561. *Il Cortegiano* takes the form of dialogues, in which knights and ladies discuss the attributes which make the ideal courtier. The picture that emerges is one of the universal man, *l'uomo universale*: like Hamlet and Chaucer's Squire, he can fight, write, sing, dance, paint, compose poetry and flirt in the approved neoplatonic fashion. He is attentive and sophisticated in conversation. Physical accomplishments are as important as intellectual ones, and much importance is placed on body language. A courtier is evaluated by the way he mounts a horse, rides, walks, gesticulates and dances. None of this should look effortful, however: an important value in Castiglione's book is *sprezzatura*, the art of excelling at something with apparent nonchalance. Disciplined practice should be kept in the background, so that performance looks easy and natural. This corresponds to the ideal in rhetoric of *ars celare artum est*: art is to conceal art. In passing, it is interesting to consider the thesis that these arts of leisure were a substitute for the older occupation of fighting: as the old courtly occupations of running the country and fighting were increasingly taken over by professional bureaucracy and soldiers, so the courtly class needed to find another identity, and this was based on display rather than productive activity.

Another interesting aspect of Castiglione's book is the importance of ladies. The court of Urbino, where *Il Cortegiano* is set, is a salon directed by the Duchess and her ladies in the absence of the Duke. Ladies are outside the world of formal politics, but as mistresses of the domestic realm they exercise a different kind of power in governing the household and establishing norms of conduct, besides acting as sophisticated judges of male behaviour: in Castiglione's dialogues, it is the ladies who judge the topics and decide who has the best of an argument. Book Three of *Il Cortegiano* is devoted to discussion of the court lady. She must embody such feminine graces as tenderness, sweetness and 'pleasing affability', and like the men strive for a happy medium: she must be modest but not coy, free but not unseemly, all such virtues appearing in her manner of moving, dressing and performing music. The ideal court lady must be able to converse with men with equal knowledge of letters, music and painting – though there is disagreement among the speakers on how different the sexes are, and whether ladies are men's intellectual equals. In addition to these Renaissance qualities, the lady must also practise the virtues of continence, magnanimity, temperance, fortitude and prudence. A comparable list of qualities is provided in Ben Jonson's epigram 'On Lucy, Countess of Bedford' (from *The Works*, 1616):

> I meant to make her fair and free and wise.
> Of greatest blood, and yet more good than great . . .
> I meant she should be courteous, facile, sweet,   [facile: affable
> Hating that solemn vice of greatness, pride;
> I meant each softest virtue there should meet,
> Firm in that softer bosom to reside.
>
> (5–6, 9–12)

The Countess of Bedford (1581–1627) is also an example of the courtly lady who not only adorns a court but actively promotes artistic creation: the writers she befriended and encouraged included Jonson, Samuel Daniel, Michael Drayton and John Donne. It has been argued that Castiglione's ideal lady is an insipid, passive figure, there principally to be impressed by men and make them feel important: we note that it is 'softness' which Jonson holds up as a great virtue. Yet ladies in great households could exercise considerable power and influence in their domain: we could find local instances of matriarchy even within a patri-archal culture.

Courtly etiquette, as described by Castiglione and others, became increasingly complex over the sixteenth and seventeenth centuries. Codes of behaviour became more precise, and the ability to discuss art and literature, with their own highly sophisticated codes, presented a real challenge. There also seems to have been a growing self-awareness and self-control. At the start of the sixteenth century, a writer like Rabelais depicts all kinds of bodily behaviour, from eating to excretion, without embarrassment. Over the course of the century, though, norms of hygiene and physical conduct were transformed: methods of eating were changed by the invention of the fork in the later sixteenth century, and soap and toothpaste were introduced. A high value was placed on politeness, seen as something which could be taught to children in works like Erasmus' *De civilitate morum puerilium* (*On the Civilising of Children's Manners*, 1526).

Perhaps one could interpret the emphasis on ceremony in Renaissance courtly life as a symbol of subjection on the part of an individual to a wider system, including the disciplining of corporal urges. Over the early modern period, the kind of physicality relished by Rabelais came to be regarded as proper to animals, and beneath the dignity of gentlefolk. Different courts had different reputations: James I's entourage apparently behaved in a coarse and disgusting manner, whereas Charles I's court was marked by more refinement.

A good deal of Renaissance literature may be read as part of the art of being a courtier: many love poems, which we would probably read in silence and alone, would have originated as songs after dinner, inextricably accompanied with music and conversation. What was originally a social act, involving several arts, is today constricted to a textual object in a very different, academic milieu. We might also note the important figure of the courtier writer: under Henry VIII the pre-eminent examples are Sir Thomas Wyatt (1503–1542), diplomat and member of the *garde du corps*, and Surrey (whose annotated copy of Castiglione survives). In the reign of Queen Elizabeth, the most famous courtier poets are Sir Philip Sidney (1554–1586) and Sir Walter Raleigh (1552–1618). In such figures it is hard, if not impossible, to draw the normal modern distinction between the real and the feigned. The biography of Sidney by his friend Fulke Greville (1554–1628) presents him as a model courtier, whose life is a work of art worthy of imitation (the text is also implicitly a critique of the present court). Raleigh played the role of courtly lover of Elizabeth, but was sent away in disgrace when he secretly married one of her ladies-in-waiting, Elizabeth Throckmorton (1591). 'The 21th: and last booke of the Ocean to Cynthia', written in the Tower of London either at this time (1592) or when he was later imprisoned by James I, uses mythological imagery to convey a passage of thought which is at once personal and political.

Life at court was notoriously precarious, and bitter reflections on the unpredictable reverses of fortune and favour are part of the stock of much Renaissance writing. Indeed, the court itself could be an emblem of the ephemeral and fleeting: the loving mistress of one day turns to 'new-fangledness' the next, in Wyatt's lyric 'They flee from me that sometime did me seek'. Alongside the courtier poets are other writers who failed to gain high positions in court. Edmund Spenser (1552–1599) only ever attained the position of a second-ranking courtier, rewarded for his poetic efforts with a pension and a post as secretary to the Viceroy of Ireland: the various dedicatory verses to *The Faerie Queene* record a fairly desperate attempt to find favour and patronage in the right places. John Lyly (*c*.1553–1606) failed to secure the post of master of the Revels. Unsurprisingly, criticism of the court is an important theme: Donne's fourth Satire portrays a foppish courtier and reveals an interestingly divided state of mind over the attractions of court life. Fulke Greville attacks court sycophants and flatterers:

> The little Hearts, where light-wing'd Passion raignes,
> Move easily upward, as all frailties doe;
> Like Strawes to Jeat, these follow Princes veines,
> And so, by pleasing, doe corrupt them too.
>
> (Sonnet 26, from Caelica, written ?c.1600,
published 1633)

Over-sophistication and pretension are satirised in the Overburian character of the courtier and in the cameo role of Osric in *Hamlet*. Behind such anti-courtier satire one can feel the competing values of plainness, sincerity and austerity, increasingly associated with the country as against the city in the Jacobean period, but present as early as the juxtaposition of old-world knight and rising Squire in *The Canterbury Tales*. Court and courtier present vital themes in Renaissance literature, and like other themes demonstrate a set of tensions rather than a coherent unitary picture. Wherever the ideal courtier is to be found, his affected, sycophantic and conspiring alter ego is never far away.

See also   *Contexts*: Court, Patronage, Women; *Texts*: Epic, Masque

Further Reading

Catherine Bates, *The Rhetoric of Courtship in Elizabethan Language and Literature* (Cambridge: CUP, 1992).

Daniel Javitch, *Poetry and Courtliness in Renaissance England* (Princeton, NJ: Princeton UP, 1978).

Steven W. May, *The Elizabethan Courtier Poets: the Poems and their Contexts* (London: University of Missouri Press, 1991).

Economy and Society

Early modern England was a rural economy. Some 90 percent of the population – roughly estimated at four million in 1600 – lived on the land and pursued country occupations: milling, baking, brewing, distilling, felling and preparing timber for houses and shipbuilding, growing barley and rye for ale and bread. Work patterns varied greatly between regions: orchards, market gardens and hops were cultivated in the South East (London, Essex and Kent); tin was mined in Cornwall, coal in Durham and Newcastle; iron was smelted in Sussex and the Forest of Dean; cattle were farmed in Devon, and East Anglia grew rich through cultivating corn and producing good-quality cloth. The Fens were still swamp (farmed on stilts), while beyond England large tracts of Wales and Scotland were moor and heath. Varieties of produce, soil, landscape, natural resources and climate were accompanied by marked regional varia- tions of culture and strong local loyalties. Communication was often precarious, and markets were limited by practicalities of transport (these facts naturally militated against any unifying consciousness of shared Englishness). Towns were small: after London, which had a population of perhaps 200,000 in 1600, the next largest town was Norwich, numbering some 20,000. Then came Bristol, York, Exeter, Newcastle and Plymouth. Some towns (Southampton, Sandwich, Hull) were in decline; others, like the cloth towns of Yorkshire and Lancashire, were growing. But none of these resembled modern urban centres in either activity or size: most townspeople were connected to the land in some way, and to us the Renaissance town would look like a large village, surrounded by countryside. To take one example, Leicester had a population of only some 4000. Early modern Englishmen and women lived in an intimate proximity to the land, with its animals and its weather, to a degree that is extremely hard for those of us in an industrialised society to imagine.

Important changes to agriculture occurred over the sixteenth century. One cause of upheaval was inflation. Steep price rises were a general European phenomenon over the sixteenth century, for a number of reasons: gold and silver bullion from the New World flooded the market; debasement of the coinage (that is, decreasing the amount of silver in each coin) under Henry VIII and Edward VI made sellers suspicious of the money offered, leading to a rise in prices; and a rising population inexorably led to an increase in the money in circulation (it has been estimated that England's population doubled in size between the reigns of Henry VII and James I, creating pressure on land and food besides a need for coins). Landholders living on fixed rental income found that they could not keep up with rising prices and sought to make as much money as possible from their land, by exploiting its natural resources or raising the rent. While many tenants were protected from rent-rises by the terms of their lease, there was still considerable criticism of the practice of 'rack-renting', a departure from fixed rents in a medieval non-inflationary economy. An important underlying conceptual shift concerned attitudes to land itself: traditional subsistence farming, serving basic needs, gave way to commercial farming, growing for the market rather than the household. Land thus became a source of income besides being a means of survival. This early capitalist thinking was also fostered by the intense market in land following the dissolution of the monasteries: former church territories were acquired for their investment value and for the social standing coming from the status of country squire.

Land, once acquired, could then be geared to the needs of the market, if necessary by changing its produce. Consequently, many areas saw a shift from arable to sheep farming. Wool production satisfied the ever-growing demand from England's main industry, textiles. Sheep farming was also cheaper than arable in terms of labour: a shepherd, a boy and a dog could look after a large herd, in contrast to the large numbers needed to plough, sow and harvest a field of corn. Sheep farming also led to an increase in enclosures – the enclosing of previously open land by hedgerows, chiefly to prevent sheep from straying. This was not a new practice, nor was it universal. But it did have significant social effects. There were various ways in which enclosure might happen. Land which was formerly occupied by open fields might be enclosed by a smallholding tenant buying up plots surrounding his or by landholders securing large plots through purchase and eviction; common ground, on which village life relied, was also sometimes enclosed by lords of the manor, leading to the complete disappearance of some communities. These changes led to a basic organisational structure of landholder, tenant farmer and labourer. They also meant that the peasant labourer, feudally bound to his lord and the land, disappeared from English life over our period. In his place arose the landless labourer, without fixed attachment to master or place.

If labour was not needed, the inevitable result was men and women roaming the highways, some searching for work, some turning to beggary or crime. These vagrants were dealt with in various ways, often punitive: the idea that beggars were incorrigible idlers showed a hardy persistence. The Poor Law of 1601 put the onus of responsibility on parishes for providing labour and masters and followed an important 1531 Statute in distinguishing between those who could not, and those who would not, work. This was an important stage in the emergence of state welfare, since it accepted that private philanthropy was inadequate to deal with the social problem of poverty and unemployment and created a system of relief funded by a compulsory poor rate.

Writers as well as legislators responded to economic turbulence. Contemporaries attacked many of the practices mentioned above: Book I of Sir Thomas More's *Utopia* (1516), which contains important satirical commentary on the issues touched on here, contains the famous observation that England's sheep 'have become so greedy and fierce that they devour men themselves', a reference to the workers pauperised and effectively driven off the land they had previously tended. Social historians have discussed how far this kind of polemic adequately describes the early modern economy: while terrible poverty existed, and crises caused by bad harvests could lead to social unrest such as the rebellion in Norfolk in 1549, there is less evidence of an extended surplus of labour leading to widespread unemployment. Some were enriched by the new conditions; many others suffered terrible poverty. Again, regional variation makes generalisation risky. It should also be noted that the shift to sheep farming was not permanent: the market peaked and fell off, and by the end of the sixteenth century food production overtook wool production.

As we have seen, cloth was England's most important early modern industry. Usually, rough cloth was produced and exported, to be finished in other countries. The cloth industry was organised on a domestic basis: the basic model was a weaver at his loom in his own cottage. One emerging practice was the 'putting-out' system. Under this kind of organisation, clothiers provided weavers with cloth, and weavers would work for the clothiers for a wage. In other words, weavers ceased to provide their own raw materials and sell their own produce on the open market, these stages in the process being devolved onto a 'middle man'. This can be seen as the beginning of industrial capitalism, though in other respects Renaissance industry was pre-industrial: while there were a few instances where several weavers would work under one roof, these were experimental oddities rather than an emerging norm. Factory work, based usually on heavy machinery and a common power supply, did not arise until after our period. The cloth trade expanded hugely from about 1460, doubling by the reign of Henry VIII, thanks in part to the debasement of coinage which made English wool relatively cheap abroad. But, in a familiar cycle, boom led to overproduction, which was followed by a slump after 1551 when the market in the Netherlands collapsed, and inevitably unemployment resulted. It was recognised that a more reliable regulatory mechanism was needed, in part to prevent opportunists taking over parts of the trade. The 1563 Statute of Artificers was an attempt to make rigid the apprentice system; a similar principle of excluding outsiders informs the charters of the new merchant companies (such as the Muscovy Company, the Levant Company and the East India Company). A further underlying conceptual change lay in the nature of money and perceptions of value: in medieval tradition, everything had a 'just price', a value set by nature. The sixteenth-century price rise, however, led to the sense of commercial value that we are used to: the value of an object is not fixed, but the function of the relation between supply and demand. Over the sixteenth and seventeenth centuries, England gradually improved at other manufactures, such as glass, copper, brass and luxury fabrics for the affluent end of the market: foreign artisans settling in England brought with them techniques from countries where skilled manufacture was considerably more developed.

Finally, we should consider the issue of class. This is perhaps an unhelpful concept, more appropriate to urban industrial life than to a pre-industrialised economy. Though an obsession with rank and order in the literature might lead us to expect a fixed class system in Renaissance England, with everyone knowing their place, the reality seems to have been much the opposite: indeed this obsession may be a register of disquiet at the amount of social mobility taking place. It is, for example, hard to draw any clear line between nobility and gentry, or between merchant and landholder. Some landed gentry invested in trade adventures, while some merchants acquired land and became country gentlemen. The custom of primogeniture (by which the eldest son inherits the family estate) meant that younger sons of gentry went into commerce. The crown could push new men, some of a humble background, into the ranks of the upper classes, and similar preferments could occur at many levels through the patronage system. Some nobility achieved wealth through land, others through court office; and of course just as people could rise by these means, they could also fall. Those with titles might have financial difficulties, while untitled merchants could be very rich. What seems to have been important as a social marker was not belonging to a definable 'class', marked by specific economic criteria, so much as the individual's rank and degree, which depended on particular circumstances. If a common theme emerges from our brief consideration of agriculture, industry and social hierarchy, it is indeed this popular Renaissance topic of mutability: all things on earth are subject to change, often violent and unforeseen. The fluctuating economic conditions of the time provide a context for this preoccupation and help to explain the yearning for a stable and ordered 'golden' society, ignorant of such vicissitudes, that we find in texts across the period.

See also *Contexts*: City, Golden Age, Travel and Colonialism; *Texts*: Pastoral; *Criticism*: Ecocriticism

Further Reading

An important contemporary source is William Harrison, *Description of England* (1577).
G. R. Elton, *England Under the Tudors*, 2nd edn (London: Methuen, 1974).
J. A. Sharpe, *Early Modern England: A Social History, 1550–1760*, 2nd edn (London: Hodder Arnold, 1997).
Keith Wrightson, *Earthly Necessities: Economic Lives in Early Modern Britain, 1470–1750* (London: Penguin, 2002); *English Society, 1580–1680*, 2nd edn (London: Routledge, 2003).

The Elements

The medieval theory of the humours informs thought and writing throughout the Renaissance period. On this model, the earth is made up of four elements: earth, water, air and fire. Earth is the lowest and heaviest, and fire is the lightest and highest. The concept of the elements is far older than the Renaissance: it has an ancient source in Empedocles (Fragment 17) and was adopted by Aristotle, whose version was passed on to the Middle Ages. Like the humours, the Chain of Being and the geocentric universe, the elements form a rich source of metaphor and imagery.

Elements are not, as in modern chemistry, discreet substances. They are not things, but qualities attributable to all matter. The elements are aspects of each substance. We cannot see them directly, but discern them from their effects. Traditionally they are defined according to their temperature and humidity, as follows:

Fire	Hot and Dry
Air	Hot and Wet
Water	Cold and Wet
Earth	Cold and Dry

As this table shows, each element has something in common with the element above. The highest element shares with the lowest the quality of being dry: thus they form a continuing cycle. Each element has a natural inclination to occupy its proper place: heavy objects fall because the preponderant element of earth gives them a natural inclination to join that element in the ground. The elements make up the matter of the earthly sphere and correspond to the four humours which make up the human physical constitution. Beyond visible fire is the invisible fire which reaches to the moon. Beyond the lunar sphere the material elements cease and the common element is the quintessence, or ether.

An even mixture of the elements, with none dominating, is a common image of inner equilibrium, or noble temperament:

> His life was gentle, and the elements
> So mixed in him, that Nature might stand up
> And say to all the world, 'This was a man!'
> *(Julius Caesar,* 5.3.,73–75)

Even when composed harmoniously, the elements are still properties of matter. Donne contrasts the material world known by the senses with the spiritual realm beyond it:

> Dull sublunary lovers love
> (Whose soul is sense) cannot admit
> Absence, because it doth remove
> Those things which elemented it.
> (Donne, 'A Valediction
> forbidding mourning', 13–16)

In these lines, 'sublunary' lovers are those in the earthly sphere: they are 'dull', since they cannot see beyond matter, and their soul is sense-bound ('sense' also has a connotation of sensuous: dull loves love the body, not the soul). Such lovers cannot be separate, because it is matter or 'sense' which unites them: they 'cannot admit / Absence', a neat wordplay on 'Absence' combining its senses of 'separation' and 'ab-sence, removal of the sensual'. In the next stanza, this earth bound relation is contrasted with the 'refin'd love' of the poet and his mistress which, as a spiritual state, transcends the elements of matter.

The doctrine of the elements on earth and the quintessence above is suited to both Christian and Platonic thought: Donne's lines depict love as a religious separation of the soul from the flesh; and the idea of a refined and higher love, transcending the dull earthly version, is clearly similar to the Platonic world of Ideas.

See also   *Contexts*: Chain of Being, Cosmos, Humours, Magic, Medicine, Science; *Criticism*: Ecocriticism

Further Reading

Alan G. R. Smith, *Science and Society in the Sixteenth and Seventeenth Centuries* (London: Thames and Hudson, 1972), ch. 1 'Science and Society in 1500', 9–27.

English Reformation

When Henry VII came to the throne in 1485, England was a Catholic nation. While some voices were calling for reformation from within the Church, the authority of Rome and the Pope in spiritual matters was generally accepted as the natural state of things, and this membership of the Catholic communion of western Christendom left its mark on people's lives at many levels. Catholic teachings shaped both people's inner beliefs, and also their external world, from the liturgy and decoration of their churches to local saint cults and pilgrimages to shrines. Time itself was given meaning by the Catholic Christian faith: each year traced Christ's passage from birth to death and resurrection, and man's path from the Fall to Salvation, through feasts, music, devotions and ceremonies. This membership of the Catholic mother Church had been the state of things roughly since the mission of St Augustine to bring the English kingdoms to the religion of Rome, starting with his landing in Kent in 597.

By the end of the sixteenth century, England was energetically Protestant. It had not only separated from Rome but was virulently anti-Catholic in much of its culture and official doctrine. This shift is a profoundly important episode in England's history, and naturally provokes the question of how it could occur. An older 'Whig' interpretation sees England's rise to the status of an international Protestant power as an inevitable course of events. More recently, revisionist historians have argued that the English Reformation was irregular, piecemeal, and far from a matter of destiny. This seems a more persuasive picture if we look at the direction of the Church in England under the Tudor monarchs, moving from the Henrician Reformation to Edwardian Protestantism to Marian Catholicism. There were tensions between Anglicans of different persuasions, from the more Calvinist at one end to the more Catholic at the other. These continued under the Elizabethan Settlement (1559) and played themselves out in the Civil War. Whatever else it achieved, the English Reformation certainly did not produce a unifying clarity of vision among the faithful.

While historians continue to discuss the details, there is no doubt that an English Reformation did happen and that it had lasting consequences for English life. Henry VIII's dissolution of the monasteries (1536–1540) affected both the English landscape, the distribution of wealth and power and the cultural manifestations of that power, from great houses built from old abbeys to the tombs and monuments by which the powerful had themselves commemorated. The policy of iconoclasm (the destruction of religious imagery, viewed as Catholic idolatry) pursued under Edward VI (*r*.1547–1553) obliterated much of the visual expression of faith in England. In this period, the religious is also political, and thus Protestant ideas are intimately bound up with matters such as the idea of nationhood, loyalty and royal propaganda: England becomes a righteous power, rescuing the purified true Church from the dark forces of Catholicism. On a domestic scale, Protestant thought shapes and informs convictions about the good life: the Protestant ethos of the individual feeling in direct relation to the divine has been seen as a fundamental part of notions of the individual self in the period, while the sanctification of virtuous toil and self-help has been related by some to rising capitalism. At the same time, the centuries of thought surrounding Catholicism still survived in manifold forms. In the mind as in real churches, the traces of Catholic images were still visible beneath Protestant whitewash. This frequently muddled and often confusing inner world of the imagination is recorded in Renaissance language and literature.

Indeed, modern notions of 'Renaissance literature' often disguise the deeply religious nature of the age. About half of sixteenth-century books were religious in content, while other kinds of writing were also imbued with religious ideas. In particular, Protestantism has been called a religion of the book: Luther's idea of *sola scriptura* – the Word of God in the scriptures as the absolute foundation for the truth – led him and other Protestant leaders to see printing as a gift from God. The mass printing of Tyndale's translation of the New Testament (1526) was impossible to suppress, and the increased availability of the Bible for private contemplation had important consequences. One of these was an intense concentration on language. Protestants were trained to give their full attention to the scriptures, visualising passages and memorising them, and basing their conduct on Christ's precepts. A biblical story might be understood in the plain and literal sense, but it could also be read as allegory. English writers could thus draw on a rich fund of commonly understood metaphors and tropes: for example, darkness and sickness might figure sin; and Christ could be represented as shepherd, physician, light, a bridegroom, among other symbols. This habit of reading narratives symbolically made possible the allegories of Spenser and Bunyan, but we also find symbols in shorter lyric poems. Sir Walter Raleigh's beautiful 'The Passionate Mans Pilgrimage' develops the traditional idea of pilgrimage as a metaphor for the journey from life to death:

> Give me my scallop shell of quiet,
> My staffe of Faith to walke upon
> My Scrip of Joy, Immortall diet,
> My bottle of salvation.

Objects that might in life be denounced as Catholic superstitions, in poetry become signifiers of truth. Underlying such writing is the habit of scripturalism – reading a simple text for multiple meanings – and the notion that the world itself is the Book of God, pregnant with divine meaning. George Herbert's poems expound ideas of man's relation to God through plain imagery, again drawing on the habit of seeking the transcendent through the familiar.

Reformation practices affected not only the imagery of texts, but also their style. This is characteristically polemical in intent and plain in expression. Like classical rhetoric, Protestant discourse has a natural tendency to argument and polemic. Unsurprisingly for an epoch marked by savage religious wars and persecutions, the literary history of the period is marked by intense controversies. An early example is the 'battle of the books' between William Tyndale (1494–1536) and Thomas More (1478–1535). In this exchange, More's Latinate English contrasts with Tyndale's pugnacious vernacular style, as seen in works such as *Obedience of a Christian Man* (1528). The plain style emerges as the voice of Puritan Protestantism and is characterised by short statements and concrete vocabulary. Foundational texts were the English translation of the Bible and Cranmer's *Book of Common Prayer* (first edn. 1549). In the first decade of Elizabeth I's reign (1558–1568), hundreds of books were written in exchanges between Catholic writers and English scholars defending the Elizabethan settlement of Church of England. From the 1560s, attacks on the English Church also came in the form of Puritan manifestos, objecting to church hierarchy, ceremony and Cranmer's liturgy. A later argument in print was the Martin Marprelate controversy of 1588: under that name a number of satirical attacks on the official State Church were published. The establishment was concerned enough at the popularity of these to commission some leading writers to answer them, including Thomas Nashe (1567–1601) and John Lyly (c.1553–1606). This episode was not only a significant interface between secular literary writers and religious contention, but also an example of how theological argument naturally drew on the language and strategies of street culture, as expressed in ballads and libels. We might also remember that written tracts and pamphlets were also closely related to the energy and rhythms of the sermon and preserve the vivid directness of the spoken address.

Most of the religious tracts of the sixteenth and seventeenth centuries are today of concern chiefly to specialists. However, some key works of the English Reformation command the attention of students of English literature. One very important text is the history of the persecution of English Protestants written by John Foxe (1516–1587). *Acts and Monuments of Ecclesiastical History*, commonly known as Foxe's *Book of Martyrs*, first appeared in Latin in 1554, and grew to millions of words in successive English editions (1563, 1570, 1576, 1583). The chief aim of this book was to praise the heroism of the Protestant martyrs who suffered under Mary. Foxe makes effective use of homely language to create an Anglican martyrology, complete with the tales of marvels and miracles familiar from Catholic saints' lives. Though Foxe used historical sources, he also seems to have omitted evidence which did not fit his initial object. The effect of his book is a matter of debate among historians: its expense presumably limited its circulation, yet it also inspired many cheaper imitators. It may, then, be taken as some guide to the popular imagination, integrating comforting tales of wonders and endurance with bitter hostility to Papist tyranny. Perhaps more restricted in its intended audience, but of far greater subtlety, is the defence of the Elizabethan settlement of the Church of England entitled *Of the Laws of Ecclesiastical Politie* (Books I–IV, 1593; Book V, 1597) by the theologian Richard Hooker (?1554–1600). This work was written in response to Puritan objections to Church governance and discipline, though it was not the last word in the ongoing arguments between moderate and Puritan Anglicans. It is regarded as a classic of English prose, its measured and decorous rhetoric distancing it from the Puritan plain style mentioned earlier.

Beyond explicitly theological works, the influence of the English Reformation can be found in much of the literature of the period. Most obvious is the propagandistic imagery representing England as the home of the

True Church, in battle with Rome, pictured as Babylon and the Anti-Christ. We find such imagery in Foxe, while part of Spenser's programme in *The Faerie Queene* is to promote the idea of the English Church representing a return to the Truth: in Book I, the Red Cross Knight is the 'Patron of True Holiness', championing simple Truth and Faith as figured by the maiden Una and combating Error and Hypocrisy. Milton's Puritan attack on what he sees as Romish superstition is explicit, without the veil of allegory. In Limbo he writes,

> Then might ye see
> Cowles, Hoods and habits with thir wearers tost
> And flutterd into Raggs, then Reliques, Beads,
> Indulgences, Dispenses, Pardons, Bulls,
> The sport of winds.
> (Paradise Lost, III.489–493)

A similarly anti-Catholic flavour can be found in the portrayal of the Pope in Marlowe's *Dr Faustus* (1604) and in corrupt Italian Churchmen like the cardinal in Webster's *The Duchess of Malfi* (performed 1614).

However, there is an interesting internal tension in English literature between avowed attacks on Catholicism and the preservation of many Catholic ideas as poetic metaphors. To take one particularly complex example, the cult of the Virgin Mary was transformed into the imagery of Elizabeth the Virgin Queen. Thus the very risky political situation of an unmarried female monarch, with no clear successor, was turned to advantage as Elizabeth could be presented as the object of traditional devotion. Meanwhile devotion and quasi-religious adoration are central to the language of much poetic writing. While praying to images was condemned as idolatry by the official Church, in poetry devotion to the beauties of the beloved takes on a religious fervour. The adoring gaze, associated with religious fervour, was too powerful an instinct to repress and was thus given a new secular home. Adoration of the beauty of a beloved can be condemned as 'dotage' – the word is applied to Antony's love of Cleopatra and Titania's spellbound devotion to Bottom (in *A Midsummer Night's Dream*). Yet in both cases, while the love is viewed as irrational and irresponsible, it is also a potent cause of beautiful language and intense experience. English texts incorporate the ideas and images of the old religion, and do so with no clearly defined value system.

In this respect, literary writing may be a better guide to the contemporary imagination than polemical tracts from either side. For though a few staunch Catholics and Puritans held to clear tenets of belief at one end or other of the spectrum, the private religious vision of most of those who lived at the time of the Reformation was probably a layered mixture of old and new. This layering is evoked by the rich and complex texture of much of the writing of the period.

See also   *Contexts*: Catholicism, Protestant Theology, The Self; *Texts*: The Bible, Non-fictional Prose, Prose Style

Further Reading

Patrick Collinson, 'English Reformations': in *A Companion to English Renaissance Literature and Culture*, ed. Michael Hattaway (Oxford: Blackwell, 2000), 27–43.

Patrick Collinson, *The Reformation* (London: Weidenfeld and Nicolson, 2003).

Brian Cummings, *The Literary Culture of the Reformation: Grammar and Grace* (Oxford: OUP, 2002).

Christopher Haigh, *English Reformations: Religion, Politics, and Society Under the Tudors* (Oxford: Clarendon, 1993).

Golden Age

A key element of Renaissance thinking was the idea of a Golden Age – an ideal state of existence in which society lives harmoniously and man can perfectly fulfil his nature without suffering. There are various sources for this idea. In classical Greek literature, the Golden Age is the first of the five ages of man in Hesiod's *Works and Days* (eigth century BC): it is a time of peace and plenty, before the human race is corrupted by impiety and greed. Cronos (the Roman Saturn) ruled, before being supplanted by Zeus (Jove). For the Renaissance, the most popular source of this story was Ovid's *Metamorphoses* (*c*.8 AD), in which there are four rather than five ages: 'The Golden Age was first; which uncompelled, /And without rule, in faith and truth excelled' (I.ii, 89, trans. George Sandys, 1632). At this time, so Ovid's account goes, humans were naturally virtuous and so had no need of law or punishment. There are no fortresses or armies, trees have not been cut down to make ships (all are content to live where they are), and there is perpetual spring: the earth brings forth its fruits without the need for human labour. Another classical version of the perfect society was Elysium, which awaited the souls of the just after death: In Virgil's *Aeneid* (*c*.29–19 BC), Aeneas sees Elysium in his visit to the underworld (Book VI).

The classical Golden Age is clearly very similar to the Christian Garden of Eden, in which Adam and Eve live in primal innocence and do not need to plough and till the land. There, too, spring is perpetual and man lives in harmony with nature. In the Renaissance, Eden was held to be a real place which had physically existed and could be placed on a map, somewhere in Mesopotamia. With this sense of Eden as a literal historical place in mind, some writers of the period argued that the pagans must have had some kind of access to the biblical description of Eden in order to conceive the idea themselves (see, for example, Sir Walter Raleigh's *History of the World*, I.iii). Milton's description of Eden in *Paradise Lost* (Book IV) explores the classical and Christian parallels – the garden is 'Hesperian fables true' – a reference to the mythical garden of the Hesperides, whose trees bore golden fruit. Milton also uses the subject of the garden to explore themes of the human condition, the ideal relation of man and woman and the integration of man and nature. The image of the Golden Age as a paradisal garden links the idea to the pastoral motif of the *hortus conclusus*, or enclosed orchard: Marvell's 'The Garden' depicts 'that happy garden-state' as a space for inner contemplation and calm. Another biblical image of an earthly paradise is the Promised Land, the 'land flowing with milk and honey' of the Israelites, who reached it after their escape from persecution in Egypt, and the subsequent hardships of exile and war (see Exodus, iii). America was heralded as just such a promised land by the Puritan Pilgrim Fathers, who saw it as a haven from persecution, where true godliness might prosper. For Michael Drayton (1563–1631), urging on the early colonists, Virginia is 'Earth's onely paradise' ('To the Virginian Voyage'); and Marvell's 'Bermudas' celebrates the 'perpetuall spring' of those islands.

Common to many treatments of the Golden Age is the idea of recovery: an ideal original state is restored after a time of bloodshed and corruption. Thus a Golden Age in historical time was supposed to have been reached in the time of the Emperor Augustus (*r*.23 BC–14 AD), under whom Roman civilisation was held to have been rescued from civil turmoil and brought to a perfect state of political supremacy and cultural achievement. This was the prophecy of Virgil in his fourth eclogue: *Jam redit et virgo, redeunt Saturnia regna* ('Now Virgo returns, and Saturn's kingdom'). In Renaissance England, the Golden Age was especially associated with the reign of Elizabeth I (1558–1603). Elizabeth, the Virgin Queen, was identified as Virgo, combining the attributes of the Virgin Mary, and of an Augustan ruler, restoring peace and justice to a previously troubled realm. Elizabeth was also identified with the classical virgin goddess of justice, Astraea, who had been the last of the immortals to abandon man in the iron age in the classical accounts of the ages of man. Another emblem associating Elizabeth with a golden age was the phoenix, which is found on numerous artefacts with the motto *Semper eadem* (always the same). To this series of associations can be added the strong Tudor connection with King Arthur, the legendary king who had presided over a time of unity. Henry Tudor (later Henry VII) stressed his Welsh ancestry to emphasise the Celtic connection with the Briton King. He also displayed Arthur's banner at the battle of Bosworth, and named his son and heir Arthur. Spenser sets *The Faerie Queene* in the time of King Arthur in order to show his loyalty to Elizabeth, or Gloriana. As Virgin, Phoenix,

Astraea and Gloriana, Elizabeth was officially depicted as a saviour who was bringing England back to an Age of Gold. Other analogous associations were made. In the so-called *Book of Martyrs*, John Foxe compares the Queen to the Emperor Constantine (*c*.280–337 AD): in ending the Marian persecutions of Protestants, Elizabeth had performed a feat comparable to Constantine's establishment of Christianity in the Roman Empire. George Puttenham (*d*.1590) celebrates the 'concord and peace' of Elizabeth's reign in a poem which visually figures her as a pillar ('Her majesty resembled to the crowned pillar'); Mary Sidney compares the Queen to the Israelite King David – both protect their people in the Promised Land against the philistines and both enjoy reigns 'Possest of place, and each in peace possest' (the first prefatory poem in a presentation manuscript of Mary Sidney's translation of the psalms, intended to be given to Elizabeth). Jonson's masque *The Golden Age Restored* praises James I in similar terms. This use of the Golden Age idea also highlights the conception of Protestantism as a return to a purer religion, literally a re-formation of what was previously mired in corruption.

The Golden Age is also associated with the Renaissance genre of the country house poem, in which a well-managed estate and household are praised as a model of good governance and living. These enclosed spaces are often contrasted with the violent world outside, and praise can function as an exhortation to behave in certain ways. For example, England is depicted as an earthly paradise in Sir Richard Fanshawe's 'An Ode upon occasion of His Majesties Proclamation in the year 1630. Commanding the Gentry to reside upon their Estates in the Country' (stanzas 9–20). The political point here is that peace and plenty can only flourish if the nobles return from the court to their country estates: 'to rowle themselves in envy'd leasure / He therefore sends the landed Heyres' (lines 33–34). The contrast between a Golden Age and a fallen one takes a poignant nostalgic tone in Marvell's poem 'Upon Appleton House', which pursues the opposites of former peace and recent civil bloodshed: England, which was 'the garden of the world', has been made a 'waste' by its people (stanza 41). Images of plenty are used in ironic similes to emphasise recent destruction: 'where, as the Meads with Hay, the Plain / Lyes quilted ore with Bodies slain' (stanza 53).

To summarise, the Golden Age is a complex figure in Renaissance culture. The challenge for the reader is to see how it is being used. Instances of it might combine classical and Christian traditions. The idea can be used as a source of metaphor for political, religious and philosophical discourse. In texts and other artefacts, the Golden Age can exist in and out of historical time, as a vanished past, a metaphor for a perfect present and a heavenly future. Apparent earthly paradises can also be illusory: another resonant classical motif was the island of Circe in Homer's *Odyssey*, where Ulysses' men are lured by pleasures and turned into beasts. Here the sensual delights of a place of plenty denature man. This lies behind *The Faerie Queene* (Book II, Canto xii) where the lovely garden of Acrasia is shockingly destroyed by the knight Guyon, apparently because its pleasures dull the moral nature of its inhabitants. In Milton's *Comus* (performed 1634), the deceiver (Comus, the son of Circe) is similarly associated with a delightful garden. In this tradition, we sense a tension between the celebration of primal purity and the erotic and sensual connotations of the uncomplicated physical pleasures a paradisal garden affords. The endless leisure of the ideal state is also at odds with a Protestant capitalist work ethic. It is precisely the licence of the paradisal garden which is playfully celebrated by Cavalier poets such as Richard Lovelace (1618–1657), who depicts the golden age fondly as a time when 'lads indifferently did crop / A flower and a maidenhead' ('Love made in the first age'). A wider consideration to bear in mind when reading Renaissance literature is the potency at that time of the notion that time was a decline from a past ideal and that great human achievement was often a turning back rather than a moving forward. While we might be inclined to see the Renaissance period as some kind of progress towards modernity, at least as strong in the age itself was the idea that any improvement was to be achieved by erasing the errors which have accrued over time to reveal a pristine original state.

See also   *Contexts*: Court, Travel; *Texts*: Bible, Epic, History, Pastoral

Further Reading
Introductory
Isabel Rivers, *Classical and Christian Ideas in Renaissance English Poetry: A Student's Guide*, 2nd edn (London: Routledge, 1994), ch. 1 'The Golden Age and the Garden of Eden', 9–19.

Full Length
A. Bartlett Giamatti, *The Earthly Paradise and the Renaissance Epic* (Princeton, NJ: Princeton UP, 1966), esp. ch. 1.
Harry Levin, *The Myth of the Golden Age in the Renaissance* (London: Faber, 1970).
David Quint, *Origin and Originality in Renaissance Literature: Versions of the Source* (New Haven: Yale UP, 1983).

Humanism

Humanism is central to the Renaissance. Yet 'Humanism' itself is a modern word (it is a nineteenth-century coinage) and is potentially misleading. Today, humanism denotes a view of life which is opposed to religion and celebrates man's rational faculties. Renaissance humanists, by contrast, lived and worked in a God-centred universe. Though several humanists wrote on man's creative and intellectual powers, they did not collectively advance a creed of 'man the measure of all things', exalting the status of the individual and his potential to control his destiny. Certainly such ideas can be found in some humanist writings, like the famous *On the Dignity of Man* by Giovanni Pico della Mirandola (1463–1494), but different views can be found in other humanist texts.

Humanists, in fact, did not elaborate any ideology or *–ism*, and applied their talents to the expression of diverse and even contradictory opinions, often in the form of propaganda for their political masters: the *Historia Anglica* (*History of England*, 1534) by the Italian Polydore Vergil (1470–1555), for example, was designed to provide support for the tenuous claim of the House of Tudor to the English throne. Renaissance humanism involved a commitment to certain *practices,* not theories, above all the study of classical Latin and its application to modern life and letters.

'Humanist' derives from Latin *humanitas*: in the context of the *studia humanitatis* promoted by humanists it means a course of study, principally of *bonae litterae* or 'good writing', through which a student reaches personal fulfilment.The Italian *umanisti* of the fourteenth and fifteenth centuries trained themselves and their pupils to write in correct classical Latin, as opposed to the Latin used in their own time, which they regarded as a degraded version of the original classical language. The most famous of the early humanists was Petrarch (1304–1374). He saw in the writings of antiquity the 'pure pristine radiance of the past' and believed that if these texts could be resurrected in the minds and hearts of the learned in his own time, then the noble values they enshrined would be released and the light of true learning would illuminate the darkness of the present. For Petrarch and for other humanists throughout the Renaissance, the supreme model of wisdom (*sapientia*) married to style (*eloquentia*) was Cicero.

Italian humanists tracked down ancient manuscripts in archives such as monastery libraries, where earlier medieval copies of Latin texts in many cases lay neglected. In this way, numerous classical writings were newly brought into circulation. Petrarch discovered Cicero's letters to Atticus, and a later exciting find (in the archive of Lodi Cathedral in 1421) was Cicero's treatises on rhetoric, *Brutus* and *On the Orator*. The manuscripts unearthed by humanist scholars were then copied and edited. Through this process, humanist scholars advanced the principles of philological study and the method of editing by critically comparing and emending texts – a contribution of far-reaching importance for future education and cultural transmission in the West. Another early consequence of the editorial process was the formation of humanistic script, a clear style of handwriting which lies behind letter forms today. Greek was also studied, though far fewer scholars mastered this than Latin.

As stated above, humanists did not have a coherent philosophy or ideology, but they did commonly stress the importance of eloquence and related it to ethics. This contrasted with Scholasticism, the system of instruction in the universities. Scholasticism was based on the rigorous mastery of logic (also called dialectic). It was a method of reaching logical certainty and sound knowledge, while the pursuit of eloquence aimed instead to achieve discourse that was plausible and persuasive. While some humanists worked as tutors in universities, most earned a living in positions such as secretaries, diplomats or private tutors. Because humanists thus operated beyond the 'ivory tower', their work was closely linked with practical affairs: humanists could provide propaganda for states, compose diplomatic letters or offer advice on good government – so-called 'civic humanism'.

Humanist ideas began to reach England late in the fifteenth century, when some Englishmen studied under Italian humanists and some Italian scholars visited England. An important development was the application of humanist techniques of linguistic scrutiny and editing to the Bible. John Colet's lectures on the New Testament in Oxford (1496) introduced the radical method of studying the texts in the original Greek in order to elucidate their message – thus bypassing centuries of accumulated commentary.

The greatest of all the northern humanists was Erasmus (c.1466–1536), who visited England on various occasions and lived there between 1509 and 1514. Erasmus edited the New Testament by returning to the oldest texts and found many errors in the Vulgate, the fourth-century Latin translation by St Jerome which was the official Bible of the Church. This kind of study was beyond the reach of all but a few, yet it was highly significant. Erasmus, Colet and others were demonstrating that an authority to understand the Bible could be acquired by diligent study and was therefore not the exclusive preserve of the Church. Moreover it was emerging that the Church was basing its teachings on a version of the Word of God which was demonstrably erroneous. The application of humanist techniques to Bible study thus prepared the way for the Reformation and Luther's far more dramatic claim that through the Bible God could speak directly to believers without the need for the mediating interpretation of the Church.

Another important early English humanist was Thomas More (1478–1535), who wrote in both Latin and English. More seemed to be temperamentally divided between medieval piety and the new learning. Early in his life he was strongly drawn to the reclusive contemplative life, yet he later committed his talents to the service of the state under Henry VIII.

Though a close friend of Erasmus, More was also alarmed at the spread of new ideas about the scriptures outside the intellectual elite and strenuously opposed Tyndale's English translation of the Bible.

Other notable English humanists include Roger Ascham (1515–68), tutor to Elizabeth I and author of a treatise on archery, *Toxophilus* (1545) – which Ascham said he would have found easier to write in Latin – and *The Scholemaster* (1570), which describes the typical humanist pedagogical system of translating a text first from Latin into English and then back again. Sir Thomas Elyot's *The Boke of the Governour* (1531) is an example of a work in the 'Advice to Princes' tradition. Other humanists took up places in the Tudor court to help in running the increasingly complex centralised bureaucracy. Sometimes they were brought in as 'new men', replacing aristocrats who had fallen out of favour. The values frequently espoused in humanist texts – hard work, sobriety and organisation – can be contrasted with the aristocratic ethos of ostentatious leisure and expense.

Humanism's most important impact in England lay in education. St Paul's School was founded by Colet in 1509 and run by the Headmaster William Lily on humanist principles. Mastery of classical Latin was regarded as the ideal way of forming the character and intellectual competence of future servants of Church and state, most particularly in the law. Humanist education could spread more easily now that printing had been introduced, and books were more widely available. Students were encouraged to keep books of *loci communes* (commonplaces) in which they would note and learn valuable lines and sentences from the classical texts; they could then use these in their own orations and compositions. This practice helps to explain the mosaic-like quality of many Renaissance texts, in which quotations and allusions are drawn together to make new works. Another important consequence of the study of classical Latin was the huge increase in translations of the classics, which in turn provided valuable source material for other writers and extended the range of literary English.

Humanism in England remained closely associated with public life and practical affairs and was thus generally directed away from purely abstract thought. We can see the influence of this in writings like the essays of Francis Bacon (1561–1626), which explore ideas in a vivid concrete way, illustrated with numerous examples and pithy sayings. The digressive and conversational flavour of the prose of a writer like Thomas Browne (1605–1682) is in keeping with humanism's emphasis on anecdotal colour over formal structure. Writers studied classical authors like Livy and Plutarch, who saw history primarily as a source of moral lessons on how to live: in English dedicatory letters, biographies and history books, we find the same use of literature to present an instructive and inspiring ideal. Under the influence of humanism, literature itself is conceived both as an imitation of past models and as a pleasingly eloquent way of describing and promoting good conduct. The poet's role becomes that of a guide to practical morality and a reminder of the goals to which we should aspire.

If we wish to study English Renaissance writing in the light of humanism, there are several lines of enquiry we can take. We might see if we can find in the texture of a piece of writing some of the qualities mentioned above: extensive citation and quotation, anecdotes which provide a moral lesson, aphorisms modelled on classical *sententiae* (sentences, or wise and instructive sayings) or the evident use of a particular classical writer as a stylistic authority. We can also ask what kind of audience a text implies in the values and assumptions it embodies. More and Erasmus quite evidently wrote books with each other in mind, for example: for there to be humanist writers, there must be like-minded humanist readers. An interesting theoretical question is how objective we can be in assessing Humanism, since some tenets of the project have formed our own outlook. The arguments that the study of past literature fits us for employment by sharpening our powers of analysis and expression and that reading great literature deepens our moral awareness and potential for useful action are still put forward to defend the study of 'the humanities' today. The spirit of the early humanists inhabits contemporary commentators who lament common errors of spelling, punctuation and grammar, seeing them – perhaps rightly – as symptoms of a civilisation in decline.

See also *Contexts*: Book Trade, Patronage, Platonism; *Texts*: Logic, Non-fictional Prose, Prose Style, Rhetoric

Further Reading

Introductory

Anthony Grafton, *Leon Battista Alberti: Master Builder of the Italian Renaissance* (London: Penguin, 2001), ch. 2 'Humanism', 31–70.

Isabel Rivers, *Classical and Christian Ideas in English Renaissance Poetry* (London: Routledge, 1994), ch. 5 'Humanism', 125–139.

English Humanism

Mary Thomas Crane, 'Early Tudor Humanism': in Michael Hattaway, ed., *A Companion to English Renaissance Literature and Culture* (Oxford: Blackwell, 2000), 13–26.

Full Length

Jill Kraye, ed., *The Cambridge Companion to Renaissance Humanism* (Cambridge: CUP, 1996).

Charles G. Nauert, *Humanism and the Culture of Renaissance Europe*, revised edn (Cambridge: CUP, 2006).

Mike Pincombe, *Elizabethan Humanism: Literature and Learning in the Later Sixteenth Century* (Harlow: Pearson, 2001).

Greg Walker, *Writing Under Tyranny: English Literature and the Henrician Reformation* (Oxford: OUP, 2006).

Humours

Like other parts of the traditional picture of the cosmos, the doctrine of the humours was ancient: it can be traced back to Hippocrates (*The Nature of Man*, 4), and was subsequently passed down through the authority of Aristotle to medieval encyclopaedias and early modern treatises. The humours correspond to the elements, and so are likewise four in number: black bile, phlegm, blood and choler. They take the form of fluids, produced in the body. Food passes through the stomach to the liver, which governs the inferior parts of the body. The liver converts the ingested matter into the four humours and sends them to the bodily organs through the blood. Different organs affect them in distinct ways. The heart is the centre of the body and is the seat of the passions. In the heart, stoked by heat and air from the lungs, the humours become vital spirits, the fuel of life. These are then carried with refined blood through the arteries. Some vital spirits pass up to the brain, the seat of the immortal, rational part of man which regulates the higher body. In the brain, they become animated spirits, working through the nerves to control the intelligence. On a metaphorical level, this picture of the body makes man a microcosm of the physical earth. Vital heat corresponds to underground fire, veins are like rivers, sighs are like the air, and passions are the human version of tempests and earthquakes.

The mixture of humours in an individual makes up his or her temperament, or 'complexion'. The better the balance, the more even-tempered a person is. When they are mixed unevenly, certain physical and behavioural characteristics will dominate. Each humour corresponds to one of the four elements, sharing with it the essential properties of temperature and humidity. A dominant humour is related to a dominant character 'type'. These correspondences can best be explained in the form of a table:

Element	Humour	Common quality	Character
Earth	Black Bile	Cold, dry	Melancholic
Water	Phlegm	Cold, wet	Phlegmatic
Air	Blood	Hot, wet	Sanguine
Fire	Choler	Hot, dry	Choleric

The following passage from Robert Burton's account of human anatomy gives some idea of the level of detail at which the subject could be treated:

> Choler is hot and dry, bitter, begotten of the hotter parts of the chylus, and gathered to the gall; it helps the natural heat and senses, and serves to the expelling of excrements.

> Melancholy, cold and dry, thick, black, and sour, begotten of the more feculent part of nourishment, and purged from the spleen, is a bridle to the other two hot humors, blood and choler, preserving them in the blood, and nourishing the bones. These four humors have some analogy with the four elements, and to the four ages in man.
>
> (*The Anatomy of Melancholy*. Section I, Member II, Subsection 2: Division of the Body, Humors, Spirits).

Burton's prose has a precise, scientific feel. But it also makes clear the Renaissance sense of fusion between mind and body: melancholy is not what we might call a state of mind, but a physical property, 'thick, black and sour'. There is a deep sense of the interconnectedness of the physical and the emotional, and of wider correspondences – here, between the elements, the humours and the four ages of man (this could be extended to include the four seasons). Through the humours and their translation into the spirits, human temperament is firmly grounded in the physical world.

In literary writing, the system of correspondences provides an unending stream of metaphorical images, in which the spiritual is represented as physical and vice versa. The body is a picture of the soul. Through the humours, inner states of character are projected into physical fluids. Ben Jonson neatly encapsulates the usefulness of this concept as a metaphor for describing traits of character:

> Why, humour (as 'tis *ens*) we thus define it
> To be a quality of air, or water,
> And in itself holds these two properties,
> Moisture, and fluxure; as, for demonstration,
> Pour water on the floor, 'twill wet and run;
> Likewise the air (forced through a horn, or trumpet)
> Flows instantly away and leaves behind
> A kind of dew; and hence we do conclude,
> That whatsoe'er hath fluxure and humidity,
> As wanting power to contain itself,
> Is humour. So in every human body

The choler, melancholy, phlegm, and blood,
By reason that they flow continually
In some one part, and are not continent,
Receive the name of 'humours'. Now thus far
It may, by metaphor, apply itself
Unto the general disposition:
As when some one peculiar quality
Doth so possess a man that it doth draw
All his affects, his spirits, and his powers,
In their confluctions, all to run one way,
This may be truly said to be a 'humour'.
(*Every Man Out of his Humour* (1599), Induction.)

The comedy of humours practised by Jonson exaggerates the dispositions by which characters are possessed to examine human psychology. The expression 'a sense of humour' means originally the ability to perceive the humour of another person in the Renaissance sense.

Like astral influences, the humours were not generally held to determine a person's character or behaviour: that would conflict with the Christian principle that man has free will. As Jonson indicates, they could be drawn on as a vocabulary with which to describe certain states of mind. The holistic picture of the physical and the moral being integrally related was eventually challenged by the new science, which divorced the moral from the physical; and in the seventeenth century, Descartes provided a system which saw mind and body as distinct – so-called 'Cartesian dualism'. At the level of metaphor, though, the humours continued to have a vigorous existence along with other parts of the traditional cosmology. Indeed, we still describe people as sanguine, bilious or splenetic. Many other metaphors attest to the intuitive link between body and personality: thus we say someone is big-hearted, lily-livered, or has guts, or the stomach to do something. Sections in bookshops today dedicated to 'Mind, Body and Spirit' indicate a contemporary concern with the interrelations of the mental and physical, which may help us to understand the theory of the humours and the metaphors deriving from it.

See also   *Contexts*: Chain of Being, Cosmos, Elements, Magic, Medicine, Science; *Texts*: Non-fictional Prose

Further Reading

Antonia McLean, *Humanism and the Rise of Science in Tudor England* (London: Heinemann, 1972), ch. 7 'Pre-Tudor Medicine and Natural History', 169–185.

Magic (Alchemy, Astrology, Witchcraft)

Magic has been defined as 'the power of apparently influencing events by using mysterious or supernatural forces' (*Compact Oxford English Dictionary*). In this sense, magic was integral to the belief structures of early modern society. For all practical purposes, this was a pre-scientific age: diseases, storm, droughts, freak accidents – indeed phenomena of every kind – could rarely be explained by natural causes, and people therefore sought other ways to understand their experiences and exert some control over their environment. Before the Reformation, the great source of this understanding was the Catholic Church: events were to be understood as the actions of the mysterious divine will; under the guidance of the Church, through prayers, the sacraments, and the many miraculous powers to be drawn from relics and shrines, Christians could influence the course of their lives (and afterlives) by connecting to divine forces.

Besides the comforts of religion, other kinds of magical belief actually increased during the Renaissance itself – a fact which should warn us against viewing the age as a steady progress towards modern rationalism. Florentine Platonism is steeped in magical ideas. Scholars such as Marsilio Ficino (1433–1499) and Agrippa (1486–1535) drew on a vast range of classical texts and sought to synthesise them with Judaic, Arabic and Christian teachings to reveal a true underlying wisdom: this syncretic vision included the presence of many good and evil spirits besides Christianity's angels and demons, and it was held that these spirits could be summoned up with the right spells. Another influential idea was that by transcending their bodily form, men could absorb heavenly perfection and intelligence. This thinking was passed onto Englishmen such as Dr John Dee (1527–1609). An underlying desire was to elevate man's power over his world; just the same urge to manipulate the physical universe lies behind the scientific enterprise.

On a popular level, the villages of England would have their cunning man or wise woman to offer services such as charms, remedies, healing, fortune telling, forecasts and searches for buried treasure. Their practices would draw on many sources from Christian prayers to herbal lore, folk wisdom going back to pre-Christian times and shrewd psychology (for example, guessing the hopes, fears and suspicions of the customer and then reinforcing them). When the Protestant Church condemned the Catholic practices referred to above as idle superstitions, such local traditions became the focus for the instinctive quest for supernatural activity and explanation. On both a 'high' and a 'low' level, magic was divided into good and bad. Good magic (*magia*) manipulates natural forces for a beneficent end such as healing, or aims to perfect the soul through communion with invisible spirits; bad magic (*goetia*) is exercised for maleficent ends such as harming through spells or trafficking with the powers of darkness. We can see, then, that 'magic' covers a vast range of activities, from herbal medicine (as practised by Friar Laurence in *Romeo and Juliet*), which may often have been more beneficial than the blood-letting favoured by doctors, to the black arts of satanic ritual. We shall now look at three kinds of activity which were important to Renaissance life and literature: Alchemy, Astrology and Witchcraft.

Alchemy

Alchemy is the quest for the elixir of immortal life (turning base metals into gold is in theory secondary to this higher purpose). Its history passes from ancient China to Arabic scholars to the West, where it was studied by the thirteenth-century scholar Roger Bacon (*c*.1214–1294) among others. Alchemy was stimulated by two preoccupations: the consciousness of mutability and complexity and a yearning for their opposite – a pure, perfect unchanging essence. Thus it was observed that the world is composed of a huge number of things which can be grouped in certain forms (animal, vegetable, mineral, metal and so forth). These forms are constantly changing – seeds turn into trees, all bodies decompose, wood turns into ashes – and this change involves a redistribution of the matter of the elements (earth, air, fire, water). In alchemical lore, these elements are themselves reducible to one basic primal matter, the quintessence. Through manipulation of matter and change, it was held, it ought to be possible to change anything into anything else. Base metals could by the right process be refined into gold which, in alchemical thinking, was constituted by all four elements in exactly the right proportions and so was eternal and indestructible. The elixir of life would bring the body into the same perfectly proportioned state, rendering it pure and indestructible. Alchemy was taken seriously at the highest levels: Elizabeth I herself provided funds for Dr Dee, who had taught her some of his mystical wisdom and, together with his crooked associate Edward Kelly, was received by four emperors. Dee was held to have conversed with spirits and discovered the philosophers' stone (used to turn base metals into gold). According to the seventeenth-century gatherer of gossip John Aubrey, Dee was the model for Jonson's *The Alchemist* (1610); but fortune, like matter, is mutable, and he died in poverty in 1608.

Alchemy is of importance to the history of Science for the instruments and experimental observations it handed on to posterity. For medieval and Renaissance English literature, it is the subject matter of two texts which demonstrate the charlatanry of practitioners and the gullibility and greed of their customers: Chaucer's *Canon's Yeoman's*

Tale and Ben Jonson's *The Alchemist*. Both texts make a play of the jargon with which alchemists dupe their victims. An interesting difference is that while Chaucer's tale is straightforwardly about the desire for wealth, Jonson's text is full of the hermetic lore surrounding Renaissance alchemy, such as the need for the souls of those commissioning the experiment to remain unsullied. The alchemical experiments supposedly taking place in Jonson's comedy take place offstage. His work can be read as a study of the magical effects not of Science but of language: words and images can be mixed to beguile the unwary and create false hopes. Beneath the gold of the alchemist's words lies the base matter of greed and human vice.

Astrology

Astronomy is the study of the movement of the stars, astrology is the study of their influence (the word 'influence' derives from the idea of power 'flowing in' from the planets to the earth). This is however a modern distinction, and in the Renaissance the two words were often interchangeable: the Renaissance term for the study of planetary influence was 'judicial astrology'.

Astrology is an ancient practice which, like alchemy, came to medieval Europe through the Arabs. It is based on the opposition between eternity and mutability. According to traditional cosmology, the heavens are perfect and constant in their operations; while on earth, all is change, corruption and decay. It was observable that the moon controlled the tides, and thus it was a natural extension to believe that the other planets affected earthly processes. Planets emit the heat, dryness and moisture which formed earthly matter; they influence the weather and the human body (anatomical maps linked parts of the body with the 12 zodiacal signs). Judicial astrology had four main branches: Predictions, concerning public events such as civil wars or bad harvests; Nativities, the config-uration of planets at a person's birth; Elections, or the decisions on the auspicious moment to do something; and horary questions, a method for answering questions according to the planetary positions when the questions were put.

Astrology provided a kind of parallel to the Church, with its inter-pretation of heavenly powers, body of ancient lore, texts (the phenom-enally complex astrological tables charting aspects, constellations, configurations, zodiacal signs in endless combinations) and sages; understandably, it was regarded with suspicion by Church authorities. Nevertheless, though sceptical voices can be found (for example, John Chambers, *Treatise Against Judicial Astrology* (1601)), most seemed to have believed in it. Dr Dee was asked to determine the most auspicious day for the coronation of Elizabeth I; university academics and even priests provided astrological advice, which was part of the stock-in-trade of the village cunning man. The wide-selling almanac – a calendar providing information, advice and predictions – was mostly concerned with astrological material; and professionals such as Simon Forman (1552–1611) commanded high fees for their personal consultations. On the basis of probability and native intelligence, some pieces of advice would turn out to be correct; while failures could easily be explained by the wide margin of error made possible by the sheer complexity of the whole art. Like any coherent belief system, astrology was self-verifying: errors could still be accounted for by the system itself, making it immune to falsification.

As C. S. Lewis points out, astrology is in a sense the opposite of magic. For where magic involves man's quest to govern his life by manipulating the physical world, astrology is determinist: man is essentially a passive creature, controlled by the stars ('We are merely the stars' tennis balls / Struck and bandied which way please them' says Bosola in Webster's *The Duchess of Malfi* (5.4)). In this respect, it is comparable to the other powerful determinist philosophy of the age, Calvinist predestination. Still, men and women, even if they did not seek to control the stars, at least attempted to work with them and so maximise their chances of happiness – for example, by ploughing or marrying (or being crowned) on a day deemed to be favourable. And while astrology diminished mankind by making him the passive object of planetary behaviour, it also linked him to the heavenly spheres and stressed humanity's part in the whole cosmic pattern. Like alchemy, astrology was an invitation to charlatanry, but while some practitioners were evidently conmen, others, like Dee and Forman, apparently took their own advice seriously. Different attitudes to astrology are recorded in literature: in *King Lear*, Gloucester declares that 'These late eclipses in the sun and moon portend no good to us . . . Love cools, friendship falls off, brothers divide . . . ' (1.3.100) to which Edmund privately responds: 'This is the excellent foppery of the world: that when we are sick in fortune – often the surfeits of our own behaviour – we make guilt of our disasters the sun, the moon, and stars . . . ' (we note here the word 'dis-aster', deriving from 'astra' or star). Astrology was variously challenged by scepticism like this and by the advance of empirical science: Newton's famous fascination with astrology in the late seventeenth century could then be seen as a fad distinct from real science. At the same time, it lent itself to vivid images and ideas, particularly when combined with classical mythology with its stories of Mars and Venus and the other planetary deities. Thus, whatever its scientific standing, astrological matter had a persistent life at an imaginative level.

Witchcraft

Witchcraft existed in early modern England principally as a lurid fear in educated minds. On the accession of Elizabeth I (1558), Bishop John Jewel declared in a sermon that 'the shoal of them is great, their malice intolerable, the examples most miserable' and implored strenuous activity against them (sanctioned by the biblical text 'Thou shalt not suffer a witch to live', Exodus 22.18). Witchcraft had been a felony in England since 1542 and The Witchcraft Act of 1563 imposed the death penalty for 'invocations or conjurations of evil . . . spirits' and for killing through witchcraft. In the same year, it was made punishable by death in Scotland. Under James I (the author of *Daemonologie* (1597)), witchcraft was pursued more vigorously than under Elizabeth I. Persecution of old women (and some men) under the law continued in England beyond our period: the last trial for witchcraft was in 1712, and the legislation was eventually repealed in 1736. Between 1558 and 1736, the courts of the Home Circuit (Essex, Hertfordshire, Kent, Surrey, Sussex) examined 513 charges, leading to 200 convictions and 109 hangings.

But laws against an activity do not prove that it is being practised; and confessions gained through torture or psychological pressure, which simply confirm the interrogator's charges, are of little value as evidence. How much witchcraft, if any, was actually going on? The figures given above are very slight compared to continental witch-hunts: in Lorrain, between 1580 and 1595 some 900 witches were burned at the stake. Witchcraft in England was lower level in terms of executions than petty theft. There is little evidence of witch scares, though the witchfinder Matthew Hopkins (for whom a fly settling on the defendant's shoulder was proof of a satanic compact) executed a high number in Essex and the other eastern counties (appropriately, he was himself subjected to ordeal by water and, since he floated, hanged as a wizard in 1647; the logic behind this particular ordeal is that the water of baptism refuses to receive a corrupt soul, making drowning an unhelpful proof of innocence). Cases are interestingly diverse but a common pattern is as follows. A lonely old woman lives in poverty, on the verge of death from starvation, perhaps with only a cat, spider or toad for company; she begs a neighbour for something – alms, milk, eggs – but is turned away. A few weeks later, the neighbour's child falls ill or his livestock are diseased. (This sequence is reflected in *Macbeth*, 1.3, 1–25.) The neighbour remembers that the old gossip he turned away muttered something as she left. He goes to the local wise man or woman who asks him whom he suspects and then confirms that suspicion. Other neighbours might then turn on the old woman as scapegoat for their own problems, and the matter could be dealt with locally or be taken to trial. The 'witch' would be accused of using magical powers for evil, perhaps with her pet as a 'familiar', exercising malevolent powers.

This is the basic template for English witchcraft trials. There is no evidence in trial records of satanic covens and other organised rituals, and only one mention of a broomstick. Some 'pacts' with the devil were confessed to, or even boasted about, and a few victims must have believed they had such dealings: perhaps a reputation for strange powers was the only defence such marginalised people had against death by total social exclusion. These themes are touched on in *The Witch of Edmonton* (1621), a Jacobean play by Thomas Dekker, William Rowley and John Ford, and based on a contemporary pamphlet recording a real witch trial. The play both sensationalises its material, depicting the 'witch' Elizabeth Sawyer, making a pact with the devil, and associating with a familiar 'devil-dog'. At the same time, the play makes clear her social exclusion, poverty and desperation, inducing a complex audience reaction.

Witchcraft is of interest to a number of disciplines. Psychologically, the accusation of someone who has been refused alms is a projection of guilt; for anthropologists and social historians, the situation points to a dysfunction in communal life, with the most vulnerable and unproductive members being turned upon. It has also been suggested that witch trials in England were affected by Protestantism, which admitted the existence of witches and evil spirits but denied any practical recourse against them, since exorcism and other Catholic charms were deemed superstitious. This intolerable position drove people to use the systems of local and official justice against the object of their fears. One positive side of this bleak story is the scepticism and humane concern for the victims voiced by writers like Reginald Scot (*Discoverie of Witchcraft* (1584), a great contemporary source on witchcraft and alchemy) who believed that accusers were simply refusing to accept common calamities: 'The fables of witchcraft have taken so fast hold and deep root in the heart of man that few or none can nowadays with patience endure the hand and correction of God'. Another is the increasing reluctance of the courts to convict: the history of witchcraft trials points to an important shift in the required standards of evidence.

The witchcraft phenomenon reported by historians is remote from the most famous literary witches, the three weird sisters in *Macbeth* (*c.*1603–1606). These have something in common with the real-life cases – for example, one of them says she was refused nuts by a woman and then took her malignant revenge – but their prophetic powers and ability to summon up spirits makes them chiefly a reflection of the fantasies of King James. As literary critics, we can ask, what do cultural representations of witches tell us about the imaginative life of the time?

The whole business is essentially a matter of individual and collective imagination. For, unless we take the view that they are factual, all the accusations and confessions of trial records, with their accounts of fantastical deeds, are documents of imaginative literature. Thus the witch has been seen as part of the construction of the 'other', a type feared by society, and against which identities are defined; witches have also been interpreted as fearful misogynist projections – the female as dominant, disobedient, destructive, armed with knowledge; but since many of the accusations came from women, they have also been interpreted as a reflection of female anxieties over maternity and expressions of rivalries between females. *Macbeth* itself could fruitfully be explored with such ideas in mind: the witches, bearded and detached from society are 'other', outside the spheres of social and natural order; they are efficient as expressions of male terrors of being controlled by women, subverting Macbeth's masculinity and code of loyalty; they are also a kind of embodiment of Lady Macbeth's rejection of her own female attributes. This kind of psychoanalytic reading would see the witches as expressions of official, communal, male and female fears, repellent but fascinating voices lurking in the recesses of the imagination. It is a notable feature of the play itself that their responsibility for events is ambiguous, and they escape all punishment. The play corresponds to Church teaching that man has free will and is responsible for his actions.

Conclusion

Magic is obviously relevant in texts dealing with the subject. We have considered briefly the cases of *The Alchemist* and *Macbeth*. We can see the figure of the Renaissance mage in Marlowe's *Dr Faustus* and Shakespeare's *The Tempest*. In both, deep scholarly study leads naturally to occult learning. Faustus sells his soul to purchase magical powers from the devil, a clear case of *goetia*. Prospero in *The Tempest* has been interpreted as practising the good magic, *magia*: in gathering those who exiled him and making them face their crimes, he uses his arts for the ends of justice; he marries his daughter to a young nobleman and blesses their union in a spiritual masque; and while he uses spirits to summon up a storm, no one is killed. All of this is implicitly contrasted to the goetic Sycorax, the 'witch' and mother of Caliban. Yet Prospero's magic is also open to question: he himself is troubled that he has tampered with the forces of nature ('Graves at my command / Have waked their sleepers' (5.1, 48–49)), and it is unclear where he gains the right to enslave Caliban and exploit the island spirit Ariel. His fits of anger unsettle our confidence in him as a benign sage; and the contrast with Sycorax is problematic, since we only ever hear Prospero's own, self-justifying, description of her.

How did a Renaissance audience respond to such works? The weight of evidence is that most would readily have believed in the existence of mages (Dr Dee's neighbours suspected him of dabbling in the dark arts), the influence of the stars, the mischievous activities of hobgoblins and fairies (malign creatures, such as we see in *A Midsummer Night's Dream*, and very far from the 'fairy' image of today), in ghosts that walked abroad or visited their murderers, in the existence of spirits and in the dangerous power of books (Faustus promises to burn his books, Prospero to drown his). In Protestant England, such beliefs might have been strengthened by the condemnation of the old magic of the Catholic Church. But beneath the specifically magical beings of individual texts, we can see general accounts of the world as being in a real sense magical. Following Aristotle, in the traditional scheme Nature herself had a purpose; and physical behaviour across the universe is described in animistic terms, impelled by sympathies, attractions, inclinations and desires. The alchemists talked of matter marrying and generating. Such language is not a series of metaphors for some more literal modern scientific understanding of matter: it indicates the way in which the natural world was imagined, before the seventeenth-century scientific revolution brought about the different, mathematical account of cause and effect and separated mind and matter. In Christian terms, all Creation was in a sense magical, pregnant with significations of the mind of God. There was thus no clear boundary between nature and supernature. The various kinds of magic thus inform much of the literature of the period – from a deliberate use of images in a poem like Donne's 'Loves Alchymie' to the thoroughly animistic account of the Chain of Being in Sir John Davies' poem *Orchestra* (1596). Spenser's description of the Garden of Adonis, where the flowers 'remember well the mightie word . . . That bad them to increase and multiply', could be read not as an escape into romantic fantasy but as a picture of the true magic of fecund Nature, *natura naturans*, which it is the vocation of the artist to uncover. Our own modern perspective on the topic is affected by the discourses of New Age writing, alternative therapy and material science (and the personal attitudes we have towards such matters); the 'Gaia' model of the earth as a self-regulating organism, of interest to ecocriticism, gives us one interesting perspective from which to view the world of early modern magic and the conception of the world which underlies it.

See also   *Contexts*: Chain of Being, Elements, Humours, Medicine, Science; *Criticism*: New Historicism

Further Reading

General

Keith Thomas, *Religion and the Decline of Magic*, 2nd edn (London: Penguin, 1973).
Brian Vickers, ed., *Occult and Scientific Mentalities in the Renaissance* (Cambridge: CUP, 1984).

Alchemy

Stanton J. Linden, ed., *The Alchemy Reader: From Hermes Trismegistus to Isaac Newton* (Cambridge: CUP, 2003).

Astrology

Eugenio Garin, trans. C. Jackson and J. Allen, *Astrology in the Renaissance: The Zodiac of Life* (London: Routledge, 1983).

Witchcraft

K. M. Briggs, *Pale Hecate's Team: An Examination of the Beliefs on Witchcraft and Magic Among Shakespeare's Contemporaries and His Immediate Successors* (London: Routledge, 1962).
Diana Purkiss, *The Witch in History: Early Modern and Twentieth Century Representations* (London: Routledge, 1996).
J. A. Sharpe, *Witchcraft in Tudor and Stuart England*, Seminar Studies in History (London: Longman, 2001).

Fairies

K. M. Briggs, *The Anatomy of Puck: An Examination of Fairy Beliefs Among Shakespeare's Contemporaries and Successors* (London: Routledge, 1959).
Diane Purkiss, *Troublesome Things: A History of Fairies and Fairy Stories* (London: Allen Lane, 2000).

Literary Criticism

John S. Mebane, *Renaissance Magic and the Return of the Golden Age: The Occult Tradition and Marlowe, Jonson and Shakespeare* (London: University of Nebraska Press, 1989).

Manuscripts

Many poets, from Thomas Wyatt (1503–1542) to John Donne (1572–1631) and Thomas Carew (1594/5–1640), eschewed print and circulated their work in manuscript form. One scholar writes,

> Of those who wrote lyric poetry in the period between Donne and Marvell, the majority preferred to restrict their work to manuscript circulation, many first functioned within a system of manuscript

transmission and then organized their work for publication, and very few took a direct route from private composition to typographical presentation of their work to a large public.

(Marotti, 1993, p. 56).

Why would a writer prefer the medium of manuscript to print? One possible reason is that a handwritten text has more of a personal touch than one set in type: a poem in the writer's own script has the intimacy of a letter and is rich with traces of the act of composition. Handwriting is a more personal and immediate medium of expression than print. It is closer to the spontaneity of speech, in the personal characteristics of the writer's script style, and in the conventions – or lack of them – in punctuation and spelling. Renaissance manuscripts often continue to use the older punctuation marks, which indicate where to pause and draw breath, in contrast to print punctuation, which became a system for the logical and grammatical organisation of written discourse. Manuscript spelling might also contain diverse and frequently phonetic orthography, suggestive perhaps of the author's individual voice.

More material reasons might also induce writers to prefer script to print. Because writers were not protected by copyright, it was extremely hard for authors to gain any financial gains from the printed book market. By contrast, a manuscript presented to a patron might earn a much greater reward for its creator, while offering particular satisfaction to the patron: while a printed book is devalued by its easy availability, a manuscript gift-book is a unique object, the result of intensive work, and an ideal article of conspicuous consumption. It might also be exquisitely beautiful: the colours and detail of manuscript illumination could not be equalled by print illustration.

The rarity of the manuscript thus gave it a particularly high value. For the aristocracy, it may also have represented a superior form of expression to the printed book, which was tainted with associations of trade. The choice of manuscript, this argument runs, expressed an aristocratic disdain for commerce, which put poetry on a level with sensational gossip, ballads and lampoons. The manuscript was the natural choice for many a gentleman amateur, wishing to distance himself from the emerging world of grubstreet hacks. It was also an acceptable practice for women poets like Katherine Phillips (1631–1664), who might have faced disapproval among their peers by going into print.

Besides looking different from printed books, texts in manuscript also circulate differently. A manuscript might be directed to a small coterie of friends and be part of an intimate dialogue between them. Once in circulation, it could be sent on, copied and altered: for example, a poem composed for one occasion might be revised for another. A text might be copied into a letter, or preserved in a manuscript miscellany. In this way, manuscripts could have a wider circulation than a print, since print-runs were generally short and print-runs of poetry rarely exceeded 1000: a poet like John Donne (1572–1631) achieved wide esteem purely through the passing around of manuscript copies. The way a literary text is transmitted also affects the way it is interpreted. Rather in the way that a piece of gossip or a joke might circulate among friends, so a lyric could move around, and be regarded as a shared social good, a showcase of the author's wit and not principally as the utterance of an individual genius.

These various general features of manuscript raise several questions. Faced by multiple copies of a poem, each with variants, which one should an editor print? A poem in an altered state might be regarded as at least as authentic as the 'original', assuming that could be identified. It is interesting to compare the different versions of a poem like Wyatt's 'They flee from me that sometime did me seek', which survives in two texts, both equally authentic. The manuscript in the period is a social phenomenon and challenges any assumption that we might excavate an 'authentic' authorial version and present it as a superior, fixed and static text. Increasingly, editors take account of the conditions of manuscript circulation and do not aim for a final, 'correct' reading – though the space limitations of anthologies, and, ironically, the implications of print might still lead us to assume that there is something particularly authorised about the text before us on the page. Reading a poem as part of a letter, or in a commonplace book or miscellany of the time, suggests certain meanings and functions which we would not consider when we see it separated from this context in a modern anthology.

See also *Contexts*: Book Trade, Patronage, Printing; *Texts*: Lyric; *Criticism*: Textuality

Further Reading

Peter Beal, *Manuscripts and Their Makers in Seventeenth-Century England* (Oxford: OUP, 1998).

Harold Love, *Scribal Publication in Seventeenth-Century England* (Oxford: OUP, 1993).

Arthur F. Marotti: 'Manuscript, Print, and the Social History of the Lyric': in Thomas N. Corns, ed., *The Cambridge Companion to English Lyric Poetry: Donne to Marvell* (Cambridge: CUP, 1993), 52–79.

Arthur F. Marotti, *Manuscript, Print and the English Renaissance Lyric* (Ithaca, NY: Cornell University Press, 1995).

Richard Jacobs, *A Beginner's Guide to Critical Reading: Readings for Students* (London: Routledge, 2004), ch. 1 (discussion of two versions of Wyatt 'They flee from me...').

H. R. Woudhuysen, *Sir Philip Sidney and the Circulation of Manuscripts, 1558–1640: The Procreative Pen* (Oxford: Clarendon, 1996).

Medicine (Medical Profession, The Mind, Women)

Renaissance medicine took place against the background of what has been called 'the worst health disaster there has ever been' (Roy Porter; see below). This was the exportation to the New World of Western diseases, against which the native peoples had no immunity: influenza, smallpox, measles and typhus devastated the populations of America, a mass death commonly ascribed to the will of God. In turn, America was the probable source of syphilis (variously called the French pox, the disease of Naples, or the great pox, among other names). This ranged across Europe, assisted by international warfare and expanding, migratory populations. Other diseases included influenza, and its variant the 'English sweat' (major outbreaks in 1485, 1507, 1528, 1551, 1578), typhus ('bloody fever'), scurvy (bred particularly on ships) and malaria (the 'ague' or 'fever', bred in such areas as the marshes on the Thames). The plague was a constant threat: there were major epidemics in 1558, 1563 (when nearly a quarter of London's population died), 1597 and 1603. Meanwhile the innumerable other diseases and conditions which flesh is heir to remained at large. Most were mysterious and incurable, and there was no anaesthetic. Life expectancy has been calculated at 30–35 for men in the better parts of London and 40 for many was the beginning of old age. Life in Renaissance England was lived in the presence, and constant threat, of terrible pain.

The Medical Profession

Medical practice was organised in three layers: Physicians, Surgeons and Apothecaries. Physicians had university degrees and the status of gentlemen. Their professional body was the College of Physicians (founded by royal charter in 1518). 'Physic' was a theoretical enterprise, based on the careful study of ancient authors, particularly the Greek Galen (129–c.200), whose texts were edited, published and translated. An important Renaissance anatomist was Andreas Vesalius (1514–1564), who demonstrated the importance of the dissection of human bodies (Galen had only studied the bodies of animals). In the period, some new advances were made in the understanding of the human body – for example, the identification of the fallopian tubes by Gabriele Falloppia (1523–1563). Along with this scientific method, Hermetic, astrological and Occult ideas of the human constitution were given prestige by the neo-Platonists, and the theory of the humours survived, though not without debate. However, the new anatomy had little practical effect on the work of surgeons, who actually treated people. Surgeons dealt with surface wounds (fractures, burns, swelling, etc.). They too were professionally organised: the Barber-Surgeons Company was founded in 1540 (merging two older guilds). As with other guilds, members had to serve a seven-year apprenticeship. Considerable knowledge was gained by surgeons through the experience of warfare, though practices remained traditional: diagnosis was commonly performed by the inspection of urine, and the most common treatment was blood-letting (purgation). The administering of drugs, which affected the 'inward' body, had to be licensed by a Physician (though in practice the Physicians had little control over Surgeons, and there was much professional rivalry). Apothecaries (who belonged to the Grocers' Company) provided medicines, both herbal and, increasingly, chemical. 'Herbs' – the word has a wider sense including leaves, seeds, fruit, bark and roots – might be applied individually ('simples') or as compounds. The world of the apothecary was rapidly changing: botanical science led to a new classification of plants, while travel brought back new drugs and vegetation from other parts of the world, including opium. Beneath apothecaries came herbalists and wise women (allowed to practise by Act of Parliament, 1542–1543), midwives (licensed by the Church), and beneath them were the quacks, pettifoggers and charlatans who filled the gaps where the inadequate number of surgeons could not reach. Besides organised professional bodies, another vital institution is the hospital. England's provision of hospital care was effectively destroyed by Henry VIII's dissolution of the monasteries: these had historically tended, if not treated, the sick and infirm. In London, the hospitals of St Thomas's and St Bartholemew's survived under the management of the City of London. But they cared for relatively few patients, and outside London the ill usually had no such shelter.

The Mind

As well as the body, the human mind was an object of great interest. Medical and theological interpretations of the soul joined with mystical, astrological and hermetic discourse. Melancholy (depression) was associated by the Florentine Marsilio Ficino (1433–1499) with the planet Saturn. This distemper of the mind is an important topic in literature, where melancholy can slip into madness. Dramas depict mad characters in a variety of modes, from comic to tragic (see, for example, Hieronimo and Isabella in Thomas Kyd's The Spanish Tragedy (1597) and Ferdinand in John Webster's The Duchess of Malfi (1612–14)). Melancholy was also analysed by two great writers who suffered from it, Montaigne (1533–1592) and Robert Burton (1557–1640). Burton listed among its causes: 'idleness, solitariness, overmuch study, passions, perturbations, discontents, cares, miseries, vehement desires, ambitions...'. For both writers, writing itself was a defence against melancholy and madness, but the uneducated had no such resources: beggars might be seen as fools or madmen (like Poor Tom in *King Lear*); confused old women might be pursued as witches; and it was common entertainment in London to laugh at the antics of the inmates of the Hospital of St Mary of Bethlehem (Bethlem, whence 'bedlam'), which had housed the mentally ill since 1403. Such visits are dramatised in two plays by Thomas Dekker and John Webster (*Westward Ho!* (1604), 5.7; *Northward Ho!* (1607) 4.3), while Thomas Middleton and William Rowley's *The Changeling* (1622) is set in a madhouse.

Women

The close sense of connection between mind and body is clear in Renaissance views of women. A prevalent view was that women were naturally inferior by reason of their physiology. While men were of hot and dry humours, women were cold and wet, and this made them prone to mood swings, deceitfulness and a generally unsteady temperament. According to the idea of the 'wandering womb', the uterus was a hungry animal, needing sexual intercourse or reproduction, and liable to cause hysteria if not kept satisfied. A woman was thus in thrall to her body and lower disorderly instincts ('Frailty, thy name is woman', says Hamlet (1.2.146)). This strand of medical thinking lies behind literary descriptions of woman's changeability and untrustworthiness (see, for example, Posthumus' speech in *Cymbeline* (2.5)) and the view that women should not take positions of power. It may also help explain the notions of witchcraft, since women were considered particularly vulnerable to 'possession' by forces unseating their reason.

Conclusion

Medicine converges with the arts on a number of levels. Study of the human body was promoted by Renaissance artists' interest in the human form and advanced by the printed illustrations in medical books. The idea of anatomy was picked up in such works as Burton's (mentioned above) and Donne's poem 'An anatomy of the World'. Literary texts provide vivid descriptions of medical practitioners (see the description of an apothecary in *Romeo and Juliet*, 5.1.37–1.57), and of disease itself: see, for example, the description of sweating sickness by Thomas Nashe (1567–1601) in *The Unfortunate Traveller* (pp. 24–28) or Timon's account of the effects of syphilis (*Timon of Athens*, 4.3.134–4.3.166 – this play generally is dense with medical imagery). As well as helping us to imagine what diseases were like, literature also helps us to understand how illness was thought about. What often emerges is a holistic picture: through metaphor, physical illness is closely related to other disorders. In Shakespeare's *Henry IV, Part 2*, for example, the sickness of the King is analogous to the fractured state of the realm and the moral sickness which we see in the disordered world of Eastcheap. In such thinking, we see a desire to make sense of the incomprehensible: bodily pain is the symptom of moral degeneration, a divine judgment, a spiritually necessary experience to be suffered patiently, a revelation of the 'sullied flesh' in which the soul is imprisoned. These ideas remained potent even as Science entered a new experimental phase in the seventeenth century. They have not entirely dissipated today.

See also   *Contexts*: Chain of Being, Cosmos, Elements, Humour, Magic, Science; *Texts*: Non-fictional Prose

Further Reading

Ian Maclean, *The Renaissance Notion of Woman: A Study in the Fortunes of Scholasticism and Medical Science in European Intellectual Life* (Cambridge: CUP, 1980).

Liza Picard, *Elizabeth's London* (London: Weidenfeld and Nicolson, 2003), ch. 6 'Health, Illness and Medicine', 99–122.

Roy Porter, *The Greatest Benefit to Mankind: A Medical History of Humanity from Antiquity to the Present* (London: HarperCollins, 1997), ch. 8, 'Renaissance', 163–200.

Douglas Trevor, *The Poetics of Melancholy in Early Modern England* (Cambridge: CUP, 2004).

Patronage

In early modern England, all offices in Church and State were controlled by patronage. Advancement depended on the support of some influential person. In his Precepts to his son Robert, Elizabeth I's Chief Secretary Sir Robert Cecil describes the gift-giving that was a normal part of this process:

'Be sure to keep some great man thy friend; but trouble him not for trifles. Present him with many yet small gifts and of little charge. And if thou hast cause to bestow any great gratuity, let it be some such thing as may daily be in his sight. Otherwise in this ambitious age thou shalt remain as a hop without a pole living in obscurity, and be made a football for every insulting companion'.

Patronage started with the sovereign, and moved in a pyramid through nobles, lesser nobles and so downwards and outwards. Favours, posts or hearing for a cause might depend on a chain of patrons, each one interceding with another higher up, and each one in turn expecting something in return for any assistance that was offered. The same person might offer patronage to someone below, while seeking it themselves from someone else.

Literary patronage was a part of this complex system. Little money was to be had from publishing books, and writers sought to attach themselves to great people, who might provide financial assistance, further useful contacts, and even subsistence. Two years in the life of the poet George Gascoigne (1539–1578) illustrate this predicament: in 1575, he was employed by the Earl of Leicester to help plan the entertainments put on for Queen Elizabeth I at Kenilworth. As part of the show, when the Queen returned from hunting, Gascoigne leapt out, 'clad like a Savage man, all in Ivie' and asked for royal patronage. In 1576, he translated another entertainment which had pleased the Queen into three languages (presumably to show his employability as a secretary) and prefaced the work with an extended plea for patronage. The next year sees him dedicating one book to Lord Grey with a preface hoping for 'speedy advauncement' and another to the Earl of Bedford asking for youthful indiscretions to be forgotten. When Gascoigne finally secured an official appointment, perhaps on the recommendation of these noblemen, he dedicated a collection of poems to the Queen in 1577, with thanks for 'undeserved favour'. The choice of subject matter would in each case have been influenced by the tastes of the patron whose help he was trying to solicit.

From the patron's point of view, a writer could be a valuable ornament to his or her household. From medieval times, great houses had employed entertainers of one kind or another. The Renaissance brought with it a need for educated secretaries and tutors. Moreover, the figure of the Roman Maecenas (70–8 BC), patron of Horace and Virgil, might influence noblemen to fulfil themselves partly through support of the arts and learning. Henry Wriothesley, third Earl of Southampton (1573–1624), is famous for being the patron of William Shakespeare, who dedicated to Southampton his poems *Venus and Adonis* (1593) and *The Rape of Lucrece* (1594). (Southampton is also a candidate for the mysterious 'W. H.', to whom the sonnets are dedicated.) He also patronised the Italian scholar John Florio (1553–1625) and Thomas Nashe (1567–1601), who dedicated to him *The Unfortunate Traveller* (1594) with the suggestive words, 'a dere lover and cherisher you are, as well of the lovers of Poets, as of Poets themselves'.

Patronage was an area where great ladies made important contributions to the culture. One example was Sir Philip Sidney's sister, Mary Herbert (née Sidney), Countess of Pembroke (1561–1621). Her brother's *Arcadia* was dedicated to her, and after his death she supervised its publication (1593, 1598) and continued to support clients who had honoured

Sir Philip. These included the many writers already in the remarkable Sidney family and household (most famously, her niece Lady Mary Wroth (c.1587–1651/3)) and some of the leading poets of the time. Though their comments are necessarily hyperbolic and formal, it seems clear that patron – client relations went beyond formalities, and that the Sidney houses at Wilton and elsewhere served as a kind of academy of writers exchanging ideas: Samuel Daniel (1562–1619) said of his poems that he received 'the first notion for the formall ordering of those compositions at Wilton, which I must ever acknowledge to have beene my best Schoole'. More succinctly, the poet Thomas Churchyard (c.1520–1604) said of Mary Sidney that she 'sets to schoole, our Poets ev'rywhere'. Her own compositions, including the metrical paraphrases of the Psalms which she completed on her brother's death, circulated outside the family in letters and were praised by other poets. Another important lady patron was Lucy Russell (née Harington), Countess of Bedford (bap. 1581–d.1627). The many writers she patronised included John Florio (who apparently lived in her house when completing his translation of Montaigne), Ben Jonson (who wrote three epigrams to her) and John Donne, who had a close and complex relation with Lucy Russell and was allowed to name his daughter Lucy (b.1608) after her. Besides writers, she also patronised music (John Dowland dedicated to her his *Second Booke of Songes or Ayres* (1600) and praised her knowledge of the art), masques, art collecting and garden design.

The patronage system not only supported writers materially. It also actively shaped literary creation. Most directly, we see this in the dedicatory letters and verses of the age, most of them tediously eulogistic, and in the associated poetry of praise, such as Jonson's epigrams. But poetry was also affected by the activity of great houses such as Wilton: there writers would meet, read their work aloud, hear lyrical poetry sung to music, dine and converse. Literature lived not in an ivory tower or garret but as part of this complex personal and social activity. This helps to explain some common elements of Renaissance writing such as the strong dramatic element in much lyric poetry (suggestive of evenings of reading aloud) and the private references produced by a coterie readership. It also helps us understand the close links at this time between poetry and public affairs: writers could not afford to live a life of seclusion and were often employed in public office, and in contact with others similarly occupied, and so naturally caught up in political events. As an instrument for the circulation of texts and ideas, patronage is comparable to printing. The patron – client relationship could take various forms, from the remote (some books were dedicated without the patron even knowing) to the affectionate. Patronage itself is depicted in *Timon of Athens* (see 1.1). In the seventeenth century, the system started to give way to the age of the professional writer, though the quest for influential help and the gift-giving recommended by Cecil continued as keenly as ever.

See also   *Contexts*: Court, Courtier, Manuscripts, Women; *Texts*: Lyric, Rhetoric

Further Reading

David M. Bergeron, *Textual Patronage in English Drama 1570–1640* (Aldershot: Ashgate, 2006).

Michael Brennan, *Literary Patronage in the English Renaissance: The Pembroke Family* (London: Routledge, 1988).

Cedric C Brown, ed., *Patronage, Politics and Literary Tradition in England 1558–1658*, Yearbook of English Studies, 21 (Detroit: Wayne State UP, 1993).

Platonism

The Athenian philosopher Plato (*c*.428–*c*.348 BC) exercised an important influence on Renaissance thought. At the centre of Platonism is the idea of two worlds: the World of Being and the World of Becoming. The World of Being is an ideal world, made up of Ideas and Forms. It is immaterial, stable and perfect; invisible to the senses, it is intelligible only by the intellect. Inferior to this is the World of Becoming, which we occupy: this world is a defective copy of the World of Being, corrupt and mutable. It is apprehended directly by the senses but can cloud our intuition of the perfect World beyond.

The notion of two worlds in turn yields other ideas, particularly those of ascent and descent. Platonism teaches that the soul is born in the perfect world but descends to the world of becoming, where it is imprisoned in the body. Thus a natural aspiration for man is to ascend from his present state to the world beyond, his original home. 'Platonic love' is this yearning for the Good, which resides beyond imperfect material objects. The Idea of Beauty may be apprehended in a state of ecstasy. The present world can be viewed with contempt, as a place of error and mutability. Alternatively, it can be an object of enjoyment and fascination since, for all its imperfection, it is a copy of – and thus a guide to – the World of Being.

In late antiquity, Plato's ideas were synthesised with traditions stemming from magic and mystery religions. In the third century, Plotinus (*c*.205–270) in his work *The Enneads* associated the World of Being with the divine mind and described the soul as the link between the immaterial and the material. Individual souls are hence equipped with both senses and intellect. Crucially, they are free to choose what course of action to follow on the basis of their perceptions. Plotinus's treatment of Platonism is not ascetic: the material world is a creation of the divine mind and reflects its creator in being orderly, beautiful and good. Plotinus in turn influenced the thought of St Augustine (354–430; see Book VII of *The Confessions*), Boethius (480–524/5) and the author known as Pseudo-Dionysius the Areopagite (fifth century). However, in the Middle Ages the knowledge of Greek was lost, and Plato's thought was known only through the handful of dialogues which survived in Latin translations – the *Timaeus*, *Phaedo* and *Meno*.

The key Renaissance figure in mediating the thought of Plato to the age of the Renaissance was the Florentine scholar Marsilio de Ficino (1433–1499). Ficino undertook the massive task of translating all 36 of Plato's known dialogues into Latin, accompanying them with his own commentary. This great work was published in 1484, and was followed by Ficino's translation of Plotinus's *Enneads* (1492), again accompanied by commentaries. Ficino also translated various mystical works of late antiquity, attributed to the figure 'Hermes Trismegistus', a supposed Greek sage and source for Plato. Besides his labours as a translator, Ficino was important for presenting Plato's dialogues as a unified philosophy. He stressed the compatibility of Platonism with Christianity and with occult and magical texts. This syncretic approach – the attempt to integrate different belief systems – was pursued by other Florentine neo-Platonists, such as Pico della Mirandola (1463–1494), who synthesises Plato, Aristotle, Christianity and the Jewish Caballah. Another characteristic of the neo-Platonic texts is the idea mentioned earlier, of ascent and descent. From the vantage point of the Soul, midway between earth and heaven, man looks upwards to the angelic mind and to God and downwards to the material world of the body. One particular form of this yearning for the Good is the idea of Platonic love, introduced in Ficino's commentary on Plato's *Symposium*. Platonic Love is in essence a quest for the Good through love, moving beyond the material to the transcendent. In his own treatise, *De Amore*, Ficino draws on the *Symposium* and fuses it with the tradition of medieval courtly love. This account of Platonic love is echoed in Book IV of Castiglione's *The Courtier* (published 1528) and rapidly found its way into the *dialoghi d'amore* (love dialogues) of Renaissance poetry. 'Platonic love' in this sense is not a search for transcendent truth but the presentation of a secular love between two humans as a spiritual experience.

Plato was studied in English universities in the sixteenth centuries, and Platonic ideas also reached English literature through French and Italian sources: Platonic love, in its literary sense, is the most obvious influence. The sonnet sequences of Spenser, Drayton and Sidney make frequent use of Platonic themes, often in conjunction with other currents of thought.

In this sonnet by Sidney we can see Classical mythology, Protestant and Platonic topics combined:

> It is most true that eyes are form'd to serve
> The inward light, and that the heavenly part
> Ought to be king, from whose rules who do swerve,
> Rebels to Nature, strive for their own smart.
> It is most true, what we call *Cupid*'s dart,
> An image is, which for our selves we carve,
> And, fooles, adore in temple of our hart,
> Till that good God make Church and Churchman starve.
> True, that true Beautie virtue is indeed,
> Wherof this Beautie can be but a shade
> Which elements with mortall mixture breed:
> True, that on earth we are but pilgrims made,
> And should in soul up to our countrey move:
> True, and yet true that I must Stella love.
> (*Astrophil and Stella*, 5)

The main idea of this sonnet is that true beauty – the 'inward light' – is transcendent, and belongs in the spiritual realm. It is the divine or 'heavenly part' of our soul which should govern us. If we exercise free choice wrongly and 'swerve' from this directive to look beyond the material world, then we injure ourselves. The image of Cupid's dart is an idol, and, in line with Protestant teaching, adoration of idols is condemned as foolish idolatry, leading to spiritual death ('starve' has its older sense of 'die'). The sestet (last six lines) is the most explicitly Platonic part of the poem: the speaker agrees that true or ideal Beauty is not to be found in material form but in the shape of Virtue. 'This Beautie', that is the beauty we find on earth, is only a poor reflection or 'shade' of the real thing, mixed and corrupted by base earthly matter ('mortall mixture'). The Platonic idea of ascent is then conveyed through the traditional idea of life as a pilgrimage to our true home ('our countrey') in heaven. Finally, after this huge series of concessions, the final line admits failure on the speaker's part: he cannot stop loving earthly beauty in the form of Stella. Her name, though, meaning 'Star', strongly suggests she is not altogether mortal; and there is the suggestion here of courtly Platonism, the idea that outward beauty is a sign of inward goodness – an idea developed in Book Four of Castiglione's *The Courtier* and another common topic in the work of courtly poets like Sidney.

In summary form, then, Sidney's poem may be taken as a rehearsal of basic Platonic ideas synthesised with Christian and particularly Protestant ideas about images. Yet when reading poems with some conceptual background in mind we should beware of reducing them to pieces of versified philosophy: the tone, texture and narrative through which concepts are delivered are as much part of a poem's effect as its basic intellectual argument. Our paraphrase of Sidney's sonnet perhaps makes it sound much drier than it is: Platonism is used wittily here, as the poem leads us from the pious solemnities of the accumulated concessions to the bathos of the final line. There is an air of self-conscious virtuosity and playfulness in the range of imagery and transitions between classical and Christian images. One wonders how hard the speaker has really tried to perceive the 'inward light' before resigning himself to the enchantment of Stella's beauties. Platonism informs the poem but does not dominate it: it is a piece of artifice, and a psychological drama, rather than an academic treatise. Love poetry tends to resist the austerity of Platonic love in its purest formulations. In the writings of a Cavalier poet like John Cleveland (1613–1658), the combat between Platonic and anti-Platonic love is an elaborate courtly game – as perhaps it already is in Sidney. Spenser uses Platonism where it suits him, but is happy to turn to other sources and to praise worldly goods like marriage and procreation (in *Epithalamion*), which are far from Platonic ideals.

Similar allusions to Plato can be found in Donne, for example in 'The Extasie', in which the poet explores the experience of love taking lovers from the mortal to the immortal realm, or in Platonic terms from the World of Becoming to the World of Being. Ben Jonson explores Platonic love in *The Masque of Beauty* (1608) and *The New Inn* (1629). Marvell's 'Dialogue Between Soul and Body' is an examination of Christian Platonism, gathering a dynamic from a fundamental ambiguity in both Platonic and Christian thought: should the mortal world be despised as corrupt and defective, or praised and enjoyed as the work of the divine Creator? The religious writers Thomas Traherne (1636/7–1674) and Henry Vaughan (1622–1695) also employ ideas of Platonism alongside Christian theology. Beyond individual texts, there is a Platonic flavour to the idea that the body reflects the soul: 'Soul is form and doth the body make' as Spenser puts it. However, the recurrence of a few common ideas does not itself denote immersion in the original texts, and several themes are consistent with Christian ideas and native traditions of writing (for example, lyrics like Sidney's have another background in the medieval devotional lyric). Recent research has suggested that Platonism was less rooted in England than in other countries such as France. Its presence in the literature is perhaps more a result of informal dissemination than applied study.

See also *Contexts*: Chain of Being, Golden Age, Humanism, Sex and Sexuality; *Texts*: Mimesis, Theory of Poetry

Further Reading

Introductory

Sarah Hutton, 'Platonism, Stoicism, Scepticism and Classical Imitation': in *A Companion to English Renaissance Literature and Culture*, ed. Michael Hattaway (Oxford: Blackwell, 2000), 44–57.

Isabel Rivers, *Classical and Christian Ideas in Renaissance English Poetry*, 2nd edn (London: Routledge, 1994), ch.3, 'Platonism and NeoPlatonism', 33–43.

Full Length

John Smith Harrison, *Platonism in English Poetry of the Sixteenth and Seventeenth Centuries* [1903] (Westport, CT: Greenwood Press, 1980).

Sears Reynolds Jayne, *Plato in Renaissance England* (Dordrecht and Boston: Kluwer Academic Publishers, 1995).

Printing

'Printing, gunpowder and the compass' make up Francis Bacon's trio of inventions that had transformed the world (*Novum Organum*, Bk 1, 129). Printing revolutionised the manufacture and appearance of books, and in so doing caused significant changes in the wider culture: as with the Internet today, the new medium transformed the circulation of ideas within society, and thereby affected social and political life.

Printing did not originate in the West, and neither did gunpowder nor the compass: together with papermaking, these make up the four great inventions of Ancient China. In bookmaking, the Chinese were using fixed woodcuts by 200 AD, and movable type by the eleventh century. Chinese technologies of paper and ink were subsequently introduced to the West by Muslims: the first paper mill in Europe is recorded in Eastern Spain in 1074. Since about 1400, many Western monasteries had been using presses to reproduce devotional woodcut images for pilgrims.

Thus the key elements of printing predated the German Johannes Gutenberg (1400–1468), who is usually credited with the introduction of this technology to the Western world. Gutenberg's achievement was perhaps not so much to invent the printing process as to synthesise and perfect its various elements, drawing on various craft traditions such as coin-minting. He developed a new kind of ink, which produced a darker colour than the water-soluble inks of medieval scribes and was also permanent. Gutenberg also replaced wooden blocks with longer-lasting metal types. The types each bore a particular letter or other character (the expression upper-case and lower-case for letters originates in the boxes where such characters were kept, so a compositor could reach for them without looking). These types were cast in a specially developed alloy which gave crisp, precisely calibrated moulds, producing exactly the same character each time. Types were arranged in frames (called 'galleys') in any order: hence the phrase 'movable type'. Where old woodblocks could only produce one specific text, movable type could be rearranged in infinite combinations to print any book. Gutenberg's press in Mainz printed rapidly on both sides of the paper. Like other early printers, he was not thinking of producing a new type of object, but the same object – the book – by different means. Gutenberg's famous 42-line Bible (c.1454) is in gothic script, making it resemble a manuscript.

The gothic type used by Gutenberg reminds us that while printing was in many ways a revolutionary change, there were also important continuities between printed books and manuscripts. 'Incunabula' (meaning 'cradle books') are books from the first 50 years of printing and follow the model of manuscripts. Moreover, the books produced were the same books as had previously been copied by scribes: texts for the universities and, overwhelmingly, religious works commissioned by the Church. Like manuscripts, early printed books also tended to be expensive items, suited to display.

From Germany, the centre of printing moved to Italy, where it coincided with the Humanist enterprise of establishing corrected texts of the classics. The humanist insistence on correctness was served by the compositors, proofreaders and copyeditors who established the texts of Greek and Roman classics which, once set in type, could be perfectly reproduced. Along with correctness went clarity of presentation: the earlier gothic typefaces were replaced by the new italic characters inspired by Roman lettering and named after the leading printers who designed them: Aldus Manutius in Venice, Claude Garamond (French) and Christopher Plantinus (Antwerp). But as always the shift was gradual: gothic black letter types were still in use in England into the seventeenth century (a famous example is the 1611 Bible).

Printing thus had important effects on a book's text: this could now be fixed in accurate form, and reproduced without scribal error (though compositors' errors of course occurred), in a clear and classical appearance in the new fonts. At the same time, printers refined the distribution and navigation of a volume's contents: glosses, commentaries, footnotes, indexes and other kinds of apparatus were presented in steadily more uniform schemes. Books were also produced in regular sizes, based on the number of folds of a single sheet: a large Folio text (one sheet folded in half, producing four printable sides), and the smaller and cheaper quarto (four folds) and octavo (eight folds) volumes. Modern punctuation marks were also introduced in this period: earlier manuscript marks, which usually gave guidance for oral delivery, indicating pauses for breath and points of emphasis, changed into logical markers indicating the function of sentences and the relations of meaning between sentence elements. Frontispieces gave details of the date and place of publication and advertised the printer responsible as well.

The first printed book in the English language was made by the diplomat and businessman William Caxton (*c*.1422–*c*.1491). This was an impression of his own translation of the French *Recuyell des Histories de Troy*, printed in Bruges in *c*.1474. Encouraged by royal and noble patronage, Caxton set up his printing press near Westminster Abbey in *c*.1476. As with printers elsewhere in this period, the hundred or so volumes which Caxton produced were expensive items for wealthy patrons. However, the book market was growing steadily to include the growing urban bourgeoisie, and this expansion can be seen in the fortunes of Caxton's own business. His assistant Wynkyn de Worde (?*d*.1535) took this over on Caxton's death and moved it to Fleet Street to be nearer to the booksellers. There he concentrated on smaller and cheaper books for this wider public.

The rise and proliferation of printing had many effects, among them regulation of the book trade through the Stationers' Company and the development of various measures of censorship. Perhaps the phenomenon most commented on, though, is the use of print to spread religious ideas, and in particular the close relation between print technology and Reformation theology. There is a remarkable coincidence, and symbiosis, between the rise of print and Reformation thinking, centred on faith in the Word of God. Doctrines based on a reverence for the word met with a means for reproducing words faster and in greater quantities than ever before.

Through printed books, the work of humanists and reformers was quickly propagated. Perhaps there are also relations between the new technology and linguistic style: the lucidity of expression favoured by the humanists was well suited to public discussion, and their editions of the scriptures presented this public with a readily understandable text of the divine Word. The translations of the New Testament and the Psalms by Lefèvre d'Etaples (*c*.1455–1536) were soon followed by others, such as William Tyndale's for English readers, and the sheer quantity and small size of these books meant they could not effectively be stopped by the authorities. Luther's tracts of 1520 and Calvin's *Institutes* (1536–1559) were published by the thousands, and their message was expressed in a different form in sermons, manuals of piety and more ephemeral publications, such as broadsides of a single sheet which could carry a simple and powerful message to less educated people. These were some of the many generic categories of writing that the medium of print made possible. The Catholic Church responded vigorously in kind through its own publications, such as hagiographies and accounts of the achievements and tribulations of missionaries. The rapidity of print reproduction made it a natural vehicle for polemic, propaganda and fierce debate, from the disputes between Thomas More and William Tyndale to the pamphlets of the Civil War. With the expansion of print went the dissolution of centralising authority and a consequent battle in words for influence over readers' minds.

The printed word, then, propagated ideas and arguments with unprecedented speed. Other writers, such as natural philosophers, could also convey their thoughts to a wider public in book form. Print further allowed the dissemination not only of words but of various kinds of illustration: woodcut prints accompanying, and explaining, texts grew in sophistication and attracted some leading artists including, in England, Hans Holbein the Younger (c.1497–1543). The printing of music brought new styles and works out of specialised centres and into the household. As European travellers and colonisers expanded the known world, they took the printing press with them, and the consequent maps and travel accounts shaped Western ideas of the configuration of the earth. One interpretation of this phenomenon is that it constituted a revolution in information and communication: important discussions moved out of specialised groups and into the public sphere, readers became progressively empowered by increased knowledge and articulacy and were consequently more receptive to innovative thought. With increased amounts of reading material came increased opportunities for education and a rise in literacy. Consequently one can argue that print effected, and accelerated, a profound shift in the way people saw and understood the world.

However, this view of the print revolution needs to be qualified. The effects of the medium were not all in one direction. For example, while printing certainly increased access to new ideas, it also perpetuated and perhaps even strengthened older habits of thought. We might recall that Caxton's first English book was not a work of radical theology or cosmology but a collection of stories of Troy – an old favourite for his patrons. A few printers, like the Venetian Aldus Manutius, might have seen themselves as in the vanguard of the new leaning, but for the most part they were not revolutionary firebrands but businessmen providing commodities for a market. Thus the most extensively printed books were not intellectually cutting-edge works but reliable staple sellers such as schoolbooks and lawbooks. London's readers purchased small cheap copies of favourite old medieval romances, like *Bevis of Hamptoun* and *Sir Degaré*. These continued to be read throughout the sixteenth century and formed part of the mental furniture of the audiences to Shakespeare's plays, together with the old lore and marvels and folk wisdom passed on in almanacs and encyclopaedias. Such works sold in far greater quantities than learned humanist productions, which often had to be subsidised by wealthy patrons, and sold very slowly.

If we concentrate our attention on London's writers and the London book market, we risk overestimating national literacy rates: England was a rural economy, and most of the population lived very far from St Paul's. In the countryside, men and women would have encountered the printed word through the offerings of a travelling pedlar, whose stock was unlikely to include the latest revision of Calvin's *Institutes*. The description given of his merchandise by the pedlar Autolycus in *The Winter's Tale* (performed 1611) reminds us of popular reading habits and hints interestingly at a perceived link between print and veracity:

CLOWN   What hast here? Ballads?

MOPSA   Pray now, buy some. I love a ballad in print, alife, for then we are sure they are true.

AUTOLYCUS   Here's one to a very doleful tune, how a usurer's wife was brought to bed of twenty money-bags at a burden, and how she longed to eat adders' heads and toads carbonadoed. (4.4)

Another tension is that between diversity and uniformity. While printing undoubtedly opened up new areas of knowledge to a larger public, to some extent it also brought about some kinds of contraction: a manuscript might take vitally different forms in drafts and copies. It could accrete meaning through commentaries in different hands and was rarely regarded as finished and 'published'. By contrast, a printed book presented a fixed, homogenised text. A unique handwritten artefact became a mechanically reproducible commodity. Standardisation in size and format was coupled with a standardising of orthography and punctuation, with the consequent diminution of dialect forms. English was privileged over other British tongues, and – then as now – common formats of presentation arguably encouraged common approaches to reading and interpretation. Such assertions need always to be tested against the evidence of particular texts, but we can securely say that the revolution in consciousness brought about by printing was one which moved unsteadily, at varying speeds in different places, and carried a complex range of ramifications.

See also *Contexts*: Book Trade, English Reformation, Manuscripts, Patronage; *Texts*: The Bible; *Criticism*: Textualism

Further Reading

Elizabeth Eisenstein, *The Printing Revolution in Early Modern Europe*, 2nd edn (Cambridge: CUP, 2005).

Lotte Hellinga and J. B. Trapp, eds, *The Cambridge History of the Book in Britain*, Vol III: 1400–1557 (Cambridge: CUP, 1999).
David McKitterick, *Print, Manuscript and the Search for Order, 1450–1830* (Cambridge: CUP, 2003).

Protestant Theology

To those who lived in the medieval and early modern period, the question 'What must I do to be saved?' had an absolute importance that many of us today find hard to imagine. The ultimate purpose of life for any individual was to secure God's grace and enter His heavenly Kingdom, and the ultimate aim for society was to reproduce God's kingdom on earth. For any Christian before the Reformation, salvation was sought through the help of the universal Church. The Church alone had the authority to interpret the Bible and explain it to the faithful. It also ministered the Holy Sacraments, through which man's life was touched by the divine. Only a priest could administer the sacraments, and through them the faithful were received into the Body of Christ.

Beyond the priesthood lay the Virgin Mary and the Saints, who could further mediate between mortals and God and intercede on behalf of a penitent sinner to ask for God's forgiveness. Thus the medieval Christian lived in a world of rich and complex imagery, which drew on Bible stories, on the lives and miracles of saints and the festivities of the Church year. Art and music glorified God, lifted man to the divine, and instructed him on the deepest mysteries of existence and the conduct of day-to-day life.

Another central teaching was that divine grace might be hoped for not only through inner feelings such as remorse, but through good works, from attendance at Mass to performing acts of charity: Shakespeare's Henry V appeals to God to consider his good works, such as the foundation of chantry chapels, to expiate the sin of his father in usurping the throne (4.1, 277). The urge to do good works lies behind the foundation of many buildings and institutions, and the patronage of much art. It also lay behind the practice of indulgences. In origin, these seem to have been an expression of gratitude for God's forgiveness. But texts like the speech given by Chaucer's Pardoner before delivering his tale present them as a way of *purchasing* forgiveness. Luther's criticisms of the Catholic Church begin with his attack on the sale of indulgences to finance the building of St Peter's Church in Rome. There is a long tradition of criticism of such malpractice coming from within the Church itself: we find it in the poetry of Chaucer and Langland, and in our period the writings of Erasmus, among others.

The Reformers Martin Luther (1483–1546), Ulricius Zwingli (1484–1531) and John Calvin (1509–1564) produced a radically different teaching on Salvation. Drawing on a long tradition of anti-clerical writing, Luther and Calvin denounced the Church as corrupt, and denied it had authority to explain God's word or to mediate between God and man. The number and nature of the Sacraments were disputed: for a Reformer like Calvin, they were outward and visible symbols of the invisible grace of God; but Calvin denied the Real Presence of God in the bread and wine of the mass. The Christian had no need of the intercession of priests or the saints, but could come to understand divine mysteries through meditating on the Bible, which was the sole basis for all true theology (*sola scriptura*). Salvation did not depend on good works. In Luther's phrase, 'The just shall live by faith alone' (the doctrine of *sola fide*). Protestants formed a 'priesthood of all believers': ministers had no special aura or power to separate them from the other faithful, since the believer could meet and know God in his inner heart.

Protestant teachings circulated through the new medium of print, supported by translations of the Bible. Protestantism is often called a 'Religion of the Book' because of the importance it places on a personal intimacy with the words of the scriptures. This stress on inward contemplation also led to an attack on imagery such as vestments, statues and stained glass. These were regarded by puritanical Protestants as superstitious idols. The reign of Edward VI (1547–1553) saw massive destruction of art in churches, an iconoclasm which was repeated under the Puritans of Cromwell's Republic.

Protestant theology draws largely on the writings of St Paul (10–67) and St Augustine (354–430), and presents itself as a return to the true faith rather than a new departure. In texts like Spenser's *The Faerie Queene*, the Church of England is depicted as a return of the Church of Christ to its pure original state, before it had been corrupted and adulterated by Catholic practices. Central tenets of the Protestant Reformation were systematised in Calvin's *Institutes of the Christian Religion* (a book of six chapters in 1536, expanding to 80 chapters by the final edition in 1559), and most strictly followed in Calvin's theocracy in Geneva. Complex differences of doctrine and discipline led to numerous different kinds of Protestant Church across Europe. An example is England, where the 'Elizabethan Settlement' sought to organise the Church in a way that would be accepted by both Anglicans – who accepted Calvinist doctrine but wished to retain some of the rituals of Catholic tradition – and the Puritans, who felt that the Reformation in England had not gone far enough. Tensions between different kinds of Protestantism in England continued and formed an important part of the causes of the Civil War in England and the Puritan Commonwealth which followed.

Some fundamental teachings of Protestantism are alluded to in the opening lines to Milton's *Paradise Lost* (1667):

Of man's first disobedience, and the fruit
Of that forbidden tree, whose mortal taste
Brought death into the world, and all our woe
With loss of Eden, till one greater man
Restore us, and regain the blissful seat,
Sing, heavenly Muse . . .

Man's first disobedience is the action of the first man, Adam, who disobeyed God's command and ate from the Tree of Knowledge. Adam was given Free Will and the Reason needed to exercise it in harmony with the will of God, by living in accordance with the Law. Through the Original Sin, represented by the act of eating the fruit, man experienced the Fall and lost the grace of God. Man became utterly depraved and corrupt and through divine Justice could only expect death. The 'mortal taste' and death which Adam 'brought . . . into the world' refers not only to the death of the body, but also to the death of the soul – the spiritual death of damnation, without hope of heaven. As Donne writes, 'sin is the root and the fuel of all sickness, and yet that which destroys body and soul is in neither, but in both together' (*Devotions*, Expostulation 22). Protestant theology starts with this picture of man as fallen, sinful and dead in the sight of God. Common to much Protestant writing is an intense dwelling on man's fallen state and the abyss which separates him from God. Man is helpless to bridge this by his own efforts. No amount of good works will earn redemption: grace is the free and unmerited gift of God. Milton's 'loss of Eden' is an image of this severed connection between man and his creator.

The next lines, which go on to describe man's Redemption, make no mention of saints, the Virgin Mary or the Holy Church. Indeed, the poet appeals directly to the Heavenly Muse – a typical feature of epic, but also a sign that Milton feels that he, prophet-like, can have direct access to divine guidance. Man receives God's mercy directly through the sacrifice of Christ, who took on human flesh in the Incarnation. Christ is described by Milton as 'one greater man' since He is parallel to the first man, Adam. Through Adam, man fell into sin, and Adam's sin was imputed to all other men – that is to say, we all share it. Through His sacrifice on the Cross, Christ takes man's sinfulness upon Himself, and man in turn shares in Christ's righteousness. By this Redemption, mankind is restored to a state of grace and can hope for Salvation.

The basic principles we have seen in these few lines are the Fall, Original Sin and man's state of depravity, and Salvation through the sacrifice of Christ. On a more detailed level, the lines are also evidence that Milton followed the doctrine of Arminianism, whereby Salvation is available for all believers: hence 'restore *us*'. Other Protestants disagreed and followed the stricter Calvinist teaching of predestination, according to which those to be saved – the elect – and those to be damned (the reprobate) are already destined by the will of God. Another source of dispute was how far man could understand divine mysteries by the light of his own reason. Milton clearly felt that God's purposes were open to human comprehension: his stated aim in *Paradise Lost* is to 'justify the ways of God to men'. Calvin by contrast emphasised the utter mystery of God.

A central text is the 39 articles printed in *The Book of Common Prayer*: these are the basic theological principles of the Anglican Church. The central tenets of Protestant theology articulated there are expressed and explored by great religious poets such as Donne, Herbert, Milton and Vaughan. Each of these poets has a distinctive voice, and there are many varying points of emphasis. Donne's religious poems have a high theatrical drama to them, while Herbert's beautiful simplicity of language expresses a quite different kind of life in faith. While a familiarity with the essentials of Protestant teaching is essential if we are to under-stand religious poetry, we should not reduce poems to mere statements of doctrine. Poems are not only documents of religious belief but also expressions of religious experience, coloured and shaped by the sensi-bility and character of each individual writer. We can see this clearly in a book like Sir Thomas Browne's *Religio Medici* (1636), which shows a particular mind of the time at work on such matters. (The title of this work, meaning 'A Doctor's Religon', was a paradox at the time, since doctors were commonly held to be irreligious people.)

See also *Contexts*: Catholicism, English Reformation, Humanism; *Texts*: The Bible

Further Reading

Harry Blamires, *Milton's Creation: A Guide Through Paradise Lost* (London: Methuen, 1971). Commentary explaining the key theological ideas.
Alister E. McGrath, *Reformation Thought: An Introduction*, 3rd edn (Oxford: Blackwell, 2000).

Race and Strangers

The word *race*, functioning as a taxonomic term, is recorded in English from about 1500. As the citations in the *Oxford English Dictionary* show, its range of reference was considerably wider than today. A principal sense was the offspring or descendants of a person (*OED*, 2a). Synonyms include *stock*, *kind* and *breed*. Fifteen of the seventeen usages of the word in Shakespeare clearly have this sense: 'Have I... Forborne the getting of a lawful race, and by a gem of women' (*Antony and Cleopatra*, 3.13.107). The group referred to as a 'race' could be relatively small – a family, kindred – or larger, as in a tribe or nation held to be of common ancestry. Thus Milton refers to 'That Pigmean race beyond the Indian mount' (*Paradise Lost*, 1.780), the term probably denoting their descent from common stock rather than any common physical attributes. This primary sense of *race* reminds us of the crucial importance of family in early modern England, particularly for the nobility. At a time when the lesser gentry were acquiring power, land and culture, the 'race' or family breeding of a nobleman was something that could distinguish him from the newly wealthy commoners. Phrases such as 'regall race', 'nobler race' and 'hevenly race' in literature of the period indicate the strong association of *race* with nobility. By extension, *race* was also used to refer to other kinds of group, from the 'human race' of mankind to plants, animals, supernatural beings, men and women – indeed, any kind of group perceived as having some shared feature. Roger Ascham talks of 'a rase of worthie learned ientlemen', Sidney of 'the race of good men' (*OED*, II.8a). Thus the term was used in a very flexible way to refer to any group or kind. It is not until the eighteenth century that we find references to 'races' as divisions of mankind defined by physical characteristics such as skin colour. Possibly the description in *The Tempest* of Caliban being of 'vild race' is an early sign of indigenous Indians being distinguished as a racial group; but the phrase could mean something like 'common stock'.

The absence of a modern sense of *race* meaning ethnic group raises important questions. Did the early moderns classify people in this way, perhaps using other terms? Can we talk of early moderns as being racist, or is that an anachronism? Like sexual orientation, race is sometimes used as a defining characteristic today ('black men' defines different individuals by their colour). But we should not assume that early moderns classified people in the same way (it seems that they did not see 'homosexuals' as a distinct group, for example). Descriptions of different ethnic groups in the period are part of a complex process of responding to relatively recent events. In 1444, the Portuguese started importing African slaves to Europe, and in 1517, slaves were exported to the Caribbean (the English admiral John Hawkins (1532–1595) played an instrumental part in this trade). Black servants living in England are recorded from 1555. At this early stage, a crude taxonomy emerges. Elizabethans appear to have distinguished vaguely between 'Moors' from North Africa, darker-skinned 'Blackamoors' from West Africa and largely imaginary 'Ethiops' from the interior. However, in the sixteenth century the terms 'Moor' and 'Blackamoor' were sometimes used interchangeably: Shakespeare's Aaron (*Titus Andronicus*) and Othello are both referred to as Moors, for example, yet they describe themselves as black. With this taxonomy comes the possibility of racist stereotyping – the assumption that all blacks (or whatever the group may be) have certain other qualities in common. We seem to find evidence of this in a 1596 letter by Queen Elizabeth I to the Lord Mayor of London, in which she declares that 'there are of late divers blackmoores brought into this realme, of which kinde of people there are already here to manie' and orders their deportation to Spain and Portugal. Nothing seems to have come of the plan, and in 1601, the Queen wrote another deportation order, referring to the 'great numbers of Negars and Blackamoors which (as she is informed) are crept into this realm'. Elizabeth describes them as 'infidels, having no understanding of Christ or his Gospel'. This text could be called racist in the sense that it creates and alienates a race-based group (a 'kinde of people'), and further separates them with the key marker of non-membership of the national faith: they are 'infidels'. However, the order seems to have been prompted by foreign policy considerations, in particular the desire to exchange the black population for English prisoners of the Spanish (hence their deportation to Spain and Portugal). It is difficult to tell to what extent these ideas were rooted in popular attitudes, and how far they were excuses to justify the proposed exchange. Elizabeth I had supported Hawkins's slave trading in England, and herself employed negroes at court – making the claim that she had just been informed they had 'crept in' somewhat disingenuous.

Aaron in *Titus Andronicus* (*c*.1590?) is a stock villain, though his own descriptions of himself remind us of associations of blackness with wickedness: 'Aaron will have his soul black like his face' (3.1.205). Othello, the Moor of Venice, is a more problematic case, and we can only point to issues in the discussion here. There is foregrounding of colour at certain points. Othello himself says, 'I am black' (3.3.267), 'begrim'd, and black as mine own face' (3.3.393), and others insult him as 'the thicklips', 'old black ram', 'sooty bosom'. There is an implication of uncontrolled sexual appetite: 'the gross clasps of a lascivious Moor' (1.1.126). Othello's marriage to Desdemona is clearly viewed by others as something unnatural, 'a gross revolt', 'foul disproportion'. For Desdemona's father, Brabantio, it is inconceivable that she could have loved Othello except under the influence of charms. These attitudes suggest a felt difference of kind between white and black, but they are themselves made problematic by context: Othello's enemies are malevolent, fearful and possessive, not necessarily representative of normative outlooks. Othello himself is both outsider and insider, a heroic defender of Christendom against the Turks. He also contrasts with a less well-known character, Eleazer, Price of Fez in the tragedy *Lust's Dominion* (*c.*1600, possibly by Thomas Dekker and others). While Othello is prone to fits and furious outbursts, Eleazer is portrayed as a cold, calculating type. Jonson's *Masque of Blackness* (perf. 1605) seems to present blackness as something exotic: in this early masque, Queen Anne of Denmark and her ladies in waiting appeared disguised in body paint as the 12 daughters of the black god Niger. They appear in the English court to be 'cleansed' of their blackness by King James (leading to *The Masque of Beauty*, a suggestive binary opposition). Colour is one marker of identity alongside others such as family, class, religion, nationality, gender, or whether one is from north or south of the Mediterranean. In interpreting representations of colour in texts, we need to bear in mind how it functions in relation to these other classificatory categories.

Besides black Africans, other groups in England were perceived to some degree as outsiders. The gypsies, held to be of Egyptian origin, were subjected to prolonged persecution and suspected of being tricksters and criminals. Acts were passed against them in 1530 and 1554; in 1564 a further 'Act for the punishment of vagabonds calling themselves Egyptians' was passed, suggesting a confusion between real gypsies and fakes. In Thomas Dekker's *Lanthorn and Candlelight* (1608) and Ben Jonson's *Masque of the Gypsies Metamorphosed* (1621), we see representations of gypsies which combine realistic elements (several children riding on one horse) with traditional prejudices and descriptions of exotic clothing and behaviour. Other groups regarded as strangers were the foreigners in England, particularly in London: these included foreign visitors, economic migrants and Protestants fleeing persecution abroad. Some residents of foreign origin were highly skilled craftsmen, but many were used for the most unpleasant jobs. Tensions existed between London merchants and foreign rivals who, it was claimed, ignored the apprenticeship system and flouted trade regulations. Returns (censuses) of strangers were periodically made: the 1593 Return listed 7013 strangers (children included), out of an estimated population of 200,000.

A somewhat different case is presented by the Jews, who had been expelled from England in 1290 and were not readmitted until 1655. Jewish populations had been evicted from other European countries in the fifteenth and sixteenth centuries. In 1516, Renaissance Venice allowed Jews to live and work in a ghetto, with highly restricted contact with Christians. Since Christians were forbidden to practise usury (charging interest), Jews were useful to them as moneylenders. In the absence of real Jews, the figure of the Jew in the West was almost entirely a creation of the imagination, and anti-Semitic prejudices abounded. These are found in the portraits in Renaissance drama, notably Marlowe's Barabas, protagonist of *The Jew of Malta* (*c*.1589) and Shakespeare's Shylock in *The Merchant of Venice*. Barabas and Shylock are depicted with many of the anti-Semitic tropes current since medieval times, principally a love of money and a capacity for murderous vengefulness. A challenge for the reader is to consider how far (if at all) this anti-Semitic portrait is offset by a certain pathos in the way they are presented, arousing the audience's sympathy, and by the portrayal of other groups, including Christians, as decadent (an aspect emphasised by several modern productions). Another play, which has attracted increasing scholarly attention, is *The Tragedy of Mariam, the Fair Queen of Jewry* (written 1602–1604, pub.1613) by Elizabeth Cary (1585–1639). This play, the first tragedy written by an Englishwoman, depicts a variety of Jewish characters, drawing on ancient history: at its centre is an opposition between the virtuous Mariam and the duplicitous Salome, bringing into play issues of gender representation together with considerations of race. Further exploration of racial depictions in early modern literary texts usually involves today the study of further texts – travel journals, legal documents, scientific treatises, sermons – making race a complex and exacting topic for interdisciplinary study.

See also   *Contexts*: Sex and Sexuality, Travel, Women; *Criticism*: New Historicism, Cultural Materialism

Further Reading

Catherine Alexander and Stanley Wells, eds, *Shakespeare and Race* (Cambridge: CUP, 2000).
Mary Floyd-Wilson, *English Ethnicity and Race in Early Modern Drama* (Cambridge: CUP, 2003).
Kim Hall, *Things of Darkness: Economies of Race and Gender in Early Modern England* (Ithaca: Cornell University Press, 1995).
Margo Hendricks and Patricia Parker, eds., *Women, 'Race' and Writing in the Early Modern Period* (London: Routledge, 1994).

Science, Knowledge and Philosophy

Throughout the Renaissance, Science is not generally seen as a distinct discipline, but as a branch of Philosophy, part of the human contemplation of the world: Latin *scientia*, after all, simply means 'knowledge'. The later part of the period, however, sees the rise of the 'new science'. With the seventeenth-century Scientific Revolution come the foundations of the modern concept of Science as a practice of observation and experiment, anchored in mathematical calculation. We should, though, avoid the temptingly simple narrative of old-to-new implied by this summary. Old interests die hard: great figures like the astronomer Johannes Kepler

(1571–1630) and, later, Isaac Newton (1643–1728) were fascinated by alchemy and astrology; and outside the intellectual elite, traditional popular ideas remained in wide circulation. Equally, observation and experiment were not discoveries of the seventeenth centuries. Trial and error were well known to craftsmen much earlier in the period: the perfection of oil as a fixing element for pigments in paint, the invention of the printing press, the adaptation of ships' portholes for guns (c.1510), improvements in the compass and advances in timekeeping instruments were among many important practical advances of the later fifteenth and early sixteenth centuries. When we speak of the Scientific Revolution we refer to the gradual emergence of a way of studying the world as a whole. This brought with it not only an increase in knowledge, but an altered view of the nature of human knowledge itself.

Notions of Science were formed in relation to classical authorities. For the ancient philosophers, knowledge was acquired through the cultivation of spiritual vision: the supreme end of man is to achieve a clear vision of the nature of things. In seeking the mental reflection of the inner structure and being of things, the philosopher looks beyond the superficial particular to the essence. The philosopher is a visionary figure, and his task is also that of the poet. Plato, whose writings were translated and intensively studied by the humanists, argues that Ideas are the true reality and that essential forms of reality are imperfectly represented in the material world. Platonic texts stress the importance of the contemplative, the pursuit of an inner vision: frequently he expounds his ideas with visual metaphors, like the story of the Cave.

The philosopher's vision depends on language. The more precisely words are used, the more they will yield a precise and clear picture of true reality. While language is an essential tool in the search for truth, ancient philosophy is also keenly aware that it is also potentially misleading: reality is not simply *reflected* in words, but *constructed* by words in linguistic and symbolic structures. We can only 'see' the world through the medium of language, which is the basis for our intuitions. This insight is at the root of philosophy's quarrel with rhetoric which, instead of clarifying language to reveal the truth, could be seen as manipulating it for ends which have nothing to do with the apprehension of true reality. The philosopher's aim must be to use language properly. Hence, for Plato, the vital importance of dialectic, through which we pursue tighter definitions. Platonic philosophy is an active reflection on language, driven by the desire to make it stable, rational and consistent.

Aristotle (384–322 BC) presents a different set of emphases. Aristotelian philosophy takes on the idea that the pursuit of knowledge is the pursuit of the inner essence of Creation. However, Aristotle aims to see these essences in actual things. Rather than the Platonic contemplation of the world of Ideas, Aristotle's writings are based on attentiveness to material objects. The final aim is always to find the universal in the particular: in any one man, for example, can be found the essence of Man. Aristotle is not interested in the observation of many particular cases, but in the common essence all cases share. It is an idealist philosophy, concerned with *a priori* knowledge – that is, knowledge which can be acquired by the application of first principles, without reference to concrete phenomena. The main tool of this philosophy is the syllogism, which explains the reason behind a certain proposition. By discursive logic, knowledge is arrived at as the necessary and universal conclusion of a syllogism. Like Plato, Aristotle sees Philosophy – which includes all science, or knowledge, attainable by man – as a fundamentally theoretical and contemplative exercise. It is a speculative discipline, without practical consequences. Indeed practical skill and knowledge were regarded as lower pursuits, beneath the philosopher concerned with learning for its own sake.

The authority of ancient figures like Plato and Aristotle was enormous in the Renaissance. New thoughts had to be justified by reference to an ancient source: Kepler supports his conclusions by reference to Pythagoras, while Machiavelli develops his ideas about modern politics through his *Discourses on Livy*. In the medieval and Renaissance period, the commentary on an older text is a key part of the world of learning: knowledge is seen as a refinement of the work of the masters, not as a departure from them. Nevertheless, such a departure did take place and brought with it a new method of discovery and learning and hence a new conception of human knowledge. A key figure in this revolution in thinking about Science was the Englishman Francis Bacon (1561–1626).

Francis Bacon is best known to readers of English literature as author of the *Essays*. For his contribution to the new method in Science, however, his most important work is the *Novum Organon* (1620; volume two of the *Instauratio Magna*). Since *Organon* traditionally referred to the combined logical works of Aristotle, the title 'New Organon' was explicitly anti-Aristotelian. This is borne out by its content. Bacon argues that the logical syllogism is not the best instrument for producing knowledge: logical science is empty of actual content, since it is concerned with explaining the content of premises and their relation to each other. Science should not be based on the induction of a conclusion from its premises, but on *de*duction from observed phenomena. Its aim is not the intuition of the universal in the particular but to arrive at an accurate and reliable representation of the material world. It should ignore textual authority and look directly at nature. Bacon stresses that the value of induction is the modern sense of repeated observation. The enquirer after knowledge should proceed by experiments, the purposes of which are to verify or correct hypotheses. This is the essential basis of modern science.

The new method in Science also required a distinction between the Aristotelian concepts of efficient and final causes. The efficient cause of something explains how it came to exist: the efficient cause of a car is the process of manufacture which put it together – the events which had as their effect the car. The final cause of something is what it exists *for*, to what *end* it exists. We could say that the final cause of a car is transport. Final causes cannot, however, be tested and examined as efficient causes can. Why does man exist? Why does life exist? These 'What is the purpose of' questions lie within the domains of Philosophy as practised by the ancients, but they lie outside the province of modern science, as it is explained by Bacon. Since Science cannot pronounce on why something exists, then it follows that it cannot comment on the best means to fulfil that purpose. Hence once consequence of the new science was to leave a clear division between the Church, which has authority on moral matters, and Science, which has authority on material phenomena. This division of labour also followed Galileo's positions on Copernicanism: the geocentric cosmos is also a symbolic picture of the purpose and design of things, while the new heliocentric one accounts only for actual observations of reality. In other words, the new science loses its authority to comment on metaphysical issues through symbolic schemes.

The revolt against Aristotelian authority led to a new image of science and nature. Science is not verbal and contemplative, but an active process. It not only gazes on nature but deliberately intervenes and modifies natural objects as part of its investigations. Man is thus no longer thought of as simply subject to nature: he has some degree of control over it, and can manipulate it to serve his ends. Once we know the efficient causes of a phenomenon we can act to prevent or provoke it. Knowledge is consequently not the result of disinterested enquiry but a means of exercising power, over the environment and one's fellow men. The value of a scientific theory lies in its predictive value.

The new science not only alters the concept of nature, but also that of man. First, man relates to nature in a different way. He is a technician, working on and testing his environment with instruments, not only with the unaided senses. The world around him is most accurately measured not with language – which is full of the affections, values and meanings of human subjectivity – but with mathematics. A mathematical picture of the world is more objectively accurate, and it also removes the symbolisms and significations carried by a linguistic description. The world as seen by the new science is hence 'disenchanted', stripped of the layers of resonance which have built up through description in language. Thus, the chief relevance of the new science to Renaissance literature might be said to be its *ir*relevance: while medieval literary works could include discussion of such things as the workings of the weather or the structure of the world through common tropes and images, in the early modern period the scientific and the literary gradually separated out into separate spheres of discourse.

See also   *Contexts*: Chain of Being, Cosmos, Elements, Humours, Magic, Medicine; *Texts*: Non-fictional Prose, Prose Style

Further Reading

Allen G. Debus, *Man and Nature in the Renaissance* (Cambridge: CUP, 1978).
Lisa Jardine, *Ingenious Pursuits: Building the Scientific Revolution* (London: Little, Brown and Co.: 1999).
Katherine Parker and Lorraine Daston, eds, *The Cambridge History of Science*, vol. 3, *Early Modern Science* (Cambridge: CUP, 2003).
Steven Shapin, *The Scientific Revolution* (London: University of Chicago Press, 1996).

The Self

The nineteenth-century French historian Michelet famously characterised the Renaissance as 'the discovery of the world and the discovery of man', a time when physical exploration was mirrored by inner examination. In newly independent minds, so this thesis goes, questing and experimental attitudes took over from submission to authority. In *The Civilisation of the Renaissance in Italy* (1860), Jacob Burckhardt argued that political conditions in fifteenth-century Italy effectively gave rise to modern consciousness:

> In the Middle Ages both sides of human consciousness – that which was turned within as that which was turned without – lay dreaming or half awake beneath a common veil. The veil was woven of faith, illusion, and childish prepossession, through which the world and history were seen clad in strange hues. Man was conscious of himself only as a member of a race, people, party, family, or corporation – only through some general category. In Italy this veil first melted into air; an objective treatment and consideration of the State and of all the things of this world became possible. The subjective side at the same time asserted itself with corresponding emphasis; man became a spiritual individual, recognized himself as such.

In support of this thesis, Burckhardt draws our attention to several phenomena: the increased use of signatures by craftsmen; the *studiolo* or private chamber in houses; commissions of portraits by merchants and courtiers and personal writings, like the diary of the Londoner Henry Machyn (1550–1563), which intersperses records of public events with accounts of his own social life. In northern Europe, Protestantism, with its emphasis on a personal relationship to God, has been seen as conducive to enhanced self-awareness; and the rise of capitalism, and social mobility, nurtured the self-seeking, individual entrepreneur. Still other causes for Renaissance subjectivity have been proposed: religious persecution led many to disguise their real beliefs, separating their genuine spiritual identity from their public image; and complex social and commercial transactions would have favoured strategies of evasion and ambiguity, as individuals hid one part of themselves and presented another.

It is certainly suggestive to read English Renaissance texts in the light of this idea of the rise of the self. In the theatre, we find internal conflict in the minds of protagonists, expressed in soliloquies. Several of Shakespeare's characters appear to support the idea that a subjective 'self' haunts their spiritual and imaginative life: 'Who is it who can tell me who I am?' (Lear); 'I have that within which passes show' (Hamlet). Lyrical writings like the sonnet dramatise the speaker's inner feelings, and the essays of Montaigne see writing as an instrument for self-discovery. The OED records how, from the late sixteenth century, many collocations with *self-* first appear: 'selfe-love . . . is not so vile a sin, / As selfe-neglecting' (*Henry V*, 2.4.75); 'A submitted soul . . . the deeper it sinketh in a self contempt' (Robert Southwell, *Marie Magdalen Funerall Tears*, 1594). Literary evidence such as this seems to bear out the idea that a new kind of self-consciousness is a feature of the Renaissance imagination.

Nonetheless, the Burckhardtian thesis has come in for much criticism. Medievalists dispute his portrait of the earlier period: the thirteenth-century spiritual exercise of the *devotio moderna*, for example, emphasises precisely the individual's subjective experience, centuries before the supposed great awakening. In the Renaissance itself, people still identified themselves through belonging to a group – such as nobles, pure Protestant believers, or the company of martyrs, perhaps. In any case, surely interiority is a complex mixture of belonging to groups and feeling individual in some way? Like all critics, Burckhardt is subject to the influences of his own time, and his portrayal of the mature self-aware Renaissance individual is influenced by romanticism, which values intense subjective experience as a purer, more authentic kind of being. The influence of romanticism persists today, and – along with Freudian psychology – might lead us into reading a modern kind of subjectivity into pre-modern texts: when Lear asks who can tell him what he is, he might not be undergoing existential angst as he searches for his authentic unique self, but experiencing the alarm of someone displaced from his social roles of king and father. 'Self' in early Modern English can refer to one's status and place in the scheme of things; the formula 'Know thyself' is not Renaissance in origin but an ancient saying, probably meaning something like 'Know your place'. Even if we do to an extent agree with Burckhardt, we might still wonder whether the rise of the self was an entirely positive experience. Renaissance texts often present the breakdown of 'general categories' with alarm: in *King Lear*, *Hamlet* and *Macbeth*, the destruction of networks of community and kinship leads to catastrophe, while the unbridled will of Tamburlaine, Richard III or Iago makes them monstrous figures.

Postmodern thought has in turn become sceptical about the very notion of an essential self, seeing this as a fiction invented in the enlightenment which obscures the shifting, contingent nature of being. In *Renaissance Self-Fashioning*, Stephen Greenblatt argues that the Renaissance self was itself a fictional persona that could be adopted and adapted according to circumstance. This is what we see in the art of rhetoric, which trained students to present themselves and their material in whatever way would best suit the occasion. Thus Hamlet puts on a different self depending on the needs of the occasion; even his 'I have that within' might be a stoical persona adopted for the situation. The popularity of acting in the period, and of plays involving disguise and the putting on and off of masks, further suggests the idea of the self as an invention for the moment, rather than an underlying continuous consciousness. According to some critics (such as Jonathan Dollimore, *Radical Tragedy*), the Renaissance self is characterised not by a confident new subjectivity, but by its opposite – a crisis of identity. The metaphysical certainties of Christianity fade away, and the enlightenment picture of man has yet to emerge: in the vacuum between, subjectivity becomes a matter of trying out one assumed persona after another, from stoic to cynic to avenger to lover and so on. We might query the rather neat overlap here of Renaissance thought and postmodernity and wonder whether we are not imposing our own mindset on the past here just as Burckhardt did. As moderns, we are perhaps also more comfortable talking about the *self*, with its modern psychological associations, than we are talking about the *soul*, which is not necessarily the same concept: the soul, for example, comes from God, while the self is surely a worldly affair. Understanding what the sense of *soul* is in Renaissance texts, and how this helped to frame the experience of self-consciousness of early modern life, is one of the greatest challenges we face as readers today.

See also *Contexts*: Courtier, English Reformation, Humanism, Protestant Theology; *Texts*, Actors and Acting, Imitation, Rhetoric, Prose Style; *Criticism*: Cultural Materialism, New Historicism

Further Reading

Stephen Greenblatt, *Renaissance Self-fashioning: From More to Shakespeare*, 2nd edn (Chicago: University of Chicago Press: 1980).
John Jeffries Martin, 'The Myth of Renaissance Individualism': in *A Companion to the Worlds of the Renaissance*, ed. Guido De Ruggiero (Oxford: Blackwell, 2002), 208–223.
Roy Porter, ed., *Rewriting the Self: Histories from the Renaissance to the present* (London: Routledge, 1997), Part I: Renaissance and Early Modern, 17–60.

Sex and Sexuality

In the study of this topic, clear use of terminology is vital. The words *sex* and *gender* have distinct meanings: *sex* refers to male/female anatomy and is a biological fact; *gender* refers to perceptions of masculinity and femininity and is a cultural construct. Notions of gender are thus contingent on a particular society. To take one example, Renaissance fashion required men to show their legs, while ladies concealed them. Today things are broadly the other way around: whether 'being a man' involves displaying shapely legs clearly depends on the norms of the time. However, the sex/gender distinction does raise the question of whether our physiology (sex) conditions our behaviour (including mental behaviour). 'Essentialists' hold that there are certain universals in human nature, and that, for example, our hormones predispose us to typically male or female conduct. Anti-essentialists, such as Michel Foucault, argue that all conceptions of what is male or female are the products of society, and normally part of a patriarchal ideology empowering men and oppressing women (this is a basic assumption of much literary theory). We shall not attempt to resolve this debate, which today involves biochemical and psychological science beyond the competence of most critics. In any case, we can study sexual behaviour in early modern society, and gender in Renaissance texts, without taking a dogmatic position on the issue. In pursuing such study, we should also distinguish gender from *sexuality*: 'being a man' may involve matters (physical courage, for example), not directly related to sex. Thus sexuality is simply one aspect of gender identity, and a certain sexual inclination (for example, wanting to be a passive partner) may not be confined to one sex or gender. In studying sexuality in other cultures, we also need to be conscious of the systems of classification that we bring with us: today we categorise behaviour as heterosexual, homosexual and bisexual, but the Renaissance did not use these terms or equivalents. We should be open to the possibility that sexuality was interpreted in different terms by early modern society, and, by extension, experienced in a different way by individuals. Sexual desire is surely a constant in human history, but the way in which it manifests itself on an imaginative and emotional level will be influenced, if not determined, by the surrounding culture.

One type of sexual behaviour is sexual abstinence. In the sixteenth and seventeenth centuries, there were several discourses exalting this state. Canon Law in the pre-Reformation Church insisted on priestly celibacy, and though Anglican priests were allowed to take a wife (on the grounds that the institution of matrimony was divinely ordained) there was a persistent view that clerical celibacy was the ideal (this was the opinion of Elizabeth I). Centuries of tradition of devotion to the Virgin Mary and female saints continued to exert an influence. Most visibly of all, at the top of Elizabethan society was Elizabeth herself, doubly strange in being a female ruler – and thus a kind of man-woman – and a virgin. The cult of the Virgin Queen permeates the literature, from Spenser's Una (*The Faerie Queene*, Book I) to the language surrounding maidens – pure, white, spotless and so forth. The personal was political: the Anglican Church was presented as pure and virginal, while Rome was a painted whore. Yet the image of the Virgin Queen was plainly unsettling, and perhaps helps to explain the cold remote ladies of the sonnet sequences or the androgynous figures of drama. Virginity is examined in texts. The life of a nun is praised in *A Midsummer Night's Dream* (written *c*.1595), but at the same time held out as a threat to a girl who will not marry the man chosen by her father: it is an object of both reverence and fear (1.1). *Measure for Measure* (written 1603/4) deals with what we would call sexual repression: in this play, illicit sexual activity is apparently thriving in Vienna, as it is in the unconscious minds of the protagonists – Angelo, a Puritan unsettled by feelings of lust; and Isabella (the object of Angelo's desire), a would-be nun who praises celibacy and condemns sex in a language which seems hysterical, at any rate to a post-Freudian audience. Both these plays also externalise inner repression as state oppression. In both, authority figures seek to govern and control sexual behaviour in society, and to ensure in particular that female desire is channelled through marriages arranged by men. Resistance to this takes various forms, from untameable comic bawdy energy to the fantasising play of a dream. Uncontrolled sexual desire is associated with licentiousness and promiscuity and threatens the state with disorder. Part of the function of comedy is to resolve this tension, and this it does through the traditional vehicle of matrimony, the harnessing of personal appetites to social ends.

As we have noted, Renaissance society did not seem to designate people as homosexual. It certainly did condemn anal intercourse, however. This had always been forbidden by ecclesiastical law, and in 1533 the prohibition was widened to include all males, in a parliamentary Act designed to punish 'the detestable and abominable vice of buggery committed with mankind or beast'. Buggery was officially a felony: punishment was death, with loss of property and without benefit of clergy. The Act was repealed by Mary, but reinstituted in 1563 in even stronger terms. Despite the fierceness of the wording, however, prosecutions were rare, and usually involved other kinds of crime: child abuse, rape, bestiality or treason. 'Sodomy' could apparently function as a general, and extremely opprobrious, term for kinds of transgression deemed unnatural. Whether the same attitude was taken to homoeroticism – intimate conduct between men – is less clear. Since women were generally deemed inferior, and marriage was primarily an economic contract, the married couple could not be held up as the ideal kind of relationship, through which partners fulfil themselves emotionally and intellectually. The male–male relation was then more likely to represent a true meeting of minds. There were positive images of this in the culture: the legacy of antiquity included exemplars of pederasty – men loving boys – in the writings of Plato; texts such as Virgil's Eclogues presented intimate friendship between male shepherds; and the scriptures provided the model friendship of David and Jonathan. Besides same-sex friendships, close homosocial relationships, perhaps involving some degree of affectionate physical contact, were a normal aspect of everyday life: master – minion or patron – client relations, for example, could be coloured by erotic language. On the other hand, homosexual behaviour does seem to have been condemned by some: it is a staple feature of Puritan attacks on the theatre, for example, which regularly include the accusation that it leads to improper love of men for boys, and assignations between them. (This is one of the accusations in John Rainolds' *Th'Overthrow of Stage-Playes* (Middelburgh, 1599).)

All this makes the reading of sexuality in Renaissance texts interestingly difficult. Close friendships like that in *The Two Gentleman of Verona* (c.1590), which might seem gay to us, could have been a normal, even ideal aspect of masculinity. The disguises of comedies like *Twelfth Night* (c.1600) – boy actors playing girls disguised as boys, with whom men fall in love – presumably raised some kind of sexual frisson (and the ire of the Puritans) at the time, but the precise dynamics of such responses are largely a matter for speculation. More clearly homosexual in orientation is the work of Marlowe (bap. 1564–d.1593), particularly his depiction of the King and his favourite Gaveston in *Edward II* (c.1593). His famous lyric 'Come live with me, and be my love' could be read as one male addressing another, on the model of Virgil's Eclogues. (And in general we should beware of the assumption that Renaissance love lyrics are a man speaking to a woman: Shakespeare's most famous sonnet, 'Shall I compare thee to a summer's day', has nothing to signify that the person being spoken to is female, for example.) The most clearly homoerotic literary text of the period is probably *The Affectionate Shepherd* (1594) by Richard Barnfield (1574–1627), who was clearly influenced by Marlowe. In this work, the Shepherd Daphnis expresses his love for the boy Ganymede in such lines as these: 'O would to God (so I could have my fee) / My lips were honey, and thy mouth a bee'. This was apparently over-explicit for some, since in the preface to his next volume, *Cynthia* (1595) Barnfield protests that his intention was 'nothing else but an imitation of Virgil, in the second Eclogue of Alexis'.

In investigating such material, we find that different norms and codes are in play: in the early modern world, sharing a bed with another male does not indicate intercourse, 'lover' can simply mean friend, and intensities now normally associated with sexual friendships (kissing, hand-holding, protestations of love) might occur within a non-sexual relationship (as they still do in other cultures). Suggesting sexuality in the course of interpretation is similarly problematic: Could Iago's hatred of Othello be in part a jealousy of the Moor's love for Desdemona? Is Caesar's preoccupation with Antony's former toughness and present Egyptian softness in *Antony and Cleopatra* homoerotic in origin? Are the amorous addresses to a young man in Shakespeare's sonnets gay, conceivably even relating to a real relationship between Shakespeare and Southampton? Or are these inappropriately modern ideas which we project onto early modern texts? In pursuing this topic, we should also be aware of two influences on us from later culture, pulling in opposite directions. One is Victorian censoriousness, which smothered the sexual content of Shakespeare and others, and hid it from editions as far as possible. The other, opposite, tendency is the erotic obsession of our own age, which is saturated in sexual imagery and perhaps inclined to find sex in places where no Renaissance audience would have seen it. Popular glossaries of Shakespeare's bawdy rescue the bard from Victorian repressiveness, but at the same time they repackage him for the age of *Little Britain*. What looks like enlightenment could be one mystification (or falsification) exchanged for another. We are ourselves inevitably conditioned by the conceptualisations of gender and sexuality shaped by our own particular culture.

See also   *Contexts*: Patronage, Race, Women; *Texts*: Actors and Acting, Lyric, Theatres

Further Reading

Alan Bray, *Homosexuality in Renaissance England* (London: Gay Men's Press, 1982).

Jonathan Goldberg, *Sodometries: Renaissance Texts, Modern Sexualities* (Stanford: Stanford UP, 1992)

Jonathan Goldberg, *Queering the Renaissance* (Durham: Duke University Press, 1994).

Bruce R. Smith, *Homosexual Desire in Shakespeare's England: A Cultural Poetics* (Chicago: University of Chicago Press, 1991).

Valerie Traub, *Desire and Anxiety: Circulations of Sexuality in Shakespearean Drama* (London: Routledge, 1992).

Stanley Wells, *Looking for Sex in Shakespeare* (Cambridge: CUP, 2004).

Stoicism

The doctrine of stoicism, which originated with Zeno of Citium (335–263 BC), addressed the question of how one ought to live. Starting with the observation that much of life is spent suffering, it praises fortitude in the face of adversity. As good stoics, we should regard with indifference anything which an accident of fortune might take from us: ephemeral goods such as status, position and worldly wealth are beyond our control and it is foolish to rely on them. True peace of mind lies in what we can control, our inner being. This calm is threatened by the emotions, or passions, which suffering, especially, arouses (*passion* derives from the Latin verb *patior* meaning 'I suffer'; the Passion of Christ means Christ's suffering). The way to keep hold over one's passions is to govern the mind with Reason, which can see beyond the immediate moment. For Stoicism, the true goods in life are not material but moral. Stoics practise the four classical virtues of Prudence, Temperance, Justice and Fortitude (Christianity adds to these the three spiritual, or Pauline, virtues of Faith, Hope and Charity).

Stoicism thus encourages moral seriousness, piety and asceticism: it commends an austere lifestyle, without need of material comforts. These values allowed a synthesis with Christian teaching, referred to as Neo-Stoicism. This could not be an entirely coherent philosophy, however, since the two ethical systems are at key points inconsistent. Unlike traditional Christian teaching, Stoicism is determinist: it asserts that all that happens is predetermined and will work itself out through human agency whatever we do. This belief encourages a passive acceptance of whatever happens – what will be, will be. The cultivation of virtuous apathy was condemned by Calvin, among others (although it might be felt that his doctrine of predestination, leaving the individual helpless to control his fate, actually encouraged it). Another clash with Christianity was the stoical admiration for suicide as the supreme act of the sovereign will; for Christians (of that time), our life belongs to God and suicides commit the mortal sin of despair (Donne's 'desperate men' in the sonnet 'Death be not proud' refers to suicides). We might consider in this context the contrary presentations of suicide in Shakespeare, from the heroic Brutus, who dies in the Roman manner, to Hamlet reminding himself and the audience that God has 'fixed his canon 'gainst self-slaughter'.

Renaissance scholars found a clear description of stoicism and other ancient ethical systems in the writings of Cicero (106–43 BC): the key texts are *De Officiis* (*On Duties*), *De Finibus bonorum et malorum* (*On the Ends of Good and Evil*) and the *Tusculan Disputations*. Another hugely influential figure was Seneca (the Younger; 4 BC–65 AD; writings include *De Constantia: On Constancy*; *Epistulae Morales: Moral Letters*), who committed suicide under Nero and was revered in the Renaissance as a quasi-divine moral teacher. The Italian poet Petrarch (1304–1374) develops a stoical discourse in *De remediis utriusque fortunae* (*On the Remedies for Fortune Fair and Foul*, 1366), in which Reason debates with the emotions on how to deal with ill fortune. Cicero and Seneca were widely read in schools, and humanists added to the corpus the writings of Epictetus (55–135) and Plutarch (46–127; especially *Moralia*) which were sympathetic to Stoical philosophy. The general flavour of stoicism was thus present in the sixteenth century; and a learned account of Senecan Stoicism was offered by the Flemish humanist scholar Justus Lipsius (1547–1606), culminating in a treatise of 1604. Though Lipsius disapproved of suicide, he admired the chief doctrines of subordinating passion to reason, and remaining constant in the face of adversity.

At the same time as Lipsius's account of stoicism was being expounded, writers in England were becoming attracted to Seneca's sententious prose style and violent closet dramas. For the English essayist William Cornwallis (*Essays*, 1600), Seneca is the 'Prince of morality'. The same Prince looms over Bacon's essays 'On Death' and 'Of Adversity', and another prose treatment of the topic is Joseph Hall's 'Heaven Upon Earth' (*Treatises Devotional and Practical*, Section 1). A stoical contempt for worldly oppression is convenient for Richard Lovelace in 'To Althea, from Prison' (*c.*1642), which enthuses over the true freedom to be found in an 'innocent and quiet' mind. In the theatre, strong-minded stoical heroes appear in plays like Chapman's *Bussy d'Ambois* (1604) and Ben Jonson's *Catiline* (1603) and *Sejanus* (1611). A particularly interesting case is *Hamlet* (*c.*1600). Hamlet struggles with his own passions and seems to move towards inner serenity by adopting a Senecan fatalism: 'There's a divinity that shapes our ends, / Rough hew them how we will'. Hamlet describes his friend Horatio as a model stoic:

> ... for thou hast been
> As one in suff'ring all that suffers nothing,
> A man that Fortune's buffets and rewards
> Hath ta'en with equal thanks.
>
> (3.2, 63–66)

Yet, typically, Shakespeare's play also interrogates this position. For Hamlet's problem is also finding the passions required for his role of avenger. Is the equanimity attributed to Horatio entirely laudable? Passions might be necessary for the furtherance of some acts, and even for the higher moral life. Passivity as a moral code is condemned by Milton as 'a fugitive and cloistered virtue, that never sallies out to meet her adversary' (*Areopagitica*, 1644). Reverence for Reason need not lead us to abandon the strenuous moral life, or to despise our own feelings. Erasmus in the *Praise of Folly* (1511) mocks stoicism for denigrating the emotions; and Montaigne, who was fascinated by Senecan Stoicism, also found its doctrine of impassivity an impossible demand. Stoicism was also convicted of pride, for placing its wise men on the level of the gods. It is Milton's Satan, the incarnation of Pride, who espouses the Stoical belief that 'the mind is its own place, and in it self / Can make a Heav'n of Hell, a Hell of Heav'n' (I.254–I.254.5). In *Paradise Regained* (1671), Christ scorns 'The Stoic last in philosophic pride, / By him called virtue' (IV.300–IV.301). Stoicism contributed to early modern thinking on ethics, while leaving central questions unresolved. Both the strength of the doctrine, and the doubts surrounding it, can be traced in the writing of the period.

See also   Contexts: Platonism, The Self; *Texts*: Epic; *Criticism*: New Historicism

Further Reading

Reid Barbour, *English Epicures and Stoics: Ancient Legacies in Early Stuart Culture* (Amherst: University of Massachusetts Press, 1998).
Audrey Chew, *Stoicism in Renaissance English Literature* (New York: Peter Lang, 1988).
Adriana McCrea, *Constant Minds: Political Virtue and the Lipsian Paradigm in England, 1584–1650* (Toronto: University of Toronto Press, 1997).
Gilles D. Monsarrat, *Light From the Porch: Stoicism and English Renaissance Literature*, Etudes Anglaises, 85 (Paris: Didier-Erudition, 1984).
Andrew Eric Shifflett, *Stoicism, Politics, and Literature in the Age of Milton: War and Peace Reconciled* (Cambridge: CUP, 1998).

Travel and Colonialism

In 1450, Western Europeans would have had only a vague idea of the extent even of their own countries: these were often fairly amorphous political entities, and in the age before printing, maps were not in general circulation. Those maps that were produced would often be symbolic: according to Christian belief, Jerusalem was at the centre of the world, and so it was placed there in traditional cartography. Travel to other countries was dangerous and expensive, and throughout the Renaissance period this remained an activity for the rich. The general mental picture of the world beyond Christendom was still more blurred. To Europeans, the continents of America and Australia, and the Pacific Ocean were unknown. No one knew how far Africa extended: beyond the northern coast it seemed to be endless desert. There was a general conception of countries far to the east, generically referred to as the 'Indies'. The widely circulated story of the experiences of Marco Polo, together with the mixture of fact and fable in travellers' tales, conjured up pictures of the exotic land of Cathay (China), and the island of Cipango (Japan) somewhere off its coast. Luxury items were brought from the East by overland caravan routes, passing through Constantinople on their way to Western markets. Together with luxuries came all-important spices: these were not dainties, but, in an age before refrigeration, essential food preservatives. The republics of Venice and Genoa grew wealthy on their management of this trade in the West and controlled shipping in the Mediterranean.

Over the Renaissance period this picture of the world changed radically, and the catalyst for this change was the Turkish conquest of Constantinople in 1453. With Constantinople fallen, trading by overland routes was extremely dangerous as caravans could be plundered. Western countries thus looked for other, marine routes to the Indies, and over time the axis of power shifted to those countries with ports on the Atlantic seaboard, who were best placed to explore sea passages for merchant shipping – Spain, Portugal, France and England. These were to become the imperial powers of the modern age.

Three possible alternative routes to the Indies were open to Western countries: one was to sail down and around Africa and then up again to India; a second was to sail north into the Atlantic and then find a route near the north pole through the so-called 'Northwest Passage' and a third was to sail West until the Indies appeared (since the existence of America and the Pacific was unknown, the globe was thought to be considerably smaller than it really is). The first route, going around Africa, was adopted by Portuguese explorers, who were enthusiastically supported by Prince Henry 'the Navigator' (1394–1460). Portuguese sailors discovered the Canary Islands and the Azores, and by 1445 knew of Cape Verde. In 1486, Bartholomew Diaz rounded the Cape, but was obliged to turn back by his crew. Finally, in 1498, Vasco da Gama reached India. For nearly a century, the Portuguese capital of Lisbon was the centre of trade with the East, until Spain conquered Portugal in 1580.

The second route, through the supposed Northwest Passage, was pursued by English explorers, but with less munificent royal patronage: John Cabot, a Venetian settled in England, sailed from Bristol in 1497 and discovered Newfoundland as part of his search; although he found rich fishing stocks, his expedition seems to have been regarded as a failure. Cabot's explorations were later continued by Martin Frobisher, who explored the coast of Greenland and North Canada in 1576–1578; but the fabled Northwest Passage eluded him, as it did John Davis and Henry Hudson, who was set adrift by a mutinous crew. Sir Humphrey Gilbert annexed Newfoundland in 1583, but his efforts to start a colony there were abandoned after a few weeks.

The third proposed route to the Indies, by sailing due West, was the one taken by the most famous of all Renaissance explorers, Christopher Columbus, who finally secured the backing of the King and Queen of Spain. In 1492 (when Columbus sailed the ocean blue) he landed on the island of Hispaniola (present-day Dominican Republic and Haiti), and then sailed on to Cuba and other islands in the Caribbean Sea. He did not reach the American mainland and believed that he had come close to Asia and the Spice Islands. (No doubt this was wishful thinking. Commonly presented as a triumph in history books, America to Renaissance Europe must have been a disappointment, next to the fabled world of the Indies.) Thus Columbus called these islands the West Indies. These first landings were followed by the discovery of the American mainland and the swift exploitation of its human and natural resources. The Spanish conquistador Cortés conquered the Aztec people of Mexico (1519–1521) and Pizarro conquered the Incas of Peru (1530–1535). Large proportions of the indigenous populations died from the illnesses such as influenza which the colonists brought with them. Survivors were forced to work in the gold and silver mines, while African slaves were set to work in the fields. Gold and silver was sent to Spain, though much of it was lost on the way through corruption, and it is a curious fact that England's great rival Spain was seriously short of money throughout the period. Of no practical value in themselves, gold and silver flooded European markets and drove up prices. This made it difficult for kings to maintain their armies during a time of almost continuous warfare. Territorial disputes between the great powers Spain and Portugal were averted by the 'Pope's line' whereby all land west of a line 370 leagues from the Azores was deemed to belong to Spain and land east of it to Portugal (explaining why Portuguese is the official language of Brazil today).

Next to the giants Portugal and Spain, England was a minor player in exploration and colonialism throughout the sixteenth century. This is a case of history being at odds with the popular image we have of swashbuckling heroes like Drake and Raleigh characterising the English spirit; but this image owes a good deal both to Victorian historians seeking a colourful narrative of the imperial adventure and to later romanticised treatments. In fact, the Tudor monarchs had very little enthusiasm for colonial expansion. Attention was indeed given to England's navy: Henry VII built the first dry dock at Portsmouth, and Henry VIII hugely expanded the country's naval power – he may also have been directly involved in the adaptation of portholes (designed for unloading goods onto ports) for cannons, one of the important innovations of the period. But the navy was regarded as a necessary defensive force for an island, not as a means of establishing territories elsewhere. Only Mary Tudor was much interested in pursuing colonial adventures, as a way of tying England's interest to Spain's.

The conception of empire certainly existed, however. The notion combined commercial, military and religious strands. Elizabeth I faced a strong body of Protestant activists, who believed that England should build its own righteous Christian empire to rival the dark Catholic forces of Spain. This was the view held by Sir Walter Raleigh (1554–1618) and Richard Hakluyt the younger (1552?–1616), who were natural allies of those such as Sir Philip Sidney (1554–1586), who wanted England to take a more aggressive stance in support of the Netherlands. However, Elizabeth I was anxious to avoid war with Spain if possible, and colonial missions in her reign were very tentative affairs. The first efforts at colonies were made by Drake in Virginia (1585) and on Roanoke Island (1584, and 1587 – the second seeing the mysterious disappearance of all the English colonists). By the end of Elizabeth's reign in 1603, England had no substantial overseas colonial holdings; the first permanent colony was established in Virginia in 1607. James I was much more sympathetic to the idea of expansion, and England's empire in America began in the seventeenth century, as Spanish power declined.

Though she was not an imperialist, Elizabeth I was, however, readier to license raids against Spanish shipping carrying goods and money across the Atlantic. Sea captains such as Sir John Hawkins (1532–1595), Sir Humphrey Gilbert (1539?–1583) and Sir Francis Drake (1543?–1596) conducted an undeclared war in the Atlantic, and profited in other ways besides from what was essentially officially condoned piracy: Hawkins traded slaves from Guinea to the Spanish colonies. The English 'sea dogs' would also sail out from the Thames and harry Spanish ships carrying supplies to the Netherlands. Drake made a momentous journey around the world (1577–1580, some time after the first circumnavigation completed by Magellan's crew in 1519–1521) and landed on what was probably California, declaring it New Albion in Elizabeth's honour. Although Elizabeth knighted Drake on board his ship *The Golden Hind*, he risked execution, since confrontations in the New World risked upsetting her foreign policy of avoiding war with Spain. From a commercial point of view, the Pacific Ocean was in any case extremely dangerous for English ships, and London merchants preferred to back voyages around the African Cape, where warships could harass and plunder the Portuguese. Commerce was gradually establishing itself in an organised way, in the form of regular companies: Sir Hugh Willoughby's expedition to Russia in 1553 led to the founding of the Muscovy Company; this was followed by the East India Company (1600), which controlled trading with India, China and Japan, and the Virginia Company (1606). New goods brought from the Americas included the potato, cocoa and, notoriously, tobacco.

The historical experience is reflected in the genre of travel literature. Important works in this category include the Spanish *Decades of the New World (De Orbe Novo)* by Peter Martyr (1516, translated into English 1555) and a *Brief and True Report of the New found Land of Virginia* (1588, 1590) by Thomas Harriot (1560–1621). From these works a complex set of ideas emerges: the indigenous Indians are on the one hand presented as innocent, and living in harmony with nature, in contrast to decadent Westerners. On the other hand, the Indian is presented as a savage, resistant to Christianity and without the finer feelings of humanity. Both views depict the American Indian as an 'other' and so sanction the colonial enterprise: according to the first picture, of the Indians as prelapsarian souls, the indigenous people in their unfallen state need only be shown the light of Christian truth, while the second picture of them as savage beasts implicitly condones the violent imposition of Western order. In English writings, an analogy was also made between American Indians and the Irish, both supposedly brutish and inferior, and in need of firm governance by their betters.

The Europeans, meanwhile, are often portrayed in travel literature as heroic and superior, but their brutality is not overlooked. Harriot's book is illustrated with images of Indians dying from imported illnesses, imputed to the 'invisible bullets' of the Europeans. More straightforwardly supportive of the colonial mission are the books of Richard Hakluyt: *A Particuler Discourse Concerninge the Greate Necessitie and Manifolde Commodyties That Are Like to Growe to This Realme of Englande by the Westerne Discoueries Lately Attempted, Written in the Yere 1584* was commissioned by Sir Walter Raleigh and presented to Queen Elizabeth I. It argues for the plantation of English colonies in North America and was intended to win royal sympathy for Raleigh's expedition. Hakluyt's best-known work is *The Principall Navigations, Voiages and Discoveries of the English Nation* (1589, published in an enlarged three-volume edition 1599–1600). Here English imperialism is presented as a grand historical narrative, told through accounts – many of them eye-witness – of discoveries made by heroic English merchants and travellers. Hakluyt's work was continued by Samuel Purchas (baptized 1577, *d*.1626), whose compilation of travel tales *Purchas, His Pilgrimage* encompassed the whole of human history and the globe: it reaches from the travels of ancient patriarchs and apostles in the near east to the latest English settlements in the Bermudas, and throughout pursues an intensely Calvinist, anti-Catholic strategy. *Purchas, His Pilgrimage* went through four editions between

1613 and 1626; and at the time of publication its four large folio volumes made it the largest work yet to be produced by the English press.

Literary texts exploring the New World are mostly from the early Jacobean period. The best known is Shakespeare's *The Tempest* (1611). This certainly bears traces of travel literature, particularly the recent shipwreck on the Bermudas of would-be Virginia colonists (recorded in William Strachey's then unpublished letter, 'True Repertory of the Wrack', and in other travel narratives). In the figure of Caliban we can see competing images of the native Indian, who is presented as a danger to Western man and a natural slave, and at the same time as sensitive to the island's habitat in ways the Westerners are not. For these matters, a key source text is John Florio's translation of Montaigne's essay 'On Cannibals' (1603). Yet Shakespeare sets his island in the Mediterranean, not the New World, and draws equally on Ovid and Virgil: the play is based on classical models as much as on present adventures. The colonial experience is reflected upon, but also transmuted in a narrative apparently focused on issues of power, art and magic. A later play, set squarely in the New World, is John Fletcher's tragicomedy *The Island Princess* (1619–1621), based partly on a history of the Spanish conquest of the Molucca Islands (the Spice Islands). A convoluted plot has at its centre Princess Quisara of the Island of Tildore. The play involves quintessential Western themes of love, honour and nobility, lent extra charm by the exotic setting. The aim is the atmosphere of romance, and we might read this as a projection of ideas of the golden age onto the exotic otherness of the New World: 'The treasure of the sun dwells here; each tree, / As if it envied the old Paradise, / Strives to bring forth immortal fruit' (1.3,19–21).

A more hard-edged sense of the exploitation of riches provides the extended colonial metaphor in Donne's Elegy 19 (discussed in the General Introduction). Donne also uses the image of the globe in 'A Valediction: of Weeping': it has 'an Europe, Afrique, and an Asia' (12) – that is, the pre-Columbine world with no America. Elsewhere colonists are saluted as heroes by Michael Drayton in 'To the Virginian Voyage', and Andrew Marvell's 'Bermudas' praises 'an Isle so long unknown, / And yet far kinder than our own', again treating the New World as an other by which to illuminate the shortcomings of old Europe. Colonial issues are present in some other texts (for example, the play *Eastward Ho!* (1605), in which the contemptible fop Sir Petronel Flash sees Virginia as a place to flee to having sold his bride's property), but direct literary explorations are sparse. Perhaps the New World was generally marginal to the interests of most people, who had no direct interest in it either imaginatively or financially and were happy to enjoy the tales in circulation without pondering the ethics of imperialism.

In general, the colourful stories and artefacts create a sense of a place which is exotic – more a place of dreams than an integral part of the real known world. English language literature in America starts with the imagery of the Promised Land taken over there by the Pilgrim Fathers. Exploration is not a passive process: as soon as Westerners discovered the New World they turned it into something else – a lost paradise, the treasure trove of El Dorado, the desert awaiting Christ, the return to the Golden Age. The discoveries of Renaissance travellers took centuries to work through western consciousness, and the processes of thought which this involved are the subject of continued discussion in post-colonial studies today.

See also   *Contexts*: Cosmos, Golden Age, Race; *Texts*: Non-fictional Prose, Pastoral, Prose Style

Further Reading

Anthony Grafton (with April Shelford and Nancy Sirasi), *New Worlds, Ancient Texts: the Power of Tradition and the Shock of Discovery* (Cambridge, MA; London: Belknap Press, 1992).

Stephen Greenblatt, 'Invisible Bullets', ch. 1 of *Shakespearean Negotiations: The Circulation of Social Energy in Renaissance England* (Berkeley: University of California Press, 1988).

Stephen Greenblatt, *Marvelous Possessions: The Wonder of the New World* (Chicago: University of Chicago Press, 1992).

Andrew Hadfield, *Literature, Travel, and Colonial Writing in the English Renaissance, 1545–1625* (Oxford: OUP, 2007).

Peter C. Mancall, *Hakluyt's Promise: An Elizabethan's Obsession for an English America* (New Haven, NJ: Yale University Press, 2007).

Anthony Pagden, *European Encounters with the New World: From Renaissance to Romanticism* (New Haven and London: Yale UP, 1993).

Kim Sloan, *A New World: England's first View of America* (London: British Museum Press, 2007).

Women

In Renaissance writing, we find man in a variety of identities, among them prince, warrior, poet, artist, scholar, merchant, priest, explorer and sage. Women, however, have fewer occupations: chiefly they are defined by family (mother, wife, daughter, sister), sexuality (typically the extremes of virgin or prostitute) and morality (saint, witch). These categories were consolidated in the Renaissance, which saw no significant revolution in the lives of women and the roles allocated to them by society. Indeed, according to Joan Kelly's famous essay 'Did Women Have a Renaissance?', Renaissance ladies were actually more constricted in their behaviour than those of the Middle Ages.

The supreme vocation of early modern woman was to bear children, ensuring the continuity of a family and its inheritance. Few vocations were so perilous or so fraught with grief. The momentous event of giving birth frequently led to complications and infections from which the mother died. Babies who survived the birth might soon be taken by plague, hunger or illnesses such as diarrhoea and tuberculosis; babies of rich mothers, who did not usually breastfeed, faced the further dangers attendant upon being fed by a poor rural wet-nurse, who might herself suffer from malnutrition. (Both Catholic and Protestant scholars insisted that a woman had a duty to breastfeed. However, the rich generally did not submit to this: men did not like the sight of breastfeeding, and it was held to diminish fertility.) Newborns might also die from maternal negligence, and unwanted babies might be deliberately killed (though the crime of infanticide was punishable by death). It has been calculated that in Western Europe only 20–50 per cent of children survived infancy, though what effect this had on the emotional lives and relations of mothers and children is largely a matter of speculation: the anguish recorded by private writings such as letters, however, should warn us against any easy assumption that hearts naturally become harder as a way of coping with loss. Wives in rich families often became pregnant again soon after birth, in the paramount endeavour of producing an heir: Charles I's wife Henrietta Maria was almost constantly pregnant between 1628 and 1639.

Women exercised a vital influence as parents in the home. Sons would stay with their mother until the age of seven, after which they were deemed to have reached manhood, and were to be deferred to. Daughters, however, remained under their mother's tutelage until marriage. Scenes of Lady Macduff and her son, and Juliet with her mother and nurse, give us brief glimpses into the kinds of relationships that must have existed. Women were encouraged to train their children in religion by Christian humanists like More and Vives (in his book *De institutione foeminae christianae* (1529)) and equally by Protestant reformers. This recognition of the influence of the mother in forming a child's character is reflected in various kinds of writing: diaries, and letters like those written between Lady Margaret Beaufort and her son the future Henry VII; and the genre of the mother's advice book (see Further Reading). Children were expected to be subservient to their parents: daughters would stand or kneel in their presence, and even as adults children would ask their parents' blessing on returning home (a convention shockingly if understandably overturned in Lear's curse of his daughter). Evidence of the emotional relations between parents and children is mixed, but parents could certainly use physical coercion to keep their children in subjection.

This is unpleasantly confirmed in the account of her childhood given to Roger Ascham by Lady Jane Grey:

> For when I am in presence either of father or mother, whether I speake, kepe silence, sit, stand, or go, eate, drinke, be merie, or sad, be sowynge, plaiyng, dauncing, or doing anie thing els, I must do it, as it were, in soch weight, mesure, and number, euen so perfitelie, as God made the world, or else I am so sharply taunted, so cruellie threatened, yea presentlie some tymes, with pinches, nippes, and bobbes, and other waies, which I will not name, for the honor I beare them, so without measure misordered, that I think my self in hell . . .
>   (*The Scholemaster*, Bk. 1, 'The Bryngyng Up of Youth').

This is dramatic testimony of the upbringing of at least one high-born daughter but, as ever, we should beware of generalising from individual cases. It can be safely said, though, that all daughters were required to preserve their chastity to maintain their value on the marriage market and guarantee the legitimacy of their children.

Women were of course expected to become mothers only having married. Marriage was essentially an institution for the transmission of property from one generation to the next. After the dissolution of the monasteries, marrying off daughters became more urgent, since they could not be sent to nunneries. At the higher end of the social scale, marriages were customarily arranged by parents for this material end, and women who disobeyed their parents' wishes were punished. Brabantio clearly sees his daughter's elopement with Othello as a kind of theft, as did the father of Anne More when she married the poet John Donne – this marriage led to years of penury for the couple. Marriage was for life, and cases of separation or annulment were rare. Life tended to be shorter for women, and many died before menopause, while second and third marriages by men were common.

The dowry that women received on marriage did not belong to them: it relieved the father of further financial responsibility, and compensated the husband for the cost of a wife who could not earn an income. In effect a dowry was a means of passing wealth from one man to another. A woman could not inherit in her own right, her property legally becoming that of her husband (though the husband was expected to preserve the inheritance for the next generation rather than spend it, to ensure the continuance of the family line). While there were no doubt loving marriages, and mutual affection was encouraged by preachers, the superiority of the husband was stressed. Some have seen in the Reformation a softening of this attitude, with the ending of the misogynist cult of virginity and some move towards a sense of equality of all the faithful before God. Yet Calvin followed the strict Pauline line that woman's subjection to man was analogous to man's subjection to God: 'he for God only, she for God in him', as Milton puts it (*Paradise Lost*, IV.299). An interesting text to put next to marriages in literature is William Whately's *The Bride Bush or a Wedding Sermon* (1617) in which separate advice is offered to husband and wife. Whately says that a wife must convince herself that her husband is superior, and though the author demurs over domestic violence he finally concludes that husbands should be permitted to beat their wives. Women's bodies, like their social positions, were subject to the will of others, a situation which also applied to sex. This was intended primarily for procreation, and secondly to prevent adultery. Female sexual desire was clearly recognised, however: Juliet's yearning for Romeo, the amours of the ladies in *A Midsummer Night's Dream* and the bawdy language of a Rosalind or Cleopatra's female entourage are all Shakespearean examples of attitudes to feminine sexuality which are less repressed than we might expect – the relative lack of privacy in houses of the period must have made silence and secrecy regarding intercourse very difficult.

As mother, wife and household manager, a Renaissance woman's place was in the home. A man's duty was to provide for the household through dealings with other men. The woman ran the home; in large houses, this was a complex task, involving saving, arranging, ordering, accounting and managing servants. Poor women might work as maids and seamstresses, but the guilds were closed to females. This order of things reflected the idea that with man's greater power came greater responsibility. From the division of labour many social and cultural arrangements followed. The education of women was largely confined to domestic labours: humanists like Vives stressed the need for honesty and chastity but saw no need for women to acquire any knowledge of science, philosophy or rhetoric. There are a few examples of highly educated women, like Elizabeth I, the unfortunate Lady Jane Grey or More's daughters; but these were exceptions. In Protestant countries, women were encouraged to read the Bible and to sing in church, but they were excluded from theological discussion. A man's education, though it increasingly involved humanist elements, was utilitarian: it was designed to equip him for his worldly business, at the same time as framing him morally to be a good subject and citizen. A husband needed to be eloquent and suitably dressed to deal with the world, while the wife should be silent and dress for her husband's pleasure. The Petrarchan female is usually silent, and persuasive women in literature tend to stand outside the normal order of things: their oratory can be subversive, as with Shakespeare's Cleopatra and Lady Macbeth, or Milton's Eve. Biblical exemplars were used to establish these roles: Eve was the type of the woman in the house, Mary of the woman in the cloister. Women who achieve in the public sphere were often desexualised as Amazons in cultural representations: *A Midsummer Night's Dream*, in the figure of the Amazon queen Hippolyta, suggests that a female ruler disrupts the natural order of things.

Of course there were exceptions to this norm, the most famous being the English monarch Elizabeth I. Beneath Elizabeth were examples of women who exercised power and influence through patronage: Lady Margaret Beaufort (1443–1509) founded two colleges, and chairs of theology at Oxford and Cambridge; Henry VIII's first Queen, Catherine of Aragon (1485–1536), was an important patron of Erasmus, Vives and Elyot. The discussions in Castiglione's *The Courtier* are presided over by the Duchess of Urbino and her ladies, and a male courtier's behaviour was clearly designed to be pleasing to such formidable mistresses.

Complexity on a mental level can be found in the various (male-authored) pamphlets debating women. It is interesting to place *The Taming of the Shrew* against *The Schole House of Women* (1541). At first, this presents a typically misogynist portrait of women as sharp-tongued, argumentative, complaining types who need to be kept in subjection: speech of any kind, and still more writing, are abnormal deviations from a woman's proper role as chaste, silent and obedient. Yet intriguingly, in a debate between an old gossip and a young wife it emerges that the husband is cruel and selfish. Women were praised – sometimes ironically – in several writings, including *The Prayse of all women, called mulierum paean* (1541), Thomas Elyot's *The Defence of Good Women* (1545) – in which women are held to be the equals of men as rational beings, *A little and brief treatise called the defence of women* (1560) by Edward More (grandson of Thomas) and Nicholas Breton's *The praise of virtuous ladies* (1597). Concerns about gender transgression are fascinatingly voiced in *Hic Mulier* (1620), an attack on transvestism at a time when women wearing men's apparel was apparently fashionable. Persecutions of alleged witches also suggests unease about females outside prescribed social roles. Though women were typically subservient and confined to the home, in the sphere of the imagination they were clearly less subject to control.

See also   *Contexts*: The Court, Medicine, Race; *Texts*: Lyric, Sonnet; *Criticism*: Feminism

Further Reading
Source material
Kate Aughterson, ed., *Renaissance Woman: A Sourcebook: Constructions of Femininity in England* (London: Routledge, 1995).

The Feminist Controversy of the Renaissance: Facsimile Reproductions (Delmar, NY: Scholars' Facsimiles and Reprints, 1980).

Betty S. Travitsky, ed., *Mother's Advice Books* (Aldershot: Ashgate, 2001). See also Travitsky's entry on Elizabeth Grymeston in *Oxford Dictionary of National Biography*.

Studies

Iona Bell, *Elizabethan Women and the Poetry of Courtship* (Cambridge: CUP, 1998).

Joan Kelly, 'Did Women Have a Renaissance?': in *Feminism and Renaissance Studies*, ed. Lorna Hutson (Oxford: OUP, 1999), 21–47.

Margaret L. King, 'The Woman of the Renaissance', in Eugenio Garin, ed., *Renaissance Characters* (Chicago: University of Chicago Press: 1997), 207–249.

2 Texts: Themes, Issues, Concepts

Introduction

'Renaissance' is a term to be used tentatively. It was introduced by the Victorians and was not employed in the period itself (the *OED's* first citation is 1840). Moreover, exactly when that period was is far from clear. 'Renaissance' is often used to mean the age of Shakespeare (1564–1623), the Golden Age of English letters which saw the flowering of literature in the latter part of the reign of Elizabeth I (*r*.1558–1603), reaching into that of her successor James I. This Renaissance starts with the publication of Spenser's *Shepheardes Calender* in 1579 and includes the achievements of Sidney and Spenser, the great works of Elizabethan and Jacobean drama and the writers who flourished at the turn of the century, such as Ben Jonson and John Donne. But 'Renaissance' can equally refer to a wider space of time, opening with the founding of the Tudor dynasty in 1485 and ending with the convulsive changes to the political and cultural landscape brought about by the English Civil War: here the focus is on the slow implantation of humanist and Reformation thought and the working out of these influences in the context of political and economic changes which shape the early modern world. But of course cultural shifts do not begin and end on certain dates. Wherever we seek to locate the Renaissance, we will find that the tides and currents of literature do not respect fixed historical boundaries.

To this problem of vagueness over period is added that of the cultural value system which 'Renaissance' implies. The Renaissance is essentially used to mean a re-birth of classical thought after the 'Dark Ages' of the medieval period, and this naturally leads us to privilege works with a classical flavour. Yet this approach excludes or downgrades much interesting writing, from the rich legacy of medieval writing to pamphlets, letters, travel accounts, and most writing by women, who were generally deprived of access to a classical education. Thus the concept of 'Renaissance' can lead us to a selective view of the age. The writings of women happily now occupy a far more prominent place in Renaissance studies, but still any account of the period is likely to be exclusive in some way, and that is certainly the case with the present book. Beyond the edges of the scene outlined in these pages are the rural areas relatively untouched by the influence of London, the literatures of Wales and Scotland and the cultural life of most of the population who had neither the ability nor the leisure to read and write literature – yet their culture might include festivities, rituals, romances and ballads, local customs and a rich imaginative account of the physical world. Only a tiny elite, virtually all of them men, actively participated in the creation of Renaissance English literature as that body of work is usually understood. And even then, we should remember that their work was by no means driven by the quest for fresh, classically inspired thinking. There are important continuities which run through the Renaissance: the mixture of jest and earnest in Shakespeare's history plays looks back to medieval theatre; Spenser mixes Italian epic with traditions of English allegory and romance; and throughout the period, Chaucer was revered alongside Virgil. Even as new currents of thought emerge, strong traditions persist. The Renaissance is not a tidily unified cultural era, but one marked by tensions and shifting balances of the native and foreign, classical and medieval, the old and the new.

However we qualify the term 'Renaissance', certain themes associated with it can be seen emerging with Henry VII's accession by force of arms in 1485. By this stage, the Italian town of Florence had almost a century of glittering achievement behind it, including great works of art and brilliant studies by humanist scholars. New ideas also blossomed in France and the Netherlands, which had produced a breathtaking new realistic art of its own. But England had been separated from this movement. The Wars of the Roses had focused the attention of the nobility on internecine struggles rather than the patronage of art. The great work of this period was the *Morte Darthure* by Sir Thomas Malory (*d.*1471). Caxton printed this magnificent collection of Arthurian tales in 1485, and its story of the rise and collapse of the unity of the Round Table of Camelot can be read as a poignant account of the end of the medieval chivalric dream. But it could equally be taken as a dream of the future: Henry VII identified himself with the figure of Arthur, the once and future king – he unfurled Arthur's banner when he landed in Wales, and the House of Tudor continued to draw on this identification with the ancient English hero in presenting itself as the salvation of a shattered realm. The Tudor–Arthur link is still a potent force in Spenser's *Faerie Queene* (1590–1596). But though it was politically useful in this way, Arthurian matter is rooted in a medieval, not a Renaissance, imagination. Malory's masterpiece weaves together English and French sources to tell the matter of Britain. But it is noticeably remote from the new forms of expression then being forged and is testament to the largely insular spirit of the late fifteenth century. As Henry sought to unify the country under a centralised monarchy, however, attention moved outwards again. The royal court was strengthened as an institution, furnished by lavish displays in the service of power and served by humanist scholars. This laid the foundations for humanist education which was to shape the minds of future writers, but had little immediate effect on vernacular literature. The principal English poet of this time was the cleric John Skelton (1460?–1529), who, though classically educated, was unsympathetic to the new learning. Often seen as a kind of bridge between the medieval and the Renaissance, Skelton is a unique voice: his jaunty colloquial 'Skeltonic' rhythms and earthy realism are quite different from the smooth and refined verse we associate with the Renaissance. Though his linguistic play, energy and observation are impressive and engaging, modern critics struggle to find the sensibility which led to Skelton being praised by Erasmus as 'that light and glory of English letters'. Yet Skelton's many writings, which include a series of satires of Cardinal Wolsey such as the play *Magnificence* (1515), provide among other things a vivid satirical picture of the early Tudor courtly life, as seen through the eyes of a moralising satirist.

Skelton is also a link between the courts of Henry VII and Henry VIII (*r*.1509–1547), whom he tutored. In his quest for an imperial image, Henry massively aggrandised the court: our picture of this is largely created through the works of Hans Holbein the Younger (*c*.1497–1543), who was brought to England to paint the English monarch and aristocracy. Henry's interests included theology, music, astronomy and literature, and he was enthusiastically greeted by humanists as a great patron who would bring England into the orbit of European intellectual and religious life. An important work from the first years of Henry VIII's reign was *Utopia* (1516) by Sir Thomas More, originally composed in Latin and assimilating the sophisticated ways that language was used by scholars such as Erasmus. The benefits of a humanist education are described in the major prose work of the period, Sir Thomas Elyot's *The Book Named the Governour* (1531), while Roger Ascham's brief treatise on archery, *Toxophilus* (1545), shows the influence of Cicero on English prose, now capable of nuances and syntactical complexities far distant from the chronicle style of Malory. Petrarchan images of lovers freezing and burning for their lady arrived – along with the sonnet form – in the lyrics of Sir Thomas Wyatt (1503?–1542) and Henry Howard, Earl of Surrey (1517–1547). Surrey's translation of Virgil also introduced blank verse into English poetry, and the first miscellanies of English lyrics date from this period. If the word 'Renaissance' did not yet exist, new currents in English writing unmistakably did. But this wave ended with the English Reformation, which once again cut the native culture off from Catholic continental culture and learning. One significant consequence of this rupture was the English Bible. Only two years after William Tyndale (1494?–1536) was executed for translating the scriptures into English, copies of his work, as revised by Miles Coverdale (1488–1568), were placed in every church in the land by royal decree. In the 'false dawn' of this early Renaissance under Henry VIII we also meet the image of the Renaissance writer – not suffering souls in garrets, but men of the world, engaged in business such as law and diplomacy and involved in the political and social life of court. For them, humanist eloquence was a useful professional asset as much as a literary skill, and much of the writing of our period is marked by the tone, persuasive strategies and knowledge that comes from engagement in worldly affairs. This presents the modern reader with the further challenge of finding other ways of reading the writings of women, whose sphere was the private one of the household rather than the public *polis*.

The turn to a more severe brand of Protestantism under Edward VI (r.1547–1553) made England still more isolated, and the most important English text of this period was also a religious one: Thomas Cranmer's *Book of Common Prayer* (1549) presented a Protestant English liturgy in superbly resonant and cadenced prose. Though treatises on the classical rhetorical figures were written in the reigns of Edward and Mary (r.1547–1553), they did not inspire much verse, and the publication of *Mirror for Magistrates* in 1555 reminds us of the persistence of older traditions: this compilation (enlarged in 1559) of the stories of the fates of princes belongs squarely to a medieval mode of instruction in vice and virtue through exemplary stories, in varied and unpolished metres. That there was a taste for the new style is shown by the popularity of the so-called *Tottel's Miscellany* (1557), which gathered together lyrics and songs that were to influence the next generation of lyric poets. However, much of the verse of the middle of the sixteenth century seems heavy-handed and stale; in his important study of English sixteenth-century non-dramatic literature, C. S. Lewis characterised this period as 'drab', before the flowering of talent in the golden years at the end of the century.

Elizabethan literature can be divided roughly into two halves: in the first two decades of her reign, literary achievement was relatively modest, while it is the second half, encompassing the 1580s and 1590s, which saw the sudden flourishing of writing that has come to be called the Golden Age. An important aspect of the first half was translation: Thomas Hoby's version of Castiglione's *Courtier* (1561) brought ideas of courtly conduct into wider circulation, while Arthur Golding's translation of Ovid's influenced Shakespeare, among others. The first part of Elizabeth's reign also saw another monument of English Protestant literature, the *Acts and Monuments* (1563) of John Foxe, better known as

Foxe's *Book of Martyrs*, which describes the sufferings of Protestants under 'bloody Mary'.

The Golden Age of letters begins just as Elizabeth's reign entered its most difficult phase. Rather than glorifying the monarch in any simple way, the works of this period often seem to explore the tensions of a nervous and fractious period. Whatever the cause for such an efflorescence of writing, famous names and works now appear in quick succession. Lyly's intricate prose work *Euphues* (1578) was followed by the publication of Spenser's *Shepheardes Calender* and Sir Thomas North's translation of Plutarch's *Lives* (both 1579). The first part of the 1580s are dominated, from the literary point of view, by the writings of Sir Philip Sidney (1554–1586), charismatic courtier and militant Protestant: between 1581 and 1584 he composed the sonnets of *Astrophil and Stella* (p. 1591), the treatise *An Apologie for Poetry* (1595; also published as *Defence of Poesie*) and the first three books of the prose romance *The Arcadia* (1590). The style and aristocratic subject matter of Sidney's writings influenced later writers and, with the publication of the first three books of Spenser's *Faerie Queene* (1590; the next three books, of a projected twelve, were published in 1596), took English literature into a new phase: classical and continental forms were imitated with confidence and transformed with English speech rhythms and habits of thought; literary creation was accompanied by eloquent self-analysis; and Sidney's depiction of the poet as a semi-divine figure and poetry as a source of moral wisdom led to aspirations of high seriousness. In Spenser we can see a Protestant identity finding a literary vehicle, as native romance and allegory are integrated with Renaissance epic. In the context of fears of Spanish invasion and Catholic plots, Lyly, Sidney, Spenser and the Marlowe of *Tamburlaine* (1587) are all concerned with finding a distinctive English voice for the definition of English virtues. Yet to a modern reader, inclined perhaps to look for instability and uncertainty in texts, 'golden' Elizabethan works also convey a sense of unease, for all their smoothness and refinement. The sonnet sequences depict in harmonious music dissonant mindsets, torn between paganism and Calvinism, passion and virtue; the pastoral realms of Arcadia and Faeryland are constantly threatened and disrupted by latent vice and violence. The fascination with order and pattern which characterises Elizabethan aesthetics suggests an anxiety to control whatever forces of disturbance lurk beneath.

Disturbance is a keynote of the 1590s. This decade saw many of the great works of Christopher Marlowe (1564–1593) and Shakespeare; and the vitality of the drama, a form based on conflict, seems closely linked to the internal religious, political and cultural debates of the age. Francis Bacon (1561–1626) led the 'anti-Ciceronian' movement, in which ornate prose was replaced by a curt, compressed style based on the Roman stoic Seneca. Bacon's own essays, first published in 1597, represent the exploratory cast of mind characteristic of this period; this questing attitude darkens into an elegant scepticism in the verse of Fulke Greville (1554–1628). In poetry, Elizabethan prettiness gives way to the passionate and intellectual dramas of thought in the metaphysical verse of John Donne (1572–1631), influenced by the mannerist and baroque tendencies of continental Europe, with their emphasis on emotional expressiveness. The end of the sixteenth century also saw the rise of satire, as practised by writers associated with the Inns of Court, notably John Davies, Joseph Hall, John Marston and Thomas Middleton. Their themes of corruption in the private and public spheres are echoed in the lively depictions of London's underworld in the pamphlets of Thomas Nashe and Robert Greene.

Jacobean literature (1603–1625) continues the dark and pessimistic tone of the end of Elizabeth's reign. Caustic satire is realised in the Jacobean tragedies of Webster, Ford and Middleton, whose malcontents rail against lust and other evils in violent narratives. Jacobean drama is also often self-consciously experimental: Beaumont and Fletcher mix the genres of tragedy and comedy; both comedy and tragedy involve new plot lines, and the densely textured writing of many plays is an intriguing mixture of the passionate and bitterly ironic. These elements are reflected in the 'problem' plays of Shakespeare such as *Measure for Measure* (c.1604), while the most dismal speculations of the age are voiced in his late tragedies. A new form of drama meanwhile arose in the court, with the Jacobean masques of Ben Jonson and Inigo Jones: these used symbol and spectacle to glorify James I and his court. The great prose work of the period is *The Anatomy of Melancholy* (1621) by Robert Burton (1577–1640), which provides an encyclopaedic account of the follies and vices of mankind in the looser, more conversational style that succeeded the compact aphorisms of Bacon. Another stylistic tension was that between the classical style of Ben Jonson (1572–1637), who aimed for a smooth, clear, 'plain' style, and the dynamic, baroque writings of Donne and his circle – though Jonson also admired and imitated Donne, and later poets drew on, and integrated, their approaches. Influential in a different way was the royally approved revision of Tyndale's Bible, known as the Authorized Version (1611). In the Jacobean period the number of female writers also increases, though, since publication was disapproved of, the writings of these educated noblewomen were usually unpublished. Significant names include Elizabeth Cary (1585–1639), whose *The Tragedie of Miriam* (1613) is the first play by an Englishwoman; Mary Wroth (c.1587–1651/3), author of the scandalous fictionalised account of

Jacobean high life, *The Countess of Montgomeries Urania* (1621); and the Scottish Elizabeth Melville (*c*.1582–1640).

Caroline literature (1625–1649) reflects the ethos of the court of Charles I. The 'Cavalier Poets' (Robert Herrick, Thomas Carew, John Suckling and Richard Lovelace) express the model courtier's sophistication and libertinism in clear and witty lyrics. The classical clarity of Jonson, and the taste for precisely phrased wit, was developed by Edmund Waller and Denham; with them, the heroic couplet began to supplant the stanzaic forms, providing the foundations for John Dryden's Restoration Neo-Classicism. Courtly manners are also explored in the work of Caroline dramatists (Philip Massinger, James Shirley and William Davenant), who also drew on the achievements of Jacobean tragedy, romance and John Marston's city comedy. The closure of the theatres in 1642, at the beginning of the Civil War, brought an effective end to drama until the Restoration. One response to courtly worldliness and political turbulence was to withdraw into the spirit: the troubled reign of Charles I and the Interregnum that followed is also a great period of religious poetry in English literature: the Anglican George Herbert (1593–1633) and the Catholic Richard Crashaw (1613–1649) drew on the metaphysical and the Baroque to find a way of expounding Church doctrines and evoking the spiritual life. A different manner of reflection on religious matters is given by *Religio Medici* (1642) by Sir Thomas Browne (1605–1682), whose writings provide a valuable and readable insight into the intellectual preoccupations of the age.

The metaphysical strain in English poetry continued into the Commonwealth period, in the mannered conceits of John Cleveland (1613–1658) and the witty artifice of Abraham Cowley (1618–1667). The great late metaphysical figure, however, was Andrew Marvell (1621–1678), whose work fuses passion with cool logical organisation, and addresses topics in philosophy, politics and religion. One preoccupation of Marvell's was the tension between the active and the contemplative life; as political strife drove many writers into their country retreats, the attractiveness of retirement and seclusion arises as a theme of the period, in such works as Marvell's 'A Garden' and Izaak Walton's prose work *The Compleat Angler* (1653). Deep spiritual meditation yields the mystical poetry of Henry Vaughan (1621/2–1695) and the writings of Thomas Traherne (1637–1674). Izaak Walton (1593–1683) was also important in furthering the genre of biography, and vivid portraits of many figures of the age can be found in the gossipy sketches of John Aubrey (1626–1697). The great prose work of this period is the *Leviathan* (1651) by Thomas Hobbes (1588–1679), an examination of human nature and the corresponding ideal state, and an example of the attempt at a dispassionate application of reason to problems which came to be the hallmark of the coming scientific age. A towering figure in both the Caroline and the Commonwealth periods is John Milton (1608–1674). His epic *Paradise Lost* (1667) reads as a summation of all the major themes of this outline account of Renaissance literature: it marries Protestant thought with deep humanist learning and classical epic with the theatrical imagination of the continental baroque. Milton also drew on Old Testament and esoteric traditions to portray the poet as a prophet, inspired to guide men in public and spiritual life. But the succeeding age looked less for mystical gravity than a refined and rational style, one which would reflect and help to rebuild the social order.

Further Reading

Sixteenth and Seventeenth Centuries

David Norbrook, *Poetry and Politics in the English Renaissance*, 2nd edn. (Oxford: OUP, 2002).

Marion Wynne-Davies, *Sidney to Milton 1580–1660* (Houndmills, Basingstoke: Palgrave Macmillan, 2003).

Sixteenth Century

C. S. Lewis, *English Literature in the Sixteenth Century Excluding Drama* (Oxford: Clarendon, 1954).

Murray Roston, *Sixteenth-Century English Literature* (London: Macmillan, 1982).

Gary Waller, *English Poetry of the Sixteenth Century* (London: Longman, 1986).

Seventeenth Century

Douglas Bush, *English Literature in the Earlier Seventeenth Century, 1600–1660* (Oxford: Clarendon Press, 1962).

Thomas Corns, *A History of Seventeenth-Century English Literature* (Oxford: Blackwell, 2007).

Bruce King, *Seventeenth-Century English Literature* (London: Macmillan, 1982).

David Norbrook, *Writing the English Republic: Poetry, Rhetoric and Politics* (Cambridge: CUP, 1999).

George Parfitt, *English Poetry of the Seventeenth Century* (London: Longman, 1985).

Actors and Acting

At the beginning of the sixteenth century, the actor was not a recognised craftsman or professional. Thus, his activities were not regulated by a guild, and his livelihood had no protection in law. Travelling players could resemble the bands of the destitute, who roamed the land foraging and stealing food. Indeed, vagrants, when arrested by the authorities, sometimes claimed to be travelling players pursuing their trade. In order to remove this defence – rather than to support the trade of acting – in 1572 an Act was passed declaring that only groups of players with a document proving the personal patronage of a nobleman were allowed to tour: hence the names of Elizabethan companies such as the Admiral's Men, or the Earl of Leicester's Company. The institution of the company led to the professionalisation of acting, which bought with it the customary practices of any guild: more secure financial arrangements and the passing on of skills from masters to apprentices.

For actors the proliferation of plays meant the challenge of learning several parts, often at the same time. Their feats of memorisation are all the more remarkable when one remembers that actors would usually only have a copy of their part with cue lines and very limited opportunities for rehearsal. There was no equivalent to a modern director and so directions are implied in the writing: a Renaissance playscript can be interpreted not only for its textual meaning but also in a practical sense: What kinds of movement, intonation, emphasis and breathing give it dramatic life? Companies would have four or five main actors taking the main parts. The Renaissance theatre created star actors, whose previous roles would be known to many in the audience. An allusion to this practice occurs in *Hamlet* (c.1600) when Polonius tells Hamlet he once played Julius Caesar, and Brutus killed him (3.2, 90–100). In Shakespeare's company, the actor who played Polonius also played Caesar, and another actor played both Brutus and Hamlet – who, in the play, is later to kill Polonius.

Like the theatre scenery of the time, acting style is likely to have included symbolic elements. Renaissance drama is generally speaking pre-realist. In theatre performance, the actor's style of delivery could signify a certain state rather than emulate it. This does not mean that the acting was crude and bombastic: symbolic acting in some non-western cultures (such as Japanese kabuki drama) shows that this art can be exquisitely subtle and refined. Hamlet's advice to the players is to resist the temptation to crudity and excess, but he is not telling them to inhabit the role either. A formal, rhetorical representation of the inner world of feeling is the working language of Renaissance drama. Here acting style works with the language. Characters tend not to be individuated by particular habits of speech. Rustics speak in the comic prose which signals they are rustic, courtiers use formal verse.

Another important aspect of Renaissance theatre was the boy actor. In the open playhouses, boys played the parts of women. There is evidence, not least in the length and density of the parts themselves, to suggest that they did this with great skill. Yet such an arrangement inevitably highlights the fact that the woman is being signified by dress, intonation and gesture by the boy playing her. In other words, it is another instance of the real actor being as patent as the acted character. There is a felt difference between signified (female) and the agent signifying (the boy), a difference played out on an ironic and narrative level through plots turning on disguise and cross-dressing: in *Twelfth Night* we see a man falling in love with a handsome boy, who in the plot is really a woman in disguise, while in a further irony the audience knows the actor is male. Actor/character, male/female, individual/multiple identity, symbolical/real: Renaissance theatre has a dynamism in blurring and deconstructing these distinctions to create a fluid event, constantly moving between the real and the pretended, the actual and the symbolical. Such an experience would not be open to a solidly realist approach.

Reading a playtext is a specially challenging activity: from a page often dense with notes we have to imagine a performance, with movement, colour, voices, gestures and audience participation. Criticism today is less liable than in the past to treat a play as a book to be read, and more interested in the interpretations provided by productions. All recent academic editions of Shakespeare plays will carry rich information on the archive of previous film and theatre performances; performance study, involving the detailed description and assessment of particular productions, is an exciting avenue of enquiry. There is also much to be learned from the directors, voice coaches and actors who have written on the ways a Shakespeare text can be vocalised in performance.

See also *Contexts*: Court, Patronage, Rhetoric, Sex and Sexuality; *Texts*: Theatres

Further Reading

John Barton, *Playing Shakespeare* (London: Methuen, 1984).
Oliver Ford Davies, *Performing Shakespeare: Preparation, Rehearsal, Performance* (London: Nick Hern Books, 2007)
Andrew Gurr, *Playgoing in Shakespeare's London*, 3rd edn (Cambridge: CUP, 2004).
Peter Hall, *Shakespeare's Advice to the Players* (London: Oberon, 2003).

The Bible

In 1500, the Bible was only permitted in Latin (the fourth-century Vulgate translation made by St Jerome, from the original Hebrew and Greek). Possession of an English version was illegal, and the Church had sole authority to interpret the scriptures. By 1611, when the Authorized Version was published, English bibles were in every parish church and countless households, and official control of scriptural interpretation was greatly weakened. The shift from a Church-controlled Latin Bible to a publicly available vernacular one had important consequences for the English people and for their language and literature.

A movement to translate the Latin Bible had already occurred at the end of the fourteenth century. At this time, it was the Mass rather than the scriptures which was at the centre of religious life; the Bible was heard in fragments in Church services, and seen illustrated in stained glass and other artefacts, but it was the Church, rather than the written Word, which was held to the guardian of salvation. This conception was questioned by the Oxford scholar John Wycliffe (c.1320–1384), who argued that the faithful would be helped to salvation by having access to 'God's Law' in their own language. An English version was made and Wycliffe's followers – known as the Lollards, or 'mumblers' – distributed it around the country. But the Church responded severely, and in 1407 all Wycliffe's works, including this one, were burned; later his corpse was disinterred and burned (1427).

For the next century, the Bible remained in Latin. The next great proponent of an English Bible was Wiliam Tyndale (1494–1536), who shared Wycliffe's vision of the scriptures rescued from corrupt and ignorant churchmen and restored to the people. Tyndale forged this vision against the background of linguistic scholarship: Erasmus's edition of the Greek New Testament (1516) had for the first time brought the original language of the New Testament to the attention of the learned; and a key element in the Lutheran Reformation was Luther's own German rendering of the New Testament, published in 1522. The invention of printing meant that these ideas could be circulated more widely and rapidly than before. However, the political climate in England was not right for Tyndale's project. Having failed to receive the patronage of the Bishop of London, Cuthbert Tunstall, he fled to Germany in 1524. Tyndale proceeded to publish his translation of the New Testament (1526) and the Pentateuch (the first five books of the Old Testament, 1530). These were banned books in England, and had to be smuggled past the authorities, who burned any copies they could find. The most famous opponent of the English Bible was Thomas More (1478–1535), who evidently feared it would cause the destruction of an entire way of life: More's debate with Tyndale through books was one of the most voluminous and vituperative polemical exchanges of the age. Tyndale – now in Antwerp – was eventually betrayed, arrested and delivered to the officials of the Holy Roman Empire. He was executed (a botched garrotting was followed by burning) in 1536. But Henry VIII's state was now turning more radically against Rome; with the support of Thomas Cromwell and the Archbishop of Canterbury Thomas Cranmer, the King agreed to an English Bible. There appeared the so-called 'Matthew's Bible' (1537) and the 'Great Bible' (1539). These, and subsequent versions, were essentially the work of Tyndale lightly revised. Though only a few years previously English Bibles were burned, they were now put into England's churches by royal command: every parish had to buy one, and the testaments were now available to anyone who could read (though a few years later, the fear of a chaos of rival independent interpretations led to a restriction of readership). Over the second half of the century, rival versions appeared, using textual choices and commentary to support different churches: the Geneva Bible (1560), composed by Protestant exiles from Queen Mary, was the official version of the Calvinist church and was the one which the Pilgrim Fathers took with them when they sailed to America in 1620; the Douai-Rheims New Testament (1582) was an English Bible for Catholics. In Elizabeth's England, the Bishops' Bible (1568) – again very largely Tyndale's work – was the official version read in churches. When James I came to the throne in 1603, Puritans anticipated that he would be friendly to their cause, and at the Hampton Court Conference (1603) supposed to unite the Puritan and Anglican parties (but in practice heavily weighted against Puritanism), a Puritan scholar suggested that a definitive English Bible should be produced. James assented, and the resulting translation – the work of teams of scholars assigned different sections – was finally printed in 1611. This is known as the King James Bible, or Authorized Version. Revisions and corrections had been made, yet it has been calculated that this is still 90 per cent the work of Wiliam Tyndale.

The English Bible was a significant episode not only in English religion and politics but also in the history of the language. Tyndale had an ear for the rhythms of English speech and for the resonances of ordinary English words. Many of his phrases remain today: the powers that be, give up the ghost, salt of the earth, a law unto themselves . . . among many others. His work was to put the Bible not only into English, but into the English of the people, rather than the Latinate vocabulary of the learned. The Authorized Version, which was designed to be read aloud to congregations, retains this use of simple concrete language. In measured rhythms and cadences, the most ordinary language becomes the vehicle for the most serious thought: 'Man that is born of woman is of few days, and full of trouble. He cometh forth like a flower, and is cut down: he fleeth also as a shadow, and continueth not' (Job 14:1–2). The parallelisms and compression of Hebrew poetry are here transplanted into English. The critic Herbert Grierson characterised this kind of imagery as 'realistic, passionate', and much Renaissance (and later) poetry in English combines the two: feelings and ideas weighted by concrete, matter-of-fact observation are more common than blurred, sensuous evocation. George Herbert's homely similitudes belong to a preaching tradition which frames passionate spiritual thought in realistic images and is rooted in biblical language; the Bible's bare style, with nouns stripped of adjectives, finds an English echo in Milton's later works *Paradise Regained* (1671) and *Samson Agonistes* (1671). In Milton we can also see on an individual level one of the stylistic tensions of the age: elaborate, ornamented classical rhetoric on the one hand and the *sermo humilis* or 'humble speech' of the scriptures on the other; the pretty and the plain.

Beyond these textures of writing, the English Bible also affected ways of thinking. It made more accessible to readers and listeners the complex patterns of biblical typology, a mode of interpretation whereby one detail in the Bible can be held to have numerous different meanings: there are connections between the ingenuity of John Donne and Lancelot Andrewes, who find multiple significances in biblical words and images, and the dazzling intellectual displays of the metaphysicals. Interpretation could also have a political edge and motivation: Christopher Hill's book on the seventeenth-century Bible (see below) shows the various uses of biblical interpretations by the factions of that age.

See also *Contexts*: Catholicism, English Reformation, Protestant Theology; *Texts*: Prose Style

Further Reading

David Daniell, *The Bible in English* (New Haven and London: Yale UP, 2003).

Gerald Hammond, *The Making of the English Bible* (Manchester: Carcanet, 1982).

Christopher Hill, *The English Bible and the Seventeenth-Century Revolution* (London: Allen Lane, 1993).

Alister McGrath, *In the Beginning: The Story of the King James Bible* (London: Hodder & Stoughton, 2001).

Adam Nicolson, *Power and Glory* (London: Harper Collins, 2003).

Conceit

The word 'conceit' comes from Italian *concetto* and means a concept or image (literally, something conceived by the mind). In criticism, the term refers to a comparison striking for its ingenuity. A conceit is a metaphor or simile which seems surprising and far-fetched, bringing together two unlike things to bring out a thought, and extending the initial idea over several lines. An example is 'A Fly that Flew into my Mistress her Eye' by Thomas Carew (1595–1640), in which the poet fancifully compares a fly to a rival for his mistress's attention:

> She did from hand to bosom skip,
> And from her breath, and cheek, and lip
> Suck'd all the incense and the spice,
> And grew a bird of paradise.
>
> (lines 13–16)

The initial conceit of fly-lover is carried right through the brief 24-line poem. The reader is invited to admire and enjoy the inventiveness which drives the writing and the curious imagery that results. Conceits such as these are ubiquitous in Renaissance poetry and are part of a taste for marrying the abstract and concrete in colourful ways. There are family resemblances between the Renaissance conceit and the emblem, in which concrete images give form to abstract concepts; extended similes also come close to allegory, in which the image corresponding to an idea is developed as a narrative. Conceits themselves fall into identifiable styles, two important ones being the Petrarchan and the metaphysical.

The Italian poet Francesco Petrarca (1307–1374) exerted a huge influence on Renaissance literature through his poetic collections *Canzoniere* and *Trionfi* and his Latin writings: Petrarchism refers to the vogue across Europe for his choice and treatment of subject matter. Petrarch's love poems develop medieval ideas of courtly love, emphasising the intense emotions and refined sensibility of the lover. They are addressed to the unattainable Laura and contrast the distress of the lover with his cold and aloof beloved. Petrarchan conceits typically depict the lover's condition as an irrational mixture of hope and despair, delight and pain, as in these lines from a sonnet in Sir Philip Sidney's sequence *Astrophil and Stella* (printed 1591). Here, it is the initial paradoxical pain – pleasure idea, rather than a particular image, which is the conceit:

> On Cupid's bow how are my heart-strings bent,
> That see my wrack, and yet embrace the same!
> When most I glory, then I feel most shame:
> I willing run, yet while I run, repent.
>
> (no. 19)

Petrarchan suffering lovers, cold mistresses and states of sharply contrasting feeling can be found in the lyrics of many of the leading Tudor poets, notably Wyatt, Surrey, Sidney, Spenser and Shakespeare. These thoughts and images inevitably became hackneyed, however. Shakespeare uses them effectively but with knowing irony in *Venus and Adonis* (1593) and memorably parodies them in sonnet 130: 'My mistress' eyes are nothing like the sun; / Coral is far more red than her lips' red'.

Metaphysical conceits deliberately turn against Petrarchism and are employed for many subjects besides love. Rather than the travails of the lover, it is the wit of the poet which is on display. The poet draws on fields as diverse as philosophy, theology, science, myth, history and everyday experience to find arresting comparisons in which, in the words of Samuel Johnson (1709–1784), 'the most heterogeneous ideas are yoked by violence together' ('Life of Cowley', *Lives of the Poets* (1779)). John

Donne (1572–1631), who is particularly identified with this style, finds a surprising image for poetic creation:

> See, Sir, how as the sun's hot masculine flame
> Begets strange creatures on Nile's dirty slime,
> In me your fatherly yet lusty rhyme
> (For these songs are their fruits) have wrought the same.
>
> ('To E. of D.')

The exotic image is arresting, but it is also precisely apt for what the poet means to convey: it combines the tropes of admiration and self-deprecation in a novel way. George Herbert (1593–1633) surprises in an opposite way with his homely picture of God as a recognisable workman: 'When God at first made man, / Having a glass of blessings standing by...' ('The Pulley'). Where Donne finds a surprising image for the stock theme of inspiration, Herbert rescues the worn idea of 'pouring out' goodness by realising it in a literal, concrete fashion. In both cases the conceit is an instrument for refreshing the language of verse. Herbert was also concerned with the tension between the contrivances of poetry and the plain truths of scripture, and explores the idea that a poem can have value through its message, without the need for ornament: 'Who says that fictions only and false hair / Become a verse? Is there in truth no beauty?' ('Jordan (I)'; see also 'Jordan (II)'). There is an irony in that these poems, which speak against elaborate conceits, inevitably use the 'fictions and false hair' of metaphoric language; but they do express a felt tension between 'plain, unvarnished truth' as exemplified in the simple language of the testaments, and the dazzling world of Renaissance rhetoric. Very much on the dazzling side of this divide is the poetry of the Catholic poet Richard Crashaw (1612/13–1649), in which torrents of comparisons express the ecstasy of meditation and prayer:

> Hail, sister springs!
> Parents of silver-forded rills!
> Ever bubbling things!
> Thawing crystals! snowy hills,
> Still spending, never spent! I mean
> Thy fair eyes, sweet Magdalen!
>
> ('The Weeper')

Not all Renaissance conceits are novel, and contemporary readers did not necessarily share Johnson's view that the vehicle and tenor (the two parts of a metaphor) were heterogeneous. Many extended similes and analogies draw on the 'topics' of tradition to express some common ideas: life is a journey; life is a theatre; the state is a body; the body is a landscape or castle and so forth. Such stock ideas (*topoi*) reach back into medieval literature and sermons and are drawn on by Renaissance writers. To a readership more familiar than we are with the comparisons used in sermons and biblical commentaries, the strategies of Donne, Herbert and Crashaw may have seemed less surprising. The conceit would also have been a more familiar use of language to an audience used to reading epics, with their extended epic similes, in which a situation or action is described as analogous to another in passages which point out a complex series of correspondences. Is an image a passing metaphor, or extended? Would it have seemed novel or commonplace to contemporary readers? What primary and secondary meanings does it suggest? What emotional colour does it cast on its subject? These are some of the questions we can usefully ask when reading the conceits of Renaissance literature.

See also   *Contexts*: Chain of Being; *Texts*: Decorum, Logic, Lyric, Metaphysical Poetry; *Criticism*: Language Criticism

Further Reading

K. K. Ruthven, *The Conceit* (London: Methuen, 1969).
Rosemond Tuve, *Elizabethan and Metaphysical Imagery: Renaissance Poetic and Twentieth-Century Critics* (Chicago: University of Chicago Press, 1947).

Decorum

The principle of decorum derived from classical rhetoric, which took as the basic model for communication the situation of a speaker addressing an audience. It is essentially the doctrine of suitability: a speaker must choose a subject suited to the occasion and audience, and then employ language which is suited to the content. Thus, appropriate content for a funeral oration would be praise of the achievements and qualities of the deceased; and the language suitable for such content would in most cases be clear and formal, though not without anecdotal humour. Criticism of the departed or obscene jokes would be regarded as a breach of decorum, a failure of eloquence (what we might call poor taste). From real-life situations such as funerals, this principle can be applied to literary composition: just like orators, poets and fictional characters are expected to talk of appropriate subjects in an appropriate way. This is straightforward in theory, but in practice approaching a text with this criterion in mind can create a challenge for the modern reader. In *Henry V*, for example, the young king makes a speech before the besieged town of Harfleur in which he warns the inhabitants that his men will rape their women and commit other atrocities (3.3). We might be inclined to see this disturbing rhetoric as some sign of Henry's inner aggression, or moral confusion. From the point of view of rhetorical decorum, though, what counts is whether content and language suit the occasion: here, a general needs to rouse his troops and scare his enemies into submission. On both these counts, Henry succeeds. It is the occasion of the speech, not the character of the speaker, which generates the rhetoric. Arguably, public oratory like this tells us nothing about Henry's character at all, only that he is trained in rhetoric and an effective general.

Decorum is grounded in classical rhetoric, and in rhetoric there is an important distinction between the matter or content of a text (Latin *res*) and the verbal form with which that content is treated (*verba*, *lexis*). Logically, content had precedence. A speaker or writer must first think about the purpose of a speech, the audience to whom it is addressed and the effects desired – whether the audience is to be persuaded, moved, outraged, shamed, frightened, or flattered. This all makes up the process of *inventio*, or discovery of the subject matter. This is then followed by consideration of language. Positive virtues of language, as prescribed by Aristotle and others, include grammatical correctness and, most importantly, clarity. Aristotle, Cicero and others emphasise that a speech should be clear and accessible, avoiding ambiguity and sticking to familiar language wherever possible. English rhetoricians similarly praise plainness of style. Again, this challenges the modern reader, schooled in critical praise of ambiguity and accustomed to difficulty to the point of obscurity in experimental modernist writing (and some literary criticism). Renaissance writers tended to aim for clarity of expression: imagery, metrical variation and other devices might intensify the effects but should not cloud the idea. It is rare to find a writer who seems to aim at ambiguity: George Chapman (1559–1634), who seems to have regarded the vocation of the poet as a vehicle for prophetic mysteries, might be an example (see, for example, his poem 'The Iliads of Homer, Prince of Poets', dedicated to James I's son Prince Henry (1611)). But in general, expressing a point clearly is a prime aim of Renaissance texts. Decorum can be seen as an extension of this idea: by using language suited to the purpose of the speech, a speaker can ensure that his point is clearly communicated. Hence, as Aristotle teaches, a solemn subject ought to be treated with solemn language, and a speaker aiming to induce a sense of outrage in his listeners should use suitably angry language. The Roman poet Horace (65–8 BC) develops this idea further in his *Ars Poetica* (*The Art of Poetry*). For a textual work of art to have unity, Horace writes, there must be consistency in the expression; thus the subject must be treated with appropriate diction, metre, form and tone – and in accordance with the age, class, temperament, moral and emotional state of the speaker. The same idea is echoed once again by Quintilian (35–100) in his *Institutes* (I.v.i): the words and presentation (such as gestures and intonation) of the speaker must suit the subject, the occasion and the audience.

The concept of decorum was enthusiastically adopted by Renaissance rhetoricians. In *The Arte of Rhetorique* (1553), Thomas Wilson (1524–1581) calls it 'aptness': 'apt words... properly agree unto that thing which they signify, and plainly express the anture of the same'. Elizabeth I's tutor Roger Ascham (1515–1568) in *The Scholemaster* (1571) calls it 'propriety': it applies 'in choice of words, in framing of sentences, in handling of arguments, and use of right form, figure, and number, proper and fit for every matter'. Puttenham (*d.*1590) devotes two chapters to decorum in *The Arte of English Poesie* (1589), calling it variously conformity, proportion, convenience, decency and seemliness – terms which suggest how literary values shade into moral ones. Perhaps with the same suggestion that the study of decorum trains not only eloquence but also wisdom and character, Milton's ideal system of education includes instruction on 'what decorum is, which is the grand master-piece to observe' (*Of Education*, 1644). Against this general agreement among Renaissance critics about the importance of decorum, writers are naturally evaluated according to their use of it: in his commentaries on Spenser's *Shepheardes Calendar* (1579), EK praises the poet for his 'due observing of decorum everywhere, in personages, in seasons, in matters, in speech'. English drama, with its continuance of medieval vernacular tragicomic mixtures, presents a problem for the rhetoricians. Gascoigne's view that 'to intermingle merry jests in a serious matter is an indecorum' (*A Primer of English Poetry*, 1575) is echoed by Sidney's criticism of English writers for 'mingling comedy and tragedy' (*Apologie*) and by later seventeenth-century criticism of Shakespeare for introducing clowns into tragedy.

The concept of decorum is certainly familiar to us: we can easily imagine what would sound inappropriate at a wedding, funeral or some other occasion – and indeed much contemporary comedy exploits the embarrassment that can occur when such 'indecorum' occurs. Yet in studying literature, the notion is perhaps not so prominent. Traditionally, exam questions on a text like Henry V will focus on theme and character: yet what does this play really tell us about the character of Henry V? He speaks disdainfully to messengers from the enemy, angrily to traitors, in prose to ordinary soldiers, rousingly just before a battle and so on. Even in a private prayer to God to forgive his father's usurpation of the throne, he is speaking in terms which are appropriate to a penitent sinner. On each occasion, the speech is suited to the occasion. His utterances do not necessarily stem from a consistent inner self, as they might in a character in a nineteenth-century novel. Nor do they necessarily add up to a systematic investigation of kingship or any other supposed theme. Yet while in this respect Shakespeare can be interpreted as writing in conformity to the rhetorical principle of eloquence, in other respects he seems deliberately to flout it – in *King Lear*, for example, there is not only a mixture of clown and King in the same scene, but numerous trans- ference of modes of speech, such as the nobleman Edgar speaking like a beggar. The doctrine of eloquence can also lead to generic stereo- types, with all old men being wise and serious, all daughters modest and beautiful and so forth. A play like *King Lear* seems deliberately to challenge this. In Goneril and Regan's false protestations of love we see how eloquence can be at once decorous and deceitful, while Cordelia's silence might suggest that a rhetorical universe leaves no space for the simple utterance of truth.

See also *Contexts*: Chain of Being, Court; *Texts*: Genre, Imitation, Lyric, Metaphysical Poetry, Mimesis; *Criticism*: Language Criticism

Further Reading

Brian, Vickers, *English Renaissance Literary Criticism* (Oxford: OUP, 1999), Introduction, 1–56 (esp. 'Criteria of Correctness').

Derek Attridge, *Peculiar Language: Literature as Difference from the Renaissance to James Joyce* (London: Routledge, 2004), ch. 2 'Nature, Art, and the Supplement in Renais- sance Literary Theory: Puttenham's Poetics of Decorum', 17–45.

Rosamond Tuve, *Elizabethan and Metaphysical Imagery* (Chicago: University of Chicago Press, 1947), ch. 9, 'The Criterion of Decorum', 192–247.

Epic

An epic is a long narrative poem, describing historical or legendary episodes which are central to a culture's identity. Typically, an epic will feature a central hero or group of heroes who represent the community or culture; the subject matter will involve heroic actions such as war, conquest or a quest, and common motifs including boasts, combats and fabulous adventures. Stylistically, epic has some characteristic devices: long, elaborate narrative; episodic structure, with dramatic set-piece scenes; elevated language to suit the high matter; invocations to the gods or muses; extended or 'epic' similes; long lists or 'catalogues'; and an abrupt beginning *in medias res* – 'into the middle of the story'.

In the West, Homer (8th / 7th c. BC) is the father of epic poetry, though his *Iliad* and *Odyssey* were only slowly discovered in the sixteenth century, since Greek was less understood than Latin, and the martial world of the *Iliad* was perhaps alien to the Renaissance ethos of courtliness. Homer was translated into English by Chapman (published 1598–1616) but the most influential writer of classical epic for the Western Renaissance was

Virgil (70–19 BC), who had himself transformed the model of Homer into the *Aeneid*, providing a foundational epic for Augustan Rome. The *Aeneid* was translated by Gavin Douglas in 1513 (printed 1553), and the second and fourth books were translated by Surrey (published 1554 and 1557). Virgil was also read in Latin intensively in the schools.

Like many other aspects of the Renaissance, the revival of epic came to England through Italy. In the fourteenth century, Italian poets adopted Virgil as a mentor in different ways. Petrarch (1304–1374) attempted to revive the Roman historical epic in *Africa* (begun 1338), describing the Punic wars in Latin hexameters. Other poets employed Italian vernacular. Dante's *Divine Comedy* (1308–1321) integrates classical and Christian traditions by having Virgil guide the poet through Inferno and Purgatory. Boccaccio's *Teseida* (1339–c.1341) makes changes to the Virgilian model which were to influence later English epic. Adopting the classical structure of 12 books from the Latin author Statius (whose *Thebaid* is the basic source), Boccaccio (1313–1375) uses epic structure to tell a medieval romance story about winning a lady: Geoffrey Chaucer (c.1343–1400) imitates this in turn in *The Knight's Tale*. Later Italian writers continued to mix themes of love and war, drawing on the Arthurian verse of the twelfth century, the *chansons de geste*: Boiardo's *Orlando Innamorata*, for example, combines stories of war and the quest for love, with magical and marvellous elements. Another important development initiated by Boccaccio is the use of stanzaic verse forms in epic: his *ottava rima* form was taken up by Boiardo (1434–1494), Ariosto (1474–1533) and Tasso (1544–1595) and the Portuguese Camoëns (1525–1580).

Together with Italian models, the English also had the benefit of continental theorists. For critics such as J. C. Scaliger (*Poetices libri septem*, 1561), the epic is the highest form of poetry since it shows human nature at its most heroically developed, depicts the noblest actions and gives eloquent voice to the finest thoughts and sentiments. Reading epic constitutes a moral education. As Sir John Harington (1561–1612) puts it: 'heroical poesy, that with her sweet stateliness doth erect the mind and lift it up to the consideration of the highest matters: and allureth them, that of themselves would otherwise loath them, to take and swallow and digest the wholesome precepts of philosophy, and many times even of the true divinity' ('A Brief Apology for Poetry', prefaced to his translation of Ariosto, *Orlando Furioso*, 1591). An important concept at work here is that of instruction through delight (though Harington's rendering of the racy delights of Ariosto caused him to be banished from the court).

These strands come together in the great epic of Elizabethan literature, Spenser's *The Faerie Queene* (published in three books in 1590, and in six books in 1596). In a letter to Sir Walter Raleigh in 1596, Spenser elaborates his scheme, which is distinctly moral in intent. Each book deals with a virtue, represented by a knight who does battle with that virtue's enemies: thus Book One is concerned with the battle of Holiness against Sin, which is also implicitly the triumph of Protestantism over Rome. Personal and public spheres are joined, making the poem a national epic. The virtues celebrated are generally taken as a glorification of Queen Elizabeth, who is figured as Gloriana, though the poem might also be read ironically, as holding up an ideal from which the Elizabethan court plainly fell short. Like Italian Renaissance epics, *The Faerie Queene* incorporates love stories and marvels, and uses stanzaic form: English medieval romance, as well as Italian models, provided models in these respects. Romance and epic modes can be seen in tension in Spenser's epic: romance digression and interwoven plot strands counter any sense of forward thrust, while musical verse and rich sensuous imagery arguably provide an aesthetic pleasure which detracts from the moral lessons. Throughout the poem, Spenser uses the medieval device of allegory, whereby each detail can have one or more symbolic meanings beyond the literal sense of the story: this allows him to explore historical, philosophical and political themes through the vehicle of the various narratives.

Next to Spenser, the greatest poet in the Renaissance period to use the epic form is John Milton. His *Paradise Lost* (published in 10 books in 1667, and in 12 in 1674) undertakes to 'justify the ways of God to men' (I.26), that is to explain the relation between man and God through his treatment of the Fall: Adam and Eve's temptation by Satan and subsequent expulsion from the garden of Eden. The work has a complex and self-conscious relation to the epic tradition: it draws upon ancient and Renaissance models, but also intends to surpass them as it undertakes 'things unattempted yet in prose or rhyme' (I.16). Milton was familiar with Italian Renaissance work but sought to transcend the frivolous world of romance marvels. He follows classical writers such as Hesiod, Lucretius and Virgil in seeing instruction in philosophy and theology as central to the epic: the poem is deliberately difficult, using complex syntax, elaborate language and a dense web of references. This is part of the training of the mind of the reader, and an expression of the labours of the writer. Milton also retains typical classical features such as digression, invocation and mythic allusions, while taking the epic simile to new lengths. Yet at the same time, *Paradise Lost* deals with a clash between Christian and classical models of behaviour: it is Satan who epitomises the ancient values of martial courage, imperial ambition and stoical defiance, while the Son of God shows the Christian values of patience and martyrdom. The epic form synthesises different currents and traditions and can be read as an encapsulation of many of the tensions and dialogues which animate Renaissance cultural artefacts: the competing virtues of the active and contemplative life, the finally unresolvable differences between classical and Christian notions of heroism and a narrative which deals with triumphant fulfilment – of Gloriana's court, or God's will for man – in a way which dramatises struggle and tragedy.

See also   *Contexts*: Golden Age, Humanism, The Self; *Texts*: Decorum, Genre, History, Imitation, Metre, Rhetoric

Further Reading

Kenneth Borris, *Allegory and Epic in English Renaissance Literature: Heroic Form in Sidney, Spenser and Milton* (Cambridge: CUP, 2000).
Colin Burrow, *Epic Romance: Homer to Milton* (Oxford: OUP, 1993).
Robin Sowerby, *The Classical Legacy in Renaissance Poetry* (London: Longman, 1994), ch. 1, 7–57.

Genre

A literary genre is a type of writing, with distinct characteristics of form (length, arrangement and style) and content (argument, function and subject matter). A writer working in a specific genre can exploit the codes and conventions of that kind of writing, either satisfying the audience's expectations or unsettling them by subverting the 'rules of the game'. Milton's *Paradise Lost* (1667) responds creatively to the models of Homer's *Iliad*, Virgil's *Aeneid* and Italian Renaissance epic, employing the motifs, structure and narrative and stylistic devices of the epic genre for its own ends. Educated readers would be expected to pick up these echoes and connections and appreciate what the poet was doing with them.

Generic classification is constantly changing, and different ideas of generic types may coexist at any one period. There is also a gap between theory and practice: by the time critics have arrived at a scheme of classification, literature itself will have moved on to new forms. Both of these points apply to the Renaissance period: several generic schemes were in circulation, and the range of texts does not fit neatly into the tidy categories advanced by theorists. Two ideas are particularly important, though: one is that literature is closest to the demonstrative branch of rhetoric, concerned with praise or blame; and second, that literary writings fall into three main genres depending on who is speaking. These three types are Lyric (in which the poet speaks in his own voice), Dramatic (comedies and tragedies, where characters speak), and Epic (where there is a mixture of the other two, combining direct narration by the author and dramatic speech by characters). This theory, which draws on Plato and Aristotle, is advanced by the Italian Sebastiano Minturno (first in Latin, in *De Poeta* (1559); and subsequently in Italian, *L'Arte Poetica* (1564)), and this formulation was rapidly disseminated across Europe. Minturno's book was very influential in the Renaissance – we find the same notions taken up in English books on rhetoric – and the doctrine of the three genres was widely known, though it was not completely established as the dominant view until the later seventeenth century.

Beneath the overarching division into three genres or 'kinds' (to use the Renaissance term), we find subgenres, species within a genre: when the editors of the First Folio (1623) divided Shakespeare's plays into Comedies, Tragedies and Histories, for example, they were grouping Drama into three separate sub-species. Under the heading of Lyric, we find poems celebrating state occasions, elegies, eclogues, poetic epistles and other kinds of writing. Epic similarly has subgenres such as *epyllion* (a short mythological narrative) and biblical epic. All such kinds have their own histories and conventions, generating expectations in the reader. There may be still further classification according to traditional subject matter: within the love lyric we find the *aubade* (a dawn song), the *basium* (a poem on a kiss) and many others. Lyrical poetry might yield the meditative poetic epistle and the poem of seduction – types so different that they can then be viewed as genres in their own right. Sometimes classification according to form – the ordering and structure of a work – overlaps with generic definition: a sonnet is a formal structure, but during the fashion for sonnet sequences sonnets were expected to treat of certain subject matter. In practice, the various possible combinations of form, tone, purpose and subject make for an infinite variety of possible 'types'.

Renaissance critics also grouped literary kinds in a hierarchy: like nature and society, literature was conceived as having its own ordered scale, from the noblest to the meanest. On this scale, epic and tragedy are the highest kinds, dealing with the highest moral matters in the grand style, and at some length. Pastoral, comedy (dealing with 'mean' subjects such as clowns) and the epigram (a very short form) were lower down the scale. According to the theory of decorum, each of these places on the hierarchy had its own appropriate style – high style for the court, middle or low style for baser matters. Genre (Kind), Form (stanzaic and metrical structure and rhyme scheme) and Style are all in theory distinct from poetic *modes*. A mode is a kind of writing which may occupy part of a work but does not define it. Satire, allegory and parody can all be called modes, and one work may involve several modes. For example, *The Shepheardes Calendar* (1579) is Lyric (Genre), Pastoral (Subgenre) and internally divides into its own specified 'kinds' of recreative, moral and plaintive, each of which can involve modes such as satire and panegyric (praise).

Renaissance literature presents a vast variety of species, impossible to classify according to any one scheme. A common practice is the deliberate mixture of kinds and styles: writers drew on, and mixed, the forms of expression available to them. While a humanist critic like Sidney believed that genres should be kept pure, writers like Shakespeare were clearly animated by the possibilities of interbreeding; thus in Shakespearean drama we find comedy mixed with tragedy from an early stage: the announcement of a death upsetting the happy resolution at the end of *Love's Labour's Lost*; the juxtaposition of King, clown and beggar in the storm scene in *King Lear* and the developed parallelisms between (high) court and (low) tavern scenes in the *Henry IV* plays. The modern concept of Shakespeare's 'problem plays' (such as *Measure for Measure* and *All's Well that Ends Well*, which do not seem to resolve on either tragic or comic lines) indicates that the effects of such mixtures can be disconcerting even today. While Shakespeare's brilliance makes him an exceptional case, the generic variety of his plays nonetheless points us to something important in the culture, namely the vitality of the native tradition. His audience, who did not generally spend hours in studies furnished with humanist texts, were familiar with abrupt shifts between high and low, or comic and tragic, in romances and mystery plays. English Renaissance writers made use of these native forms together with the revived classical genres, and the resulting work often offends against prescriptions based purely on classical models. A supreme example of such generic mixing is Spenser's *The Faerie Queene* (I–III, 1590; second part 1596): this takes the form of a vast Arthurian romance, is divided like an epic into separate books and encompasses numerous genres and modes from pastoral to satire to descriptive lyric. It invites us to read it as an encyclopaedia of genres rather than as a single type of work.

A different kind of generic mixture is stylistic or rhetorical: Donne, for example, typically writes love poetry (demanding the rhetoric of praise) in a witty argumentative style (drawing on deliberative rhetoric, dealing with persuasion). The *suasio*, an act of clever persuasion, is ubiquitous in Renaissance poetry, and can mix with other modes: in Donne's 'The Flea', we hear a sharply witty voice, while in 'A Valediction: Of Weeping' the logical mind appears to be energised by deep feeling. We could say in general of Renaissance writers that they used whatever material was available, generically and stylistically, to do the job in hand, without being restricted to the box of a particular Kind. The same kind of English genius can be seen in the buildings of the period: Elizabethan country-houses comfortably mix elements of Italian and Flemish origin with those of traditional vernacular architecture. Against this, some writers and other artists consciously tried to follow classical models. A famous example is Ben Jonson (1572?–1637), who consciously adopted the classical notion of the poet's vocation and sedulously modelled his work on the style and forms of ancient literature. Later in the seventeenth century this classicising-humanist approach was to become the school of neoclassicism, with its prescriptions for correct writing according to the supposed precepts of Aristotle and other sages.

Shakespeare famously parodies generic categories through the mouth of Polonius: 'the best actors in the world, either for tragedy, comedy, history, pastoral, pastorical-comedy, historical-pastoral, tragical-historical, tragical-comical-historical-pastoral, scene individable or poem unlimited' (*Hamlet*, 2.2). Such irreverence should not be taken as an invitation to dismiss the subject, however, for Shakespeare, like other Renaissance writers, was deeply familiar with generic conventions, and we will appreciate their work much better if we ask questions raised by this topic: What is the form of a text, and how does this relate to its subject matter? What is its function? What other works of this kind can we relate it to? Are the conventions of the genre being conformed to, or departed from, and what are the implications of this for our interpretation?

A useful exercise in becoming familiar with Renaissance kinds is to read several of the poems by Robert Herrick (1591–1674), collected in *Hesperides* (1648). Here, the different kinds of lyric are compressed into short, epigrammatic texts. Often, the titles make the kind of poem clear: 'Upon Julia's Voice' (praise of the beloved), 'To the King . . . ' (praise of a public figure), 'Dean-Bourn, a Rude river in Devon . . . ' (description of place) and so forth. With longer texts, it can be fruitful to ask not what genre they belong to, but what genres and modes are being employed: Milton's *Lycidas* (1645) is an elegy in praise of the departed Henry King: through a web of allusions and other devices Milton aligns his poem with Greek and Latin pastoral elegy, and in so doing announces his own grand poetic ambitions. The elegiac genre at the same time leaves room for the satirical mode as the poem criticises the corrupted clergy of the time. Through his deployment of generic convention, Milton positions himself as both private friend expressing his grief and authoritative public voice denouncing the vices of the age. His adoption of classical elegy for this purpose also gives an air of venerability to his argument, as the weight of classical tradition is aligned to protestant Puritanism. Milton has appropriated the classical Italian form of elegy to use against the Italian Roman Church and what he sees as Romish tendencies within the Anglican establishment. The choice and deployment of genre is thus not merely an aesthetic matter, but can be a formative part of the personal and political strategies working through a text. Such strategies are particularly interesting in the work of women writers, who are constrained to work through the genres of a male literary tradition to articulate female experiences. 'To her unconstant Lover' by Isabella Whitney (fl. 1567–1573), for example, adopts the familiar type of the love complaint, with its devices of classical allusion and clever argument; yet it uses them to voice the distinctively female predicament of a woman discovering her lover was married. Against the acrobatic verbal anguish of the male-authored love sonnets, the speaker of Whitney's poem comes over as movingly wry and dignified:

> You know I always wisht you wel
> so wyll I during lyfe:
> But sith you shall a husband be
> God send you a good wyf.
>
> (5-8)

See also   *Contexts*: Humanism, Platonism; *Texts*: Epic, Lyric, Pastoral, Non-fictional Prose

Further Reading

Introductory

'Index of Genres', Appendix 1 to David Norbrook and H. R. Woudhuysen, eds, *The Penguin Book of Renaissance Verse* (London: Allen Lane, 1992), 853–856.

Longer Works

Rosalie Colie, *The Resources of Kind: Genre Theory in the Renaissance*, ed. Barbara K. Lewalski (Berkeley: University of California Press, 1973).

Alastair Fowler, *A History of English Literature: Forms and Kinds from the Middle Ages to the Present* (Oxford: Blackwell, 1987).

Alastair Fowler, *Kinds of Literature: An Introduction to the Theory of Genres and Modes* (Oxford: Clarendon, 1982).

John Frow, *Genre*, The New Critical Idiom (London: Routledge, 2006).

History and the Nation

History is a frequent subject of Renaissance writing. Besides the well-known examples of Shakespeare's history plays there are many other texts which draw on the histories of England and the ancient world for their subject matter. Recent histories of Italy and France exerted a similar fascination on Renaissance writers and their audience, while the popular imagination was shaped by biblical history and the countless stories of miracles, saints and martyrs. The various kinds of historical writing we find in the Renaissance were not simply source material for literary writers, however. They themselves may be regarded as literature: rather than a dispassionate record of events, they tend to present a meaningful narrative, using literary techniques to shape and delineate their material. This approach gradually shifted in the sixteenth and seventeenth centuries into the practice of history as an empirical discipline, such as we know it today; but for our period there was generally no clear distinction between history and story. History was a story to be read, like others, for its message and moral content: it was a deliberately artful composition, and its lessons had a prescriptive intent. The historical writing of the period is thus of interest to the student of literature for several reasons: it provides sources for well-known canonical writings; historical texts are also literary works, inviting and rewarding literary analysis; and in their treatment and interpretation of their subject matter they suggest important currents of thought which run through the culture: the present is shaped by the images it makes of the past.

One distinct category is the history of Britain. Much of this must have existed in oral form, as folk memory, often local and anecdotal. Such matters were given written form in the many town chronicles of the period. A different kind of record was required by the Tudors, though: they needed to legitimise their dubious claim to the throne, and at the same time construct the idea of a single nation, centralised on and embodied by the monarchy. Hence Tudor historical writing is concerned with constructing a nation and with it a narrative presenting the Tudor dynasty as the inevitable holders of power. The *Anglica Historica* by the Italian scholar Polydore Vergil (*c*.1470–1555) was undertaken with this propagandist intent. This treats the history of England by reign, equating the history of the land with that of the ruling dynasties; historical figures are agents in a moral drama, idealised or demonised; and the history of the land is seen as passing through the internecine struggles of the Wars of the Roses to the salvation offered by the Tudors. At the same time, Virgil was also concerned with some degree of objective assessment, dismissing the legends of Arthur and the myth of the Trojan foundation of Britain as unhistorical. His work was completed in 1513, but not published for some 30 years. Thomas More's *History of Richard III* (*c*.1513) further sanctions Tudor rule in its portrayal of Richard as a demon, while his use of literary devices such as rhetorical oratory and irony also makes his account a piece of self-conscious artistry. The Tudor writing enterprise was further continued by Edward Hall (*The Union of the two Noble and Ilustre Families of Lancaster and York*, 1548), Richard Grafton (whose *Chronicle at Large* of 1568 was a continuation of Hall) and John Stow (*Summary of English Chronicles*, 1565). Best known to modern students of literature is *The Chronicles of England, Scotland and Ireland* (1577), a composite work though usually known as 'Holinshed'.

The Tudor impetus for historical writing helped to stimulate ideas of national and regional identity: notions of England and Britain were also given form in cartography, as in Saxton's *Atlas* of the counties of Britain of 1579. A closely related genre is chorography, which combines the study of landscape and geography with history. The antiquarian William

Camden (1551–1623) set out 'to restore antiquity to Britaine, and Britaine to its antiquity' in *Britannia* (1586): this popular work went through seven editions by 1607 and was translated into English by Philemon Holland in 1610. Camden's fellow antiquarian John Stow (1525–1605) produced, among several other works, a *Survey of London* (1598), describing in great detail the architecture and life of Elizabethan London. Chronicles, cartographies and chorographies established a sense of England in time and space. They also contributed to a patriotic sentiment: Camden said he was motivated in his labours by 'the glory of my country', a sentiment not too dissimilar from John of Gaunt's famous 'this England' speech in Shakespeare's *Richard II* (2.1, 31–68). As antiquarians sifted material evidence of the distant past, the matter of ancient Britain became disputed territory. Polydore Vergil had dismissed the old stories of Arthur, but these were defended by the antiquarians John Leland and John Bale and by the Welsh. The old stories, and the ideas which went with them, lived on in popular belief and in poetry: Michael Drayton's *Poly-Olbion* (1612, 1622), which versifies Camden, includes 236 lines on ancient British history; and *The Faerie Queene* both uses and venerates the Arthurian legend (see Proem.2/III).

But how far were the English people self-conscious of an English or British identity? Tudor histories, and the plays which followed them, could impose to a degree an official version of Englishness and obscure the nation's past: crucially, it was Henry VIII's project to disconnect Englishness from a thousand years of history in which culture followed the religious authority of Rome. The cult of the Virgin Queen necessarily involved adverse description of Spain and other enemy nations; the Protestant refugees who filled London's labour market were seen as an economic threat and stimulated stereotypes of national difference. Yet the degree to which people identified themselves in some meaningful and positive way as English, with defining characteristics, is difficult to judge. Other identities were in play, both wider and narrower than nationality. Protestants could regard themselves as part of the community of true believers, and professionals might feel a deeper affiliation to their guild than to their country. Most of the population lived far from the intellectual circles around the London court, and might have had a far sharper sense of belonging to a village, town or region than to a nation. Extended families and households were a further source of identity. Then as now, notions of Englishness could be deliberately created for a political and propaganda purpose, and do not necessarily portray the complex, multi-layered senses of identity in play in the culture at large.

See also *Contexts*: City, English Reformation, Protestant Theology, Race, Travel and Colonialism; *Texts*: The Bible, Epic

Further Reading

Patrick Collinson, 'History' in: *A Companion to English Renaissance Literature and Culture*, ed. Michael Hattaway (Oxford: Blackwell, 2000), 58–70.

Edwin Jones, *The English Nation: The Great Myth* (Thrupp, Gloucestershire: Sutton, 1998).

F. J. Levy, *Tudor Historical Thought* (San Marino, CA: Huntington Library, 1967).

Claire McEachern, *The Poetics of English Nationhood, 1590–1612* (Cambridge: CUP, 1996).

Imitation

Imitatio is the use of a model as an aid to writing well, and is distinct from *mimesis*, the literary representation of an external reality. In schools, pupils were taught to copy the style and matter of the best authors as a means of learning to write good Latin. The imitation of Latin and Greek models was also seen by many theorists as a way of expanding the resources of the vernacular. Indeed, creative imitation of a revered authority was held to be a criterion of literary excellence: a writer was judged by the assurance and skill with which he made use of antique models. These are a rather different set of aesthetic criteria than our modern ones of originality and sincerity. Where we might praise an artist for departing from convention, a Renaissance reader would be more likely to appreciate the creative adoption of the form, content, style and generic patterns of ancient authorities. It is an interesting challenge for us to adjust to, and sympathise with, this pre-romantic mode of judging literary art.

In seeing imitation as a key aspect of the writer's craft, the writers and critics of the Renaissance looked back to the Romans. As the Roman empire expanded into Greece, they realised that the achievements of ancient Greek culture across all the arts were superior to their own and set about learning from them by attentive imitation. Virgil absorbed the lessons of Homer through writing the *Aeneid*, and Greek literature provided the model for many other kinds of writing, from comedy, lyric and pastoral to the prescriptions of rhetoric. This appropriation of models was endorsed by Roman theorists. Cicero (*De Oratore [On the Orator]*, 2.22.90 ff) comments briefly on the wisdom of choosing the best authors judiciously, though he also notes that some writers have a natural ability to express themselves without such imitation. Quintilian is more prescriptive. In his *Institutes of Oratory* (10.2), he states that 'although invention came first and is all-important, it is expedient to imitate whatever has been invented with success'. It should be remembered that 'invention' here does not have the modern sense, but is the classical rhetorical concept of *inventio*, meaning finding appropriate material. In the *inventio* stage of a composition, the writer is concerned with finding the right ingredients for the task in hand. These may be phrases, ideas or arguments drawn from wide reading and noted down and remembered (just as Hamlet notes down useful things in his 'tables'). Quintilian is saying that in the second, ordering stage, models should also be used. He specifies which Greek and Latin authors make the best models, and encourages the writer to identify particular excellences of a wide range of authors and transform those into a new context. *Imitatio* thus leads to *aemulatio*, or emulation, as the modern writer seeks to absorb the lessons of the masters into his own work. Seneca provides analogies for this process of absorption in *Epistulae Morales* [Moral Letters], no. 84: the writer is like a bee gathering pollen to turn into honey; and the writing process is similar to digestion, in that it takes in one material and makes it into something new. Thus, *imitatio* is conceived not as slavish copying but as a creative process of transformation. 'Longinus', the anonymous author of the first-century treatise *On the Sublime*, similarly recommends the 'imitation and emulation of the great prose writers of antiquity'. Longinus stresses the value of the model as a stimulus, inspiring the modern writer to new heights: the source text or texts provides both pattern and inducement to make something new. By inspiring a writer to emulate and transform his model, the process of imitation actually releases creative energies and leads to fresh and original work.

Renaissance writers largely endorse this Roman view of the creative process. In this, they also followed the medieval veneration of *auctoritee*, or authority, in the great books of the past. Thomas Wilson states in his *Arte of Rhetorique* (1560): 'before we use either to write or speak eloquently, we must dedicate our minds wholly to follow the most wise and learned men'. Roger Ascham in *The Scholemaster* (1570) similarly directs the student of Latin to use imitation, though he places a supreme value on Cicero: 'form...your speech and writing to that excellent perfectness which was only in Tully, or only in Tully's time'. This takes us into the so-called 'Ciceronian controversy': should a writer use Cicero above all, or regard him as one of several masters? Erasmus's *Ciceronianus* (1528) satirises the slavish reproduction of Ciceronian Latin, and Sidney in his *Apologie for Poetry* (pub. 1595) criticises the Ciceronians for excessive verbal ornament: 'they cast sugar and spice upon every dish that is served to the table'. A more common view was that the writer should draw on many sources for his own act of making: Erasmus's rhetorical treatise *De Copia* (On Plenty) is concerned with how multiple sources can be selected from and recombined in a composition. Gabriel Harvey (1545–1630) in his annotations on Quintilian clearly sees imitation as a form of competition: 'the better the author, the better the emulation required, and in addition the more diligent the emulation'. The modern practitioner should aim to be 'not similar, but equal, or even better' than his master. Harvey reports that Spenser's *Faerie Queene* was an *aemulatio* in this sense of Ariosto's *Orlando Furioso*. Ben Jonson provides a clear statement in English on the value and purpose of imitation in his notebook, *Timber: or Discoveries made upon men and matter* (1615–1635):

> The third requisite in our poet or maker is imitation, to be able to convert the substance or riches of another poet to his own use. To make choice of one excellent man above the rest, and so to follow him till he grow very he, or so like him as the copy may be mistaken for the principal. Not as a creature that swallows what it takes in crude, raw or indigested, but that feeds with an appetite, and hath a stomach to concoct, divide, and turn all into nourishment. Not to imitate servilely (as Horace saith) and catch at vices for virtue, but to draw forth out of the best and choicest flowers, with the bee, and turn all into honey: work it into one relish and savour, make our imitation sweet, observe how the best writers have imitated, and follow them: how Virgil and Statius have imitated Homer, how Horace, Archilochus; how Alcaeus, and the other lyrics; and so of the rest.

The Renaissance practice of creative imitation is evident across its literature. Writers draw constantly on the common body of topics handed down from classical literature. To these were added the newer stock of ideas, for example the imagery of Petrarchan love poetry. A great deal of Renaissance literature is in recognisable genres, each with its own built-in motifs and patterns, which writers could develop and sometimes turn in new directions. To the use of generic patterns we can add modelling on specific texts, giving rise to a body of writing (and a method of reading) that we today would call intertextual. One text not only echoes another but sets up a dialogue with it. Renaissance theorists were adept at this kind of comparative reading: Roger Ascham, for example, demonstrates how Cicero made creative use of a model speech of Demosthenes, emphasising some points and editing out others. He recommends the habit of eclecticism, for example by using passages from Plato to illustrate Aristotle. In the same spirit, More's *Utopia* (1516) draws on and reworks Plato and Lucian. A learned work like Burton's *Anatomy of Melancholy* (1621) is a gigantic and complex patchwork of quotations, and references to other authors similarly form part of the texture of the essays of Montaigne (1533–1592) and Bacon (1561–1626). When reading Renaissance works, we might usefully think that we are in a sense not reading one work but several, engaged in an internal dialogue.

This is a kind of effortful, self-conscious imitation which the reader is supposed to recognise. Jonson's writing is saturated with allusions to classical authors, to the point of repeating whole lines if they contain suitable matter: his Epigrams, modelled on Martial, might be called free translations. Jonson himself annotated his play *Sejanus* (1603) to show the range of reading from the classics it incorporates; EK's notes to Spenser's *Shepherd's Calendar* (1579) have the same function. The density of allusion and echo creates a particularly self-aware kind of writing and establishes a special kind of bond between writer and reader, not the least pleasure of which is the reader's satisfaction in noticing the sources of lines and ideas. There is also an interesting correlation between the intellectual self-consciousness evident in the allusive texture of a Rabelais or Montaigne or Burton and the developing mode of self-analysis in Renaissance literature. Both suggest a mind alive to, and delighting in, its own journeys.

This self-conscious, self-advertising mode of imitation may be contrasted with writing which has, as it were, silently absorbed a model and does not go out of its way to draw our attention to its own allusiveness. Shakespeare is an example of a writer who answers to Seneca's description of the bee transforming pollen to honey: Prospero's speech on his magical powers is based on a speech by a sorceress in Ovid, yet this source does not seem to be of the first importance (Prospero's speech occurs in 5.1, 34–57; it is closely based on Medea's incantation in Ovid, *Metamorphoses*, VII, 179–219). The famous adaptation of Plutarch in Enobarbus's 'barge speech' in *Antony and Cleopatra* (2.2, 195–210) equally does not depend for its effect on us recognising the immediate source. This sort of 'quiet' imitation corresponds to Castiglione's *sprezzatura*, a difficult operation made to seem effortless. It also avoids the dangers of affectation and over-ingenuity which attend on the virtuosic allusive style of learned writers like Jonson.

We have noted that Renaissance imitation challenges the modern value placed on originality (even if that value is largely a matter of advertisement rhetoric, concealing the deeply derivative nature of most cultural products). It is also an issue in defining the concept of the author. In a text like *Sejanus*, we might see the author less as the originator than the transformer of pre-existing material. Add to this the fact that the author was not recognised in the form of copyright and we can soon arrive at the notion that 'author' is too modern a notion for the Renaissance craftsman with words, who is constantly collaborating with others, whether living or dead. Yet there is evidence that writers of the period were indeed conscious of their own individual authorship: plagiarism is the object of attack in Donne's Second Satire, for example. For the reader today, a useful exercise is to study in depth a particular text against its source(s), which are often pointed out in glosses to editions. Once scholars have answered the question of what model is being used, the critic can ask how that model is being employed, and why, or with what effect. What kind of rebirth, or renaissance, are we faced with?

See also   *Contexts*: Golden Age, Humanism, Platonism, The Self; *Texts*: Decorum, Genre, Metre, Prose Style

Further Reading:

Jonathan Bate, *Shakespeare and Ovid* (Oxford: Clarendon, 1993).

Thomas M. Greene, *The Light in Troy: Imitation and Discovery in Renaissance Poetry* (New Haven: Yale UP, 1982).

Brian Vickers, *English Renaissance Literary Criticism* (Oxford: Clarendon, 1999), 'Originality and Imitation', 22–39.

Logic

'To be or not to be: that is the question'. Shakespeare's most famous line reminds us of the centrality of logic in Renaissance education: along with grammar and rhetoric, logic (also called dialectic) was one of the three arts of language studied in the *trivium* of the curriculum. To hone their skills as logicians and orators, schoolboys and students debated *quaestiones* through formal disputations. A *quaestio finita* would involve a single, specific decision: 'The question then Lord Hastings, standeth thus – / Whether our present five and twenty thousand / May hold up head without Northumberland' (*2 Henry IV*, 1.3.15–1.3.17). A *quaestio infinita* deals with more abstract and general matters. 'To be or not to be' is an example of this category. Renaissance literature is consequently full of debate, reasoning, persuasion, argument, justification and explanation – flights of logic in a register of tones. Many of the great prose works, like Hooker's *Laws of Ecclesiastical Polity*, are composed of argument (in Hooker's case, to convince readers of the wisdom of the 1559 Elizabethan Settlement). Milton describes *Paradise Lost* (1667) as a 'great argument' with a lofty aim: 'to justify the ways of God to men'. Here he uses 'argument' in the sense of both narrative and a case presented to the reader. Many of the great writers of the age exercise their art in meeting the lawyer's challenge of presenting a case, convincingly and memorably. Some, like Milton, finally rely on prophetic powers of insight, which go beyond logic to another plane of understanding.

In plays, characters debate with each other or in their own minds: Should Faustus summon up the devil? Should Macbeth kill Duncan? Soliloquies broadcast these internal conflicts, in which rationality may be swept aside by deeper forces: Macbeth stacks up reasons why he should not assassinate his King, only to admit that these are overriden by his ambition. Lyrical poems are very often apostrophes, addressed to a specific listener whom the speaker tries to convince. A popular situation is a lover trying to seduce a lady: examples are Donne's 'The Flea' and Marvell's 'To his Coy Mistress'. In a sonnet the speaker may respond to an imagined reader or ponder a matter alone: the endings of sonnets and other poems often have a forceful sense of closure as a conclusion to this process of ratiocination is reached. At the lighter end of the spectrum, logic is parodied and played with in the chopped and false logic of clowns and rustics like the gravediggers in *Hamlet*. Emotional expression is very often made through argument, not as an effusion of sentiment: a poet like Donne can convey a passion through the very act of tough, convoluted logical discussion.

Logic concerns itself with the form of arguments. A basic structure, as formulated by Aristotle, is the syllogism. In a syllogism, a proposition is made [P], and then supported by two *rationes* or reasons [R1, R2]; these reasons make up the major and minor premises and produce a conclusion [C] which restates the proposition. Juliet's mother uses a crisp syllogism to explain to her daughter that it is her duty to marry Paris.

> [P] Well, think of marriage now. [R1] Younger than you,
> Here in Verona, ladies of esteem
> Are made already mothers. [R2] By my count,
> I was your mother much upon these years
> That you are now a maid. [C] Thus then in brief:
> The valiant Paris seeks you for his love.
>
> (1.3.70–1.3.75)

The first sentence here is the proposition. The major premise is that many other ladies of Juliet's age have already married; the minor premise is that she, Juliet's mother, had married by this time. The last line has the effect of an implied conclusion: you should marry Paris.

For the sake of naturalness and drama, literary writings often use a relaxed version of the syllogism known as the enthymeme. An enthymeme is a syllogism with one or more of its parts missing: it may simply be a proposition followed by a single reason, or two reasons implying a proposition which is not actually stated. Hotspur moves from proposition to *rationes*, or proofs, when he insists that Mortimer is a faithful subject:

> Revolted Mortimer!
> [P] He never did fall off, my sovereign liege,
> But by the chance of war: [R] to prove that true
> Needs no more but one tongue for all those wounds,
> Those mouthed wounds, which valiantly he took...
>
> (*1 Henry IV*, 1.3. 92 ff.)

Hotspur then describes Mortimer's supposed fight with the Welsh rebel Glendower, 'When on the Severn's sedgy bank...'. This line, and the account that follows, meets the rhetorical criterion of *enargia*: this is the art of depicting a scene with immediacy and vividness. Logically, the single point is that Mortimer could never have been wounded voluntarily, and the speech ends with a restatement of the opening: 'Then let him not be slander'd with revolt' (whence the expression QED, standing for *quod erat demonstrandum* – 'that which had to be demonstrated' has been shown to be true). There are problems with this, however. Juliet's mother's speech is a syllogism in the Aristotelian sense, in that the premises are actually true (or could easily be proven). For Aristotle, the premises of an enthymeme are only probable: but Hotspur's premise, that Mortimer was terribly wounded, is not even likely. Mortimer is not there for others to see, and sceptical listeners might suspect that Hotspur is simply making the whole thing up. This suspicion would only be strengthened by his hyperbolic language, which breaks the principle of decorum for parlance with a monarch. King Henry simply responds by calling Hotspur a liar.

A very different tone is sounded by Katherine Phillips (1631–1664), in a poem marking Cromwell's defeat of Charles II at the battle of Worcester. Phillips reflects on the fall of great men and concludes that virtue rather than greatness is the more reasonable aspiration:

> Who would presume upon his Glorious Birth,
> Or quarrel for a spacious share of Earth,
> That sees such diadems become so cheap,
> And Heros tumble in a common heap?
> Oh give me Vertue then, which sums up all,
> And firmly stands when Crown and Scepters fall.
> (On the 3. of September, 1651)

This is not an original idea. Training in argument provided not only the basic forms of syllogism and enthymeme but a huge stock of commonplace thoughts which could be endlessly varied according to situation. When confronted by a familiar piety like this, our attention is drawn to the manner of delivery. Phillips's organisation of ideas into tidy couplets with end-stopped lines conveys a measured, reasonable voice which is part of the poem's persuasiveness. This language is moving in the direction of Augustan poise as practised by Dryden, who said, 'I am of opinion that they cannot be good poets who are not accustomed to argue well'.

There are other ways of arguing besides enthymemes, proofs and propositions. Citing authorities, as Bacon frequently does in his essays, lends weight to a point, as does the display of erudition in texts like the sermons of Lancelot Andrewes. Proverbs, commonplace *sententiae* or wise sayings, have a persuasive force. In prose from the 1590s on, when writers imitated the compressed wisdom of Seneca, arguments could depend entirely on the strength of lapidary, proverbial and epigrammatic statements:

> Vita Recta [Upright Life]
> Wisdom without honesty is mere craft and cozenage. And therefore the reputation of honesty must first be gotten, which cannot be but by living well. A good life is a main argument.
> (Ben Jonson, *Timber or Discoveries* (printed 1641)).

Argument can also be implicit, as in the branch of rhetoric called epideictic, concerned with praise or blame. A particular genre which affords examples of this is the country house poem: Amelia Lanyer's 'The Description of Cooke-ham' (1609–1610) praises Margaret Clifford, Countess of Cumberland, through celebration of the royal manor of Cookham and its environs. Ben Jonson's praise of Sidney's country estate, 'To Penshurst' (printed 1616), similarly implies the virtues of its owners – and the deficiencies of less responsible landowners – through a eulogistic description of house and estate.

See also *Contexts*: English Reformation, Humanism, Patronage; *Texts*: Conceit, Imitation, Non-fictional Prose

Further Reading
Edward P. J. Corbett and Robert J. Connors, *Classical Rhetoric for the Modern Student*, 4th edn (Oxford: OUP, 1999), 38–71 on logic as a form of persuasion.

Lyric

Traditionally, Lyric is one of the three genres of imaginative literature, alongside Drama and Epic. In Lyric, the poet (or poetic persona) speaks directly, rather than through other characters. The word 'lyric' is derived from the Greek for lyre: historically lyrical poetry is song, often accompanied by dance. Indeed, in the Renaissance many lyrics were still set to music, as lute songs or madrigals, and published in songbooks (and thus we still talk about the lyrics to songs today). But in this period the lyric was also advancing as an autonomous verbal artefact without musical accompaniment; the carefully wrought sound effects that we find in Renaissance lyric can be seen as deriving from its long relationship with song, imitating musical patterns on a verbal level. The idea that lyric poetry expresses a particularly intense subjective experience is a later

Romantic concept. In the Renaissance, a verse epistle on a philosophical matter or a laconic epigram is as much a lyric as a love sonnet. Below are some of the important subgenres of Lyric which we find in this period.

Eclogue

An eclogue is a debate among shepherds, in an idyllic setting, usually singing of love. In classical poetry, it is distinguished from the *georgic*, which realistically describes countryside tasks. See the section on 'Pastoral' for further discussion.

Elegy

Elegies express grief for the death of a loved one, combined with praise of their merits. In classical poetry, elegies are composed in a specific kind of metre called elegiacs, but in the Renaissance they take many different verse forms. A famous example of this kind of lyric is Milton's *Lycidas* (1645), published in a volume of elegies for the drowned Cambridge student Edward King. More simple and plain in expression are the moving elegies for deceased children: examples are Ben Jonson's 'On my First Sonne' ('Farewell, thou child of my right hand, and joy') and Katherine Phillips's two poems on her dead infant Hector ('Epitaph. On her son *H. P...*' and '*Orinda* upon little *Hector Philips*'). However, Renaissance elegy did not depend on the poet having a close personal knowledge of the deceased: Donne's two 'Anniversary' poems are long contemplative poems commemorating the death of Elizabeth Drury, whom he did not know; and it does not appear that Milton was as close to King in life as he was in verse. A death can thus be the occasion for a poem expounding ideas and extolling various kinds of excellence, often as a result of commission by a patron or the requirements of a public event. As poems about suffering, elegies can also describe the sufferings caused by love: Donne's *Elegies* are of this nature.

Epigram

In the classical world, epigrams were public inscriptions carved onto a monument. In poetry, epigrams are characterised by brevity and concision – short words and short sentences are favoured, tied up with simple rhyme schemes. Ancient models were the Roman satirical poets Lucilius (*c*.180–103 BC) and, in particular, Martial, author of over a thousand epigrams, published in 12 books (86–103 AD). Ben Jonson (1572–1637) collected 133 poems as Epigrams in his *Works* (1616), most of them praising the noble persons to whom they are addressed. Epigrammatic utterance was particularly in vogue in the late sixteenth century, when the terse Senecan style was in fashion: the aim is to compress a thought neatly, precisely and memorably. Another writer famous for his epigrams was Robert Herrick (1591–1674), whose poems can address great subjects in a small space, sometimes no longer than a couplet: 'Love is a circle that doth restless move / In the same sweet eternity of love' ('Love, what it is'). Epigrammatic expression is also a feature of many other poems – for example, the couplets concluding Shakespeare's sonnets and many so-called 'metaphysical' poems, giving those texts a strong sense of closure. The epigram is the verse equivalent to the prose aphorism. Close to the epigram is the *epitaph*, originally an inscription on a funeral monument and in Renaissance poetry a very brief piece of verse commemorating a deceased person. Epitaphs can be very personal in nature, but, like the epigram, their terseness also invites a satirical tone, as in the anonymous epitaph for the Duke of Buckingham, notoriously corrupt favourite of James I and Charles I: 'This little Grave embraces / One Duke and twentie places'.

Epistle

Based on ancient models such as Cicero, the prose epistle (letter) was important for the humanists. The verse epistle is addressed to a specific person and communicates ideas on a particular matter, usually moral or philosophical in nature. Thus the epistle combines a personal tone with a universal theme: it conveys a dual relationship – to the person addressed and to the subject being explored – and reads as both private and public discourse. One poet who used the verse epistle form on several occasions was John Donne; his famous poems on 'The Storm' and 'The Calm' at sea were written to his friend Christopher Brooke when Donne was serving under Essex in an expedition to Spain in 1597; while these poems stem from a particular friendship, Donne's epistolary poem 'To Sir Henry Wotton' belongs to a wider debate among a particular circle about the merits of life in court and in the country. Robert Herrick's 'A Country Life: To His Brother, Master Thomas Herrick' is another verse epistle on this perennial theme. Verse epistles can often be placed in this coterie context. As well as writing to friends and equals in this manner, poets would also address their musings in a suitably flattering manner to patrons: Samuel Daniel's 'To the Ladie Lucie, Countesse of Bedford' is one among many examples of this kind of text. A further context to consider is the closeness at the time between the letter and the poetry, since many poems would be written and circulated in manuscript among friends, often as part of longer letters.

Hymn

A hymn expresses collective feelings and ideals. These may be religious or secular – for example hymns of patriotism, praising heroes and celebrating victory in war. The Renaissance inherited from the Middle Ages the use of religious hymns in the liturgy. Typical of hymns are a regular stanza form and emphatic metre, and a rousing tone. 'A Hymn on the Nativity of my Saviour' by Ben Jonson (1572/3–1637) and 'A Hymn of the Nativity, sung by the Shepherds' by Richard Crashaw (1612/13–49) invite comparison. John Donne writes hymns dealing with private spiritual experience ('Hymn to God my God in My Sickness', 'A Hymn to God the Father'). An important influence was the Psalms, the Hebrew hymns of the Jewish people: metrical psalms were sung in Church, and many writers tried their hand at translating and paraphrasing them. A particularly fine translation, using varied forms, was made by the Sidneys – Mary Sidney, Countess of Pembroke (1561–1621), completed the work started by her brother Sir Philip. Hymns were also adopted to non-Christian uses, as in Ben Jonson's Hymn to Diana ('Queen and Huntress, chaste and fair') from the masque *Cynthia's Revels* (1600).

Ode

The Ode (the word means simply 'song') eludes close description, but it is usually substantial in length and treatment and serious in tone. The Renaissance inherited two main types of classical Ode, the Pindaric and the Horatian. The Theban poet Pindar (*c*.522–*c*.443 BC) left four books of choral chants. These were public works, designed to be sung and danced to, written to glorify the noble attributes (social, physical, athletic and spiritual) of the victors of Olympian and other competitions. Their purpose is to celebrate and uplift, and their tone is correspondingly intense and exalted. Separated from their original ceremonial context, the metre, formal structure, and meaning of Pindar's work is frequently obscure, but the energetic, ecstatic mood is clear enough. To Renaissance writers these served as models for passionate, bold and extravagant writing, suiting perhaps the aristocratic qualities of audacity and splendour. Milton's 'On the Morning of Christ's Nativity' (started on Christmas morning 1629) could be considered a Pindaric Ode for the force, richness and beauty of its expressive imagery and allusion, its asymmetric structures and energetic rhythms – qualities which we also associate with the art of the baroque. Ben Jonson makes a careful attempt to follow the ancient tripartite structure of a Pindaric Ode in his eulogy 'To The Immortal Memory and friendship of that Noble Pair, Sir Lucius Cary and Sir H. Morison'. The vividness and intensity of the Pindaric ode also commended it as a vehicle to religious poets including

Henry Vaughan (1622–1695; 'Resurrection and Immortality', 'The Holy Communion', 'Affliction') and Richard Crashaw (1612/13–1649; 'Prayer, an Ode'). Abraham Cowley (1618–1667) wrote a series of 'Pindaric Odes in the Style and Manner of the Odes of Pindar' (*Poems*, 1656).

The Roman poet Horace (65–8 BC) wrote in a quite different style to Pindar. Where the Greek poet delivers high-flown praise, Horace is precise and measured. His odes, written in the poet's country estate, express the values of calm, moderation and quiet reflection, values much needed in Augustan Rome after the upheaval of civil war. Both Horace's verse forms and themes were largely traditional – typical topics are the fleeting passage of time and the pleasures of good company – but in his treatment of these he achieved an exquisite artistry in the management of rhythm and the subtle interplay of ideas. Horace's Odes were read in the Middle Ages and studied in schools, and many poets of the Renaissance sought to imitate his qualities of tranquil, thoughtful tone, refined sensibility and restrained economical style. Ben Jonson was saturated in the influence of Horace: the speaker of a Jonson poem like 'To Penshurst' embodies a certain Renaissance notion of the urbane, civilised poet who observes and reflects, and celebrates what is good with moderation rather than loud effusiveness or sentimentality. This measured voice is as much a part of the meaning of the text as its content. Horatian odes commemorating public events include 'An Ode Upon Occasion of His Majesties Proclamation in the Year 1630' by Sir Richard Fanshawe (1608–1666), commending the sweet reason of the monarch in ordering the gentry to leave the court for their country estates, and 'An *Horatian* Ode upon *Cromwel*'s Return from *Ireland*' by Andrew Marvell (1621–1678), in which in the course of hailing Cromwell the poet seems unable to resist praising the dignity with which Charles I faced his execution. Robert Herrick wrote an 'Ode to Sir Clipseby Crew', but as with Jonson the Horatian voice is an animating presence across his work, as indeed it is in much Renaissance literature. The Horatian Ode was a model not only of a certain kind of writing, but also of a style of living, aspired to by an educated gentry who wished to live cautiously but decently on their country estates.

Odes in turn can be subdivided according to subject, and two important kinds to note are the *prothalamion* (celebrating a betrothal) and the *epithalamion* (in honour of a wedding). Lyrics of this kind were regularly commissioned, or offered, to honour state weddings. The best-known examples from the Renaissance, however, are the *Prothalamion* and *Epithalamion* of Edmund Spenser (*c*.1552–1599). These poems celebrate his own marriage in elaborate mythological imagery and rich verbal music (and employ a complex symbolic numerological scheme). Their 'golden' richness of image and joyful tone make a striking contrast with the later Jonsonian voice.

Satire

Satire can be a mode of writing which can occur in the course of a work but not define it. When it describes a whole work, we can consider it as a genre, concerned with the critique of human vices and customs. Satire may involve techniques of caricature and ridicule, but it is not necessarily comic. Donne's *Satire III* is a serious meditation on the merits of the different Christian churches. It uses such devices as satirical personification to depict those who adhere to different confessions, such as the Calvinist Crants who 'loves her only who at Geneva is call'd / Religion, plain, simple, sullen, young . . . ' (50–51). The aim of formal satire like this is not to mock but to present a vivid and effective depiction of certain kinds of social and personal defect, for both the enjoyment and also the moral edification of the reader.

Sonnet

A sonnet is a particular form of poetry which in the vogue for sonnet sequences took on the expectations associated with a genre. See the entry on Sonnet for discussion.

Conclusion

These types of lyric occur frequently in Renaissance poetry, but they certainly do not encompass it. As in all writing of the period, alongside the classical heritage the native stock of genres was influential. An important and popular kind of longer poem was the ballad, a narration of an historical or legendary incident, usually anonymous, which employs epic motifs of narration and a sentimental tone – moving, for example, from great sadness to great joy in a way a measured Horatian would not approve. The devotional poems of George Herbert and others look back to the medieval stock of carols and the vital model of the private prayer. As we have noted, other lyrics took the form of madrigals and other kinds of song. The same poem could belong to several generic categories – we might find a satirical epistle, for example. Context will accentuate one generic membership over another: the edition in which we read Renaissance poems will have a strong influence on the generic aspects which we look for, and Renaissance readers, too, will have been affected by the placing of a work: the popular miscellanies in which lyrics were usually printed must have made encountering various modes and genres together a common experience.

In any overview of the Renaissance English lyric, some points become clear. One is the astonishing technical range and inventiveness of poets, particularly from the 'Golden Age' of the 1580s onwards. There is an apparent restlessness in trying out different schemes and patterns: in the 164 poems of *The Temple* (1633), Herbert uses around 140 different stanzaic forms. There is an evident fascination in the possibilities of rhythmic, musical and structural effects, and a close reading of a selection of lyrics using the methods of Practical Criticism can be deeply rewarding. With this comes a corresponding complexity in tonality and the identity constructed for the speakers of texts. Scholars continue to decipher the subtle political nuances carried in and between the lines of poems, and critics attempt to respond to the play of voices which can be discerned often within the lines of the same speaker. If the Lyric is essentially defined as the poet/persona speaking directly, then an intriguing task for the reader is to try to understand who that persona is, and to what extent his or her utterance is indeed direct.

See also *Contexts*: Catholicism, Court, Courtier, Humanism, Platonism, Women; *Texts*: Conceit, Decorum, Genre, Metaphysical Poetry, Metre, Pastoral

Further Reading

James Biester, *Lyric Wonder: Rhetoric and Wit in English Renaissance Poetry* (Ithaca, NY: Cornell UP, 1997).

Ann Baynes Coiro, *Robert Herrick's Hesperides and the Epigram Book Tradition* (Baltimore and London: Johns Hopkins UP, 1988).

Thomas N. Corns, ed., *The Cambridge Companion to English Poetry, Donne to Marvell* (Cambridge: CUP, 1993).

Dennis Kay, *Melodious Tears: The English Funeral Elegy from Spenser to Milton* (Oxford: Clarendon, 1990).

Bruce Pattison, *Music and Poetry of the English Renaissance* (London: Methuen, 1970).

Masque

The masque was a court event involving song, dance, symbolism and pageantry. In the fourteenth century, a 'masque' was any kind of entertainment involving a mask: these included masquerades, acrobatics and the Christmas mummings and dances provided by medieval masquers, who would proceed through the streets on holidays and enter ordinary houses. The Renaissance masque, however, was a courtly spectacle: it not only entertained the court, but glorified and idealised it. Masques were composite creations – designer, choreographer and composer were just as important as the writer – performed for a special occasion such as a marriage. A performance would end with the Revels, when courtiers would join with the masquers in a dance. After some early development under the Tudors, the masque became more sophisticated in the court of James I (r.1603–1625) and is particularly associated with the writer Ben Jonson (1572–1637) and the designer Inigo Jones (1573–1652).

Henry VIII (r.1509–1547) loved music and dancing and wanted to emulate the Renaissance courts of Europe at home. He participated in perhaps the first court masque in England, the Epiphany Spectacle performed on Twelfth Night, 1512. Another example is a masque of 1527 entertaining the French ambassadors: singing and dialogue led to the usual dance, which was linked to the themes of union and harmony. Masques were prepared by the Master of the Chapel Royal: they were designed as ephemeral, specific to certain occasions, and functioned as examples of conspicuous consumption. Later Tudor monarchs were less enthusiastic: little is recorded under the austere reigns of Edward VI (r.1547–1553) and Mary (r.1553–1558), and the thrifty Elizabeth I (r.1558–1603) did not patronise them, though she was happy to enjoy masque-like entertainments paid for by others, such as the lavish spectacles put on at Kenilworth by her favourite Robert Dudley, Earl of Leicester in her royal progress of 1575. Two masques appear in Spenser's *The Faerie Queene*: the procession of the Seven Deadly Sins (I,4) and the Masque of Cupid (III, 12).

James I (r.1603–1625) took court masques a great deal more seriously, partly no doubt because his wife Anne of Denmark loved lavish spectacles. James employed professional writers, most notably Ben Jonson, who wrote 25 court masques between 1605 and 1625. *The Masque of Blackness* (perf. 1605) marked the start of his partnership with Inigo Jones. Jonson added to the revelry of masques a concern for lyric beauty, poetic form and coherent allegorical narrative: Jacobean masques are hence moral in content, leading the audience to an ideal world. They are also, in the first years, explicitly erudite: arcane symbolism is employed in the text and in Jones's ingenious illusionist scenery. Scene changes themselves become part of the symbolic action of the drama; in this way the spectacle of the masque was integrated into its meaning and structure. Jonson himself provided copious scholarly notes on the masques: this self-consciously clever, 'witty' Jacobean style is visible in other forms, such as the sermons of Lancelot Andrewes (1555-1626) and in styles of ornament. Jonson also introduced the antimasque, a grotesque prelude designed to make the masque proper seem more dignified: *The Masque of Queenes* (1609) begins with an antimasque of 12 witches cavorting in hell. This scene symbolically vanishes – thanks to Jones's stage machinery – to reveal the House of Fame with 12 ladies, including the Queen, representing the moral virtues.

From about 1611 the masque under Jonson and Jones aspires to the principle of classical order, as Jonson's classical scholarship combines with the influence of Italy, from which Inigo Jones returned in 1614. Jones's surviving designs show Palladian architectural features and a concern for formal harmony. Action, setting and text are unified, and the court itself is celebrated as a place of order. Classical character types and plots are employed. The principle of the action is often a classical contrast, and drama is sacrificed to make the abstract meaning clear: *The Golden Age Restored* (1615) shows the Iron Age banished by the Golden Age of poetry in a sequence of lyrics; *The Vision of Delight* (1617) moves from town to pastoral, dark to light and winter to spring in both verse and spectacle; *Pleasure Reconciled to Virtue* (1618) achieves Aristotelian unities of place and action in being set entirely on a mountain.

The spectacle progressively incorporated illusionist as well as emblematic scenes, until by 1620 Inigo Jones had arrived at the proscenium stage. This arrangement in which the stage area is a total self-enclosed picture working backwards from an invisible 'fourth wall' is the theatrical experience we are most used to today, but at its time it was revolutionary. A proscenium stage brings the perspective introduced by Italian art into the theatre: like perspectival painting it presents an illusionist setting, representing the real world rather than an emblematic space depicting ideas. This realism in turn favours the worldly genre of comedy, diminishes symbolism and encourages rounded characters rather than abstract ciphers. The visual experience comes to be at least as important as the auditory one, and the audience are thus turned into spectators, physically removed from the scene of action where before they had the role of semi-participants. The refined and exclusive world of the courtly masque thus brought about a technological change that was to have ramifications for the whole of English theatre. The change was not a sudden one, however: it was not until 1634 that an English play was presented in an entirely proscenium space.

The masque was attractive to playwrights. It carried a courtly flavour and the influence of France and Italy in its esoteric symbolism. Furthermore its highly stylised and dramatically inert actions, and thin characters, provided an interesting counterpoint to the action of the main drama. Shakespeare's *Timon of Athens* includes a stage direction for 'Cupid, with a mask of Ladies as Amazons, with lutes in their hands, dancing and playing' (1.2). *The Tempest* includes a hymeneal (marriage) masque to celebrate the betrothal of Miranda and Ferdinand; interestingly, this play also draws attention to the illusion of the masque itself as Prospero summons up and then dissolves the spirits who play it. One attraction of the masque may have been that it suited the self-consciousness we find in Renaissance theatre about its own illusory nature: 'All the world's a stage, and all the men and women merely players', as Jaques famously puts it in *Twelfth Night*.

After the era of Jonson and Jones, further court masques were written by Thomas Campion, Sir William d'Avenant and Aurelian Townshend. The last court masque in England was *Salmacida Spolia* (1640) by Jones and Sir William d'Avenant (1606-1668), an unprophetic work in which Charles I banishes discord and ushers in harmony. The influence of the masque appears in pastoral plays such as Milton's *Comus* (1634) and Jonson's *The Sad Shepherd* (1641). Songs and verses from the masques also stand as separate lyric poems. But the masque as a form of drama disappeared with the Civil War of 1642. Nonetheless, the creative achievements of Jones and Jonson had a lasting influence: the notion of theatre as a space for the integration of music, text and spectacle; the use of theatrical space to create a coherent imagined world imitating real space; the use of spectacular scenery and effects both to create an illusion and suggest a meaning – all of these concepts owe much to this specifically Renaissance form of dramatic spectacle.

See also   *Contexts*: Court, Courtier, Golden Age, Race; *Texts*: Actors and Acting, Theatres

Further Reading

David M. Bevington and Peter Holbrook, eds, *The Politics of the Stuart Court Masque* (Cambridge: CUP, 1998).

David Lindley, ed., *Court Masques: Jacobean and Caroline Entertainments, 1605–1640* (Oxford: Clarendon, 1995).

Stephen Orgel, 'The Masque', in *English Drama to 1710*, ed. C. Ricks (London: Sphere, 1971).

Linda Levy Peck, ed., *The Mental World of the Jacobean Court* (Cambridge: CUP, 1991).

Metaphysical Poetry

The 'metaphysical poets' were a group of seventeenth-century poets who rejected many Elizabethan poetic conventions and composed a new kind of verse. Their poetry is characterised by a markedly intellectual frame of reference, ingenious imagery and a dramatic, 'rough' use of metre. Prominent among the metaphysicals is John Donne (1572–1631); others are Andrew Marvell (1621–1678) and Abraham Cowley (1618–1667), and the religious poets George Herbert (1593–1633), Richard Crashaw (1612/13–1649), Thomas Traherne (1637–1674), and Henry Vaughan (1622–1695). Like many critical terms, 'metaphysical' was not used in the period itself. It was devised later, as a term of disapprobation, to describe poetry which offended against post-Restoration canons of taste. John Dryden (in his *Discourse Concerning Satire* (1693)) says of Donne: 'He affects the metaphysics, not only in his satires, but in his amorous verses, where nature only should reign'. By metaphysics, Dryden means the dry, academic language of scholasticism which is for him an inappropriate diction for love poetry. Samuel Johnson believed that poetry ought to be smooth, decorous and uplifting, and felt that the intellectual material of Donne and his circle conflicted with that purpose: 'The metaphysical poets were men of learning, and to show their learning was their whole endeavour' ('The Life of Cowley', in *Lives of the Poets* (1779)). Romantic and Victorian arbiters were similarly hostile, but over the twentieth century a major revaluation took place, led by T. S. Eliot and the New Critics of the 1930s – though clear definition of what 'metaphysical poetry' actually means remains elusive, and there is much variety among writers designated with that label. Currents in critical discussion are reflected in the anthologies by Herbert Grierson (1921), Helen Gardner (1957), and Colin Burrow and Christopher Ricks (2006). In the last of these, some rediscovered female writers, such as Anne Bradstreet and Katherine Philips, are included under the metaphysical heading.

That Donne and others were revising and extending the language of poetry was recognised at the time. Other Renaissance writers criti- cised what they called 'strong lines'. Strong lines compress meaning into epigrammatic form, and express it through vivid and startling images which sometimes have to be decoded, like a riddle. For example, in declaring that grief in verse is artificial, John Cleveland (1613–1658) comes up with this piece of obscure artifice: 'Verse chemically weeps: that pious rain / Distill'd with art is but the sweat o'th' brain' ('An Elegy Upon the Archbishop of Canterbury', 3–4). Knowing that 'Chemically' means 'alchemically', which is then taken up in the reference to distillation, does not make this a great deal clearer. Objectors to strong lines like this felt that ordinary ideas were being translated into needlessly obscure indecorous images. William Drummond of Hawthornden (1585–1649) called such writing 'scholastical quiddities'; Michael Drayton (1563–1631) referred to 'strong-lined writers' as 'chamber poets', a knowing coterie writing to impress each other. Robert Burton (1577–1640) gives an idea of the confusion of tastes: 'He respects matter, thou art wholly for words, he loves a loose and free style, thou art all for neat composition, strong lines, hyperboles, allegories' ('Democritus to the Reader', *Anatomy of Melan- choly* (1621)).

The compressed style of strong lines came into fashion in the 1590s. The mellifluous music of Spenser and the stock comparisons of love lyrics had come to seem dated, and the metaphysicals sought to invig- orate the language of poetry with a less familiar mode of expression.

In prose, writers were turning from the Ciceronian model to the terse style of Seneca and Tacitus. Poetry similarly turned in the direction of economy, treating rich matter with economical means. The verse form in vogue at this period was the lapidary form of the epigram, which is intended to say a lot, memorably, in a few words. Longer poems were modelled as extended epigrams, conveying a tough argument concisely, in self-consciously artful stanza forms. This tense and concentrated mode appealed to a coterie readership, but at its best it reaches beyond a specialised audience to convey an intensity of inner experience: in poems like the lyrics collected in Donne's *Songs and Sonets* or Marvell's 'The Garland', emotional and intellectual processes appear to energise each other. This intensity is also highly dramatic: metaphysical poetry coincides with the great age of Renaissance theatre, and poems often read like dramatic speeches. They are frequently set on a specified occasion and favour abrupt openings in the form of an address. These openings often signal that smooth metre is to be rejected in favour of the jagged rhythms of emotive speech. As in the great dramas, thought is given voice immediately, as it is felt by the speaker: 'For God's sake hold your tongue, and let me love!', 'Busie old fool, unruly sun', 'Batter my heart, three-person'd God' are famous first lines by Donne. There are no particularly 'metaphysical' subjects, though the style is suited to the short and intense world of the lyric rather than extended allegory or epic: Donne himself wrote love poetry, satires, verse letters and religious poetry, employing ingenuity not simply to grab attention but to pursue a line of thought to a definite conclusion. Like the dramatic openings, the endings of metaphysical poems are important, providing a strong sense of closure after a passage of argument.

Having announced itself in such a fashion, a metaphysical poem will then typically elaborate a tight piece of meditation, or argument, employing logical rigour and highly complex syntax, moving across verse lines to create shifting rhythms. The thought processes of Donne, Herbert and others also involve the extensive use of figures of thought like pun, paradox and hyperbole. Highly figurative language is also employed in the shape of ingenious conceits, yoking together unlike objects in extended similes. Johnson calls this 'a kind of *discordia concors*; a combination of dissimilar images, or discovery of occult resemblances in things apparently unlike'. The most famous example of this is Donne's comparison of lovers to the feet of a draughtsman's compass in 'A Valediction: Forbidding Mourning'. But the poetry of the period offers many other examples. If we turn to the lesser-known Cleveland again, we find these similes for tears in his elegy for Edward King (printed with Milton's 'Lycidas' in *Justa Eduardo King* (1638), a collection of poems by different hands commemorating this brilliant student who drowned at an early age):

> I like not tears in tune, nor do I prize
> His artificial grief who scans his eyes.
> Mine weep down pious beads, but why should I
> Confine them to the Muse's rosary?
> I am no poet here: my pen's the spout
> Where the rainwater of mine eyes run out
> In pity of that name whose fate we see
> Thus copied out in grief's hydrography.

Weeping is compared to music, scanned verse, rosary beads and rainwater – and the simile is further extended in the course of the poem. The poet stresses the immediacy of his effusion by saying he eschews artificial, planned verse, yet we might well feel that the self-conscious cleverness of his writing makes the grief seem insincere; that the ludicrous image of a pen spouting rainwater moves the wrong kind of response in the reader; and that the learned reference to 'hydrography' is gratuitous showing-off, and quite distant from the evocation of real, lived grief. Lines like this offend both against Augustan classicism and the Romantic emphasis on sensuous imagery – noticeably absent here. Yet a Renaissance reader was not bound by this frame of reference. Scriptural commentaries and practices of meditation included imagery that would seem bizarre to us, and this was continued in the outpouring of religious writing which is given such low priority in literary studies today. Metaphysical verse was also in tune with the European baroque, which is characterised by intense emotional dynamics across the arts. The *culteranismo* and *conceptismo* of seventeenth-century Spanish poetry (exemplified by Francisco de Quevedo and Luis de Góngora), for example, are also characterised by surprising images, emphasis on abstract thinking, and metrical and syntactical complexity. Mannered and highly gestural forms of expression were in the cultural currents of the time, in a way it is difficult for us to recover imaginatively. Moreover, sixteenth- and seventeenth-century writers did not have a settled idea of 'poetic diction'. Thus we find Herbert, for example, using very homely images to expound the most sublime ideas of the divine. What counted was the idea conveyed by a text, and the effect it induced, and any words or images could be used to serve this end. If we find 'rainwater' and 'hydrography' unpoetic we may, then, be revealing our distance from the sensibility of the time. Modernist poets like T. S. Eliot were also inspired by such writing to explore their own surprising similes: they saw *discordia concors* as a means of defamiliarisation and of rupturing settled habits of vision, and as an indicator of the strange subterranean mental links that do not conform to approved 'poetic' norms. 'Metaphysical' is admittedly a vague term, but it usefully focuses our attention on aspects of seventeenth-century style and on wider aesthetic issues of artistic creation and critical reception.

See also *Contexts*: Court, Manuscripts; *Texts*: Conceit, Decorum, Genre, Logic, Metre, Rhetoric, Sonnet

Further Reading

Robert Ellrodt, *Seven Metaphysical Poets: A Structural Study of the Unchanging Self* (Oxford: OUP, 2000).
Richard Willmott, *Metaphysical Poetry* (Cambridge: CUP, 2002).

Metre

The Renaissance saw important developments in English verse metre. The iambic foot (an unstressed syllable followed by a stressed one, as in *decíde*) was established as the basic unit, and a line of five iambs – the so-called 'iambic pentameter' – became the standard verse line. Iambic pentameter lines appear in a huge variety of rhyme schemes, from the sonnet to the complex stanzaic forms composed by Donne and Herbert and others. Blank verse – that is, verse in unrhymed pentameters – was introduced early in the sixteenth century by Henry Howard, Earl of Surrey, and became the staple line for the great Elizabethan and Jacobean dramatists. Traditional metres continued, and two of the most popular (poulter's measure and fourteeners) are well worth becoming acquainted with; experiments were also made in 'quantitative' metre, which is the attempt to write English verse according to Latin metrical forms. Though this experiment is generally regarded as a failure, it was an important chapter in the history of thinking about metre in English. Careful analysis of English rhythm was also made by writers of rhetorical manuals and treatises about verse, and their findings provided an important methodical underpinning to the composition of poetry.

In the story of Renaissance verse metre, Sir Thomas Wyatt (1503–1542) and Henry Howard, Earl of Surrey (1517–1547) are pioneering figures. Their work first appeared to a wider public with the publication of *Tottel's Miscellany* in 1557, and it was this book which made clear the possibilities of iambic metre in English. Wyatt seems to have been the first modern English poet to use the iambic pentameter line (Renaissance readers had difficulty scanning Chaucer, with his sometimes silent and sometimes pronounced final 'e'), though he was clearly anything but a slave to it. Often Wyatt disregards metrical smoothness to bring an idea across forcefully. In all metrical analysis, we become alive to the tension between the rhythm of a speaking voice – often jagged and jolting – and the smoothness of regular metre. Every poet finds a voice by playing the rhythms of deliberate artistic pattern and natural speech off against each other. Wyatt's writing tends towards the pulse of real speech, and thus we often get the effect of immediate feeling, speeding up and slowing down according to the actual movement of thought.

> Who so list to hount I knowe where is an hynde   [hount: hunt
> but as for me helas I may no more
> the vayne travail hath weried me so sore
> I ame of theim that farthest cometh behinde
> yet may I by no meanes my weried mynde
> drawe from the Deere but as she fleeth afore
> fainting I folowe I leve of therefore . . .

This is in iambic metre, but varied according to the actual mental action being depicted: 'Who so list to hount' is trochaic (stressed-unstressed), and brings across the weariness of the speaker, as does the interjected 'helas' (alas) of the next line. Succeeding lines give examples of effects which were to be deployed by generations of poets: enjambment (the syntax crossing from one line to the next) and trochaic inversion ('drawe from', 'fainting'); the last line quoted above seems to stumble in line with the poet's own fainting: 'fainting I folowe'. Such effects show the poet using his basic iambic line in supple and inventive ways, creating a feeling of pattern and measure without letting it become dull and repetitive. We notice, too, that the minimal punctuation leaves it to the reader to decide on the phrasing of lines: this reminds us that Renaissance poetry is explicitly to be read aloud and performed, and this is as true of a sonnet like this as it is of theatrical writing. We could well imagine this piece being read to a small group of friends. The sum effect is to transpose an original sonnet by Petrarch into English, without it seeming derivative or stilted.

Surrey's lyrics are metrically more regular than Wyatt's. Often the iambic pattern is clear and uninterrupted, with consonants deployed in alliterative groups and vowels organised into pleasing cadences. Metrical pattern rather than speech rhythm is predominant: 'The soote [sweet] season, that bud and blome furth bringes, / with grene hath clad the hill and eke the vale'. Here we can sense the Renaissance fondness for measure and order, and also the close relation at that time between poetry and singing. Indeed, all of these topics were felt to be related: in Renaissance theory, music embodied the mathematical patterns which underlay all creation, and poetic metre was also integrated into these patterns, which had a mystical relationship to divine harmony. Surrey's pointed alliterative phrasing is part of this picture of the divine cosmic ordering of seasons, time and space. His other great contribution to English metrics, as we have noted above, was the introduction of blank verse. This was one of the lessons of his partial translation of Virgil's *Aeneid* (Books 2 and 4). Here are the opening lines from his rendering of Book Four, describing members of Dido's court gathering for a morning hunt:

> Then from the seas, the dawning gan arise,
> The Sun once up, the chosen youth gan throng
> Out at the gates: the hayes so rarely knit,   [hayes; nets for hunting
> The hunting staves with their brod heads of steele
> And of Masile the horsemen fourth they brake
> Of senting hounds a kenel huge likewise.

This is 'blank' because there is no end rhyme, leaving the poet free to extend a syntactical idea over several lines (the *arise / likewise* rhyme does not set up any pattern, and may be accidental). The lines illustrate some of the effects that Shakespeare and other dramatists were to use to such effect on stage: the enjambment of 'gan throng / Out . . . ' evokes the youths surging through the gates as the sentence surges across the line break; the pause after 'Out at the gates' is a caesura, providing a rhythm in counterpoint to the pentameter; *brod* falls under a stressed syllable, and the resulting lengthening of the syllable helps to emphasise how 'broad' the spearpoints are. At the same time as we admire this flexible handling of rhythms, though, we might also notice some slightly wooden moments as Surrey tries to fit the iambic template: the redundant *gan* in lines 1 and 2 seems to be there merely to pad out the metre. The syntax is hard to follow as the word order is so unnatural: the sense of the last lines seems to be 'the horsemen of Masile brake forth [ie unleashed] a huge kenel of senting hounds' (*likewise* is again padding, ending the line lamely), but even that leaves the previous phrases unresolved. It was to remedy this stilted syntax that the poet and critic George Gascoigne (1525–1577) wrote *Certayne Notes of Instruction Concerning the Making of Verse or Ryme in English* (1575). This is the first English manual on prosody, and in it Gascoigne urges poets to follow natural English word order wherever possible.

We have spent some time analysing these early poets, partly because it indicates the kinds of effects one can investigate in metrical analysis, and partly because later Renaissance verse was to play out the essential difference between Wyatt's rough naturalism and Surrey's polished, patterned writing. Very generally speaking, in the 'Golden Age' writing of Sidney, Spenser and Marlowe the quest is for a perfect, polished performance. Writers such as Marlowe (1564–1593) were searching for a 'golden line', one which used the pentameter to achieve an utterance as rich, vivid and mellifluous as possible:

> The outside of her garments were of lawne,   [lawne: fine linen
> The lining, purple silke, with guilt starres drawne,
> Her wide sleeves greene, and bordered with a grove,
> Where Venus in her naked glory strove . . .
> > (Marlowe, 'Hero and Leander', 9–12)

Images conform to the rhetorical principle of *enargaia* or vivid description, and the verse is as finely wrought as the clothes being described: iambs are used to lay stress on the rich sequence of vowels so that words like *garments* and *starres* are given their full weight, bringing out the assonance; there is half-rhyme (*lawne . . . lining*), repeated rhythmic patterns (the triple stress of 'guilt starres drawne' is echoed by 'wide sleeves greene'); and the 'g' alliteration threads across the lines. The aim seems to be to make the lines as densely 'poetic' by such means as possible. Jonson also follows the iambic template to compose verse of a chiselled, classical perfection, expressive of the control of the balanced and rational mind over the material. Going in the other direction, Shakespeare in his later plays, and the metaphysical poets, developed a highly irregular metrical style, expressing the dramatic movements of thought and speech as they actually occur. In this way, this school of 'baroque' seventeenth-century Renaissance verse returns to its sixteenth-century roots in the rough textures of Wyatt. When we read Donne, it often feels as though we are overhearing a real voice, exclaiming and thinking aloud:

> Busie old foole, unrulie Sunne,
> Why dost thou thus,
> Through windowes, and through curtaines call on us?
> > ('The Sunne Rising')

Through such means, Donne takes a conventional genre of poetry, the *aubade* (a love poem set at dawn), and makes it something immediate and fresh.

Both Marlowe's golden lines and the expressively varied metrics of Donne and others had far-ranging influence on later English verse. In the Victorian era we can find, for example, the harmonies of Tennyson making quite different effects to the broken, energetic lines of Browning. Part of the modernist project of T. S. Eliot, Ezra Pound and others was to break into this iambic fortress and identify other musical contours in the language.

Analysis of iambic lines and their effects is a basic skill of today's student, but we are less familiar with the popular Elizabethan metres of poulter's measure and fourteeners. Briefly, poulter's measure consists of feet arranged in the pattern 3 + 3 + 4 + 3. For example:

Láyd in my qúiet béd, | in stúdy ás I wére, |
I sáw withín my tróubled héad, | a héap of thóughtes appére:
(Surrey. Tottel, I, 29)

To a modern reader, this has a jingling effect: the units do not allow for flexibility or inversion, and the rhythm soon starts to seem insistent, and distract from the content. The consequent nursery rhyme feel makes it unsuitable for any serious or subtle expression. Yet it was a popular verse rhythm of the middle sixteenth century, as was the similar fourteener, which alternates groups of eight and six syllables:

No vainer thing ther can be found
amyd this vale of stryfe,
As auncient men reporte haue made
Then truste uncertayne lyfe.
(Barnabe Googe)

This, too, has a sing-song effect that works against the seriousness of the idea: the caesura will always fall between eight and six, creating a feel of monotonous predictability. These metres, though, feature heavily in *Tottel's Miscellany* and were used extensively by the poets Barnabe Googe (1540–1594) and George Turberville (1544–1597). It is an interesting test of sympathy to spend some time with such writers and see if we can find a feel for this kind of writing, which many intelligent Elizabethan readers clearly enjoyed. Equally clearly, others were alive to its deficiencies: the fourteener is the measure parodied at the end of *A Midsummer Night's Dream* in the play put on by the mechanicals. But it was also used in at least one highly important work, Sir Arthur Golding's translation of Ovid's *Metamorphoses* (1565–1567). This work was hailed as a masterpiece by Ezra Pound (in *An ABC of Reading*), though other modern readers have been less rapturous. In any case, we gain by reading verse beyond the pentameters we are used to; and we can better appreciate the superb handling of iambic pentameter by Shakespeare, Donne and others against the background of these popular, apparently jog-trot metres.

Finally, we can note the experiment in quantitative metre. The theoretical issues involved here are perhaps more interesting than the resulting verse. For Tudor Humanists and other ardent classicists such as Roger Ascham (1515–1568), the highest aim of the poet should be to emulate the ancient masters: only by adopting the noble metre of Virgil and other greats would poets achieve true verses, in preference to the 'rude beggarly ryming' (Ascham) of Chaucer, Wyatt and Surrey. Poets of the distinction of Spenser and Sidney duly attempted to write English verses according to the Latin hexameter (eight of the poems in Sidney's *Arcadia* are in this measure). The difficulty is that there are fundamental differences between Greek and Latin on the one hand and English on the other. Latin metre is called 'quantitative' because syllables are measured by their quantity – whether they are short or long. But English is accentual, and metres natural to English are concerned with whether a syllable is stressed or not, rather than its length. The hexameter (six feet) of Latin combines spondees (long long: slów páirs) and dactyls (long short short: sú-dden-ly), though in English hexameters it is dactyls that tend to predominate. This tends to produce a falling, 'feminine' ending at the ends of lines which again becomes monotonous. Here is a rendering of the same lines of Virgil which we looked at earlier in Surrey's translation, this time in English hexameter as written by Richard Stanyhurst (1547–1618):

Thee whilst thee dawning Aurora fro the Ocean hastned,
And the May fresh yoonckers [noble youths] to the gates do make there assemblye
With nets and catch toyls, and huntspears plentiful yrond:
With the hounds quicksenting, with pricking galloper horsman.

This is not without vividness, and, as with anything unfamiliar, we should read it for a while, not rush to judgment. It is certainly the case, though, that the experiment was not followed up (though later poets like Tennyson and Auden tried out Latin metres from time to time) and it was generally felt that the measures of Virgil are unsuited to the particular rhythms of English speech. This particular chapter in English verse reminds us, though, of the importance of the concept of translation in Renaissance culture: the Italian of Petrarch, the French of contemporary lyricists, the Latin of Virgil and Ovid and the Scots of the Scottish Chaucerians – all fed into the literary language of Renaissance English. The metres of the great poets of the age are a result of a long and thoughtful encounter with other tongues, mixed with English traditional materials, and adapted to the shape and texture of the language as spoken by the English people.

See also   *Contexts*: Humanism; *Texts*: Epic, Metaphysical Poetry, Mimesis, Prose Style, Rhetoric, Sonnet, Theory of Poetry

Further Reading

Derek Attridge, *Well-Weighed Syllables: Elizabethan Verse in Classical Metres* (Cambridge: CUP, 1974).
John Thompson, *The Founding of English Metre* (New York: Routledge, 1961).
George T. Wright, *Shakespeare's Metrical Art* (Berkeley: University of California Press, 1992).

Mimesis

Mimesis is the representation of reality in writing (or any other artistic medium). A literary text is mimetic if it presents to us a copy of something – for example, a portrait of a person or landscape. These would be examples of the representation of a concrete, physical reality. As with a painting, the verbal description may also improve on the real landscape, to give us an ideal picture, one which brings across the idea of a landscape in its purest form: thus, a poem about spring may not copy any actual landscape, but give us a picture of the notion of spring, typically full of rebirth and hope and new growth. Next to realistic and idealistic representations, a text may also portray something abstract, such as a feeling or an idea: love, or jealousy, or honour perhaps. Much Renaissance writing is to do with finding a way to represent such experiences, in the form of an image we can contemplate. In this work of 're-presenting' the original subject, a writer may employ all possible verbal means: Donne's sonnet opening 'Batter my heart, three-person'd God . . . ' aims to give a verbal representation of an inner, spiritual event. To do this, the poet employs an extended (and traditional) metaphor: the soul is like a fortress for God (the Trinity) to break into. We are further helped to picture this scene, and feel its drama, by the rough rhythms and hard consonants.

There are, then, various kinds of mimesis. The accurate description of things in words we shall call 'realistic' mimesis. The attempt to capture the essence of something like Spring we can call 'ideal'. Realistic description often takes the form of simply naming and listing things, and this mode of language was held to be suitable to the low, earthy world of comedy. We can take as an example a few lines from *Henry IV, Part Two*. Here, the Hostess accuses Falstaff of promising to marry her and then reneging (so-called 'breach of promise'). Her speech paints a scene in precise realist language, with nothing being tidied up or idealised:

> Thou didst swear to me upon a parcel-gilt goblet, sitting in my Dolphin chamber, at the round table, by a sea-coal fire, upon Wednesday in Wheeson week, when the Prince broke thy head for liking his father

to a singing-man of Windsor, thou didst swear to me then, as I was
washing thy wound, to marry me, and make me thy wife.
(*Henry IV 2*, 4.1.82)

The writing is simple in the sense that it is full of concrete nouns and
adjectives, yet it is interesting to note its effects. One of these is to
make the account more emphatic: this is a formal accusation (breach
of promise was against the law for many centuries), and the Hostess
wants to make her account as credible as possible. But the seemingly
unending sentence, with its accumulated details, also gives the actor
plenty of opportunity to bring across complex feelings: there is a mixture
of poignant recollection and present anger, carried in the rhythm as well
as the content of the writing. For the modern reader, this comic realism
also has the fascination of bringing us a 'slice of life' of the age; the
speeches of the nobles in this play will generally be much more abstracted
and removed from the actual textures and sensations of experience.

For discussion of 'idealist' mimesis, we can turn to some famous lines
of Hamlet. Here he is advising the players who come to Elsinore not to
overact. In so doing, he articulates a theory of drama, which could be
extended to the other arts.

For anything so o'erdone is from the purpose of playing, whose end
both at the first and now, was and is, to hold as 'twere the mirror up
to nature; to show virtue her own feature, scorn her own image, and
the very age and body of the time his form and pressure.
(*Hamlet*, 3.1.15)

'To hold . . . the mirror up to nature'. But how should art do this? Hamlet
does not seem to mean a mirror showing an exact copy of how things
look. In this speech, 'nature' probably means something like 'essence'
(as in 'it's in the nature of teenagers to be easily distracted'). The art of
the players, then – and other arts, including poetry – is to capture the
essence of something, going beyond the particular instance to find the
general truth. Thus, when Hamlet says that art should show envy her
own image, he means that it should provide an image which shows us
the essential idea of envy. He puts this into practice himself, when he
confronts his mother Gertrude with two 'counterfeits' or portraits of her
two husbands, his father and Claudius (3.4). Hamlet senior is portrayed
not as he looked, but as the image of the noble, martial king:

See what a grace was seated on this brow –
Hyperion's curls, the front of Jove himself,
An eye like Mars, to threaten or command . . .
(3.4.56–3.4.58)

No doubt Hamlet's own strong feelings are at work in his interpretation of the picture. Yet Renaissance portraits and poems do work in this way, depicting the 'nature' or idea of something in an artistic medium, rather than attempting a photographic copy. Portraits of Elizabeth I (which only a few approved artists were authorised to make) are usually about what she signifies (justice, chastity, love of the realm), rather than how she looks; and in any case how she looked, with make-up and vestments, was itself a carefully constructed symbolic image.

Idealist mimesis has ancient sources. The philosophy behind Hamlet's lines comes largely from Aristotle (see *Poetics*, xv). The idea is that something is most fully itself when it realises all its potentialities. Thus, a tree is most tree-like when it is vigorous and full of leaves. A man is most manly when in full vigour of mind and body. Renaissance poetry is full of idealised imagery, showing the created world living out its nature to its fullest potential:

> What time the groves were clad in green,
>   The fields drest all in flowers,
> And that the sleek-haired nymphs were seen
>   To seek them summer bowers.
> Forth rov'd I by the sliding rills,
>   To find where Cynthia sat,
> Whose name so often from the hills
>   The echoes wonder'd at.
>   (Michael Drayton, 'The Quest of Cynthia')

The governing concept is that this is Nature as it really is, behind the local distortions of mud, weeds and clouds. To the Renaissance mind, it is not a fictive fantasy, as we might see it, but a higher reality. Drayton is showing us what Nature is really like, in its fullest being – teeming, graceful, echoing in harmony with the universal order. So we often find in Renaissance lyrics that trees are always leafy, gardens blossoming and rivers gently flowing – and when they are not, some interference or blight is being referred to. In the Renaissance conception, Art does not take a photo of the world before us, but, by appealing to our imagination, it lifts our minds and spirits to a higher and truer reality beyond. We might reflect that such a movement towards idealisation is fairly inevitable in writing anyway, since language itself is an abstraction: 'tree' does not signify any particular tree, but the general concept of tree that we carry in our minds. One has to work hard, as the Hostess does, to locate a description in a very specific place and time.

Besides Aristotle, this poetry also has roots in Platonic philosophy: in this current of thought, images are Ideas. Their beauty can help us to understand divine Beauty and perfection. Drayton's verses, in which images are linked by melodic and measured lines, present us with an imitation of divine harmony, beyond the vicissitudes of our ever-changing, fallen world. Great Renaissance works, like *The Faerie Queene*, aspire to present a unified theory of the universe, and offer a vision of the rational ordered pattern according to which the cosmos is constructed. The complex numerological schemes employed by Spenser are a further poetic means of locking the work of art onto this deep pattern of Creation: in this way, even formal devices such as stanza lengths and rhyme schemes can be mimetic.

For the artist, mimesis starts in the mind, in the contemplation of the Idea. In his *Apologie for Poetry*, Sidney refers to 'that Idea, or fore-conceit of the work', the starting image which must then be transposed into language. In the first sonnet of *Astrophil and Stella*, his inner voice tells him 'look in thy heart and write'. We could take this as a rather modern injunction – say what you really feel. But something more on the lines of what we have discussed may be intended: the poet is to look inside himself, and find in his heart the store of images where true reality may be contemplated. These Ideas are not only pleasant and delightful, but are also instructive. They help us to understand Envy, Nature, Manhood, Beauty – or whatever the topic might be – by showing them in their true colours. The poet is hence a teacher, and will naturally use the devices of exaggeration and amplification. In lyric and heroic poetry, the beautiful becomes more beautiful. In satire and comedy, faults are similarly painted boldly to show vice in its true colours.

Certain kinds of description fall into their own generic categories. One of these is the *blazon*. In the Renaissance, this term generally designated the praise of a woman's body (or part of it), typically from head to foot. This topic was used in sonnets (see Sidney, *Astrophil and Stella*, 9; Spenser, *Amoretti*, 64), shorter lyrics (for example, Campion's 'There is a Garden in her face') and longer poems (see Spenser, 'Epithalamion', 148–203; Donne, Elegy 19). Renaissance blazons encompass a variety of tones, from religious rapture to wry parody; technically, they involve inventive conceits in their figuration of the woman. Since they are essentially itemisations and evaluations of women by men, they are of particular interest to critics studying the poetics of gender. Another descriptive genre is the *ekphrasis* (Greek for 'description'), which in post-classical poetry usually means the description of a work of art. In Renaissance literature, we find extended descriptions of tapestries (Spenser, *The Faerie Queene*, 3.11.29–3.11.46; Shakespeare, *The Rape of Lucrece*, 1366–1561), sculptures (John Marston, 'The metamorphosis of Pigmalions image') and buildings (Milton's description of Pandaemonium in *Paradise Lost*, I, 670–730). Exercises in *ekphrasis* are closely modelled on classical examples, and in their selection of detail and choice of epithets are also useful guides to Renaissance attitudes to the visual arts. Closely related is the description of the 'lovely spot' or *locus amoenus* (Spenser's Bower of Bliss, Milton's Eden, Marvell's garden), developed in the particular genre of the country house poem (for example Ben Jonson's 'To Penshurst', Aemilia Lanyer, 'The Description of Cooke-ham'). A criterion of much description was the rhetorical concept of *energeia*, or 'vividness'. The speaker or poet appeals to the audience's imagination by conveying a sight and texture as vividly as possible. The figure helps to explain the colour, detail and clarity we often find in Renaissance poetic description; its source in rhetoric also reminds us that these images are often meant to have a persuasive value – for example, by making a political or moral point – above and beyond being pleasing pictures in themselves.

See also *Contexts*: Golden Age, Humanism, Platonism; *Texts*: Conceit, Decorum, Genre, Lyric, Theory of Poetry

Further Reading

Gunter Gebauer and Christoph Wulf, *Mimesis: Culture. Art. Society* (Berkeley: University of California Press, 1995).

A. D. Nuttall, *A New Mimesis: Shakespeare and the Representation of Reality* (1983; reprinted New Haven and London: Yale UP, 2007).

On *ekphrasis*, see William H. Race, *Classical Genres and English Poetry* (London: Croom Helm, 1988), 56–85.

On number symbolism: Isabel Rivers, *Classical and Christian Ideas in English Renaissance Poetry*, 2nd edn (London: Routledge, 1994), ch. 13 'Numerology', 170–182.

Non-Fictional Prose

Biography

Early modern biographies provide moral instruction. Foxe's 'Book of Martyrs' continues the ancient tradition of hagiography (lives of saints) with a Protestant content; the Greek writer Plutarch's *The Lives of the Noble Grecians and Romanes* (translated from a French version by Sir Thomas North in 1579) had a similar aim: the life of a great person is an example of virtues and vices in action. Renaissance biography is also shaped by epideictic rhetoric (concerning speeches of praise or blame). Fulke Greville's *The Life of the Renowned Sir Philip Sidney* (written c.1610–1612, published 1652), for example, depicts his friend and patron Sidney as the exemplification of aristocratic virtue: 'Indeed, he was a true model of worth: a man fit for conquest, plantation, reformation, or what action soever is greatest and hardest among men' (ch. 3). It is unrewarding to read such a work with modern criteria and decide it falls short of a properly balanced or 'warts and all' account. The chief function of such encomiastic (praise-giving) writing is to praise the virtues, delineating them through the portrait of an individual, who is naturally perfected to suit that purpose. From the biography as panegyric, we learn about the particular kinds of personal excellence admired (if not actually practised) by educated people of the day.

A similar affectionate and laudatory tone is found in the charming life of John Donne by Izaak Walton (1593–1683; *The Lives of Dr. John Donne, Sir Henry Wotton, Mr. Richard Hooker, Mr. George Herbert* (1675)) who is depicted as the model churchman: 'Thus variable, thus virtuous was the life; thus excellent, thus exemplary was the death of this memorable man'. *Exemplary* is the key word here: the subject is an example, or model, which we should follow. Walton's life of Donne is the record of personal friendship more than the product of methodical research; there is no pretence of objective distance. It is also part of Walton's longer project of supporting his beloved Anglican Church. In a much longer work, the vices and virtues of individual men are integrated into an account of the Civil War in *The History of the Rebellion and Civil Wars in England* (1702–1704) by Edward Hyde, Earl of Clarendon (1609–1674). Here, demonstrative rhetoric is combined with a serious desire to record the royalist Clarendon's account of these tumultuous years, through portraits of the men he admired and detested. Clarendon's magnificent handling of a complex prose style allows for nuanced psychological descriptions. His ardent service of the House of Stuart lends passion both to his description of individuals, such as the villain of his story, Oliver Cromwell ('the greatest dissembler living', Book X), and to his moving narrative accounts of key episodes such as the Trial and Execution of Archbishop Laud (Book VIII) and Charles I (Book XI).

Character

The Character, or Charactery, is a genre of early Stuart literature. The classical model is the Greek writer Theophrastus (*c.*371–*c.*287 BC) whose sketches of various corrupt types were published in France with Latin versions in 1592, and translated into English in 1616. Joseph Hall (1574–1656) published his *Characters of Vices and Virtues* in 1608: his stated aim is to help the reader 'learn to know virtue and discern what to detest'. He does this by describing types rather than individuals, anatomising moral qualities using a terse and pithy Senecan style, and sharply vivid imagery. Hall's Hypocrite, for example, 'comes to the sickbed of his stepmother and weeps, when he secretly fears her recovery'. The so-called 'Overburian Character' (*Sir Thomas Overbury His Wife*, several editions 1614–1622) is an anthology of character sketches by various hands, named after the unfortunate Sir Thomas Overbury (1581–1613). Overbury served his patron the royal favourite Robert Carr (Earl of Somerset), but when he became obstructive to Carr's plans, he was murdered by poison. (The case was one of the great scandals and trials of the seventeenth century.) Another important writer of characters is John Earle (1601–1665), whose *Microcosmographie* (1628) provides witty and observant descriptions. His description of Paul's Walk (the nave of St Paul's Cathedral), for example, brings us close to several character types of the time, from unemployed captains, men seeking patrons and criminals: 'All inventions are emptied here and not a few pockets... it is the thieves' sanctuary, which rob more safely in the crowd than a wilderness'. Charactery is close to the essay: it deals in lapidary fashion with moral topics and is always brief, though the author tends to take a more objective stance than the subjective essayist, and relies more on external observation of the current world than on the reflections of other authors.

Dialogue

Ancient texts like Plato's Socratic dialogues and Cicero's books on Friendship (*De Amicitia*) and Old Age (*De Senectute*), which are written as conversations, gave a distinction to the dialogue as a mode of enquiry. By following these models, humanists could distinguish their work from the medieval treatise. They were also no doubt attracted by its rhetorical possibilities: different styles could be employed for different speakers; jokes and popular material could be incorporated alongside elevated discourse; and by using different voices the writer could keep an ironic distance from the ideas expressed. Sir Thomas More's *Utopia* (1516) is a dialogue: through the main speaker Hythloday, he is able to make criticisms of English society and suggest an ideal alternative; yet in the voice of his own character, More, he dismisses Utopia as illusory. A different kind of dialogue by More is the beautiful *A Dialogue of Comfort Against Tribulation*, an exercise in consolation and moral comfort (in the older sense of 'comfort', meaning 'strengthening') written when the author was awaiting execution. An Elizabethan example of the dialogue form is Spenser's *A View of the Present State of Ireland* (written 1596, published 1633), a work often avoided by critics since in it the great poet of chivalry advocates, among other measures, starving the rebellious Irish to death. Dialogue translates naturally into verse: examples are Margaret Cavendish's 'A Dialogue betwixt Man, and Nature' and Marvell's 'A Dialogue Between the Resolved Soul and Created Pleasure' and 'A Dialogue between the Soul and Body'. Over the sixteenth and seventeenth centuries the possibilities of dramatic dialogue are explored through secular drama, while the internal debate is absorbed into the Essay, though the form is still attractive to Dryden as a way of expounding critical ideas.

Essay

The essay comes into being with Montaigne's *Essais* (1580). It is quite different from the kind of essay which readers of this book will probably have had to write. For Montaigne, *essai* – meaning 'attempt' from the verb *essayer* – is not so much a literary form as an intellectual process, in which the author burrows into his own mind and thereby discovers where thinking about a subject will take him: as a kind of conversation held by the author with himself, it is a method of self-discovery (or self-invention), and to plan it in advance would be to defeat the object. In the Renaissance essay, the author maintains a subjective stance, and embraces different modes of discourse: an essay can be logical and expository at one moment and digressive the next. An essay makes no attempt to be exhaustive on a subject – as a treatise might be – and can end abruptly, without arriving at a conclusion. Its aims are multiple: it is reflexive – the author communing with himself – but also communicative and didactic (concerned with teaching the reader). Essays draw on the oral tradition of civilised conversation and are characterised by concise thoughts expressed in proverbs, axioms, maxims and apophthegms. These succinct individual statements play against a loose overall argument. A collection of essays will typically range over a wide number of themes. In English, the most famous essays are those of Francis Bacon (first 10 published 1597), who employs a terse, balanced Senecan style quite distinct from the Montaigne's genial persona. Bacon's aphorisms are often instantly memorable: "What is truth?" said jesting Pilate, and would not stay for an answer' ('On Truth').

Sermons and Homilies

In the Protestant service, the sermon rather than the liturgy is the central point of the service: the minister leads the faithful to the truth not through administering sacraments but by expounding the Word. Consequently sermons and homilies are an important part of English Renaissance culture and literature. Church attendance was compulsory, which meant that every Sunday most English people would hear a homily from the pulpit of their local church. What they heard was not necessarily the personal view of the speaker. Both Catholic and Protestant states regarded it as normal to enforce on people both outward conformity and inner beliefs. The English Church was thus a part of the power of the state, and part of the purpose of the Sunday sermon was to ensure that the beliefs of the people were the approved ones, conducive to obedience to the civil powers. Alongside the prescribed words of the *Book of Common Prayer* (whose 39 articles describe the elements of the Anglican Confession) were centrally published homilies which ministers were obliged to deliver (*Certayne sermons or homilies* (1547); *The seconde tome of homelyes* (1563)). Sometimes subjects would be prescribed: Lancelot Andrewes among others had to give a number of sermons on the gunpowder plot (1605), and under Laud priests were required to teach their flock that the King was a divinely appointed authority. Others would be banned as too dangerous. Sermons which strayed from the official line could land their speakers in serious trouble. A particularly important pulpit in London was St Paul's Cross, just outside the Cathedral, where speakers would discourse on the issues of the day to large crowds.

Within the restrictions of this carefully monitored discourse there was still scope to elaborate imaginatively on the scriptures, with all the skills of voice and gesture required of the orator. Key elements of the Renaissance sermon are knowledge and eloquence. In the late sixteenth and early seventeenth century the sermon rises to heights of extraordinary sophistication in the 'witty' Jacobean style favoured by the court, in which intellectual brilliance is joined to devotional passion. One of the greatest exponents from this time is Lancelot Andrewes (1555–1626), whose sermons display dazzling erudition – citations from Greek and Latin are part of his usual flow of thinking – as he draws out multiple meanings from short texts. Yet the learning does not appear dry but rather a source of energy for developing powerful ideas on his central preoccupations: the Incarnation, the Resurrection and the Holy Spirit. John Donne (1572–1631) is today more read for his poetry than his homilies, yet his *LXXX Sermons* (1640) are equally rewarding of attention. His friend and biographer Izaak Walton describes him as 'a preacher in earnest, weeping sometimes for his auditory, sometimes with them, always preaching to himself like an angel from a cloud but in none, carrying some, as St Paul was, to heaven in holy raptures...'. Something of the ecstatic intensity of these hour-long performances in the pulpit of St Paul's can be felt in the printed sermons, which are evidently the fruits of long meditation and mastery of the rhetorical art. Vivid and often extraordinary images are delivered with a natural sense of rhythm and cadence which can still speak directly today: 'all our life is a continual burden, yet we must not groan; a continual squeezing, yet we must not pant' (Sermon 66). These qualities can be found at shorter length in his *Devotions upon Emergent Occasions* (1624), meditations to be read in private. The same qualities of erudition and rhetorical skill are to be found in the sermons of Jeremy

Taylor (1613–1667), who also applied his preaching talents to written discourse in his books of spiritual instruction, *The Rule and Exercises of Holy Living* (1650) and *The Rule and Exercises of Holy Dying* (1651). The high rhetoric of Jacobean sermons gave way to a plainer style, illustrated by the Cambridge Platonist Ralph Cudworth (1617–1688). His sermon preached before the House of Commons (March 31, 1647) argues for a return to an uncomplicated faith based on following the commandments, and the style appropriately eschews grand Ciceronian periods for shorter sentences: 'The gospel, that new law which Christ delivered to the world, is not merely a letter without us, but a quickening spirit within us'.

Treatise

The treatise is a catch-all term for any full-length study which 'treats of' a subject in a substantial manner. The Renaissance treatise is certainly not the same thing as a modern academic book: personal reflection can sit alongside objective study, the tone may be stridently polemical (indeed violent argument is a characteristic of the period), and the discussion will often meander. In the spirit of learned conversation, Renaissance treatises are often quite short and unerudite, approaching the feel of the essay. Some illustrative examples of topics and titles are Rhetoric (Puttenham, *The Arte of English Poesie* (1589); Hoskins, *Directions for Speech and Style* (1599?), Peacham, *The Garden of Eloquence* (1577)); Poetry (Daniel, *A Defence of Rhyme* (1603)); Education (Ascham, *The Scholemaster* (1570)), Philosophy (Hobbes, *Leviathan* (1651)); Religion (Hooker, *The Laws of Ecclesiastical Polity* (1593)). Two books which are treatises of a looser kind are Thomas Browne's *Religio Medici* (1642; first authorised edition, 1643) and Robert Burton's *Anatomy of Melancholy* (1621). The first, containing the author's reflections on different religious beliefs, among other matters, can be read as a series of essays, loosely joined together as a single work. The second, written to distract Burton from his own melancholy, is a huge book. But to read any 50 pages from it is to be in the presence of an extraordinarily capacious and energetic intellect. In their endlessly inquisitive and digressive manner, these works exemplify the 'ragbag' polymathic mentality of much Renaissance literature, unhampered by modern discipline boundaries; we find a similar spirit in Montaigne and Rabelais. In their copiousness and desire to fit everything in, these texts perhaps also give us a clue as to how to appreciate the rich visual arts of the period. Beyond the countless English treatises is still another forest of books in Latin, an important part of the intellectual culture of the time but now the province of a few specialists.

The types of writing described above by no means exhaust the non-fictional writing of the period. Another rough category is that of fragmentary thoughts, brief reflections or apophthegms collected together, as in Ben Jonson's *Timber, or Discoveries* (1641), a series of thoughts on a variety of topics, drawing on and often translating texts Jonson had read. But genre boundaries are permeable: *Timber* can be read as short essays, and Bacon's essays can conversely be read as sequences of aphorisms. Another group of writings may be broadly called subjective, including letters, memoirs, mothers' advice books, the autobiography and diaries – including the important genre of the spiritual diary of Puritans, recording the actions of the soul. The seventeenth century also saw the rise of journalism: the first English newspaper, *The Courant or Weekly News*, was founded in 1622. At the learned level, we see purely informative works such as dictionaries and the topographies of the antiquarians, and at the popular level the almanac – calendars combining facts with predictions, advice and accounts of marvels – which comfortably outsold every other kind of writing mentioned in this entry. Throughout the age the contest between Protestant and Catholic, Puritan and Anglican establishment, was fought out in a stream of religious tracts. Beyond writing entirely was the oral discourse of the speech: some of these, such as Elizabeth I's famous address at Tilbury as England awaited the Great Armada (1588), are preserved in print.

A traditional approach to all such writing is to see it as the background to the privileged fictional genres: thus we might read excerpts from Burton as a way of understanding Hamlet's depressive condition or characters from Hall and Earle alongside the rogues' gallery of Jonson's *dramatis personae*. Such exercises can be valuable, though we can also dispense with the idea of 'background' and read other writings as literary texts in their own right. It is tempting, though dangerous, to look across the various kinds of prose writing for common themes of the age: certain recurring topics, however, include the sense of 'drift' from one subject into another, the importance of the aphorism as a mode of expression, the constant reference to previous authority, and the pervasive influence of the rhetorical arts of praise, blame and persuasion in giving texts their tone and direction.

See also   *Contexts*: Book Trade, English Reformation, Humanism, Printing, Protestant Theology; *Texts*: Genre, Prose Style, Rhetoric

Further Reading

Elizabeth Nugent, ed., *The Thought and Culture of the English Renaissance. An Anthology of Tudor Prose, 1481–1555* (Cambridge: CUP, 1956).

Herschel Baker, ed., *The Later Renaissance in England: Nondramatic Verse and Prose, 1600–1660* (Boston: Houghton Mifflin, 1975) has generous selections of prose.

On Latin writings: J. W. Binns, *Intellectual Culture in Elizabethan and Jacobean England: The Latin Writings of the Age* (Leeds: Francis Cairns Publications, 1990).

Pastoral

The word 'pastoral' comes from 'pastor', the Latin for shepherd, and pastoral works typically feature shepherd swains and nymphs in a pleasant rustic setting. The word conjures up images of shepherds reclining in the shade of a tree, piping songs of love while their flocks graze. This simple picture, however, has a complex ancestry in classical, medieval and continental sources. Complexity also marks the handling of pastoral by English writers, who use it to explore a variety of artistic effects and intellectual preoccupations. In general, Renaissance writers use pastoral allegorically, for the display of eloquence and for the purposes of ethical edification.

The pastoral genre begins with the Sicilian poet Theocritus (c.316–c.260 BC), whose 'idylls' (literally 'scenes') defined its principal conventions: pastoral scenes feature the songs of herdsmen and fishermen, whose effusions usually concern love complaints, debates and merge mythological and contemporary reference. Sometimes there is a singing contest, and a paradoxical contrast emerges between the uneducated simplicity of the shepherd-speaker and the virtuosity and sophistication of the verse-utterance. In the idyllic world, the loss of primal innocence is lamented, and there is a yearning for a Golden Age. An opposition is drawn between the simplicity and the innocence of rural life and the pressures and artifice of court and city (a topic particularly enjoyed by courtly and urban readers, whether in Greek Alexandria or Elizabethan England). At the same time, the labours of the countryside are described with some degree of realism. From the beginning, there is a tension between the conception of the pastoral setting as an imagined, ideal world and as a real place of labour. The Greek origin of pastoral also accounts for several of the words associated with this kind of writing: *Arcadia*, an area of Southern Greece from which many colonists in Sicily came, was appropriated by Virgil to mean the pastoral place in general, and retained this sense in later centuries; *Doric*, the dialect of the Arcadians, similarly came to be used as a general term for the homely language of rustic folk; pastoral writings are often called *bucolics*, from Greek 'bukolos', meaning herdsman.

The Roman poet Virgil (70–19 BC) modelled his *Eclogues* on Theocritus ('ecologue' literally means 'selection', though Elizabethans often called their works 'Eglogs' in the belief that the etymology was from 'aix' or 'goat', and the word thus meant 'goat-song'). Virgil's first eclogue explores the ideal/real divide in the personae of the two shepherds, Tityrus and Meliboeus. Tityrus, who seems to stand for Virgil himself, enjoys an enviable life of ease, while Meliboeus is a farmer who has been driven from his land, which Augustus has confiscated to give to his troops (a real historical event). Pastoral is thus opened up to different tones and subject matter. Through the voice of Tityrus, it lends itself to poetry of praise and celebration; while in the voice of Meliboeus, pastoral is a setting for satire and social criticism, often through veiled references. The Renaissance critic George Puttenham comments in *The Arte of English Poesie* (1589) that Virgil wrote 'under the veil of homely persons and in rude speeches to insinuate and glance at greater matters'. In the *Eclogues*, Virgil widens the pastoral mode to incorporate social, philosophical and political issues. As they were apparently his first works, pastoral writing was also held in the Renaissance to be suitable apprentice work for a poet, before ascending, like Virgil, to the highest genre of epic. Thus we find Spenser and others often starting their literary careers with pastoral. Another classical convention adopted in the Renaissance was the presence of the poet under a shepherd's name. This leads to a complex coterie situation, in which poets under the personae of shepherd songsters communicate with each other through a series of codes and allusions.

Like other forms of classical origin, Renaissance pastoral was enriched by the native medieval tradition. While Virgilian reclining shepherds were at odds with the values of Christian austerity, other uses were made of the pastoral motifs of countryside, forest and garden. In the popular tradition, we find woodland as the setting for resistance to authority in the Robin Hood tradition and for various kinds of adventure in the forests of medieval romance; homage was done to nature in the Mayday and Whitsuntide festivals. Pastoral could also be brought within the Church's scheme of values: Christ himself was after all the good shepherd, tending his flock, and good parish priests did their pastoral work in this spirit. The Bible, too, appeared to sanctify rural labour: Abel, a shepherd, was favoured by God; the Old Testament King David was both herdsman and poet (as the presumed author of the Psalms); the Annunciation was often depicted against a garden setting and the Nativity was set in a humble stable. Dramatisations of the latter, particularly in the Towneley plays (*c.*1470–1520), combine a comic depiction of Mak and his fellow shepherds with a sense of reverence for the fact that simple pastors were summoned to witness the infant Jesus. A key use of pastoral in the Middle Ages was the 'Piers Plowman' tradition. In this, the ploughman is the emblematic figure of the rural labourer; but in place of the classical shepherd lolling under a tree, the ploughman type is marked by the Christian virtues of poverty, toil, humility and piety. In William Langland's *Piers Plowman* (*c.*1360–1399) and the many other works in this tradition, Piers also stands for the oppressed peasant: his simple dignity and honesty contrast with the corruption of Church and state. From medieval literature, then, the Renaissance inherited the Christian use of pastoral imagery, and a rich stock of vernacular work where rural labour is the site of realism and polemical and satirical social critique.

Continental writers drew on Virgil and other ancient sources to produce pastoral writing of sophisticated expression and strong sentiments, from love to lament to indignation. The Carmelite monk known as Mantuan (1448–1516) wrote a series of Latin eclogues in which satire of Church vices figures largely. This theme made his work particularly agreeable to Protestant English readers. Mantuan was variously rendered into English (by Alexander Barclay, 1515; Barnabe Googe, 1563; George Turberville, 1567) and also read extensively in Latin in schools. A French master of pastoral was Clément Marot (1496–1544), while in Italy the new form of the pastoral tragicomedy was developed by Torquato Tasso (1544–1593) and Giovanni Battista Guarini (1537–1612). Examples of the prose pastoral romance are *Arcadia* (written 1480s, published 1504) by Giacomo Sannazaro (1458–1530) and *Diana* (1559) by the Portuguese poet Jorge de Montemayor (*c.*1521?–1561). All of these were influential models for English writers and were admired for their virtuosity of expression and skilful manipulation of the form's conventions.

In England, Renaissance pastoral begins with the publication of Edmund Spenser's *The Shepheardes Calendar* (1597). This work is a self-conscious attempt by Spenser to present himself as the English Virgil. Accompanying apparatus by 'EK' provides a history and definition of eclogue, and the poems deploy all the modes of pastoral provided by classical and continental models. This range is given generic form by their division into three kinds: 'plaintive' (January, June, November, December), moral (February, May, July, September, October) and 'recreative' (April). The recreative eclogue is a poem in praise of Queen Elizabeth I, while the moral poems include satire, drawing on the medieval 'plowman' tradition of critique of the Church. Like the virtuous ploughmen of medieval poetry, Spenser's shepherds live a life of godly labour (which includes the labour of poetic composition) rather than Arcadian ease, and their tasks are realistically depicted. Spenser further extends the expressive range of pastoral in the autobiographical 'Colin Clouts Come Home Again', which, in a familiar Renaissance trope, contrasts rural life with the court, while 'Daphnaida' and 'Astrophel' (the latter on Sidney) are pastoral elegies. The eclogues of *The Shepheardes Calendar* are also notable for their stanzaic and metrical ingenuity and the use of obsolete language – a prominent and self-conscious location of the work in a specifically English tradition.

Spenser's linguistic extravagance was disapproved of by Spenser's great contemporary Sir Philip Sidney (1554–1586). Sidney's *Apologie for Poetry* includes an important definition of pastoral, while his great prose work *Arcadia* (1590) is, as its title suggests, set in a Virgilian rural space. Sidney's *Arcadia* includes the usual poems and song contests, in a wide variety of verse forms; at the time it was celebrated for its eloquence and regarded as a handbook for gentlemen wishing to improve their skill in rhetoric. But the *Arcadia* also has important philosophical and political preoccupations and increases even further the voices and themes of pastoral writing. A central theme is government, including self-government, or control of the passions. Sidney's Arcadia is at times idealised, but it is also disrupted by discord and violence, the prose narrative allowing room for a variety of genres. We can find similar polyphonic versions of pastoral in the works of Shakespeare: the forest of *A Midsummer Night's Dream* is a place of love but also madness and malevolence; while the Arden depicted in *As You Like It* (performed *c.*1600), which is based on Thomas Lodge's prose pastoral romance *Rosalynde* (1590), is a place of both aristocratic leisure and the hunger, cold and poverty suffered by the rural poor. In *The Tempest* the pastoral space of the island is also a setting for the exploration of ideas of government. This play links pastoral ideas to the New World, and through different characters and scenes the island is variously imagined as a utopia, a place of growth and beauty, and a source of terrifying punishments visited on the wicked.

This diversity of treatment characterises later Renaissance English pastoral. Most traditional are the Spenserian poets Michael Drayton (1563–1631), Samuel Daniel (1562–1619), Phineas Fletcher (1582–1650) and William Browne (?1590–?1645), who write in a clear and measured diction which is distinct from the angular thoughts and strong lines of the metaphysicals. An ideal Arcadia, where man lives in harmony with nature, is presented in Drayton's *Idea, the Shepherd's Garland* (1593; extended and revised in subsequent editions to 1619) and *The Muse's Elysium* (1630). The anti-courtly satirical strand is developed in seventeenth-century pastoral: in the 1606 revision of *Idea*, Drayton describes Sidney 'laughing even kings, and their delights to scorn / and all those sots them idly deify' (Eclogue 6). A similar temper is evident in the important anthology *England's Helicon* (1600; second edition, 1614). William Browne's *Britannia's Pastorals* (1613) is a pastoral epic on the theme of England. Book I (1613) draws on Spenserian and Italian traditions to celebrate England's greatness, while Book II (1616) uses satire and elegy to lament England's present state under James I. In an incomplete third book (not published until 1852), the poet is in exile. *Britannia's Pastorals* is noted chiefly for its vivid descriptions, particularly of the poet's native Devon, and for its bewildering generic diversity, as a combination of voices and forms is experimented with in an attempt to find a poetic shape for Britannia. *Genera mista*, or generic diversity, is also a feature of pastoral tragicomedy, popular in this period. Examples are Daniel's

The Queen's Arcadia (1606) and John Fletcher's *The Faithful Shepherdess* (performed 1608, published *c*.1610). In these, the poet shows control over potential confusion in his handling of multiple plots and voices, while an analogous moral discipline is an important theme, as virtue is shown battling against adversity. English pastoral tragicomedies imitate the refined feelings and elegant expression of their Italian models, and ideas are regarded as more important than individual characterisation. They were better received at court than on the popular stage.

Pastoral is such a protean discourse that in its various manifestations it embraces many central Renaissance topics. As we have seen, from its earliest origins there is a tension between the rural spot as an imagined paradise or a real place of work and tribulation. In its idealist guise, the shepherds' Arcadia is linked to the themes of the lost paradise of Eden, the Golden Age, and ideas of natural nobility and human dignity which were associated by Montaigne and others with the recently revealed Arcadia of the New World. Pastoral works express ideas about the relationship of art and nature, and place instinctive sensual delights against the customs of organised society. The close connection between pastoral ease and libertinism gave rise to moral debate; the latter is celebrated in the lyrics of the Cavalier poets. In *The Faerie Queene*, Book VI, the ambiguity of pastoral calm is suggested by the story of Sir Calidore, who is drawn to but resists the pleasures of Arcadian ease. Pastoral can be perceived as irresponsible escape from the obligations of knighthood, according to which virtue takes the form of strenuous activity; alternatively countryside *otium* can allow a spiritual serenity which transcends worldly concerns. The Eden of *Paradise Lost* (Book IV) involves deep consideration by the Puritan Milton of the relationship of the paradisal garden with human labour and of the nature of sexual desire before the Fall.

Renaissance pastoral is also explored through treatments of mythological stories, as in Marlowe's *Hero and Leander* and Shakespeare's *Venus and Adonis* (1593), where sensuality and desire figure highly. The various intellectual preoccupations inherent in pastoral writing are wittily explored in the various garden poems of Marvell, who radically revises Spenserian tropes. Beyond the diversity of tones and moods of particular texts, the very status of the pastoral mode is paradoxical. In terms of Renaissance literary criticism, it is a low genre, since it deals with low subject matter and thus demands an appropriate idiom; yet pastoral texts also celebrate the key marker of courtly and gentle life, which is leisure, and allow for the self-indulgently eloquent description of refined feeling. Simplicity, *sprezzatura* or easy accomplishment, and sensitivity to nature are after all quintessential courtly affectations. Critics have also considered the social and political function of pastoral. It could be seen as validating the new wealth gathered through sheep farming, which was achieved at the expense of severe rural poverty. Thus literary Arcadias present a comfortingly peaceful fictional version of the countryside which could serve as a pleasing distraction from the real thing. The critic Louis Montrose has argued that pastoral also validates class distinctions at a time when these were under threat, naturalising social constructs by depicting them as timeless. Others have noted the openness of pastoral to various functions: it can indeed naturalise class divisions and underpin the ideology of the court, while at the same time containing subversive satirical elements.

See also *Contexts*: Golden Age, Humanism, Sex and Sexuality, Travel; *Texts*: Decorum, Genre, Lyric

Further Reading

Articles

Louis Montrose. ' "Of Gentlemen and Shepherds": The Politics of Elizabethan Pastoral Form', *English Literary History*, 50 (1983), 415–459.
Michelle O'Callaghan, 'Pastoral', in Michael Hattaway, ed., *A Companion to English Renaissance Literature and Culture* (Oxford: Blackwell, 2002), 307–316.

Books

Sukanta Chaudhuri, *Renaissance Pastoral and its English Developments* (Oxford: Clarendon, 1989).
Helen Cooper, *Pastoral: Mediaeval into Renaissance* (Cambridge: D S Brewer, 1977).
Andrew V. Ettin, *Literature and the Pastoral* (New Haven and London: Yale University Press, 1984).
Annabel Patterson, *Pastoral and Ideology: Virgil to Valéry* (Oxford: Clarendon, 1988).

Prose Style

Prose style develops within a cultural context. Tudor prose grew up in the court, as the later fifteenth and early sixteenth centuries saw an increase in the power of the monarch. This centralisation of power required a competent bureaucracy to oversee government business. Civil servants, lawyers and diplomats who were competent in humanist Latin became the 'new men' of the courts of Europe. To begin with, such men were in short supply in England and Henry VII (r.1485–1509) had to import scholars from abroad. But by about 1550, humanist education had become established in England, producing a supply of highly articulate functionaries. Noblemen were also often educated in the humanist fashion.

With a humanist education came humanist prose. Expertise in writing consisted first in a mastery of good Latin, but training in rhetoric soon came to have its effect on the writing of English. Unsurprisingly, humanist English was solidly based on Latin, in the conviction that modern languages ought to imitate the Roman models. Consequently, we find the importation of many Latin words in this period: Thomas Elyot (*c.*1490–1546) wrote that he was 'constrained to usurpe a latine worde for the necessary augmentation of our language' (typically of humanist writers, he seems here to be naturally employing as many Latin-derived words as possible). Many of these so-called 'inkhorn' terms have become familiar. Elyot's own contribution includes *modesty, mediocrity, frugality* and *industrious* – all new words in the 1531 *Boke Named the Governour*. Edward Hall (*c.*1498–1547) uses inkhorn terms lavishly in his 1542 *Chronicle*: 'what mischief hath insurged in realmes by intestine devision' gives the flavour. A stylistic tendency of this period is the pairing of words, very often one Latin and one English, to express the same idea or neighbouring ideas. This technique is ubiquitous in Cranmer's *Book of Common Prayer* (1549): 'Ye that do *truly and earnestly* repent you of your sins, and are in *love and charity* with your neighbours', 'We *acknowledge and bewail* our manifold *sins and wickednesses*'. Skilfully used, the use of Latin and English words in combination creates a rhythm of long words against short ones, a balance of abstract and concrete vocabulary, and a variety of rhythmic and musical effects.

The integration of Latin into English also affected syntax. One effect of humanism was a transformation of the shape and rhythms of English prose under the influence of the classics. We can see this if we compare two pieces of writing. Here is a passage from Sir Thomas Malory's *Morte Darthure* [cf 125] (printed 1485):

> And so they yode unto kynge Arthurs lodgynge all togydir, and there was a grete feste and grete revell. And the pryce was yevyn unto sir Launcelot, for by herowdys they named hym that he had smytten downe fifty knyghtys, and sir Gareth fyve-and-thirty knyghtes, and sir Lavayne four-and-twenty.
>
> (*Launcelot and Guinevere*, XVIII: iii)

In Malory's prose, simple sentences either stand alone or are chained together with the co-ordinating conjunction *and*. This is called the paratactic style, in which statements are rarely in a subordinate position to each other. We find the same kind of writing in medieval chronicles, and this gives Malory's storytelling a vigorous, unpretentious quality. The influence of Latin brought a shift from Malory's paratactic prose to a more complex syntax: in grammatical terms, it is a movement from *parataxis* to *hypotaxis* (multiple subordination). Cicero was regarded as the supreme model, and Ciceronian English is characterised by long, complex sentences. Sir Thomas Elyot again provides an example:

> And verily I suppose that before crossbows and hand guns were brought into this realm, by the sleight of our enemies, to the intent to destroy the noble defence of archery, continual use of shooting in the long bow made the feat so perfect and exact among Englishmen, that they then as surely and soon killed such game which they listed to have as they now can do with the crossbow or gun, and more expeditely, and with less labour they did it.
>
> *(The Boke Named the Governor* (1531), I:17)

Elyot's sentence tells a whole story: the English used to practise with the longbow, and managed to use it excellently without too much hard work; but then the crossbow and gun were introduced by our enemies, and the noble art of archery has fallen in decline. Elyot's sentence retains this clarity but changes the chronology, so we look back nostalgically from modern contraptions to the good old longbow days. Ciceronian prose is an intricate, artful exercise. Long, periodic sentences are built up from clauses. These clauses were called *cola*, and punctuated by a semicolon or colon: a gathering of cola ending in a full stop is a *period*, representing a whole passage of thought. These clauses or *cola* are composed by the best writers with rhythm as well as logic in mind. Often, the sense of a period is only resolved in the very last clause or phrase, an effect known as suspended syntax (because we are kept in suspense until the end). A particularly fine writer in Ciceronian English is Richard Hooker (1554–1600), who uses the resources of classical rhetoric to pursue a point forcefully and clearly, not principally to make spectacular effects. In these sentences we can see the use of balancing clauses, couplets and an arrangement of ideas that builds up to a conclusion:

> Against such Ceremonies as are the same in the Church of *England* and of *Rome*, we see what hath bene hitherto alleaged. Albeit therefore we do not finde the one Churches hauing of such things to be sufficient cause why the other should not haue them: neuertheless in case it may be proued, that amongst the number of rites and orders common vnto both, there are particulars, the vse wherof is vtterly vnlawful in regard of some speciall bad and noysome qualitie: there is no doubt but we ought to relinquish such rites and orders, what freedome so euer we haue to retaine the other still.
>
> *(Of the Lawes of Ecclesiasticall Politie*, Bk 4, 11)

Albeit... neuertheless... there is no doubt. This is the sound of *thinking*. Hooker's prose conveys the processes of measured thought, balancing one idea against another, qualifying, refining and moving to a conclusion. A period is a composition, arranging such thoughts in a coherent and effective way; and the challenge for the reader or listener is to hold all the various parts of the period in the mind. Later writers in this style are Milton (sometimes his prose is obscure: but shorter texts like *Areopagitica* repay close attention), and the royalist Henry Hyde, Earl of Clarendon (1609–1674) in his account of the Civil War, *The History of the Great Rebellion*.

Ciceronian prose allows for infinite variations. Sometimes a piece of writing may be constructed with statements balancing each another. Alternatively, a sentence might build up in a progression of clauses, leading to a climactic ending. As Renaissance writers became more experienced at using the rhetorical tropes described by Cicero and Quintilian, so they used these devices to colour and organise meaning. At one end of the stylistic spectrum we find John Lyly (?1554–1606). His book *Euphues* provided a model of highly artificial, rhetorical style, ornamented with every possible device. Balanced clauses, classical allusion, rich imagery, alliteration and carefully controlled rhythm make it ostentatious art prose, where simple content is built into dazzling patterns of expression. Euphues, a rich youth, has just settled in Naples, and is soon visited by many wishing to take advantage of him:

> There frequented to his lodging as well the spider to suck poison of his fine wit as the bee to gather honey; as well the drone as the dove; the fox as the lamb; as well Damocles to betray him as Damon to be true to him. Yet he behaved himself so warily that he singled his game [picked out one from the herd] wisely. He could easily discern Apollo's music from Pan his pipe, and Venus' beauty from Juno's bravery, and the faith of Laelius from the flattery of Aristippus.

Today Lyly is more admired for his plays, but this prose style, known as *Euphuism*, was the fashion among writers in the late sixteenth century and took complex rhetorical prose to an extreme.

So far, we have concentrated on the use of classical models and rhetorical precepts. However, English writers could not achieve the most effective results simply by emulating the vocabulary and syntax of Latin. There are too many differences between the languages for one to be successfully mapped on to the other. While fine Ciceronian writing continued, another strand of English lay in continuity with native colloquial style. Sermons, cony-catching pamphlets and religious controversies catch the direct, energetic style of spoken delivery. The sermons of

Bishop John Jewel (1522–1571) or Hugh Latimer (c.1485–1555), or William Roper's (1496–1578) biography of Thomas More are much simpler and plainer than the elaborate periods of the Ciceronians. Thomas Nashe's writings, among them *Pierce Penniless* (1592) and the writings of Robert Greene (1558–1592), pick up on the energies of street language. The humanist writer Thomas More (1478–1535) could combine a mastery of Latin with an ear for English to produce a style which suggests the movement of real conversation in his *Dialogue of Comfort Against Tribulation* (written in 1534–1535 while he was awaiting execution). Other learned humanists interested in exploiting the natural strengths of English included scholars at St John's College, Cambridge, a centre for Renaissance humanism and Reformation ideas. Elizabeth I's tutor Roger Ascham (1515–1568) commends 'plaine naturall English' in *The Schole-master* (pub. 1570), and makes a point of using English vocabulary and constructions in his digressive little book on archery, *Toxophilus* (1545). Through works like these, Latin and English were integrated to form a prose that does not seem stilted. Archbishop Thomas Cranmer (1489–1556) discovered in English idiom what he needed to find a style for the *Book of Common Prayer*, grave and unhurried but at the same time direct and free from mannerist verbiage.

Ciceronianism continued as a dominant style in 'art' writing in the late sixteenth and early seventeenth century: as we have noted, Milton was a notable late exponent of the style. At the turn of the century, though, the tide turned against Ciceronianism, and Tacitus (c.56–c.117) and Seneca (c.4 BC–65 AD) became the preferred classical models. Their style is characterised by briefer statements, with one idea following another in a looser way. In Senecan writing, statements are more independent of each other grammatically; individual words count for more and the rhythms are more compressed. Ben Jonson (1572–1637) praises the virtues of the concise, snappy style in his commonplace book *Timber, or Discoveries*. Bacon's later essays draw on this style of writing; in these pieces the journey from one sentence to the next seems to suit the enquiring, sceptical cast of mind of the essay writer. The compact Senecan sentence also suits brief, aphoristic statements:

An ant is a wise creature for itself, but it is a shrewd thing in an orchard or garden. And certainly men that are great lovers of themselves waste the public. Divide with reason between self-love and society, and be so true to thyself as thou be not false to others, specially to thy king and country.

(Bacon, 'Of Wisdom for a Man's Self')

John Donne (1572–1631) and Robert Burton (1577–1640) similarly use staccato statements, each one making independent sense but adding to the cumulative force of the whole. The fashion for the tight Senecan style was also an important influence on the metaphysical poets, who were deliberately trying to break away from the 'golden' sound of Spenser and Sidney and find a verse style more suited to the evocation of hard thinking.

Any style can become monotonous through overuse, and the Senecan snappiness, once a refreshing antidote to Ciceronianism, in its turn threatened to become a manner. So we find in the early seventeenth century writers like Thomas Browne (1605–1682), Donne and Jeremy Taylor (1613–1667) building up longer rhetorical paragraphs, and using some vivid and surprising metaphors and similes in their imagery. This style, which avoids Ciceronian symmetries on the one hand and lapidary Senecan statements on the other, has been called baroque. It is deliberately ornate, rhythmically varied and conspicuously artful. Baroque art, however, foregoes classical symmetry and harmony for the drama of contrast and surprise.

In this short sketch of the course of English prose, a certain pattern, or set of binary oppositions, has emerged: between English and Latin; between the spontaneity of speech and the artifice of writing. In the seventeenth century, there was once again a return to writing based on the patterns of speech, with a turn from the baroque to plainer modes: the diaries of John Evelyn (1620–1706) and Samuel Pepys (1633–1703), and the gossipy sketches of John Aubrey (1626–1697), all convey the feel of real chatter. This style suits the particularly personal genres of diary and letter. It also owes something to the plain talk of the scriptures. This colloquial current is discernible in the literary writings of Izaak Walton (1593–1683), John Bunyan (1628–1688) and the philosopher Thomas Hobbes (1588–1679). John Dryden (1631–1700) employs a conversational style, eschewing out-of-the-way vocabulary and other dazzling effects. Where the sixteenth-century virtuoso like Lyly displayed his wit extravagantly, the seventeenth-century gentleman like Abraham Cowley (1618–1667) and William Congreve (1670–1729) is more concerned to carry his learning lightly. The new science brings the clear prose needed for the scientific enterprise, in the disciplined publications of the Royal Society (founded in 1660).

We have commented on some major stylistic labels of the period: Ciceronianism, idiomatic English, the Senecan style, the Baroque, the polite conversational style of the seventeenth century. It should be remembered that these are merely convenient labels, and that some terms (like 'baroque') applied to prose have occasioned debate. It is tempting to put each writer in a stylistic category, but the best authors can draw on different styles and achieve something unique of their own. The features we have looked at – vocabulary, rhythm, the construction of sentences, the type of imagery employed – are what we would naturally look for in our reading; and we would consider their relation to the subject matter of the writing in question.

See also   *Contexts*: Court, Humanism, Manuscripts, Printing; *Texts*: Genre, History, Metre, Non-fictional Prose

Further Reading

Stanley E. Fish, ed., *Seventeenth-Century Prose: Modern Essays in Criticism* (Oxford: OUP, 1971).

Ian A. Gordon, *The Movement of English Prose*, English Language Series, 2 (London: Longman, 1966).

Ian Robinson, *The Establishment of Modern English Prose in the Reformation and the Enlightenment* (Cambridge: CUP, 1998).

George Williamson, *The Senecan Amble: A Study in Prose Form From Bacon to Collier* (Chicago: University of Chicago Press, 1951).

On *cola* and punctuation, see: M. B. Parkes, *Pause and Effect: An Introduction to the History of Punctuation in the West* (Berkeley: University of California Press, 1993).

Individual Studies

Brian Vickers: *The Artistry of Shakespeare's Prose* (London: Methuen, 1968); *Francis Bacon and Renaissance Prose* (Cambridge: CUP, 1968).

Rhetoric

On any page of any Shakespeare play, we will find characters trying to persuade each other. Like us, they use a battery of methods, from logical argument to cajolement, flattery, lying and intimidation. Only rarely will a character be attempting a truthful account of some reality: usually, we find language being used strategically, to create a particular impression and sway the listener in some way. At the same time, arguments may also express emotional states: Renaissance sonnets, for instance, often present inner emotional dramas in the form of a carefully argued case. Texts can also seek to persuade us in a more general sense, by moving us to share a feeling towards some subject – admiring or despising an action or an individual, for example.

The general term for this art of persuasion is Rhetoric, a skill in which all Renaissance schoolboys were rigorously trained. Rhetoric was thus a part of the consciousness of writers and readers in the period, and a knowledge of its history, theory and practice is vital if we are to appreciate Renaissance literary discourse.

Rhetoric originated in ancient Greece, as a method for arguing a case effectively in lawcourts and before a public assembly. An important early study was made by Aristotle in his *Rhetoric* (fourth century BC), where he lists the kinds of contents suitable to particular subjects, and calculates the likeliest way of winning over different types of audience. The Greek tradition was then absorbed into Roman education. For the Romans, rhetoric was chiefly seen as a practical skill which would prepare young men for a successful career in politics and the law: rhetorical training (as explained in textbooks like the *Ad Herennium*, a first century BC work attributed during the Renaissance to Cicero) involved detailed analysis of the ordering of arguments, and the choice and arrangements of words. Cicero (106–43 BC) became for the Renaissance humanists the exemplary rhetorician, speaking wisely and eloquently on many subjects, in the style demanded by the occasion, and in this way contributing to the good of the state. Throughout the Middle Ages, many of the terms of rhetoric continued to be taught, alongside grammar and logic, as part of the *trivium* in the syllabus of the seven liberal arts. Humanist interest in the eloquence of ancient Rome was stimulated by the discovery of important manuscripts, in particular Cicero's *Brutus* and *De Oratore* and Quintillian's encyclopaedic *Institutio Oratoria* (first century AD). An assurance in persuasive speech and writing was regarded as an essential attribute in the professions, while poets were studied for the valuable moral maxims they enshrined in beautiful and memorable utterances.

In ancient Greece, Rhetoric came into conflict with philosophy (or Dialectic), as practised by Plato (*c*.428–*c*.348 BC). This led to two rival educational philosophies. For while both Rhetoric and Logic concern argument, they seem to conceive it differently. Rhetoric aims at what is persuasive and plausible; but Dialectic pursues truth and formal proof. This dispute was partly resolved by Aristotle (384–322 BC), who pointed out that Rhetoric is a fact of social life and can be applied to good or evil ends. Rhetorical persuasion – by whatever means – clearly has great dramatic possibilities, and we can find in Elizabethan and Jacobean plays many examples of the ways language can be manipulated, and listeners tricked, by a masterful speaker. Equally, we could find examples of eloquence put to good use, in conveying statements of wisdom, beauty and truth.

Aristotle divided Rhetoric into three types: judicial (legal orations), deliberative (speech in decision-making bodies, such as a parliament or council) and demonstrative or epideictic (speeches of praise or blame). He also defined three basic ways in which a speaker may appeal to his listeners: *ethos* (appeal to ethics), *pathos* (appeal to feeling) and *logos* (appeal to reason). This scheme was followed by Cicero, who said that a speaker must aim to do three things: to move his audience (*movere*), to instruct (*docere*) and to delight (*delectare*). These concepts were familiar to Renaissance writers and can provide us with a conceptual framework with which to approach texts: sermons, for example, aim to teach

Christian truths in ways which are delightful to listen to, and which move us by engaging our imagination. Shakespeare gives us many examples of all three kinds of Rhetoric: when Brutus and Macbeth contemplate killing the head of state, or Hamlet ponders whether or not to be, they follow the standard training in forensic (legal) rhetoric of arguing *in utramque partem* – on both sides of the case. The meetings of court and rebels in the History Plays offer rich examples of deliberative oratory; Enobarbus's famous 'barge' speech describing Cleopatra (*Antony and Cleopatra*, 2.2) is an instance of epideictic rhetoric.

Renaissance schoolboys learned the five parts of Rhetoric: finding the right material for the matter in hand (*inventio*), organising a speech (*dispositio*), finding the right way of expressing the ideas (*ornatus*), memorising it (*memoria*) and performing it with the right gestures and facial expressions (*actio*). They learned that ideas could be expressed in three styles, depending on the subject: the grand style was suitable for tragedy, the middle style for satire, the low style for pastoral and comedy. After this, pupils learned an exhaustive list of rhetorical terms for the ways in which language could be arranged or 'figured' (hence 'figurative language'). These are divided into two types: *schemes* involve the way words are arranged in a sentence and *tropes* involve the deviation of words from their usual sense. The following lines by Sir Philip Sidney (1554–1586) give us an example of how this could work in practice:

> Some lovers speak, when they their muses entertain,
> Of hopes begot by fear, of wot not what desires,
> Of force of heavenly beams, infusing hellish pain,
> Of living deaths, dear wounds, fair storms and freezing fires.
> Some one his song in Jove, and Jove's strange tales, attires,
> Broidered with bulls and swans, powdered with golden rain.
>
> (Astrophil and Stella, 6)

In these few lines we can see a number of schemes: unusual word order (*anastrophe*) in placing the object before the verb in lines 1 and 5; *parallelism* in the similarly structured phrases of line 2; *isocolon* in the exactly similar phrase shapes of 'dear wounds, fair storms'; *anaphora* in the same word beginning lines (*Of*) and clauses (*Some*). Line 3 gives us an instance of *antithesis*, placing contrary ideas together (*heavenly ... hellish*). More familiar to us is *alliteration*, or repeated consonants: here we have *Broidered with bulls* and also the subtle repeated pattern in **F**orce *of* **h**eavenly **b**eams, *inf*using **h**ellish **p**ain. Meanwhile, the idea of attiring a song (line 5) is the trope of *metaphor*; *hopes begot by feare* is a *paradox* (a figure of logic), and *wot not what* is a sound repeated until it sounds comic (*cacemphaton*). Above all in these lines, Sidney parodies the Petrarchan *oxymoron* or pairing of contrasting terms (*living deaths*, etc.) in descriptions of the experience of love.

Familiarity with the figures of Rhetoric gives us a means of describing texts in terms which were employed at the time and appreciating their skill. The brief analysis above also illustrates the important Renaissance idea of copiousness. A popular text by Erasmus (1466/69–1536), known as *De Copia*, shows pupils how to express the same idea in different ways, varying the style and register: Erasmus gives over 150 ways to say 'I enjoyed your letter this morning' in Latin. As an exercise, this improved pupils' handling of Latin. In English writing, we see time and again the delight in using the resources of vocabulary to express the same idea in different ways. Here is Sidney again, playing on the theme of the curative property of sleep:

> Come sleep, O sleep, the certain knot of peace,
> The baiting place of wit, the balm of woe,
> The poor man's wealth, the prisoner's release . . .
> (*Astrophil and Stella*, 39)

Besides the opportunity to learn and apply some of the figures, Renaissance Rhetoric provides the modern reader with some interesting problems. Where modern readers, heavily influenced by Romanticism, tend to feel literary expression should originate in the original expression of genuine feeling, Rhetorical education provided a way of composing poetry by methodically applying a scientific system of linguistic formulae. We might expect a poem to be in some way a sincere expression of an authentic experience; a rhetorical poem may be treating a timeworn theme (the pleasures of the countryside, the need for order) by trying out and playing with different tropes and voices. We place a high premium on novelty, while Rhetoric taught its users to draw on the sayings and arguments of the past. To see Renaissance poetry from the perspective of the time, we thus need to understand ideas like contrived, derived and artificial as positive terms of praise. In the craft of the making lies part of the meaning. Equally, rhetorical patterns can be mimetic of what they describe: perhaps in the repeated pattern of Sidney's lines on peace we get the feel of a mind turning an idea round and round as it waits for sleep to come.

At the same time as Renaissance discourse may challenge our preconceptions about what literary language involves, there are other ways in which we may feel fellow feeling with Rhetoric. Aristotle pointed out that Rhetoric is a given fact of society, and sixteenth-century analysis also applies to today's practices like advertisement and spin. Arguments about the use of language to dupe and mislead continue: like Othello and

King Lear, we are extremely vulnerable if we are not skilled in seeing how others may be using language to manipulate us. Equally, Renaissance Rhetoric shares some preoccupations with modern literary theory: the problematic relation between language and truth, the capacity for a discourse to have several meanings at the same time, and the need for new discourse to be constructed to meet each fresh occasion – these are all points at which the modern reader and the Renaissance rhetorician are on common ground.

See also *Contexts*: Court, Courtier, Humanism, Manuscripts; *Texts*: Conceit, Decorum, Imitation, Logic, Mimesis, Theory of Poetry

Further Reading

Edward P. J. Corbett and Robert J. Connors, *Classical Rhetoric for the Modern Student*, 4th edn (Oxford: OUP, 1999).

Richard Lanham, *A Handlist of Rhetorical Terms*, 2nd edn (Berkeley: University of California Press, 1991).

Peter Mack, *Elizabethan Rhetoric: Theory and Practice* (Cambridge: CUP, 2002).

Arthur Quinn, *Figures of Speech: 60 Ways to Turn a Phrase* (Davis: Hermagoras Press, 1993).

Debora K. Shuger, *Sacred Rhetoric: The Christian Grand Style in the English Renaissance* (Princeton, NJ: Princeton UP, 1988).

Thomas O. Sloan and Raymond B. Waddington, eds, *The Rhetoric of Renaissance Poetry* (Berkeley: University of California Press, 1974).

The Sonnet

The following sonnet is by Samuel Daniel (*c*.1563-1619), from his sonnet sequence *Delia* (1592):

> Look, Delia, how we steem the half-blown rose [steem: esteem, value
>   The image of the blush and summer's honour;
> Whilst in her tender green she doth enclose
> 4   That pure sweet beauty Time bestows upon her.
> No sooner spreads her glory in the air
>   But straight her full-blown pride is in declining;
> She then is scorned that late adorned the fair:
> 8   So clouds thy beauty after fairest shining.
> No April can revive thy withered flowers,
>   Whose blooming grace adorns thy glory now;
> Swift speedy Time, feathered with flying hours,
> 12   Dissolves the beauty of the fairest brow.
>   O let not then such riches waste in vain,
> 14   But love whilst that thou mayst be loved again.

This illustrates several typical features of the form, subject matter and style of the Renaissance sonnet. Its 14 lines of iambic pentameter verse are linked by the intricate rhyme scheme of the English (or Shakespearean) sonnet. This consists of three cross-rhymed quatrains and a couplet (*abab cdcd efef gg*). These structural blocks correspond to the main units of sense: each quatrain contains an idea and comes to a full stop.

The ideas follow in a logical sequence: in the first quatrain (Q1) the speaker presents the rose to his beloved Delia as a picture of youthful beauty, not yet in full bloom; in Q2 the rose blossoms, but as soon as it has done so, it starts to fade; in Q3 Delia is reminded that, like the rose's bloom, her beauty too will soon pass. The couplet, in conclusion, urges Delia not to waste her beauty, but to return the speaker's love. The sonnet is typical of scores of Elizabethan sonnets in giving us a limited dramatic situation – the lover speaking to a silent mistress – providing a very simple argument which touches on favourite themes: love, beauty, 'mutability' or the transience of earthly pleasures, and the consequent exhortation to 'seize the day'.

Intellectually, we might say Daniel's sonnet is light: the argument is derivative, and the sentiments of the speaker are unsubtle. The basic analogy – beauty is a rose – is also traditional and explicitly marked. Indeed, if we have read some other works in the genre, from the first line of this poem we can virtually guess what the speaker is going to say in the rest. This 'lightness' in turn then draws our attention to the poem as a verbal artefact: if the poet is not trying to surprise us with his ideas, then he may be trying to charm us with his craft. Thus we notice that the lines and sections of the poem are linked by a pattern of words and sounds: Q1 alone contains internal rhyme (*steem, green; rose, bestows*) alliteration (*blown, blush, bestows*) and assonance (*green, sweet*). Other cohesive devices across the poem include simple repetition (*Time, blown, adorns, fairest, glory*), the thread of *g* and *b* sounds throughout, the use of binary opposites (*pride / scorn, clouds / shining*) and the regular placement of *beauty* somewhere in the last line of each quatrain (4, 8, 12), both linking them and bringing their melody to a close. This patterning is continued on a larger scale, as the last line of this sonnet then becomes the first of the next in the sequence.

Daniel's combination of clever construction with the expression of emotion is typical of Renaissance lyric: where we might see fragmented speech as a sign of strong feeling, this kind of discourse operates on the premise that strong feeling raises our thoughts to a more intense and lucid pitch. This is registered both in the appropriately 'pure' vocabulary and imagery, from which everyday scenes are excluded, and in the elaborate acoustic, syntactic, semantic and metrical configurations in which those thoughts find form.

A traditional stock of ideas allows for infinite variation. Here is Shakespeare dealing with much the same ideas as exercised Daniel:

> Like as the waves make towards the pebbled shore,
>   So do our minutes hasten to their end;
> Each changing place with that which goes before,
> 4   In sequent toil all forwards do contend.
> Nativity, once in the main of light,
>   Crawls to maturity, wherewith being crowned,
> Crooked eclipses gainst his glory fight,
> 8   And Time that gave doth now his gift confound.
> Time doth transfix the flourish set on youth
>   And delves the parallels in beauty's brow,
> Feeds on the rarities of nature's truth,
> 12   And nothing stands but for his scythe to mow.
>   And yet to times in hope my verse shall stand,
>   Praising thy worth, despite his cruel hand.

The structure and the theme of mutability are the same, though the conclusion reached in the closing couplet is clearly different. The poet's declaration that his verse will last may seem conceited to us, but it is a standard feature of many Elizabethan sonnets, and part of the larger topic of how art can rescue worth and beauty from the ravages of time.

In this sonnet, Shakespeare has moved beyond the conventional expression of love, to give a more philosophical reflection on time and art. What is perhaps most strikingly different in his treatment is the much wider range of imagery. We start with the picture of the waves, but then come to:

> Nativity, once in the main of light,
> Crawls to maturity, wherewith being crowned...

Like a beam of light hitting a prism, one principal idea is here refracted into different metaphors, all working simultaneously. We have the image of the ages of man: a baby crawls to manhood and is 'crowned' in his prime. At the same time, the picture is of the sun moving across the sky from the light of morning to noon before descending. The *main* (expanse), picking up on the waves of Q1, also suggests the ocean main, glittering under the sun; next, the mature man seems to have become a real King fighting against *Crooked* (wicked) enemies, before personified Time appears, to relieve him of his glory. In the next quatrain the imagery shifts again: Time transfixes (kills), delves, feeds and mows – all different pictures, loosely connected by the idea of agriculture. Yet so strong is the main theme, that this Shakespearean stream of associated images does not confuse us. Instead, it serves to orchestrate a simple idea, lending it a varied tonal and emotional texture. A fairly formulaic idea thus comes over as a profound psychological event. To turn something simple and potentially dull into something dazzling in this way was a challenge relished by many Renaissance sonnet writers, though Shakespeare represents this art at its peak.

Our close reading of these two sonnets should warn us against generalising about this form, which seemed to meet exactly the Renaissance need for vehicles of expression which were at once traditional and flexible. The sonnet in English derives chiefly from Petrarch's *Canzoniere*, love poems to 'Laura' in which the subjective self of the lover is the real topic, typically expressed through paradoxes and oxymorons: he burns and freezes, suffers and delights, is in prison and free, all at the same time, under the spell of his beloved. Petrarchan sonnets are divided into an *octave*, rhyming *abbaabba* and a *sestet* (of varying schemes, of two or three rhyme sounds), often with a 'turn' or change of intellectual and emotional direction between the two. This form was translated and imitated by Sir Thomas Wyatt (1503–1542) and Henry Howard, Earl of Surrey (*c*.1517–1547).

Elizabethan literature includes many sonnet sequences, a kind of writing which came into vogue in the 1580s. In these, individual poems are connected in a larger whole, offering a prolonged analysis of a lover's experience. Two of the finest are Sir Philip Sidney's *Astrophil and Stella* (written ?1582, published 1591) and Edmund Spenser's *Amoretti* (1595). (Spenser also elaborated his own rhyme scheme, *ababbcbc-cdcdee*.) Love is still the theme in sonnet sequences, but as the conventions become worn, they are often made the subject of parody. In Shakespeare's *Sonnets* (published 1609), an intriguing set of personae appear, and the expression of feeling seems so convincing and so much the result of particular circumstances that some critics have searched for sources in Shakespeare's life. As we have seen from our reading above, Shakespeare's sonnets acknowledge the tradition but renew it, and often look beyond the immediate situation to larger themes, such as Time, Death and Art. Later poets take the sonnet out of the sphere of courtly love altogether. It is used to describe religious experience, by Donne in the sequence *Divine Sonnets*, or Herbert, in poems such as 'Prayer', in which all logical sequencing and argumentation is thrown off to give a series of contemplative images. Milton employs the sonnet for topics ranging from autobiography ('On his blindness') to religious polemic ('On the late Massacre in Piedmont').

Whatever their subject matter, sonnet writers tend to use the form to describe profound emotional situations (which they may or may not have experienced themselves), dramatised through compact narrative or argumentation: the sonnet thus gives expression to the Renaissance concern with the tension between Passion (in the content) and Reason (in the form), working together in a model of the Platonic ideal of self-governance. It also appeals to the Humanist interest in the artful deployment of individual words, in which the skill of the poet can be measured by the careful attention he gives to their properties of sound, association and sense – a poetic which in turn makes the Renaissance sonnet sympathetic to modern readers trained in the school of Practical Criticism.

See also   *Contexts*: Court, Humanism, Platonism, Sex and Sexuality, The Self; *Texts*: Conceit, Decorum, Genre, Lyric, Rhetoric

Further Reading
Michael Spiller, *The Development of the Sonnet: An Introduction* (New York: Routledge, 1992).
Barry Spurr, *Studying Poetry* (Houndmills, Basingstoke: Palgrave Macmillan, 1997), ch. 5 'The Renaissance', 61–89.
Helen Vendler, *The Art of Shakespeare's Sonnets* (Cambridge, MA: Harvard University Press, 1997).

Theatres

The Renaissance saw the introduction of the purpose-built theatre, which attracted the talents of many of the greatest writers of the day. Drama itself, though, was certainly not new: public performances of mystery and morality plays had established the theatre as a popular art form, though religious plays had been in decline from late in the fifteenth century. This change was exacerbated by politics. When Henry VIII became head of the Church in England (1533/4), juris-diction over religious drama passed from the Church to the crown. The pre-reformation mystery cycles, so closely associated with Rome, became politically dangerous material. This situation was formalised in a 1543 Act which prohibited the performance of plays which inter-preted the Bible 'contrary to the doctrine set forth' by the King. The centralising of censorship in the institution of the crown made religious theatre effectively impossible, and Renaissance playwrights turned to other material, Italian or classical or native in origin. Besides the great medieval open-air spectacles, plays had also been performed indoors, in university halls, Inns of Court, schools and private houses. The fare on offer varied from knockabout humour to moral lessons, from energetic spectacle to academic dialogues. The Renaissance playwright, as much as the poet, had a rich tradition to draw on.

Before the first purpose-built theatres, permanent spaces existed at taverns. At least two inns in London (the Saracen's Head in Islington, and the Boar's Head in Aldgate) were being used for performances by professional companies in the 1550s. There was only one door from the street into the inn yard, and, as they entered, members of the audience put their money in a box fastened to a wall or post (the origin of 'box office'). Besides this assurance of income, inn yards also offered performance possibilities. In the central yard (normally used as a parking and storage space), a platform would be erected for a stage, and the players would perform in the round. The space beneath the platform could be used for special sound effects. The public would either stand before the stage or look down from balconies before the rooms, so actors had to perform to a split-level audience. Sometimes a gallery might also serve as a secondary acting space. As well as the street entrance, there was a second door, to the inn itself: these provided two entrances and exits. A curtain could be hung across the inn wall to create a backdrop or create a further space behind. Some inns also had a tower, which could be used to house a pulley or raise a flag. All of these features can be found in a modified fashion in the playhouses: effects in later plays, like the God hoisted down in *Cymbeline* (pub.1623), or the bodies revealed in Webster's *The Duchess of Malfi* (perf. 1614) have their background in tavern performances.

London taverns fell under the control of the city authorities, who disapproved of these public performances, since they drew large and potentially disorderly crowds. In 1574 an Act made it compulsory to obtain a licence to perform. In this Act, the Corporation of London complains that:

Sundry great disorders and inconveniences have been found to ensue to this City by the inordinate haunting of great multitudes of people, specially youth, to plays, interludes, and shows; namely occasion of frays and quarrels, evil practices of incontinency in great Inns, having chambers and secret places adjoining to their open stages and galleries, inveigling and alluring of maids, especially orphans and good citizens' children under age to privy and unmeet contracts, the publishing of unchaste, uncomely and unshamefast speeches and doings, withdrawing of the Queen Majesty's subjects from divine service on Sundays and holidays, at which time such plays were chiefly used, unthrifty waste of money of the poor and fond [foolish] persons, sundry robberies by picking and cutting of purses, uttering of popular, busy, and seditious matters, and many other corruptions of youth and other enormities.

Doubtless, all of these complaints had some justification. Perhaps behind them is a deeper unease at the whole idea of illusion and pretence; as well as inducing a disorderly scene, a stage might represent a disorderly imagination. Among his many other objections to the theatre, the Puritan John Rainolds cites the excitement caused by lady's costume:

> The apparel of women is a great provocation of men to lust and lechery. A womans garment being put on a man doeth vehemently touch and move him with the remembrance and imagination of a woman; and the imagination of a thing desirable doth stirr up the desire (*Th'Overthrow of Stage-Playes*, 1599).

Rainolds's book was one of several attacks on the immorality, as the Puritans saw it, of the theatre. Other titles in this vein include Stephen Gosson's *Plays Confuted in Five Actions* (1582) and Philip Stubbes's *The Anatomie of Abuses* (1583).

Faced with the disapproval of the authorities, some companies sought licences: the Earl of Leicester's Company, led by James Burbage, was given a Royal Patent to perform on weekdays in London. Another option was to move beyond the jurisdiction of the city authorities, and this Burbage did by building a theatre in the ruins of the disused Priory of Holywell in Shoreditch in 1576. This he called The Theatre, and it was soon imitated by The Curtain (1577), The Rose and The Swan (*c.*1596). The most famous Elizabethan theatre of all, The Globe (1599), was a reconstruction of The Theatre on the South Bank of The Thames when the lease on the site of The Theatre ran out. Burbage claimed that while the land was rented, the theatre was not, and while the courts investigated the affair the whole theatre was dismantled.

These early theatres took the large spaces of game-houses, used for bear-baiting, and put in them the rectangular stage of inn yards and halls. More detailed evidence for their design is patchy. A famous document is the drawing of The Swan, made by the Dutchman Johannes De Witte in 1596. This shows a structure of three floors, with a stage backing onto the wall and projecting out into the audience. This forms an 'apron stage', visible from three sides. Upper floors are roofed, as is the stage, which rests on two columns. The yard, occupied by standing spectators, is not roofed. The yard is thus open to the elements, but a corresponding advantage is that the acting space is lit by natural daylight. Also in de Witte's drawing there is a balcony above the stage, and a tower (with a flag raised when a performance was on). Other evidence includes a drawing of London by Wenceslas Hollar in 1640 showing a distant view of the rebuilt Globe (the original burned down during a performance of

Henry VIII on 29 June 1613), and the contract for the Fortune Theatre (1600). The Fortune was a square structure, but otherwise similar to the round Globe. This contract does not give the dimensions for the stage (this is 'to be fashioned like unto the stage of the said playhouse called the Globe'), but this can be roughly inferred from stage directions, stage action and continental theatres. A space of about 14 metres by 8 would seem to be a reasonable estimate.

The Renaissance playhouse must have had a popular feel. It imitated not only the tavern yard but also the round game-houses, used for bear-baiting. The penny charge for admission as a 'groundling' to the yard meant that the public theatre was always rooted in mass entertainment. This partly accounts for the use of comic language and events, even in the serious plays. A work set in the refined world of the court, like *King Lear* (c.1606), can still include the language of ballads, riddles and fishermen. The porter in *Macbeth* (c.1606) appeals to the guffaws of groundlings, while at the same time providing a serious commentary on the nature of the proceedings: the mixture of tragedy and comedy is rooted in the spaces of the plays themselves. In the English Renaissance, the drama of the public theatre never withdraws from its popular base into a refined and purely aristocratic dimension.

The institution of the playhouse also brought a huge increase in the demand for new plays. London had a population of about 200,000. Taking away such groups as children, the old and the infirm, we are left with a potential audience for a play of about 30,000. A theatre like The Globe could house an audience of some 2000–3000. Therefore after 10–15 performances of a play the potential audience was exhausted and new material had to be found. If a play was a success, it might be revived later, perhaps in a revised fashion. A repertory system developed, with companies performing several works in quick succession: a company like The Admiral's Men could perform 11 works over 23 days. For audiences, this kind of production line meant a constant stream of novel entertainment. In their turn, companies responded quickly to public reception.

The shape of the playhouse also brought a fundamental difference in the relation between audience and actors. Actors step in and out of role. Spectators, fully visible in daylight, cluster around the stage, with no proscenium arch separating them from the stage-play world. The distinction between the real and the pretended world is therefore blurred. Actors might step in front of one of the columns supporting the roof in order to deliver an aside. In doing this, they would create a transitional space, somewhere between the imagined space of the dramatic scene and that of the audience. Interaction and improvised response by actors would make the audience part of the spectacle. The plays themselves, with their plots turning on disguise, pretence and illusion, bear witness to this fascination with the fluidity of persona and role, and the confusion of the real and the feigned. *Hamlet* (*c*.1600) takes the play within a play as a plot element. But many other plays have similar layers of illusion: the conmen of Jonson's *The Alchemist* (perf. 1610) put on theatrical spectacles – plays within the play – to gull their victims. One reason for the Renaissance interest in madness on stage might be that it is a state in which the real and imagined worlds are no longer distinguished.

Another result of the increased demand for plays was increased supply: educated men like university wits had an opportunity to make some money providing scripts for the acting companies. The theatre was thus also an important element in the rise during the Renaissance of the professional writer.

Playhouses used few decorations, so places had to be established by means of words. The texts of the plays themselves had to convey the idea of scenery to the audience's imagination. To persuade an audience to imagine it was daybreak or night in the middle of the afternoon (plays would start at two and last two or three hours), for example, intense dramatic imagery was needed. Such stage properties as were used had a suggestive or symbolic function: they were not used to 'fill in' a scene realistically. A throne suggested a palace, a tree indicated a forest. Other symbolism included colours: a black curtain was used for tragedy, a coloured one for comedy. Gestures, postures and configurations of characters on stage could all carry meaning, sometimes deriving from older traditions: Falstaff with a wooden sword recalls the Vice of misrule from the morality plays. Costumes were the most extravagant part of the visuals of a performance. Often they were sold on by courtiers moving on to the next fashion, and we know from the accounts of the theatre entrepreneur Philip Henslowe (*c*.1550–1616) that investment in costume could be one of the most expensive outlays of a theatre manager. Like props, costumes could have an essentially symbolic function, signifying that a character is regal, ludicrous or wretched. No attempt at consistent historical realism was made: this is suggested by a 1595 drawing of a performance of *Titus Andronicus*, which shows Titus in a toga and others in elaborate contemporary dress. What is important is presumably to indicate the roles in the drama each figure had. In music, spectacle meets sound. In the playhouses, an upper exists above the main stage – reminiscent of minstrels' galleries in houses or the upper tiers of an inn – where musicians would play. Music and dance formed an important part of the dramatic entertainment. Where our modern texts of Renaissance plays come to a definite close, at the time the play would usually be followed by a jig or other dance.

Besides the great public theatres like The Globe were the private, indoor theatres. At the same time as Burbage built The Theatre in Shoreditch, Richard Farrant, Master of the Children of the Chapel Royal, acquired the Dominican Convent of Blackfriars, near St Paul's. This had been a ruin since it was confiscated in 1538. Like Burbage's Theatre, Blackfriars was outside the jurisdiction of the city authorities. There, plays written for the children of the Chapel Royal were performed, with all parts being played by boys between the ages of 9 and 13. Covered halls were protected from the weather, and so more attractive for actors; but they housed fewer spectators and so had to charge more for admission (fourpence, considerably more than the penny for a place in the pit, but competitively priced compared to the more expensive gallery seats in the open theatres). Higher admission prices in turn created a different kind of audience, and so plays of a more self-consciously academic and literary content were produced to suit their tastes: John Lyly (c.1553–1606), for example, wrote a number of plays for the boys of the Chapel Royal and St Paul's, characterised by refined and didactic moral content, with little of the vigorous drama of the public spaces. Blackfriars was closed in 1584, but Burbage constructed a second Blackfriars in 1596; from 1608 it was used by his company instead of The Globe. Indoor spaces require lighting, and the private theatres of the period encouraged advances in special effects. To the skill of the boy actors, illusionist spectacle and comfort of the indoor theatres was added music, in the form of concerts and interludes. These proved attractive to audiences, and plays of the period testify to the rivalry between the different kinds of company.

The moment of the Renaissance playhouse was relatively short-lived. They were regularly closed in times of plague, and in 1642 all London theatres were closed by Act of Parliament. Under the Commonwealth, theatrical performances were banned, and when the theatres opened again at the Restoration they played not to the mixed crowds of The Globe but to the small coterie audiences of private theatres. The drama forged in the playhouses depended on constant and complex interplay with a common audience; it became a public forum through which concerns and desires of the time were given expressive shape. In Restoration London, theatre became what it still is to a great extent today, a leisure activity for the more affluent. Restoration theatre, and the theatre that followed, departs from this earlier close contact with the common spectator and marks a sharp change of direction in English drama.

See also *Contexts*: City, Court, Humanism, Patronage, Race, Sex and Sexuality; *Texts*: Actors and Acting, Masque

Further Reading

Andrew Gurr, *The Shakespearean Stage, 1574–1642*, 3rd revised edn (Cambridge: CUP, 1992).

Tanya Pollard, ed., *Shakespeare's Theater: A Sourcebook* (Oxford: Blackwell, 2003).

Stanley Wells, *Shakespeare and Co.: Christopher Marlowe, Thomas Dekker, Ben Jonson, Thomas Middleton, John Fletcher and the Other Players in his Story* (London: Allen Lane, 2006).

In addition to reading, it is enjoyable and instructive to see a performance at the reconstructed Globe Theatre on the South Bank. This is not on the location of Shakespeare's Globe, and is about half the size of the original; but it is still highly suggestive of the kind of theatrical experience a Renaissance audience might have had.

Theory of Poetry

Literary production in the Renaissance period was accompanied by a strong body of writing examining the theory of literature itself. What is the essential nature of poetry? What is its purpose? What are the defining features of poetic language? In considering such questions, Renaissance thinkers advanced a conception of poetry which was distinct at many points from that of the Middle Ages.

While medieval poetic theory is itself a complex topic, its chief assumption is clear. This is that poetry has a certain form – metrical verse – and a proper content, fiction. The poet is a versifier and a fabulist (story-maker). A poet's work has no distinctive value in itself, but may be useful for communicating moral lessons. Thus Boccaccio (*c.*1313–1375; in *Genealogy of the Pagan Gods* (1360)) defends poetry as a means of delivering the truths established by theology, in the form of allegorical fiction. Next to Theology, the queen of the sciences, poetry was deemed by the learned to be an essentially secondary kind of expression.

This conception was closely tied to the system of Scholasticism, which placed formal logic and theology at the summit of intellectual life. But with the rise of humanism came a stronger interest in eloquence: truth, asserted the humanists, may be discovered by formal proof, but it may also arise through the practice of civilised discourse. Humanism conferred a higher status on communication, pursued through the discipline of rhetoric. In turn, humanist rhetoric did not serve the passive contemplation of truth, but was directed towards the active pursuit of virtue, through informing and inspiring good actions.

This position was further elaborated through study of classical texts. Chief among these was Horace's *Art of Poetry* (which Ben Jonson translated), the main source of the notion of decorum. Cicero did not leave any treatise on poetry, but his work as a whole showed that rhetoric could be applied to any subject. Thus we find Renaissance poetry directed to a wide range of subjects, from moral philosophy to politics to the theory of knowledge: poetry is an art of eloquence, and eloquence knows no subject boundaries. Platonism was a further influence. Plato himself was ambiguous on poetry: he uses poetic devices in his dialogues and wrote of the poet's *furor divinus* or divine frenzy; yet he also found no place for poets, who deal with illusions, in *The Republic*. Nonetheless, Neoplatonism advanced the idea that art and poetry, through providing beautiful images, could help the mind to reach the divine Good. A final pervasive influence on Renaissance poetic theory was St Augustine (354–430), specifically his position on rhetoric in *On Christian Doctrine* (Bks I–III, 397; Bk IV, 426). For St Augustine, the role of the preacher was to explain the Scriptures in such a way that it moved the listener to lead a good and holy life. Much Renaissance verse – Spenser's *Faerie Queene* is a supreme example – is a secular version of the sermon, using stories and pictures to guide us towards the morally good life.

On these foundations, a new theory of poetry could be built. Starting in Italy, comprehensive theoretical works were written in both Latin and vernacular languages. But, then as now, English writers did not seem to go in for monumental theoretical works on the continental model. There were various defences of poetry composed in Latin (authors include John Jewel (1522–1571) and John Rainolds (1549–1607)), but the best known today – and the most accessible to the modern reader – is the *Apologie for Poetrie* by Sir Philip Sidney (written *c.*1579, and published posthumously in 1595; it was also published in that year with another printer as *A Defence of Poetry*, hence it is referred to by both titles). While no one work can fully represent the complex tidal patterns of ideas about literature in the period, through a summary of the *Apologie* we can see the main themes of the Renaissance theory of poetry.

Sidney's *Apologie* is brief and readable. It is not an academic treatise, but a rhetorical exercise, an oration that a lawyer might make, defending poetry against the charges of its enemies. The style is witty and conversational, dealing with deep subjects in the courtly mode of graceful language, modesty and an unforced conversational ease. Its chief conception of poetry is rich in implications, but refreshingly straightforward. In Sidney's own words:

> Poesy therefore is an art of imitation . . . that is to say, a representing counterfeiting, or figuring forth – to speak metaphorically, a speaking picture – with this end, to teach and delight.

The poet provides a figure or picture of something which teaches and delights us. The nature of the picture itself is discussed in the entry on

Mimesis: briefly, it is not a realistic representation of the world as we see it with our senses, but an image of the ideal which is disguised by the real (see the entry on Imitation). Poetry gives us a 'golden world', which is more truthful and helpful than either the factual account of history or the abstract logic of philosophy. Through this 'fiction' or golden composition of images, we readers can discern the truthful and rational pattern in Nature, and reach a better understanding of our own nature. And once we understand ourselves better, and the world of which we are a part, then we can understand our duty and fulfil our natures by performing good actions. Thus poetry teaches us, and, as it does so, it moves us (in the Renaissance sense of persuades or inspires) to live a morally good life. With its skill, eloquence and musical qualities, poetry also delights us; and delight is a natural part of learning the truth. But this delight is instrumental to the end of teaching and 'moving'. Just as an advert is not designed to be the object of our attention but to persuade us to buy something, so a poem, in Sidney's account, is not designed to be an end in itself, but to persuade us to do something – for example, to live more piously, or serve our country, as loyal subjects or valiant soldiers (Sidney himself died fighting for the Netherlands in its struggle for independence against Spain). Sidney therefore disapproves of poetry which draws attention to itself with excessive verbal artifice.

Sidney's account of poetry is thus strikingly active. In the humanist model, poetry is part of the actively useful life, something that can help us to be better Christians or subjects. It is quite different to the idea of 'learning for its own sake', according to which the study of literature is a valuable and enriching exercise in itself without any need for utilitarian justification. We can see the legacy of these ideas later in a writer like Milton, who in *Areopagitica* (1644) says he 'cannot praise a fugitive and cloistered virtue': for both writers, literary production is related to the strenuous pursuit of virtue through action, and to public service.

The *Apologie* is also an aristocratic work. Sidney himself was a nobleman and courtier, and the qualities he values are correspondingly noble ones. Popular verse dealing with 'low' themes is for him not poetry at all, and his theory does not encompass the vigorous native traditions of ballads and romances. How far such ideas were consciously applied to the writing even of courtly poetry is perhaps impossible to determine: poet-theorists themselves, whether they are Sidney or Wordsworth, do not always follow their own counsel. But the conviction that the poetic art should serve practical moral ends helps us to understand why courtiers like Sidney, who were deeply engaged in public affairs, should find the cultivation of poetry a natural part of their role. As a nobleman, Sidney is careful to present himself as an amateur in the field, and his approach is certainly different to that of a scholar like Julius Caesar Scaliger

(1484–1588). This kind of tension continues. In its description of the uses of poetry, Sidney's *Apologie* is radically different from any prospectus description of an English Literature degree today. Contemporary poetry anthologies which aim to help the reader deal with occasions of everyday life tend to be viewed askance by today's intelligentsia. Yet they are in a continuum with Sidney's conviction that poetry should serve us in our daily lives, not simply as a source of self-indulgent sophisticated pleasure in the library. Paradoxically, Sidney's aristocratic outlook has its most vigorous legacy in the democratic end of literary life today.

See also *Contexts*: Humanism, Patronage, Platonism, Stoicism; *Texts*: Conceit, Decorum, Imitation, Mimesis

Further Reading

Arthur F. Kinney, 'The Position of Poetry: Making and Defending Renaissance Poetics': in *A Companion to English Renaissance Literature and Culture*, ed. Michael Hattaway (Oxford: Blackwell, 2000), 340–351.

James Jerome Murphy, *Renaissance Eloquence: Studies in the Theory and Practice of Renaissance Rhetoric* (Berkeley: University of California Press, 1983).

Glyn P. Norton, ed., *The Cambridge History of Literary Criticism, Vol III: The Renaissance* (Cambridge: CUP, 1999).

Heinrich Franz Plett, *English Renaissance Rhetoric and Poetics: A Systematic Bibliography of Primary and Secondary Sources* (Leiden: Brill, 1995).

Sir Philip Sidney, *An Apology for Poetry*, ed. Geoffrey Shepherd, 2nd edn (Manchester: Manchester UP, 1973), Introduction, 1–92.

3 Criticism: Approaches, Theory, Practice

Introduction

Renaissance texts present a record of other ways of seeing both the external, physical world and the internal world of the mind, with its ideas, beliefs and values. The changes are registered in language: we find old words which have vanished and familiar ones which have changed their meaning; even words which have broadly the same meaning as today still have an altered frame of reference: consider, for example, what the word *journey* implies to someone in the modern west (trains, planes and automobiles) and what it meant to someone using the treacherous roads of the sixteenth century. Much of the excitement of literary study comes from this discovery of alternative ways of seeing the world. Scholars will help us to understand the Renaissance court, or views of religion, or Puritanism; but we have to read authors like Sidney, Hooker and Milton to get a first-hand idea of what it felt like to be a courtier, or Elizabethan churchman or seventeenth-century Puritan. The challenge of understanding this distant frame of mind is at the heart of literature studies; through immersing ourselves in another age, we try to read the texts of the past as far as possible in terms of their own time.

In reading, then, we go back to the past. But we are also bringing works from a previous age into our own time and reading them with a modern mentality. We interpret *Hamlet* in the light of modern psychology; we evaluate relationships from a perspective informed by modern Western ideas of sexual equality – ideas which were unavailable in the time of Philip and Mary Sidney. Reading with a consciously modern mentality has its dangers: we will soon become bored by a book if we expect it to reflect our own interests and values back at us. Renaissance texts are windows to another world, not mirrors to our own. Nonetheless, some idea of relevance clearly informs our reading, not least in the texts we choose to study: we read Donne and Herbert not simply out of antiquarian curiosity, but because we respond to them personally. We select texts which seem to speak to us, and see most clearly those aspects of them which correspond to our own preoccupations. Our interpretation of what we read is inevitably marked by the currents of thought in which we live.

One such current is determinism. This is at least the popular view of Marxism, Psychoanalysis and Darwinism. Over the last century or so, these schools of thought have cast doubt on the model of the individual as an autonomous agent. Instead, humans are often described as the vehicles through which external impersonal forces work. Marxism views culture (the superstructure) as the function of underlying economic forces (the substructure). In this account, individuals are not masters of their destiny but to a great extent the product of their environment. Psychoanalysis describes the human self as being shaped by infant experiences and stresses the importance of the unconscious. Darwinism, and its later developments, creates a powerful picture of complex beings modelled by their genetic inheritance. All of these schools of thought have influenced literary studies. Writers are not the sole creators of works, but vehicles for the dominant and marginalised voices of the time. The emphasis is on the contextual – the social and historical picture and the ideological cross-currents which are both created and recorded in texts. The text is not seen as a self-contained verbal artefact but as a kind of website with multiple links to other discourses, from race to gender to science. A great deal of recent literary criticism models itself on the social sciences in its attempt to analyse these large social and cultural patterns, as they manifest themselves in writings. The author is by no means comprehensively dead, however, as the popularity and quality of biographies of Renaissance writers makes clear.

Studying literature 'in context' inevitably raises questions about what 'context' is. The word, suggesting something about or around the text, still gives a central importance to the written work; and it also suggests some meaningful distinction between text and context, something which New Historicists and others deny is viable. One view is that we should forget this distinction entirely: 'context' or 'historical background' is simply the accumulation of other discourses, from legal records to travel journals and non-verbal discourses like furniture design and costume. (In this sense, a 'text' or 'discourse' is simply anything which can be interpreted.) Literary texts, the argument goes, are simply one discourse among these, with no necessary claim to privileged attention. One avenue of enquiry open to the literary student is not to write a study of an individual text, but to take a theme like space, sin, motion, or the body, and explore it through study of these various kinds of discourse.

Commonly, such study will not see 'context' as a neutral setting for literary work but as an active process connected to the functioning of power. This is a central preoccupation of our own time: how does any given society keep in subjection the mass of people who have little power over their own lives and are therefore a potential threat? The law, official iconography, dress, codes of etiquette, officially approved versions of history can all be seen as instruments by which certain structures of thought and behaviour are normalised and made to seem 'natural'. In the Renaissance, it might be argued, very few objected to a 'patriarchal' culture, in which power is massively invested in the male, because patriarchy was projected as normal by the culture of the time. Such contextual criticism may not be neutral, motivated only by curiosity. Some criticism today has an explicit political intention, linked to wider movements such as feminism and the campaign for homosexual rights. Politically motivated criticism seeks to uncover the processes by which a governing class maintains its power and to recover the voices of the marginalised and oppressed, commonly labelled as deviants, heretics or other terms denoting them as falling outside the prescribed norms of the time. While classical liberal reading of literature may salute it as promoting civilised values, politicised contextual reading can be adversarial – essentially accusing literary texts of complicity in the injustices of their age (but also looking for ways in which they might also present a challenge to received thinking). Contextual study is also concerned with uncovering contradictions and tensions within a culture, rather than finding a unitary 'world view'; on the Marxist model, it is these contradictions, occasionally amounting to physical clashes, which generate historical change. An internal contradiction we find in turn in some criticism is between scepticism and certainty. There is scepticism about the possibility of universal truth, of moral and aesthetic values or of identifiable authorial intentions and linguistic meanings, for example. But at the same time, there are firmly held convictions about the rights and dignities of the oppressed.

Another object of scepticism is the notion of identity. Many readers of this book will probably at some point have had to answer a question on a literary character (would Hamlet have made a good king?). Such questions are normally based on the assumption that characters have a consistent identity. One objection to this approach is that it projects later ideas of character onto the early modern period: while a character in a Henry James novel might be internally consistent, with certain regular personal attributes, this is not necessarily the case with Renaissance texts. Depending on where he is, Hamlet speaks the language of the courtier, fool, lover and theatre enthusiast. Is there a detectable, 'essential' Hamlet linking all of these? A postmodern response would be that there is not: the subjective self does not precede speech or action but is constructed by these various discourses. To put it another way, a character is courtly not because that is his real inner personality, but simply because he or she is in a situation of speaking and acting in the courtly fashion. Another situation, and another discourse, may be discontinuous with the previous one: identity is marked by the discourses of race, gender, class, spirituality by which the early modern person is defined. This idea that the self is not stable but created through language (which is itself, as deconstructionists remind us, slippery and indeterminate) interestingly coincides with the Renaissance rhetorical practice of adopting the persona suitable for the matter and purpose of a speech. For the critic, the rejection of comfortable ideas of stable character should help with the identification of the types of self constructed in early modern culture, revealing the deep structures of thought underlying individual works. One important aspect of this structure will be the perception of an 'other' against which dominant identities can assert themselves: the presentation of Catholics, the Irish, witches, New World Indians, vagabonds in Renaissance writing typically has the function of asserting a 'normal' self, more towards the centre of power, in distinction with these threatening, marginal 'others'.

These are some of the themes which recur in critical studies today. Criticism itself has a context, which is in most cases the university environment, with its politics, economics, academic presses, conferences and career paths. This institutional setting naturally influences, if not conditions, the kind of work being done. For example, one aspect of this environment is the prestige accorded to the sciences. The history of English as an academic subject is bound up with attempts to present itself as being as rigorous and difficult as other disciplines, and today this involves a certain amount of emulation of scientists. Quasi-scientific practices among critics include the preference for looking at material and impersonal subjects, using impersonal methodologies and a disinclination to make personal and subjective judgements. There is also the need to show that new studies constitute measurable progress, and this brings with it the unfortunate consequence of an enormous condescension towards critics of the past. Tropes in critical writing include the elevation of other critics to the role of scientific discoverers ('as x has shown'), when all that is being alluded to may be an unsubstantiated speculation.

This influence of the sciences on critical writing has certainly involved the development of exciting new methods of enquiry and sharpened thinking about literary texts and their connection to larger cultural patterns. At the same time, it has drawn critics away from the traditional task of evaluating works on aesthetic and even moral grounds, an activity which is inevitably subjective; indeed, appreciating and discussing the value of works has been dismissed by some as a waste of time. Similarly, in subjecting texts to various analytical procedures such as Marxism of

Feminism, critics are in danger of treating all writing alike. Our attention is distracted from the unique form and imaginative experience offered by an individual poem as it is subsumed into some larger thesis. On a more banal level, critical studies in which the conclusion is known in advance can simply be dull ('in this chapter, we will see how patriarchal structures of authority are inscribed into lyrical structures'), and we may sometimes have the same sensation of a dizzying variety of material being used to prove the same few points. A further theme is that trends in critical writing can in subtle ways be enforced: students may feel they are being encouraged to have open minds, provided they are open in the correct manner. Universities have a valuable role to play in resisting the oppressive conformities of thinking of the day, but they themselves can create powerful institutional orthodoxies of their own, as is sometimes suggested by the imperatives of critical writing. A sentence like 'Today's student must study contextually' is a straightforward imperative, which will characteristically be followed by a promise of the riches to be gained from the exercise. But it is an imperative nonetheless.

Yet another issue is the relation of academic discourse to ordinary discussion: academia is presumably supposed to do something above and beyond everyday intelligent conversation, yet the more self-conscious academic critical writing becomes the more it vanishes into the speech of a tiny coterie with no connection to general conversation. This may be to cut itself off from something rich, not least the requirement to be clearly understandable. Under such circumstances, criticism can end up talking about itself, with only passing reference to the primary material of imaginative literature. Counterintuitive ideas of the death of the author, the intentional fallacy and the non-existence of character are at once bracingly challenging and a severing of the links between discourse inside and outside the ivory tower.

Of course, the above is an exaggerated picture, and it is open to any reader to test these points against actual critical writing. Students of literature today do not all subscribe religiously to the ideas we have considered; they may adopt them but with certain qualifications, or they may query strongly some of the presuppositions of much modern criticism. 'New Aestheticism', for example, takes issue with the disinclination of some critical writers to make value judgements. If we read a book like C. S. Lewis's famous study of sixteenth-century literature, we find a writer who clearly feels it is the business of the critic to venture personal judgements with which the reader may or may not agree. The need is for a language of discrimination and evaluation which eschews the vague or vacuous.

It is probably a mistake for the student of today to follow reverently the teachings of any particular critical school, or to be pro or anti-theory, which scarcely means anything. Good literary criticism can broaden our mind by helping us to think about texts in new ways; and it can sharpen our intelligence if we engage with it critically rather than submit reverently. Meanwhile, the age in which we live brings with it new concerns – climate change, the possibility for peaceful coexistence of different faith groups – and these concerns will affect what and how we read. If discussion which goes beyond the pieties and formulae of mass media has value, then it matters that our conversation about the past and its literature continues; but what form that conversation takes is for readers of this book, and others like it, to determine.

Further Reading

On application of literary theory to criticism, see:

Ewan Fernie et al., eds., *Reconceiving the Renaissance: A Critical Reader* (Oxford: OUP, 2005).

Cristina Malcolmson, ed., *Renaissance Poetry*, Longman Critical Readers (London: Longman, 1998).

Andrew Mousley, *Renaissance Drama and Contemporary Literary Theory* (Houndmills, Basingstoke: Palgrave Macmillan, 2000).

Patricia Parker and David Quint, eds, *Literary Theory / Renaissance Texts* (London: Johns Hopkins UP, 1986).

For more adverse approaches, see:

T. McAlindon, *Shakespeare Minus 'Theory'* (Aldershot: Ashgate, 2004). Brian Vickers, *Appropriating Shakespeare: Contemporary Critical Quarrels* (New Haven and London: Yale UP, 1993).

On the question of aesthetic value, see:

Richard Chamberlain, *Radical Spenser: Pastoral, Politics and the New Aestheticism* (Edinburgh: Edinburgh UP, 2005).

Cultural Materialism

A materialist approach to culture denies that art has any transcendent significance. It insists that a poem or other artefact does not transcend its historical context to enunciate universal truths. Indeed, cultural materialists maintain there are no such eternal verities, for our concepts are social constructs, which belong to a specific culture. For example, a seventeenth-century Puritan and a twenty-first-century liberal will hold radically different ideas about female identity. But neither is in possession of any transhistorical truth on the matter; rather, their ideas are contingent upon their social context and intrinsically related to their society's material processes. The apparently immaterial world of ideas and imagination reflects, reinforces – and at times challenges – a society's distribution of power and goods. Thus, all cultural works – including supposedly timeless masterpieces like the works of Shakespeare – are contingent upon the material conditions of their time.

Materialist analysis, as defined above, may seem a restricting approach. Its denial of transcendent truths can certainly induce a feeling of disenchantment in a reader who feels affection for literary creation. But materialists would argue that their approach is ultimately a liberating one. For the very idea that there are universal truths, enshrined in art, in the materialist view of things is a much more constricted vision. In Marxist terminology, such idealism is a product of false consciousness. This arises as we have instilled into us a set of illusory beliefs that prevent us from perceiving the present configurations of power. To take a simple example, we might be led by various media and normal social behaviour to believe, say, that a real man drives that, or a real woman wears this, based on these conceptions of what men and women are or should be like. These packaged ideas of manliness or femininity are then disseminated through the whole cultural environment. They become thinking habits which then translate into buying and living habits, effectively underwriting the behaviour of corporations and the political institutions which support them, by making that behaviour seem like the natural state of things. In the normal state of affairs, our notions of identity, gender, justice and even meaning thus tend to protect the prevailing arrangements of power.

Literary texts are part of this intellectual ecosystem of processes and practices which embody socio-political arrangements, arrangements which inevitably depend on others being losers and victims (those who are poor or of minority sexual orientation may be implicitly stigmatised as not so 'real' as men and women who conform to cultural norms). For the materialist critic, literary writing is one social practice among many others, with no special access to supposed higher truths. Indeed, one of the particular roles of high culture may be precisely to purvey the idea that there are such ideal, universal truths, in this way deluding us into thinking we have escaped the contingencies of our own historical predicament and arrived at some state of superior understanding. Cultural materialist analysis, its advocates argue, allows us to penetrate this matrix-like illusory consciousness, in order to see the underlying structure of power and be in some position to reform it, or at any rate draw some attention to its inequities. In this sense, reading and criticism are not an indulgent cultivation of the intellect but self-consciously political interventions.

Cultural Materialism has several sources, the main one being Marxism. A father figure is the intellectual historian Raymond Williams, who (in works like *The Long Revolution* (1961)) challenged the prevailing methodology of reading texts formally, with reference to some separable 'background' of secondary status. Instead, Williams posited the study of culture as a whole system, with no privileged aspects, and in *Problems in Materialism and Culture* (1980) he coined the phrase 'cultural materialism' to describe this strategy. At the same time as Williams was working on this conceptual model, social historians like E. P. Thompson (1924–1993) and Richard Hoggart (*b*.1918) were studying literary production in terms of the material conditions of working-class culture. Other historians approached subjects like the rural economy, witchcraft or marriage, producing studies in which literary material might be considered alongside other kinds of evidence like population statistics or trial records. The disciplines of ethnology, sociology and anthropology were similarly approaching culture as a single system, in which, again, cultural practices were not considered as special cases but in relation to the whole picture.

Another influential thinker who received increasing attention at this time was Michel Foucault (1926–1984), whose studies were much concerned with the distribution and cultural dynamics of power. To these roots in Marxism and the social sciences was added in the 1980s the influence of continental theory: feminism, poststructuralism and psychoanalysis all led many of those concerned with academic English to question the purposes and assumptions of the discipline, creating an atmosphere propitious for the emergence of a critical school whose procedures were concerned with reading as a kind of unmasking of the relations of production. The materialist approach found its definition in *Political Shakespeare* (1985), a collection of essays edited by Jonathan Dollimore and Alan Sinfield; the introduction to this volume is a clearly stated manifesto for the project. In its intellectual origins, and its explicit concern with power and its cultural representations, Cultural Materialism has close connections with New Historicism, and the two are often treated together as transatlantic cousins in accounts of critical theory. There are, however, differences in tone and emphasis: Cultural Materialism is sometimes more earnest in feel (while New Historicism can feel like a highly sophisticated game), and it usually has a more explicit and self-conscious political engagement, mixing French theoretical language with British polemical traditions of non-conformity and class struggle. Besides their distinct flavours, both Cultural Materialism and New Historicism have focused very largely on the Renaissance as the site of their operations, and separate treatment thus gives us more space to consider their particular contributions to the field.

A key concept for both schools is culture, in the wider sense of how a society organises and makes sense of itself. Examination of the internal dynamics of a culture reveals a complex reality very different from any uniform, monological 'world picture'. Rather than a single vision collectively shared by the community, the Renaissance world – in its material structure and the internalised version of that structure in contemporary consciousness – was in constant motion and characterised by internal conflicts, uncertainties and contradictions. Cultural materialists and new historicists follow social scientists in seeing culture as being typically a dynamic process rather than a static picture, heterogeneous rather than neatly cohesive. At any point, there will be a dominant force within a culture, legitimated by the 'world picture' purveyed in discourses from law to costume to prayer. The dominant culture will incorporate both the old and the new or, in the terms established by Raymond Williams, residual and emergent elements. For example, in the Renaissance period, the residual geocentric cosmology was only gradually supplanted by the emergent heliocentric one, and the residual ideology of knowing and keeping your place in the social hierarchy was challenged by an emergent ethic of individual enterprise linked to Protestantism and burgeoning capitalism.

On a less abstract level, a culture is comprised of many individual agents and articulated by their innumerable actions. Here we find a key issue in materialist analysis. How autonomous are individual human agents? 'Soft' materialism might admit that individuals can under the right circumstances think and operate independently; they can, for example, be 'alternative' agents, representing a different kind of existence, or 'oppositional' agents, working consciously to change the order of things. But 'hard' materialism emphasises that these allegedly independent ideas will themselves be formed by the cultural matrix; social and ideological structures are prior to individual experience and to a great extent determine it. We might see a play like *King Lear*, for example, as an account of a violently disruptive cultural shift. The dominant paternalist culture, represented by Lear and Gloucester, is challenged by Goneril, Regan and Edmund, who do not conform to the idea of 'natural' filial piety. The 'world picture' of the kingdom collapses as it is divided. The imagined pleasant world described by Lear (1.2) conflicts with the wasteland, populated by the poor and the desperate, which we see in the storm: a mental construct is subverted by brute economic reality. Through disguise, Edgar becomes an alternative agent, evoking a different order through the ravings of Poor Tom; Edmund is an oppositional agent, exploiting the very ideology which condemns his bastardy to support his ruthless and self-aggrandising actions (the play is a warning against the facile assumption that any opposition must be virtuous). This suggested reading would need to be developed, and challenged, but perhaps it indicates the way in which materialism can help us to see literary texts as sites in which the tensions and fractures of a culture are articulated and given narrative shape – a shape which may leave the tensions unresolved. It would certainly be difficult to deduce from *King Lear*, with its fierce conflicts of value and conduct, any coherent endorsement of a 'world picture' which its audience supposedly shared.

A materialist analysis of culture is inevitably largely concerned with power. Who has what kind of power over whom? Where is this power located and how is it expressed? As we have noted, the dominant culture will endorse the present order of things by representing it as natural: this process is referred to as consolidation. An ideology which depicts the monarch as analogous to God, overseeing a hierarchically structured cosmos, represents autocratic monarchical government as the natural state of affairs. The insistence on order in Renaissance culture can be seen not as an expression of the collective imagination but as a result of latent conflicts within the culture. The Renaissance was a period in rapid transition: Reformation theology, the new science, the discordance at key points between Christian and classical philosophies, and social and geographical mobility stimulated by economic turbulence presented a serious challenge to the governing order. In such a situation, the dominant culture responds by subtle and forceful assertion of its own cultural model. Minds as well as bodies have to be kept under control as this model is consolidated. The process involves multiple producers of meaning, from law to etiquette to ritual. Francis Bacon (cited by Dollimore in the Introduction to *Political Shakespeare*) makes this clear in his advice to circuit judges in 1617: 'There will be a perpetual defection, except you keep men in by preaching, as well as the law doth by punishing'. Men are 'kept in' by constructs of reality which label some forms of behaviour deviant, marginal, 'other'. Historical narratives portray the current order as inevitable, as in the state propaganda which presented the Tudor dynasty as the inevitable and divinely ordained salvation of a ravaged kingdom.

The obverse of consolidation is subversion, the attempt to undermine the dominant model. The critic is faced with the interesting question of whether literary texts inevitably collude in the dominant paradigm or whether they can be a force for subversion. In *The Tempest*, we see Caliban as a treacherous monster, suitably categorising him as the New World 'other' who can justifiably be exploited by a superior culture. Yet we also see that Caliban has a great sensibility to the beauty of his surroundings (which Prospero does not), and the play gives ample evidence that the 'superior' culture is corrupt, from drunken sailors to perfidious noblemen. The work simultaneously seems to sanction and invite us to question colonial exploitation. Similarly, *King Lear* might be read as a consolidation of the notion of patriarchy by showing the calamitous consequences of children turning against their fathers; yet it also shows Lear and Gloucester as weak-minded and irresponsible, leaving us room to see the flaws in a patriarchal system. Renaissance literature, and in particular drama, seems to be characterised by such conflicts, ambiguities and paradoxes. Does *Henry V* glorify war or expose the duplicities of monarchs? Does *The Alchemist* plainly condemn the gaining of easy money by trickery, or show respectable society in the unflattering light of satire, prey to greed and vanity? Whether a play or other work functions to consolidate or subvert the dominant discourse depends not only on the text but also on the context of articulation – under what circumstances it is read or performed. A performance of *Richard II* apparently commissioned by supporters of the Essex rebellion constitutes a challenge to the monarch by implicitly equating Queen Elizabeth with the deposed Richard; conversely, a performance of *Macbeth* before James I consolidates his claim to the crown by identifying him as the latest in a line of rulers stemming from Macduff.

In another twist, subversion can itself be appropriated by authority for its own purposes: this is the process of containment. The traditional festivals of misrule, in which the world is turned upside down for the day and servants become masters, contain latent forces of anarchy by ritualising them. Politically, it is always useful to the governing order to have spectres with which to frighten the people into submission: in Elizabethan England, an example was masterless men. Vagabonds wandering the highway were whipped, put into the stocks and sent back to their place of birth to find a master to employ them. These wretched figures were useful to the dominant culture as they could be demonised as idle vagrants. Containment is another principle that carries over easily to the world of literature. Comedy summons up anarchic energies in order to dispel them: Volpone, Sir Toby Belch and Falstaff are in the end contained by power. Spenser's *Faerie Queene* is a catalogue of the nightmares of Renaissance governments, from Error – unlicenced ideas – to luxurious desires to rebellious Irishmen. All of these forces of subversion are brought into the story in order to be contained, sometimes by shocking violence.

Cultural materialist analysis is implicitly political. It is deeply interested in the voices of dissidence which challenge power and the culture which naturalises that power. As Frank Lentricchia puts it, 'ruling culture does not define the whole of culture, though it tries to, and it is the task of the oppositional critic to re-read culture so as to amplify and strategically position the marginalised voices of the ruled, exploited, oppressed, and excluded' (*Criticism and Social Change*, 1983). Materialist criticism is oppositional in another sense, in that instead of building up pictures of coherent systems it looks for gaps and contradictions: it opposes any cosy picture of stability and coherence. An example of the insights such an approach can yield is Jonathan Dollimore's *Radical Tragedy* (1984). Dollimore argues (chapter 10 provides a useful summary of the main case) that modern ideas of the self as radically unstable and amorphous have parallels in Renaissance culture. In this period, the older metaphysical picture of man's place in the universe, framed by Christianity, was eroded, by internal quarrels among Christians and the challenge of the new science. Neither could a stable idea of self be found in classical philosophies such as stoicism. Thus writers like Montaigne and Machiavelli conjure up in different ways the idea of personality as something which is self-inventing, anti-essentialist. It is only the later enlightenment period, Dollimore maintains, which constructed the liberal humanist model of man: when we read Renaissance texts with the assumption that there is some kind of continuous and consistent 'character', we anachronistically bring eighteenth- and nineteenth-century preconceptions to bear on this material. The dislocated, unstable self, unsure of its social or religious foundations, is a central issue in Elizabethan and Jacobean tragedy: they do not add up to a world picture, but rather a picture in a state of disintegration. Dollimore's thesis is developed through close readings of a number of plays, with reference to theological and philosophical ideas of the time. It reminds us of the centrality of rhetoric in Renaissance thinking – the assumption of a personality for a certain situation. Who is Hamlet? Does he have defining characteristics which we trace in each scene or does he reinvent himself for each new situation? Rhetorical Renaissance man is not 'centred' but makes himself up as he goes along.

Works like *Radical Tragedy* or Sinfield's *Faultlines* (1992) richly reward close reading and critical engagement. They are, of course, open to critique. The use of social science concepts to examine aesthetic works leads to a denial of the existence of aesthetic values: in other words, it is simply denied that a poem can be good or true or beautiful. This may rescue us from complacency and yield sharp new insights, but it could equally be criticised as a category error – using concepts developed for the field of A (objective science) to describe the field of B (the subjective values in play when we respond to art). There is also a sharp difference between cultural materialist vision and earlier Marxism as practised by Raymond Williams. Where an earlier school saw the project as being the pursuit of social goods like justice and equality, radical materialists question all such supposed universal principles. And while they argue persuasively that the assertion that there are universal truths can be misused to exploit people, it may equally be argued that other regimes have committed terrible crimes in the belief that humans are blank slates and their natures can be moulded from scratch. 'All Values are Contingent' is not a very inspiring banner under which to march against tyranny. Meaningful dissidence must surely be mounted on certain principles. And what is a critic committed to rescuing the other and the marginal to do when faced by another culture that, for example, denies women equality before the law? Celebrate the otherness of the different culture? Or speak up for those that culture has repressed, in the name of universal values and rights? These are ongoing debates within the left, in science and in philosophy.

See also   *Contexts*: City, English Reformation, Humanism, Patronage, The Self; *Texts*: History, Mimesis, Theory of Poetry

Further Reading

John Drakakis, ed., *Alternative Shakespeares*, revised edn (London: Routledge, 2002).
Jonathan Dollimore, ed., *Political Shakespeare: Essays in Cultural Materialism*, 2nd revised edn (Manchester: Manchester UP, 1994).
Jonathan Dollimore, *Radical Tragedy*, 3rd revised edn (Houndmills, Basingstoke: Palgrave Macmillan, 2003).
Alan Sinfield, *Faultlines: Cultural Materialism and the Politics of Dissident Reading* (Oxford: Clarendon, 1992).
Raymond Williams, *Marxism and Literature* (Oxford: OUP, 1977).

Ecocriticism

Ecocriticism is the study of the relationship between literary cultural artefacts and the natural environment (this is the definition given by the Association for the Study of Literature and the Environment). This is a relatively new critical approach, reflecting contemporary preoccupation with green issues; a foundational text (see below) was published in 1996. Inevitably, given its recent appearance, the precise scope of ecocritical practice remains a subject of debate, but broadly speaking it brings ecological concerns to bear on the study of texts and related productions. In literary study, ecocriticism is concerned with how writings give meaning to the natural environment, which includes beasts as well as physical geography. (It will be seen at once that terms like 'nature' and 'beasts' are themselves complex cultural formulations calling out for definition, and ecocriticism is particularly involved in tracking the senses and uses of such concepts.) Typical questions which might be addressed by an ecocritic are: What does the animal imagery in this text suggest about ideas concerning human and animal nature? How might conceptions of class or national identity be expressed through landscape description? Thus, literary treatment of environmental topics is viewed not only as an aesthetic creation, but as embedded in social and political contexts.

The Renaissance period is a particularly interesting one to study from an ecological perspective, since it saw significant shifts in the way the natural world was perceived. The early modern economy brought with it enclosures, the rise of urban spaces and greater mechanical control over land: such alterations leave traces in the imagination of the age. Critics have also seen in the early modern period an emerging mechanistic mode of scientific enquiry, which supplanted earlier medieval conceptualisations of the natural world. From being in important senses holistically and organically related to the environment – man in a popular medieval motif is 'earth upon earth' – humans come to be seen as differentiated from the rest of creation. The early modern sense of nature, it has been argued, thus involved a sensation of alienation, a phenomenon which has had enormous consequences for the present generation. As this process unfolded, the Chain of Being, as a conceptual model, came under strain and new strategies of imagery were adopted. Alienation brought with it a yearning for some kind of return to nature, and we find this expressed in such forms as nostalgic pastoral and the recreation of the ungoverned wilderness in the poetic imagination.

Like much modern cultural study, ecocriticism is interdisplinary, and its concerns often join fruitfully with other critical schools. Some feminist critics, for example, have traced relations between attitudes to nature and the representation of women. Like the natural world, runs one line of thinking, women were regarded as passive and existing to be dominated and exploited by men. An interesting female writer to study in the context of such ideas is Margaret Cavendish (1623–1673), whose writings are informed by a strong interest in chemistry and natural philosophy. Her poem 'A Dialogue betwixt Man, and Nature' considers how man's desire to understand the physical workings of nature leads to an exploitative relation to it. Nature protests 'that Tree by me was made to stand,/Just as it growes, not to be cut by man'. Such notions could be interpreted as making an implicit association between nature and woman, who is similarly powerless to resist man's appetite for dominance. Cavendish's interest in atomic theory illustrates the emerging 'mechanistic' view of creation at the time. A text concerned with nature can thus be read as a part of wider discourses in sexual politics and intellectual history.

The ways in which texts present the natural world suggest, too, the many compartmentalisations and distinctions by which reality is ordered in the human mind at a given time. What is the distinction between man and beast, between the human and natural cycles of growth and decay? Exploring such questions can lead us to genres which are often marginal to mainstream literary study. Agricultural writings on the care of the land, for example, have been seen as defining, and legitimating, the respective roles of labourer and landowner. Texts on hunting have been read as implicit affirmations of class distinctions and boundaries. Landscape description can also be a site in which conceptual configurations of reality are articulated. Both literary and real gardens have been read for what they suggest about Renaissance views of other types of distinction: between the private self and the public world, or the contemplative and active life. Exterior spaces, like interior ones, are also symbolic manifestations of social and political codes: garden design, for example, has been studied as a symbolic system closely linked to the image and institution of monarchical government. In all such studies, Renaissance writing which engages with the environment is seen not as an inert reflection of contemporary conceptions of the world, but as part of the process by which those conceptions were built up. Like all complex material representations, this process may involve a degree of internal incoherence and contradiction.

A brief summary of some other research topics provides a fuller idea of the scope of ecocriticism. Animals are an important object of study. Beasts might be identified as an 'other', an obverse of the human, for example through the mental pictures of monsters. Yet anthropomorphosis is a potent force: Renaissance culture includes speaking animals in satire, animals on stage, bears tormented in bear-baiting arenas who were given names and had a kind of 'star status' and beasts as emblems of human passions. All of these practices and representations arguably subvert the distinction between the human and the bestial. Individual species of beast, meanwhile, can be the centre of multiple and complex semantic fields. The horse, for example, has been seen as a source of metaphors for class, race, national identity, antiquated chivalry and good governance. Similar metaphorical patterns have been traced in topics of landscape: the forest has symbolised Arcadian calm, the madness of love and the alternative to a decadent court. Studies of topics like these draw on traditional practices of close reading of imagery. Individual authors and texts have also been investigated for their use of environmental tropes. Inevitably, Shakespeare studies are central. Other rich fields include Spenser's elaborate emblematic use of animal and landscape imagery and Milton's deep consideration of the meaning of the natural world in *Paradise Lost* (particularly in his descriptions of the Creation and of the Garden of Eden).

Ecocriticism provides exciting opportunities to connect texts with a variety of contexts, from agricultural economics to land estate management, forestry and garden design. It draws on what is for many a passionate concern with the state of the earth and our relation to it and channels that energy into detailed investigation. Ecocritical study can bring together the older practices of close thinking and recent theoretical thinking about ecological concepts. It can cast a new light on well-known texts and lead us to unfamiliar writings – the poetry of less studied writers such as Margaret Cavendish, perhaps, or non-literary texts like manuals on horses and falconry. Possible problems in ecocriticism include difficulties over definition, as mentioned earlier: Is a careful study of equine imagery in a Shakespeare play a work of 'ecocriticism' or an exercise in practical close reading given a new name? Definition matters because it gives a focus and sense of purpose to an individual study. As students of literature, we might also wonder about the relation between green reading and green activism: Does an interest in the field commit us to a particular set of beliefs or programme of action, and should critical study be regarded as part of a larger ecological programme? This might commit us to certain conclusions before we have even started our research. Deeply held beliefs about ecology might also lead us to be very critical of the behaviour of previous ages. However justified this indignation may be, we should remember that applying our own values to another age can also be an obstacle to gaining insight into other modes of thinking. The question of the relation between literary study and activism also arises in other schools of criticism closely connected to political activism, such as Marxism and feminism.

See also   *Contexts*: Chain of Being, Cosmos, Elements, Golden Age, Humours, Magic, Science; *Texts*: Conceit, Pastoral

Further Reading
Cheryl Glotfelty and Harold Fromm, eds, *The Ecocriticism Reader: Landmarks in Literary Ecology* (Athens: University of Georgia Press, 1996).
Karen Raber, 'Recent Ecocritical Studies of English Renaissance Literature', *English Literary Renaissance*. Winter 2007, 37:1.
Keith Thomas, *Man and the Natural World: Changing Attitudes in England 1500–1800* (London: Allen Lane, 1983).
Robert N. Watson, *Back to Nature: The Green and the Real in the Late Renaissance* (Philadelphia: University of Pennsylvania Press, 2005).

Feminism

Feminism is a movement committed to securing equal rights for women. It challenges all forms of patriarchal oppression, from media images which reduce females to sex objects to institutional, social and legal practices which subject women to inferior status; it is also interested in the historical development of these phenomena as well as in their present manifestations. Feminism has its roots in theories of universal human rights developed from the late seventeenth century and in pioneering writings of the nineteenth and early twentieth century. As an organised movement promoting women's liberation it can be dated from the 1960s. Analysis of literary texts and other cultural works has always been central to the feminist project, since it is recognised that the portrayal of females in different media plays a crucial part in constructing society's ideas of gender. One aspect of feminism in literary criticism, then, concerns the study of depictions of women in texts usually written by men. Studies of gender representation range from traditional close reading to theoretical works which draw on other methodologies, particularly Marxism and Psychoanalysis. At the same time as women are studied as the object of the male gaze and male representations, their role as real persons and agents has also been increasingly explored. Historians have sought to reconstruct the experience of women in history, and while there is much evidence of their subjugation in a male-dominated society, such studies have also widened our awareness of ways in which early modern women could be important agents in certain spheres: as mistresses of large households, patrons of the arts and religious visionaries, for example. Most importantly, over recent years many writings by women have been edited, bringing a wide range of new texts into the canon.

As one might expect, the literary representation of women in the Renaissance period corresponds to the prevailing view of that time that women are naturally inferior and should be quiet, submissive and obedient to their masters. Shakespeare's *The Taming of the Shrew* belongs to a tradition which views talkative women ('shrews') of an independent will as a threat, needing to be 'tamed' by a husband to be brought into their rightful social role. To remain with Shakespearean examples, eloquent women (Cleopatra, Lady Macbeth, Goneril and Regan) frequently exert a dangerous power over men's minds, with a lethal combination of rhetorical prowess and feminine enchantment. Virtuous women, by contrast, are often depicted as meek and silent (Cordelia). In *The Tempest*, the very name of Prospero's daughter Miranda, which means 'to be wondered at', suggests a key idea of the woman's role – to be the submissive object of men's attention and, ultimately, a man's possession. Love lyrics elevate women to the status of goddesses and in so doing depersonalise them. The qualities praised in sonnets – usually physical assets of milk-white breasts and flashing eyes – tell us nothing about the particular lady in question, and everything about the male idea of female perfection which is projected onto them. Physical beauty (of a certain prescribed kind) is praised, while feminine judgement and mental agility are feared. In a long medieval tradition, women are viewed through the polar opposite images of the Virgin Mary and the Whore of Babylon: incapable of recognising female sexuality, the male culture either perfects women as asexual virgins or brands them as whores. Love poems often verge on being hate poems, since they normalise attacks on the beloved as faithless and cruel mistresses of their wounded victims. In poems such as Donne's 'The Apparition' such attacks are explicit.

While such depictions might fairly be said to be misogynist, this is a concept which needs unpacking. Misogyny has many sources and modes, from conscious personal feelings on the part of the author to a set of unconsciously held presumptions which are normalised at a social and cultural level, and embedded in traditions of discourse. Judging the responsibility or sincerity of an utterance is a difficult matter. Literary expression is shaped by its particular codes and conventions, one of which is playful irony. Male authors of love lyrics may be parodying the male lover's voice, and keeping themselves at a distance from the text. Furthermore, misogyny is more easily discovered than its obverse: while male distortions of women are not hard to find, it is less clear how women *should* be represented. Feminist critics are themselves far from unanimous on what constitutes the proper image of female gender or the ideal of female behaviour. For example, some argue that women should celebrate their special qualities of imagination and their transcendence of the phallocentric symbolic logical order. We might call this 'separatist' or essentialist feminism since it emphasises qualities allegedly distinct to women. Other critics, however, point out that this quasi-mysticism comes perilously close to the view, central to Renaissance thinking, that women are less capable than men of rational thought and are prone to emotional waywardness. Anti-essentialists hold that all supposedly special 'female' qualities are culturally produced, working to the benefit of men in a male-dominated society. Starting from the reasonable premise that women, in life and literature, were subjugated to the will and desires of men also carries certain risks. We may implicitly be falling in with the idea that women are essentially passive and of secondary status, and thus miss evidence of the ways in which women had a shaping influence through their behaviour in, for example, the management of a great estate or in parish life. As a critical procedure, finding ways in which women are represented and reconstructed by the male gaze can also become a totalising, repetitive exercise which ignores other angles of vision and overlooks the special qualities of individual texts.

Besides being the subjects of literary texts written by men, early modern women might also be writers themselves. Perhaps the most important area of recent studies of the period has been the editing, and subsequent discussion, of female-authored texts. A brief review of some of these can hope only to suggest the remarkable range of subjects and genres that we find in the field of early modern women's writing. At the very top of society, the monarch Elizabeth Tudor (1533–1603) produced translations of Plutarch, Horace, Boethius and Petrarch and composed a number of poems. This must have served as a model for other noble ladies. Mary Herbert, Countess of Pembroke (also referred to as Mary Sidney (1561–1621)), composed several poems, among them the continuation of the metrical translations of the psalms left unfinished on the death of her brother, Sir Philip. The Sidneys' niece Lady Mary Wroth (c.1587–1651/3) was the author of the first known romance by an Englishwoman, *Urania* (1621) – whose allusions to various society figures caused a scandal – and, in the same volume, of the first female-authored sonnet sequence, *Pamphilia to Amphilanthus*. Another aristocratic female writer was Elizabeth Cary, Viscountess Falkland (1585–1639), who wrote closet dramas (plays designed for reading rather than for performance), among them *The Tragedy of Miriam* (1613). Lower in the social scale was Isabella Whitney (fl.1567–1573), who eschewed religious subject matter (traditionally the most respectable material for women) and published two poetic miscellanies, *The Copy of a Letter* (1566–1567) and *A Sweet Nosgay* (1573). These seem to be semi-autobiographical, as the poems refer to misfortunes which caused Whitney to leave London. They also express female experiences (such as being deceived by a faithless lover) and provide lively descriptions of London in ballad metre. Emilia Lanyer (c.1569–1645), the daughter of Italian Jews who emigrated from Venice, produced in the volume *Salve Deus Rex Judaeorum* (1611) the first original poetry published by a woman in the seventeenth century. Similarly pioneering was Anne Bradstreet (1612–1672), who emigrated with her Puritan family to New England in 1630 and became the first New Englander to publish a collection of poems, with *The Tenth Muse* (1650). Some lines by Bradstreet make clear how literary composition was still regarded as an inappropriate activity for women:

> I am obnoxious to each carping tongue
> Who says my hand a needle better fits,
> A poet's pen all scorn I should thus wrong,
> For such despite they cast on female wits.

Also later in the seventeenth century we find the poet Katherine Phillips (1632–1664) and Margaret Cavendish, Duchess of Newcastle (1623–1673), whose varied writings extend from plays to natural philosophy. A diverse range of women's writings appears beyond the traditional genres. The *Examinations* (1546–1547, edited by John Bale), recording the trials of the Protestant martyr Anne Askew (1521–1546), together with Askew's autobiography, published in Foxe's *Acts and Monuments*, are important documents of female spirituality. *Miscelanea: Meditations, Memoratives* (1604) by Elizabeth Grymeston (c.1563–c.1604) is an example of the mother's advice book. Rachel Speght (b.1597?) published under her own name – an unprecedented move – a pamphlet defending women, *A Mouzell for Melastomus* (1617), as part of the early seventeenth-century pamphlet war on the nature of womankind. From the various religious sects of the mid-seventeenth century emerged a number of female voices (perhaps women's imagination was channelled in this way since they were forbidden to preach in the established church): an example is Anna Trapnel (*c*.1622–?), whose prophetic visions were published in *The Cry of a Stone* (1654). And beyond the world of published texts lie still more writings that were either unpublished because printing was deemed inappropriate for women or never intended for publication to begin with: prayers, meditations, recipes, accounts of dreams, diaries, letters, journals.

The study of early modern women's writing raises several questions. One concerns our own formation as readers. Perhaps we need to step outside traditional academic traditions to understand and evaluate such writings from a non-patriarchal viewpoint. Do we, that is, need to recalibrate the methods and criteria of criticism to take account of the specific qualities of women's writings? Similarly, the particular nature of manuscript evidence requires new approaches to the task of editing (preparing an edition of a book of recipes or prophecies is clearly a quite different activity to editing a book of lyrics, and must anticipate different reader needs). Then we must consider whether early modern women may be enlisted to a modern cause. Can we speak of a Renaissance feminism, or is that to attribute to Renaissance persons notions of equal rights not yet available to them in the conceptual world of the time? In the texts themselves, does women's writing subvert the poetic language and genres of a patriarchal culture to give voice to experiences marginal to that culture? Conversely, the gender of these different writers might be over-emphasised: to define writers primarily by their sex is also to confine our interest in them principally to matters of sexual identity and to advance the condescending view that women writers are somehow unusual. Moreover, in treating early modern women's writing as a specific field we may be placing women in a reductive subset and missing the opportunity for interesting comparisons. For example, we may gain insights from reading the plays of Elizabeth Cary or the poems of Emilia Lanyer as, primarily, drama and poetry rather than *women's* drama and poetry. Women writers should also be considered in the other groups to which their work affiliates them: as religious poets, Puritans, philosophers, writers of closet plays and so forth. Furthermore, as with any classification, the notion of women writers as a distinct category also groups together individuals who are in other respects extremely different – the aristocrat Mary Sidney and the prophet Anna Trapnel have little in common, one might feel.

Another area of enquiry concerns the conditions of writing itself. Scholars are interested not only in what women wrote but how they wrote: What opportunities for privacy and reflection were available to women in the households to which they were confined, and how did this daily existence shape their thoughts? Lastly, we may challenge the emphasis given in critical books (including this one) to works which happen to have been published, especially when dealing with a period when there was so much pressure against female publication. If we open up the concept of literature to mean all substantial writings, whether published or not, then we include the many texts referred to above, bringing new kinds of discourse to our attention and perhaps revising our picture of the whole period. Critical questions like these will be refined by the ongoing work in social history which is giving us a steadily clearer picture of the lives lived by early modern women. Feminism is a multidisciplinary activity, which has already moved through several stages and revolutionised our picture of early modern culture.

See also   *Contexts*: Court, Magic, Medicine, Patronage, Sex and Sexuality, Women; *Texts*: Lyric, Sonnet; *Criticism*: Textualism

Further Reading

Dympna Callaghan, ed., *The Impact of Feminism in English Renaissance Studies* (Houndmills, Basingstoke: Palgrave Macmillan, 2006).
Lorna Hutson, ed., *Feminism and Renaissance Studies* (Oxford: OUP, 1999).
Anita Pacheco, ed., *A Companion to Early Modern Women's Writing* (Oxford: Blackwell, 2002).
Paul Salzman, *Reading Early Modern Women's Writing* (Oxford: OUP, 2006).

Language Criticism: Practical Criticism, Stylistics, Rhetoric

All critical methods pay some kind of attention to language, but the approach known as Practical Criticism is distinct in its exclusive concern with the 'words on the page'. Practical Criticism, also known as close reading, approaches the text as an independent artefact, or 'verbal icon', which can be formally analysed with minimal reference to its context. We shall consider this method through discussion of the poem below.

To the Lady Arabella

Great learnèd lady, whom I long have known,
And yet not known so much as I desired;
Rare phoenix, whose fair feathers are your own,
With which you fly, and are so much admired;
True honour, whom true fame hath so attired

In glittering raiment shining much more bright
Than silver stars in the most frosty night.

Come like the morning sun new out of bed,
And cast your eyes upon this little book.
Although you be so well accompanied
With Pallas and the Muses, spare one look
Upon this humbled king, who all forsook,
That in his dying arms he might embrace
Your beauteous soul, and fill it with his grace.

Emilia Lanyer (1569?–1645)

In this piece, Lady Arabella is addressed in various flattering terms, and then asked to contemplate a little book (we imagine the Bible, or a prayer book) and 'this humbled king' (presumably Christ), thus balancing her classical learning and accomplishments with due Christian piety. A close reading of this text might start with the verse form: the poem is composed of two stanzas of 'rhyme royal', an arrangement of seven iambic pentameter lines rhyming *ababbcc*. This form, which can be traced back to Chaucer, was employed by several Renaissance poets. In 'To the Lady Arabella', the two stanzas follow the logical binary division of the poem's argument: first the address, then the supplication. The opening quatrain of the poem feels heavy and ponderous: the lines are end-stopped (that is, punctuation or sense makes each one a distinct unit), inviting us to pause rather than move on; the 'masculine'-stressed endings in rhyme position have a similar effect of closure; and the caesura, or mid-line pause, falls clearly after three or four syllables. This slowness helps to create a sense of solemn reverence and is emphasised in the metrical effect of substituting a spondee (stress – stress) for an iamb (unstressed – stressed) in the phrases of address in lines 1, 3 and 5: '**Great learn**èd', '**Rare phoe**nix', '**True hon**our'. We note that these phrases are connected not only by the logic of repetition in the first of each pair of lines but also by their common rhythmic pattern. A further acoustic pattern is achieved by alliteration, which helps to define the three sections of the first stanza (2 lines + 2 lines + 3 lines): '**l**earned **l**ady . . . **l**ong', '**ph**oenix . . . **f**air **f**eathers . . . **fl**y', '**tr**ue . . . a**ttir**ed . . . gli**tter**ing', '**s**ilver **s**tars'. After the heavy first four lines, a shift occurs with the extended enjambment in lines 5–7, a syntactical expansiveness which helps to convey the idea of being dressed ('attired / In glittering raiment' wraps itself like a robe around the lines) and the vastness of the night sky. Then a sharp contrast in imagery, from night to morning, suggests a dramatic change of direction as we move to stanza 2. The pulse is faster: after the trochaic inversion of the first line, accentuating the imperative ('**Come** like'), the line beginnings are regular iambics, propelling us forward, in contrast to the earlier spondees. This sense of forward motion is also achieved by the enjambment linking the quatrain to the final three lines (in the first stanza these two sections are syntactically separate). The contrast in imagery continues with 'little book' and 'humbled king' replacing the grand pictures of the first stanza: we sense that the imaginary world of the text is turning from the classical to the Christian, just as Arabella is being persuaded to do. We note once again the use of enjambment in conjunction with sense: 'embrace / Your beauteous soul' emphasises the action of embracing by having one line, as it were, embrace the next. The concluding 'grace' echoes the poem's opening word 'Great', creating an acoustic frame, while also suggesting the radical distinction between earthly greatness and spiritual grace.

The comments above are not intended as a complete analysis, but as examples of the kind of observations a practical critical approach to the poem would involve. Another way of discussing the language of the text is offered by stylistics, the application of modern linguistic analysis to literary texts. Stylistic analysis would pay close attention to grammatical structures. We note, for example, the frequent collocation of adjective + noun in noun phrases across the text: 'Rare phoenix', 'fair feathers', 'true honour', 'glittering raiment' and so forth. Noun phrases which take a different form, like the unaccompanied concluding 'grace', are foregrounded by their departure from this formula. Another pattern in the opening stanza is the sequence of address ('Rare phoenix') + relative clause (lines 1, 3 and 5). In each case, the relative clause puts the lady in a passive, object position: 'whom I long have known', 'whose fair feathers... are so much admired', 'whom true fame hath so attired'. As the recipient who 'suffers' these various actions (which appear in the rhyme position at the ends of lines), the lady appears as immobile object rather than agent, a perception that the comparison to stars in the night sky does nothing to displace. She is indeed depicted as an active agent in the clause 'With which you fly', but the force of this is diminished by its grammatical subsidiary position: it is a sub-clause dependent on another sub-clause ([*whose* fair feathers [*with which* you fly]]). In the second stanza, there is more verbal action, but only in the imagination, indicating things wished by the writer. These actions are expressed first through the imperative ('Come... cast .. spare') and finally through the subjunctive mood ('That... he *might* embrace'). Deictic, or 'pointing', words lend a dramatic urgency to the exhortations to think of Christ: '*this* little book', '*this* humbled king'. The repeated passive constructions in the first stanza and the lack of an active verbal mood anywhere create a sense of inertia throughout: the Lady Arabella is herself a passive object, existing to be admired, or to have her vacuous 'beauteous soul' filled by grace.

Again, these are only some of the lines of enquiry a stylistician might take. Careful linguistic analysis such as that attempted above helps us to focus on a text and explore it in great detail: it helps us to become aware of nuances of meaning and effect and appreciate the artistry of the writer. The method is especially valuable for the study of Renaissance writing, since both Practical Criticism and Stylistics belong to the tradition of Rhetoric, the focus on the particular arrangement of words, sounds and phrases which was central to Renaissance humanist thought. Familiar terms like metaphor and simile are only some of the hundreds of figures of speech listed in rhetorical handbooks, and the attention brought to grammar by Stylistics is not unlike the early modern study of classical texts. In spirit and practice, then, language analysis can bring us closer to Renaissance ways of thinking.

However, although they have been presented here as partner disciplines, Practical Criticism and Stylistics have not always had the easiest relationship. Some stylisticians have criticised traditional close reading for a kind of self-regarding vagueness: Can the assertion that a line of verse is 'heavy and ponderous' be verified, or is it essentially a whimsical personal impression masquerading as an academic finding? What, if anything, does it mean to say that parts of a poem are 'defined' by alliteration? Through the use of the science of linguistics, Stylistics aims to provide a clear and objective record of data, subjecting poetic texts to the same kind of attention that would be brought to, say, sports commentary or the language of advertising and producing clear observations in precise language. This is a demystifying practice, which can, it is argued, usefully dispel some of the mystique which has built up around liberal humanist parlance. In return, some practical critics have retorted that the scientific aspirations behind Stylistics make the practice at odds with the aesthetics of literary expression: to regard a poem primarily as a collection of noun phrases and sub-clauses and the like is to take dryness to a parodic extreme. This is how a poem might be read by a computer, but not by a person with any sensitivity to poetic language and convention.

For all their differences, both the techniques of close reading discussed here are open to other objections. Sometimes analysis of poetic language is presented as a practice outside, and superior to, critical theory. Yet this cannot be the case. The assertion that a poem can be usefully studied when it is extracted from its context is a highly contentious theoretical proposition: studying a butterfly pinned to a card, we might feel, teaches us less than observing it in its natural habitat. The basic assumption that close reading is a valuable primary strategy also invites scrutiny: we simply do not see everything better from close up. Nor need we accept unquestioningly the divorcing of a text from its historical and biographical surroundings. Leaving context aside might be a sensible preliminary manoeuvre, allowing us to concentrate on the text, but a poem like the one we have discussed will stir other kinds of curiosity: with its presentation of the lady as object rather than subject, what does it add to our understanding of gender construction? We note that its argument that salvation can be attained by private contemplation of the Word is a Protestant idea and might wonder if there is some sensed tension between aristocratic 'glitter' on the one hand and Anglican theology on the other, or whether the poem captures a consciousness of a fracture between the acquisition of classical learning ('Pallas and the Muses') and the humble reading of the scriptures. Is the text a register of certain points of tension in the culture, among them contending ideas of feminine roles (we note, contextually, that in this poem one woman addresses another)? We can, and should, use the techniques of Practical Criticism to inform our handling of these questions. But, more dangerously, we can also use it to retreat from such matters, confining ourselves to the safer activity of linguistic commentary, on the questionable premises that the 'well-wrought urn' of the poem stands ineffably aloof from its historical environment.

A further problem faced by close practical commentary is the so-called hermeneutic gap. This is what we leap over when we move from observation to interpretation, and it is an issue across the humanities: How can an objective scientific methodology deal adequately with the sphere of human creativity, a sphere which is imbued with the subjective world of values, both moral and aesthetic? At some point we seem to cross from objective to subjective. For example, it is objectively the case that 'attired / In glittering raiment' is an enjambment, but what are we to make of my suggestion that this evokes the action of attiring the lady? The school pupil's question 'How do we know the author meant this?' is both interesting and difficult. We might reply that authorial intention is unknowable and so not worth looking for (the 'intentional fallacy'), but even if we accept this (another theory underwriting our supposedly theory-free activity), it simply raises the further question: 'How can we verify or falsify this reading of the line?' By what external criteria can my interpretation be tested? We might agree that the reading is plausible since Renaissance poets thought a good deal about rhetoric and metre; but this need not apply to the specific instance of this line, and it is moreover an extremely convenient way of supporting any interpretive claim we might choose to make. I need to face the possibility that I read in this way simply because I found that making such comments won the approval of my teachers, and that I am now perpetuating this custom, essentially supporting my claim with the authority of tradition rather than with demonstrable knowledge. Can claims about the effect of enjambment be verifiably right or wrong? And if not, are they anything more than private acts of the imagination? Stylistic reading raises the same issue. It is uncontroversial to say that a sentence is passive (assuming we are competent at grammatical terminology). But is it not an unscientific sleight of hand to turn from the terms 'passive' and 'object' in their technical sense and say that the lady is presented as a 'passive object', which uses the different, everyday sense of these words? There is no necessary link between passive verbal constructions and the suggestion of a passive character; or if there is, it needs further demonstration than this.

A final objection we shall consider here is that the historical dominance of Practical Criticism, especially at pre-university level, has narrowed the canon. Close reading techniques work better at some texts than others, and so short lyrics occupy more student attention than, say, ballads and broadsheets. Consequently, a canon of both text and methods soon establishes itself, leading to a fossilisation of the discipline and the disappearance of any genuine kind of evaluation from the process of study, since we are led to presuppose the excellence of the books chosen for our attention. This excellence is also primarily a matter of technical dexterity rather than truth, beauty or moral excellence, concepts with which much modern criticism is uneasy.

Having conceded such difficulties, we can nonetheless assert that Practical Criticism, Stylistics and rhetorical analysis are certainly invaluable foundational skills which can be integrated with other kinds of literary study. It might also be pointed out that Practical Criticism is at least honest enough to declare what it does not do, whereas contextual study is open-ended and sometimes wildly unrealistic in its vast multidisciplinary aspirations. It is not the least virtue of close reading methods that they can be systematically taught and used from an early stage to do valuable work. But we should not believe that close reading provides a placid harbour, sheltered from the stormy waters of theoretical debate. For it does no such thing. And even if it did, why would one want to go there?

See also   *Contexts*: Humanism; *Texts*: Conceit, Decorum, Imitation, Metre, Mimesis, Prose Style, Rhetoric, Sonnet, Theory of Poetry; *Criticism*: Textualism

Further Reading

Geoffrey Leech, *A Linguistic Guide to English Poetry* (Harlow: Longman, 1973).
Brian Vickers, *Classical Rhetoric in English Poetry* (London: Macmillan, 1970).
Katie Wales, *A Dictionary of Stylistics* (London: Longman, 1989).

New Historicism

Closely related to Cultural Materialism, New Historicism represented a turn in the 1980s against formalist approaches to literature, such as New Criticism and Structuralism. Where these involve the study of the literary text as an autonomous artefact, isolated from its surroundings, New Historicism seeks to historicise the text by locating it in its cultural, political, economic and social environment. By making the text in history the object of its attention, New Historicism also involves distanciation – the awareness of the difference of the past and the challenges this distance poses to our understanding. At the same time, its motivations and key points of interest are recognisably those of radical liberal humanism: New Historicist writings are frequently explicitly committed to challenging established authority and rescuing marginalised and suppressed voices. Consequently it is perhaps not surprising that New Historicist works are very often concerned with the literature of the sixteenth and seventeenth centuries: besides representing the key reference point of literary studies, as the age of Shakespeare, this period is also far enough in the past to seem unfamiliar while offering sufficient points of emerging modernity to seem relevant to present-day political engagements.

New Historicism is closely associated above all with the figure of Stephen Greenblatt (b.1943), whose *Renaissance Self-Fashioning* (1980) is often seen as the foundational text. Greenblatt coined the phrase 'New Historicism' two years later, while insisting that the movement is a practice, not a doctrine – that is, it is realised through doing work on texts, not through applying a pre-formulated theory. Nonetheless, there are implicit concepts about literature and history which are present in this work, and which have been articulated by theorists such as Jean Howard and Louis Montrose. To begin with, New Historicism challenges the binary concepts of text and context, literature and history. Works of the 'old historicist' school, by scholars such as Dover Wilson and E. M. Tillyard, discuss literary texts in terms of how they reflect the background of ideas and events of their time: literature and history are conceived as separate, the one reflecting the other. This approach has various limitations. It can make reading a reductive process, one which regards texts as the passive mirrors of their time, uncomplicated representations of something external to them: to put it crudely, it invites us to see, for example, Macbeth as 'really about' the gunpowder plot and Jacobean kingship. Furthermore, metaphors of 'background' privilege the literary text and draw our attention away from elements of that 'background' which might reward closer investigation.

Against this approach, New Historicism urges us to look at history not as a given body of facts but as an archive of textual evidence, all of which is open to interpretation. At the same time, we should see what we designate as literary texts as part of that archive, not simply passively reflecting culture, but also creating it. As Louis Montrose famously put it in his essay 'New Historicisms', the approach involves 'a reciprocal concern with the historicity of texts and the textuality of histories'. The object of study is not the transcendent text, either removed from its context or conceived as a reflection of that context, but some aspect of the culture of an historical moment, for which literary texts are one kind of evidence among others. In Jean Howard's words, 'Literature is one of many elements participating in a culture's representation of reality to itself, helping to form its discourse on the family, the state, the individual, helping to make the world intelligible, though not necessarily helping to represent it "accurately"'. Applied to today, this might involve the study of how films, texts and media both reflect social attitudes to something like race or wealth, but in turn foster those attitudes and the behaviour which springs from them in their audience: films depict heroes and terrorists, but heroic and violent behaviour is in turn consciously or unconsciously modelled on films. In the Renaissance, an example might be representations of Elizabeth as the Virgin Queen: the monarch and the court are represented in various artefacts, but these representations in turn inform and inspire actual behaviour. Literature – among other forms of representation – is thus to be seen as an agent of social and political practice, not merely as its static repository. In this reformulation of the concepts of literature and history, an important influence has been the work of the social anthropologist Clifford Geertz (1926–2006), whose practice of 'thick description' involves the study of some aspect of a culture across different kinds of evidence.

New Historicism is also much concerned with the issue of power. It is here that the approach overlaps most closely with Cultural Materialism. For both, a key figure is the French writer Michel Foucault (1926–1984). Foucault analysed cultures as closed systems, in which the dominant discourses constitute a vocabulary by which society is organised and the powerful institutions are endorsed. What we take as knowledge is the subjectivity created by these discourses. For example, the vocabulary of capitalism invites us to perceive, and discuss, material goods as the means towards happiness; this is part of the subjectivity which makes the power of corporations and credit-lending institutions seem like part of the natural fabric of things. Knowledge is equated with power, and social subjects collude in the system which controls them. This model of society is different from the cruder formulation of Marxism which sees art and literature as part of the 'superstructure' of ideology created by the substructure of economic conditions. In the Foucauldian analysis, the two layers cannot practically be separated: a portrait of a wealthy

Renaissance merchant is not only a creation of the trading economy but part of the discourse by which that system, and the role of the merchant within it, is validated and promoted. This development of Marxist thought informs the work of Louis Althusser and is adopted by other Marxist literary theorists such as Pierre Machery and Mikhail Bakhtin.

The portrait of the merchant and the poetic eulogy of a nobleman make up part of the dominant discourses of Renaissance society, legitimising and glamourising the values most useful to those in power. This does not mean a gigantic conspiracy among painters, poets and their patrons, but the naturalisation of a certain way of thinking about the world, one which is part of the life of the society and often operates at an unconscious level. But a consequence of the resulting ideology, or framework of thought, is to privilege some features of the system and exclude others. The powerful are likely to be extolled and the powerless vilified, rather as a newspaper today may depict the poor as welfare scroungers or suspicious immigrants in its front pages and describe reverently the deals of business executives in the finance pages at the back. Foucault's argument that masterful discourses operate to silence those at the margins of society influenced studies of violence, madness and vagrancy in early modern England by scholars such as Francis Barker, William C. Carrol and C. T. Neely.

More generally, the concentration of power and the function of culture in cementing it provide Cultural Materialism and New Historicism with a focus of critical attention. The approach also raises important questions: Is culture a completely closed system, or is it possible for a writer to step outside and interrogate it? It has often been noted, for example, that the slave Caliban in *The Tempest* is given especially rich poetry which conveys his sensitivity to the island now ruled by his master the European Prospero. We could read this as Shakespeare 'thinking outside the box' of the dominant ideology and providing an alternative image of the enslaved indigenous peoples of the new colonies: our sympathy is aroused, and Prospero's treatment of him seems cruel. By this reading, the text has opened up a rift between the dominant colonialist discourse and a dissident, humane alternative. Yet the play could still be seen as supporting, and indeed voicing, the masterful discourse: we can only recognise Caliban's sensitivities from a position of superiority – he is still a slave – and his feeble attempted rebellion against his master, in the ludicrous service of two drunken sailors, reassures the audience that indigenous peoples are after all only subhuman, with no moral compass to guide their sensibilities towards the pursuit of good. We can feel gratified with ourselves for our spasm of sympathy and then go on supporting the exploitation of other worlds by the West. In a closed system, it is important for different views to be expressed, but chiefly so they can be contained and drained of danger. The efficient system produces and manages its own internal opposition. Yet whether a text or other work can seriously resist and destabilise ruling discourses and whether a system can be truly closed or can be infiltrated from without or subverted from within remain open questions. The question of whether some of the values in a system might actually be good and true does not arise in this theory's particular discourse, since it is taken as a given that all values are contingent on the 'system' as it is at any given point: that is, they are functional in value and there is no transcendent truth to which they can attain.

New Historicism, then, aims not only to return literature its historical context but to abolish the notions of text and context and see all texts as co-texts, simultaneously representing and constructing the reality – or one of the realities – fashioned at a particular historical moment. And a premise of such investigation is that the shape of this reality will support the powerful, denigrate the victims and either silence opposition or appropriate it as part of the dominant ideology. But how does a New Historicist in practice approach literary texts with these ideas in mind? Typically, the subject chosen will not be a specific book or author but a much wider semantic field: concepts of race and racial attributes, madness, the self, acquisition. In the earlier essays in New Historicism, this subject was then approached by taking an unfamiliar, non-literary document, studying it in close detail – indeed drawing on the techniques of close reading developed by the New Critics – and juxtaposing it with a text from the canon. For example, Stephen Greenblatt in *Renaissance Self-Fashioning* introduces his discussion of Marlowe's plays with a discussion of a short passage from the journal of John Sarracoll, describing a village in Sierra Leone, at first inspected and then set on fire by the Englishmen. This then leads to a discussion of Renaissance attitudes to time and space, taking Sarracoll and Marlowe as comparable kinds of evidence (though in fact spending more time on Marlowe, in a discussion which is in many ways a piece of traditional close verbal analysis). The choice of Sarracoll's texts also illustrates New Historicism's predilection for texts describing very specific events in great detail: there is the sensation of moving from the close-up to the long shot of wider assertions. Similarly, Louis Montrose ('A Midsummer Night's Dream and 'Shaping Fantasies': Figurations of Gender and Power in Elizabethan Culture', *Representations* 1:2 (1983)) and Bruce R. Smith (*Homosexual Desire in Shakespeare's England: A Cultural Poetics*, 1991) analyse a dream recorded by Simon Forman in 1597, moving from this very particular incident to much wider considerations of the image of royalty and perceptions of sexual desire in Elizabethan culture.

As with any other school of criticism, a summary account such as this one runs the risk of making it seem arid and formulaic. This is especially a risk with New Historicism which, as we noted above, is more a group of interests one can bring to the exercise of reading and thinking than a set of prescriptive theoretical formulae to be rigidly applied. One refreshing aspect of New Historicism is its readability and approachability: in the minimal reference to previous critics, the startling juxtapositions of material and appetite for ideas, there is the air of the performance of the star lecturer about much of the work. Communication to the reader really does seem to matter. Summaries of New Historicism such as this one tend to concentrate on the early, pioneering essays, but I would recommend reading a later work such as Greenblatt's *Hamlet in Purgatory* (Princeton University Press, 2001). Here the speeches of the ghost in *Hamlet* are circled around as Greenblatt considers diverse texts and artefacts, from a record of a ghostly visitation to illustrations and prayers. No theoretical scheme is being grimly adhered to, and there is no sense of working towards a predictable conclusion; what emerges instead is a vivid sense of visiting a foreign and fascinating world and imbibing something of its cultural atmosphere. This book compares interestingly to the study of purgatory by Jacques Le Goff, a founding father of the French 'Annales' school of history (*The Birth of Purgatory*, 1981; English translation 1984). The Annales project has much in common with New Historicism, notably an interest in studying the culture and consciousness of a period through integrating different kinds of materials and methods. To both, the commitment to clear writing and a passion for the subject are manifestly clear, without compromising a sharp analytical edge. These qualities have brought New Historicist approaches into the wider field. A recent popular book like James Shapiro's *1599* (2005) looks contextually at Shakespeare in a single year, in the process describing vividly such topics as theatre-building (it was the year of the construction of the Globe), court emblems and the complex composition history of *Hamlet*. Shapiro's writing is clear and often has a colloquial flavour. Programme notes in theatres now typically combine documents on economic, social and literary topics in a kind of New Historicist collage. The importance of the contextual, or rather co-textual, in approaching literature no longer needs to be argued for. Through such works as those mentioned here (to which one might add Greenblatt's own recent biography of Shakespeare, *Will in the World* (2004)), New Historicism has moved from the ivory tower of academic theory to the mainstream of literary criticism and flourishes in the popular book market, an area from which literary criticism – in comparison with history, science or biography – is often notably absent. For the student who wishes to try the New Historicist project of examining 'non-literary' texts alongside the classics, materials are to hand in anthologies like Kate Aughterson's *The English Renaissance: An Anthology* (1991).

See also *Contexts*: English Reformation, Humanism, Race, Self, Sex and Sexuality, Travel, Women; *Texts*: History, Non-fictional Prose, Pastoral; *Criticism*: Cultural Materialism

Further Reading

Catherine Gallagher and Stephen Greenblatt, *Practicing New Historicism*, 2nd edn (University of Chicago Press: 2001).

Paul Hamilton, *Historicism*, New Critical Idiom (London: Routledge: 2003).

Jean Howard, 'The New Historicism and Renaissance Studies', *English Literary Renaissance*. 16 (1986), 24–30.

Duncan Salkeld, 'New Historicism' in *The Cambridge History of Literary Criticism*, vol ix, *Twentieth-Century Historical, Philosophical and Psychological Perspectives*, ed. Christa Knellwolf and Christopher Norris (Cambridge: CUP, 2001), 59–70.

Textualism

'Textualism', as used in this entry, refers not to any particular school of theory or criticism, but to the general tendency, shown by diverse students of literature, to pay close attention to the materials and process of Renaissance literary production. The close comparison of manuscripts and early printed texts, once regarded as the specialised province of the editor, is now regarded as central to critical studies of the literature of the period. Close examinations of manuscripts (palaeography) and printed books (bibliography) have similarly informed the enterprise of critical interpretation.

There are several reasons for this focus on the material text. One is the revolution in information and communication of our own age: working and living with digital technology and the Internet makes us more attuned to the implications of the printing phenomenon for how texts were conceived and received. At the same time, modern technology has also made Renaissance books in their earliest forms more available to students than ever before, in the form of facsimiles and electronic reproductions. Study of these has revitalised debate about what we mean by concepts such as 'author' and 'text', a discussion which coincides with the preoccupations of literary theory. In turn, technology, critical and theoretical work have fed back into the work of editing itself, leading to searching reconsiderations of the ways in which Renaissance texts can, and should, be presented to a contemporary reader.

An important new chapter in the editing of Renaissance texts was opened with the movement known as New Bibliography, in the early twentieth century. Scholars such as E. K. Chambers, W. W. Greg and A. W. Pollard sought to place editing, principally of the works of Shakespeare, on a methodical scientific footing. Their procedure started with careful investigation of the material printed evidence. By detailed examination of the quarto and folio editions of Shakespeare, the New Bibliographers sought to establish the best possible texts of the plays, which represented as closely as possible the original creations of the author. In *Shakespeare Folios and Quartos: A Study in the Bibliography of Shakespeare's Plays, 1594–1685* (London: Methuen,1909), Pollard divided the quartos into good and bad: the 'good' quartos, which seemed to correspond closely to the author's original, were deemed 'of good average morals and utility', while 'any desirable amount of scorn and contempt' may be heaped on the bad ones, in which the author's text had been excised and corrupted by various interventions, from unreliable actors to sloppy typesetters. W. W. Greg's 1910 edition of *The Merry Wives of Windsor* added the important hypothesis of 'memorial reconstruction': Greg argued that the First Quarto of this play was based on the actor who played the Host reciting it from memory to the printer (though the full process as imagined by Greg was considerably more complex than this outline suggests). Central to the work of the New Bibliographers was the First Folio (F1), the edition of Shakespeare's works compiled by his fellow actors Heminge and Condell in 1623: this was generally regarded as the most complete and reliable text, though in some cases the good quartos provided a better reading.

The New Bibliography has had a huge impact on English studies, and its influence continues today. Because of the work of Greg and Pollard and others, later scholars and critics have operated with a much clearer idea of the complex and problematic processes by which a text, having germinated in the mind of an author, eventually takes the form of a printed book. The process of arriving at a reading through study of the various early versions remains standard. It is still common practice for editors of Shakespeare plays to present 'conflated' editions, for example taking F1 (the 1623 Folio) as a base text but correcting or adding to it from earlier quartos to provide a composite text of the play, one which as far as we know was never read or performed in the Renaissance itself. Editors also examine the work of earlier editors, for example to find plausible accounts of lines which seem to have been mangled into unintelligibility by compositors' errors in the earliest printed versions. These editorial processes are made clear in the apparatus usually given today on each page of academic editions, together with text and commentary. To a modern reader of a student edition, the editor is in fact a very visible presence. Key New Bibliographical notions such as memorial reconstruction, 'good' and 'bad' quartos and an author's posited 'foul papers' are still frequently employed. Thus the procedures and assumptions of the New Bibliography underlie much of the editorial work of the century that followed and have helped to determine the texts, particularly those of Shakespeare, with which we are familiar today.

At the same time, the work of the New Bibliographers has also been subjected to thorough critical reassessment. One issue has been the dominance in their work of the most celebrated writer of the period. As elsewhere in Renaissance studies, the monumental status of Shakespeare has arguably disfigured our view of the rest of Renaissance literature, not only in terms of the themes and ideas we concentrate on but also with regard to our notion of the texts themselves. As we have seen, New Bibliographers based their work on the evidence of F1. But the F1 is in fact quite untypical of the way in which plays and other Renaissance texts were presented in the seventeenth century; indeed, the only similar volume is the Folio of Jonson's *Works* of 1616. So, even leaving aside the many problems surrounding the editing of Shakespeare, it may be doubted whether the methods used for that author are the right ones to use for editions of other writings. Different kinds of text require particular editing skills. Women's writings, cony-catching pamphlets, travel accounts, autobiographies, letters and many other kinds of writing pose distinct challenges. There may not be one method which suits them all. Equally the same text can emerge with radical differences if it is edited according to different criteria: an edition of Milton which preserves his original spelling and punctuation is substantially different from one which modernises them. Today, we find scholars specialising in the edition of different kinds of text and often debating with each other the dangers and opportunities associated with each proposed editorial method. The particular procedures of New Bibliography have been followed by a wider range of editorial techniques, which aim to be sensitive to the nature of different kinds of text. As a result of this work, textual issues have come into the centre of critical discussion, and the modern student has access to a far greater range of original material, often in different editions, than ever before.

Textualism, as a topic in criticism, has not only emphasised the various kinds of text but also raised questions about the fundamental concepts of 'author' and 'text'. As we have seen, the New Bibliographers studied minutely the printed versions of Shakespeare, but they did this in order to establish a text hidden behind what they famously called the 'veil of print'. This phrase suggests a pure, idealised authorial text sullied by its material incarnations. In this conception of a literary text, the work is born as an authorial creation, and error and corruption creep in during the book-production process. Undoubtedly there are such errors: names are muddled in different scenes, compositors miss out words or even whole lines and so on. The editor's job then becomes something like a restorer of paintings: to locate and correct these errors and thus rescue the authorial version underneath. This process is clearly based on the assumption that there *is* an original, authorial text. The whole procedure is designed to bring the reader as close as possible to the original text of the author. But who is the author? Can we assume that a play originates in a single mind? As Jeffrey Masten has pointed out, dramatic texts are essentially collaborative: in the papers of the theatre manager Henslowe, two-thirds of the plays mentioned specify the collaboration of more than one author. Further changes take place from one performance to the next, involving, for example, extempore clowning, actors' interpolations, topical references added and removed and other kinds of revision. A writer like Thomas Middleton (1580–1627) is known to have worked in numerous kinds of collaboration, making the attribution of a work to him as the single author-creator highly contentious. The situation is similar to that of a medieval or Renaissance artist's workshop, where various people could be involved in the creation of a work, subsequently attributed to the master alone; just as an assistant may have painted the sky, so another hand could have added the song in a play.

Even beyond the realm of drama – which may be regarded as a special case – we encounter similarly complex textual histories in other kinds of writing. A manuscript poem may be circulated, copied and changed as it is passed round: glosses and marginalia may later be incorporated into the main text, and different versions could be made for different occasions. Who is the 'author' of these variants? What is the 'correct' version? We are today familiar with the way that jokes, gossip and anecdotes are embellished and varied as they move around, with no one asking who the 'author' is. Similar processes can operate with the production and dissemination of literary texts. Scholars like Masten have argued that we are apt to work with a contemporary notion of the single author as creator and 'authority' for a particular text. Originality, uniqueness and individuality are important items of contemporary mental furniture, but they may mislead us when we look at the culture of the past: the author was not, after all, given intellectual ownership of his work until the Copyright Act of 1709. Before then, more social forms of creation, involving several agents, may have been regarded as the norm. In looking for a single, isolable and idealised 'author' of Renaissance texts we may overestimate the status of that figure and underestimate the oral, social and communal aspects of literary production in the period.

Just as 'the Author' may be a misleadingly simple term, so 'the text' is a dangerously neat word to denote a highly complex reality. Editors seek to arrive at 'the text' of a particular work – an enterprise which goes back long before the New Bibliography. When an edition is published, the work will be established, fixed, stabilised in a particular form. In the age of mass print, we are accustomed to this idea of a text as the final product of a particular process. We may be impressed by publishers' claims that an edition is authoritative or definitive, suggesting that it has been refined to its most authentic form. Yet the more we study Renaissance literature as it actually appeared at the time, the more this idea of a final, fixed and singular text is challenged. The Renaissance text, as has often been noted, is a 'liminal' entity: it exists within the world of both print and manuscript, the amateur writer and the professional author, the coterie audience and the wider audience empowered by print. It may originate as an oral and performative event before the court, theatre audience or congregation, but then take on a different manifestation as a script or print directed at the private reader. In this environment, a text may be regarded as something more malleable and 'fluid', mutating from one occasion to the next, with each fresh stage in its history being part of the creation rather than a 'corruption' of the original version: dance forms, which constantly change in style and take on regional variations, or songs which are reinterpreted by jazz musicians, provide suggestive analogies. Looked at in this light, the terminology of the New Bibliography – good and bad texts, fair and foul papers, and the author's supposedly recoverable first intentions – seems unhelpfully value-laden and judgemental.

This fluidity and branching afterlife of a literary artefact may lead a 'work' to exist in a number of texts, and the differences between these may lead us to regard each text as a distinctive work in its own right. Perhaps the different texts had different functions. An interesting example of research in this area is Lukas Erne's work on Shakespeare. His discussion of *Hamlet* focuses on the well-known differences between the first Quarto (Q1) and the second Quarto and Folio (Q2, F1). Q1 is significantly shorter than Q2 and F and presents scenes in a different sequence. Erne argues that the best explanation for this is that Q1 constitutes a shorter, faster version for the stage, while the longer and differently structured texts are better appreciated as texts to be read. We should be especially aware of the criteria we bring to bear on evaluating the different versions: in preferring rounded characters with internal struggles, we may be influenced by the kind of work which a print culture produces. Scholars such as Walter Ong have similarly argued that the complex personality with an inner life and subtle motivations is a creation suited to the private world of the reader: the interior life of the 'rounded' character speaks to the interiority and reflective consciousness of the reader in a study. Conversely, theatrical representations – and the texts that represent them – are in the tradition of oral narratives and present simpler characters, drawing on types familiar in popular culture. It is interesting that functional speech prefixes in the shorter Quartos (such as 'Servant') often become named characters in the longer texts. Erne's conclusion is that Shakespeare was aware of the new audience for print, and the emerging reading habits that went with it, and that in the texts of *Hamlet* we see him writing for both performance and print, stage and page, producing distinctive *Hamlet*s in the process: to find one better than the other, or to conflate the two in the effort to provide a unique text for a modern edition, is to ignore the actual culture, and its diverse kinds of text and reader, in which Renaissance writings had their life.

So far we have approached Renaissance texts as essentially verbal artefacts. We have noted that the diverse range of texts probably requires similarly diverse editorial approaches and that the nature of the material in its earliest state challenges assumptions about the author and the text – assumptions that may be reinforced by the editions we use. However, the text as verbal icon cannot be separated from the material form it takes, whether that is a manuscript, a carved epitaph, a printed book or a digitised text on screen. The medium in which a work is presented is itself part of the meaning of that work: a text is not a transcendent entity but a physical thing, or, as Marshall McLuhan put it, 'the medium is the message'. We may, for example, be more liable to believe a report in one publication rather than another. In our own field of literature, a poem in an academic book, chosen by an eminent authority and accompanied by erudite glosses, may speak to us in a different way from the same poem printed in a handsome coffee-table book. The verbal artefact is the same, but everything else from typography to layout and surrounding material to the weight, commercial value and even smell of the book are all different. They are also inseparable in our consciousness from the poem. These physical features are thus part of the work and integral to the relation we form with the text. The 'veil of print', we might say, *is* the text, not some tantalising screen between it and us. Thus another aspect of textualism in contemporary criticism aims precisely to study the 'veil'. Some criticism follows paleography and bibliography in studying the book as object, and considering the resonances of a text's objective features. It has been pointed out, for example, that Renaissance paper was made from rags, gathered by rag-pickers all over Europe and mashed into paper in mills: an early printed book is thus located in, and takes ideological significance from, the economic circumstances of its production. Since England had to import a lot of its paper, this drove up the price of bookmaking and gave books the status of luxury, foreign bodies. They were bodily in another sense, too, being inked with presses whose leather casings were soaked in urine: the finest humanist prose was ineluctably 'earthed' in the most basic excremental processes. Beyond these observations on books as a whole, scholars and critics have also studied the detailed features of particular volumes, among them colophons, title pages, owners' signatures and marginalia, binding, evidence of sales, choice of typeface and organisation of contents. Such physical features are all richly suggestive of the functions and meanings that books had in the culture of their time.

One particular task of criticism informed by textual concerns is to study the work of editing itself. Editors are not neutral servants of the reader, but inevitably work within an ideological mould: selection and arrangement of texts, principles of anthologies, choices of one reading over another will all at some level be a function of the particular value system of an editor, and also of the publisher and institution which oversees that editorial work. Even a seemingly innocuous title like 'Women's Writing' carries with it the implication that this is an unusual phenomenon (there are no anthologies of 'Men's writing', because men are not 'other'). As feminist critics have pointed out, this kind of anthologising, while it is enormously valuably in rescuing texts from oblivion and rectifying our vision of the culture of the period, also has attendant risks. Simply seeing the two texts in the same volume might lead us to interpret a village midwife's recommendations as having some kind of shared agenda with a noblewoman's translation of French lyrics, an assumption which might have surprised the authors themselves. Not only literary texts but their process of transmission, right up until the latest edition today, is inescapably ideological, as are our own judgements and interpretations.

Ideology is itself in part at least a function of economics. From today's perspective, the New Bibliography's assumption of a 'pure', individually authored and definable text might be seen as an expression of the high value placed by a modern capitalist economy on private property, including intellectual property. The editor returns the object (the play) to its rightful 'owner' and thus provides a better value good for the consumer/reader. The point is a difficult one to judge because this same economy, albeit at a later stage, is also the matrix for later editorial work. Whatever doubts we may have about the notion of single authorship or the fixity of text, these concepts are an integral part of contemporary law and market forces. Intellectual property is customarily patented and copyrighted to individuals and their estates, or to companies having the legal status of individuals. The book market also demands distinctive, 'fixed' books: publishers will promote their 'definitive' versions to compete (though it is a good commercial gambit always to leave room for works to be reissued in slightly revised form to maximise sales potential, ensuring a kind of 'fluidity' about at least some titles). Authorship also matters to many on a professional and financial level: to put it crudely, professional academics arguing for collaborative creation in the Renaissance might be less willing to forego the credit for their own research papers. Hence debates about the nature of author and text are inevitably going to be conditioned by, and in some senses in tension with, the current frameworks of intellectual labour. And however much theoretical reflection may make us doubt the existence of the pure, transcendent text, which the New Bibliographers sought, that holy grail may remain on the horizon of our thoughts: the idea of a better text, or a better relation with the texts that exist, may continue to inspire the editorial enterprise because the notion of some kind of progress is psychologically impossible to dispense with.

One of the attractions of Textualism in criticism is the provocative nature of the enterprise, with regard to both material analysis and larger theoretical debates. Critics and scholars working in the field are far from unanimous. Assertions always need to be tested against specific examples: Is authorship such a new concept? Even before the age of print, Chaucer was concerned at the fate of his original text at the hands of copyists – hardly the picture of cheerfully selfless collaboration. The artist as genius and hero is evidently a concept familiar to the Renaissance itself, as we see in works like Vasari's *Lives of the Artists* or contemporary lives of figures such as Sidney and Donne. The committees who established the Authorized Version were clearly accustomed to establishing a best possible text, where every word and punctuation mark mattered. Endless malleability might apply better to some works and genres than others. Discussion is ongoing, as it is on the best way forward for editors: some enthuse about the possibilities of electronic texts, which might best reproduce the multiplicity and interactivity of Renaissance writing; others see them as expensive (particularly because of a rapid obsolescence cycle), limiting in terms of texts and access, and, insofar as they are outsourced to cheap labour, an instance of enlightenment underwritten by exploitation – like Renaissance paper and the rag-pickers, perhaps. Textual criticism spans a wide range of activities, from technical skills of edition and bibliography to discussion of some fundamental elements of Renaissance and contemporary culture. Some of the first questions we might ask of a Renaissance text we have in our hands are who selected and published it, who besides the author made it the way it is, and how, and why.

See also *Contexts*: Book Trade, Manuscripts, Printing; *Texts*: The Bible; *Criticism*: Cultural Materialism

Further Reading

Lukas Erne, *Shakespeare the Dramatist* (Cambridge: CUP, 2003).

Jeffrey Masten, *Textual Intercourse: Collaboration, Authorship, and Sexualities in Renaissance Drama* (Cambridge: CUP, 1997).

Andrew Murphy, ed., *The Renaissance Text: Theory, Editing, Textuality* (Manchester: Manchester University Press, 2000).

Ramona Wray, 'Textuality': in *Reconceiving the Renaissance*, ed. Ewan Fernie and others (Oxford: OUP, 2005), 13–84.

On the texts of Hamlet, see:

James Shapiro, *1599: A Year in the Life of William Shakespeare* (London: Faber, 2005), ch. 15 'Second Thoughts', 339–358 and Colin Burrow 'Conflationism', *London Review of Books.* 29:12, 21 June 2007, 16–18.

Chronology

Historical and Political Events	Literary and Cultural Events
1455–85 Wars of the Roses between the Houses of York and Lancaster	
1469 Union of Spanish kingdoms of Castile and Aragon	
1476	Caxton: printing press in Westminster
1485 Henry Tudor defeats Richard III at Battle of Bosworth, and is crowned Henry VII. Tudor dynasty established.	Malory, *Morte dArthure*
1492–1504 Voyages of Columbus	
1492 Moors expelled from Spain.	
1499 Perkin Warbeck executed	
1503 Henry VII's daughter Margaret Tudor marries James IV of Scotland	
1509 Henry VII dies, succeeded by Henry VIII. Henry VIII marries Catherine of Aragon	Colet founds St Paul's School

Historical and Political Events	Literary and Cultural Events
1513 Scots invaded England, heavily defeated at Battle of Flodden.	Machiavelli, *Il Principe* [*The Prince*] More, *History of King Richard III* (published 1543)
1516	More, *Utopia* Erasmus, edition of Greek New Testament
1517 Luther's Wittenberg theses	
1519	Erasmus, *Moriae encomium* [*Praise of Folly*]
1520 Henry VIII and Francis I of France meet at Field of Cloth of Gold.	
1526	Tyndale's translation of New Testament
1527 Sack of Rome by Imperialist troops	
1528	Castiglione, *Il Cortegiano* [*The Courtier*]
1529 'Reformation Parliament' called	
1530 Cardinal Wolsey arrested	Tyndale, translation of Old Testament (first five books)
1531	Sir Thomas Elyot, *Boke Named the Governour*
1533–1535 Acts of Succession and Supremacy	
1534 Henry VIII Supreme Governor of Church in England	

Historical and Political Events	Literary and Cultural Events
1535 More executed	
1536 Pilgrimage of Grace Dissolution of monasteries Anne Boleyn executed Tyndale strangled and burned	Calvin, *Christianae Religionis Institutio* (first ed.) [*Institutes of the Christian Religion*]
1537	Miles Coverdale's *Bible* published Hans Holbein active in English court
1540 Thomas Cromwell executed Jesuit Order founded	Sir David Lyndsay, *Ane Satyre of the Thrie Estaits* acted (pub. 1602)
1542 Pope Paul III establishes Inquisition in Rome	
1543 Index of Prohibited Books	Nicolaus Copernicus, *De Revolutionibus Orbium Coelestium*: Heliocentric theory advanced
1545 Council of Trent opens	Roger Ascham, *Toxophilus*
1547 Henry VIII dies, succeeded by Edward VI. Surrey executed	
1548	Loyola, *Spiritual Exercises* John Bale, *Kynge Johan* acted: first historical drama in Eng Lit
1549 Fall of Protector Somerset	First Prayer Book of Edward VI
1550	Udall, *Ralph Roister Doister* Vasari, *Lives of the Artists*
1553 Edward VI dies. Lady Jane Grey 'Queen for nine days' Mary I proclaimed Queen.	Thomas Wilson, *The Art of Rhetorique*

Historical and Political Events	Literary and Cultural Events
1554 Wyatt's rebellion (against Mary's proposed marriage to Philip II of Spain) Lady Jane Grey executed Roman Catholicism restored in England Tobacco first brought from America to Spain	
1557	Tottel's *Miscellany* Surrey's translation of Virgil's *Aeneid*, I and IV
1558 Mary dies, succeeded by Elizabeth I	John Knox, *The first blast of the trumpet against the monstrous regiment of women*
1559	*Mirror for Magistrates*
1560	William Whittingham publishes Geneva Bible
1561	Sir Thomas Hoby's translation of *The Courtier* Julius Caesar Scaliger, *Poetices libri septem*
1562	*Gorboduc* – earliest English tragedy in blank verse
1563	Foxe, *Acts and Monuments*
1564	Golding's translation of Ovid, *Metamorphoses*, I–IV (completed 1567)
1567 Mary Queen of Scots abdicates	
1568 Mary Queen of Scots flees to England	The Bishops' Bible
1570 Pope Pius VI excommunicates Elizabeth I	Barbour, *Brus*; Robert Henryson, *The Moral Fables of Aesop*

Historical and Political Events	Literary and Cultural Events
Potato introduced to Europe from Spanish America	Ascham, *The Scholemaster*
1571 Turks defeated by Don John of Austria in naval Battle of Lepanto	
1572 St Bartholemew's Day Massacre	Camoens, *Os Lusíados* [*The Lusiads*] Nicholas Hilliard, miniature of Elizabeth I
1574	Gate of Honour, Caius College, Cambridge: first entirely Classical building in England
1576	Jean Bodin, *Les six livres de la République* Burbage opens The Theatre
1577 Drake starts round-the-world voyage in Golden Hind	Ralph Holinshed and others, *Chronicles* Curtain Theatre opens
1578	John Lyly, *Euphues*, part one
1579	Stephen Gosson, *The Schoole of Abuse* (Puritan attack on theatre) Thomas Lodge, *A Defence of Poetry, Music and Stage Plays* (response to Gosson and Puritans) Edmund Spenser, *The Shepheards Calender*
1580 Drake completes round-the-world voyage	Michel de Montaigne, *Essais*, 2 vols
1586 Babington Plot (implicates Mary Queen of Scots in Catholic Conspiracy)	Sir Philip Sidney dies in Netherlands
1587 Mary Queen of Scots executed Sir Francis Drake attacks Cadiz, and 'singes the King of Spain's beard'	

Historical and Political Events	Literary and Cultural Events
Raleigh's second settlement in Roanoke, Virginia, under Governor John White	
1588 Defeat of Spanish Armada	Martin Marprelate tracts, supporting Presbyterianism
1589	Richard Hakluyt, *The Principall Navigations, Traffiques and Discoveries of the English Nation* (enlarged 1598, 1600)
1590	Marlowe, *Tamburlaine the Great* Sidney, The Countess of Pembroke's *Arcadia* Spenser, *The Faerie Queene*, books I-III
1591	Sidney, *Astrophil and Stella*
1592	Samuel Daniel, *Delia* (sonnets) *Arden of Feversham* (anon) Thomas Kyd, *The Spanish Tragedy* Thomas Nashe, *Pierce Penniless*
1593	Theatres close because of plague Shakespeare, *Venus and Adonis*
1594 Earl of Tyrone's Rebellion in Ireland	Marlowe, *Edward II* Nashe, *The Unfortunate Traveller* Theatres reopen (May)
1595	Sidney, *An Apologie for Poetry* Spenser, *Amoretti*; *Epithalamion*; *Colin Clouts Come Home Again*
1596	Spenser, *Faerie Queene*, books IV, V Blackfriars Theatre opens.
1597	John Dowland, *First Book of Songs* Sir Francis Bacon, *Essays: Civil and Moral* (10 essays, expanded to 58 in 1625 edition) Shakespeare: *Richard II*, *Romeo and Juliet*, *Richard III*

Historical and Political Events	Literary and Cultural Events
1598 Death of Philip II of Spain Edict of Nantes	George Chapman's translation of seven books of *Iliad* John Stowe, *A Survey of London* Marlowe, *Hero and Leander* Shakespeare: *Henry IV (Part One)*, *Love's Labour's Lost*
1599 Earl of Essex signs peace with Tyrone. Essex arrested on his return to England	Globe Theatre built (with timber from The Theatre) Shakespeare: *Julius Caesar* acted James VI of Scotland: *Basilikon Doron* (on divine right of kings)
1600 English East India Company founded	Ben Jonson, *Everyman Out of His Humour* Shakespeare: *As You Like It*, *Henry IV (Part Two)*, *Henry V*, *Merchant of Venice*, *A Midsummer Night's Dream*, *Much Ado About Nothing*
1601 Essex Revolt	Jonson, *Everyman in His Humour* Shakespeare, *Twelfth Night*
1602	Thomas Campion, *Observations on the Art of English Poesie* (anti-rhyme)
1603 Elizabeth I dies, succeeded by James I Tyrone's Rebellion put down by Lord Mountjoy	Florio's translation of Montaigne Shakespeare: 'bad' Quarto of *Hamlet*
1604 Hampton Court Conference: proposal for new Bible translation accepted	James I, *Counterblast to Tobacco* Marlowe, *The Tragicall History of Dr. Faustus* John Marston, *The Malcontent* Shakespeare: *Hamlet* 'good' Quarto; *Measure for Measure*; *Othello* acted
1605 Gunpowder Plot (5th November)	Sir Francis Bacon, *The Advancement of Learning*

Historical and Political Events	Literary and Cultural Events
	Cervantes, *Don Quixote*, Part 1 Jonson, *Sejanus His Fall* Shakespeare, *Macbeth*
1607 Jamestown, Virginia founded under Captain John Smith	Chapman, *Bussy d'Ambois* Thomas Heywood, *A Woman Killed with Kindness* Jonson, *Volpone* Shakespeare, *Timon of Athens* Tourneur, *The Revenger's Tragedy*
1608	Joseph Hall, *Characters of Virtues and Vices* Thomas Middleton, *A Mad World, My Masters* Shakespeare, *King Lear*; *Coriolanus*
1609	Shakespeare, *Troilus and Cressida*; *Pericles*
1610	John Donne, *Pseudo-Martyr* Jonson, *The Alchemist* Shakespeare, *Cymbeline*; *A Winter's Tale*; *The Tempest*
1611 First English settlement in India, near Madras	Donne, *An Anatomy of the World* Jonson, *Catiline* *The Authorized Version of the Holy Bible*
1612	John Webster, *The White Devil*
1613	Beaumont and Fletcher, *The Knight of the Burning Pestle* Shakespeare, *Henry VIII* Globe Theatre destroyed by fire
1614	Raleigh, *The History of the World* Ben Jonson, *Bartholemew Fayre* acted Sir Thomas Overbury, *Characters*
1615	Cervantes, *Don Quixote*, Part 2
1616	Ben Jonson, *Works of Benjamin Jonson* Architecture: Inigo Jones, Queen's

Historical and Political Events	Literary and Cultural Events
	House, Greenwich Shakespeare dies; Cervantes dies
1617 Raleigh leaves on expedition to Guiana	
1618 Raleigh executed. Defenestration of Prague: start of the Thirty Years War	
1619	Kepler, *Harmonia Mundi* William Harvey lectures on the circulation of the blood
1620 Pilgrim Fathers sail from Plymouth, England to Plymouth, Massachusetts	Bacon, *Instauratio Magna; novum organum*
1623	First Folio of works of Shakespeare Webster, *Duchess of Malfi*
1624	John Donne, *Devotions Upon Emergent Occasions*
1625 James I dies, succeeded by Charles I	Bacon, *Essays: Counsels Civil and Moral* (58 essays – 3rd and last edition) Thomas Middleton, *A Game at Chess*
1628 Charles I's favourite Duke of Buckingham assassinated	William Harvey publishes paper on circulation of the blood
1629 House of Commons passes resolutions against Laudian religious reforms, and tonnage and poundage. Charles I dissolves parliament, begins personal rule. Parliament does not meet again until 1640	Philip Massinger, *The Roman Actor* Lancelot Andrewes, *Sermons*
1630	Middleton, *A Chaste Maid in Cheapside*

Historical and Political Events	Literary and Cultural Events
1632	Shakespeare: second Folio
1633 Witch trials in Lancashire William Laud Archbishop of Canterbury Thomas Wentworth (later Earl of Strafford) appointed Deputy of Ireland	Abraham Cowley, *Poetical Blossoms* John Donne, *Poems* (posth.) John Ford, *'Tis Pity She's a Whore* George Herbert, *The Temple: or Sacred Poems* (posth.) Massinger, *A New Way to Pay Old Debts* Francis Quarles, *Divine Poems*
1634 Charles I issues first writs for Ship Money in coastal towns	Milton, *A Masque* [*Comus*] presented at Ludlow Castle
1635 Ship Money collected in entire realm	
1637	René Descartes, *Discours de la méthode*
1638	John Milton, *Lycidas*
1639	First Bishops' War in Scotland
1640 Long Parliament meets (lasts until 1653)	Thomas Carew, *Poems* Izaak Walton, *The Life of Donne*
1641 Strafford executed	The Episcopacy Controversy: Joseph Hall, *Humble Remonstrance . . .* 'Smectymnuus' [response to Hall] Milton, *Reformation Touching Church Discipline . . .*
1642 Outbreak of English Civil War Theatres in England closed by order Galileo dies, Isaac Newton born	Sir John Denham, *Cooper's Hill*

Historical and Political Events	Literary and Cultural Events
1643	Sir Thomas Browne, *Religio Medici* [unauthorized edition published 1642]
1645 Archbishop Laud executed Several Royalist defeats in Civil War	Milton, *Poems*
1646	Browne, *Pseudodoxia Epidemica* Richard Crashaw, *Steps to the Temple* Henry Vaughan, *Poems*
1647 Conflict between Army and Parliament	Beaumont and Fletcher, *Comedies and Tragedies* [34 unpublished plays]
1649 Execution of Charles I	John Gauden (?), *Eikon Basilike* – defence of monarchy Milton, *Eikonoklastes*
1650	Jeremy Taylor, *Rule and Exercises of Holy Living*
1653	Izaak Walton, *The Compleat Angler* (largely rewritten in second ed. 1655)
1655 Oliver Cromwell dissolves Parliament	James Shirley, *The Gentleman of Venice*; *The Polititian*
1656	Abramah Cowley, *Poems*
1658 Oliver Cromwell dies; Richard Cromwell succeeds as Lord Protector	Browne, *Hydriotaphia, or Urne-Buriall* William Rowley, *The Witch of Edmonton*
1659 Richard Cromwell resigns; Commonwealth re-established	Richard Lovelace (d.1657), *Lucasta* (Posthume Poems) Dryden, *Poem upon the Death of his late Highness Oliver Lord Protector*
1660 Restoration of Charles II	Dryden, *Astraea Redux*

Further Reading

Useful reference books

Annals of English Literature, 1475–1950, 2nd ed. (Oxford: Clarendon, 1961).

Michael Cox, *The Concise Oxford Chronology of English Literature*, 2nd revised ed. (Oxford: OUP, 2005).

Neville Williams, *Chronology of the Expanding World, 1492–1762* (London: Cresset Press, 1969).

Bibliography

Reference

Campbell, Gordon, *The Oxford Dictionary of the Renaissance* (Oxford: OUP, 2003).

Dobson, Michael and Stanley Wells, *The Oxford Companion to Shakespeare* (Oxford: OUP, 2001).

Donno, Elizabeth Story, ed., *The Renaissance Excluding Drama* , Great Writers Library (London: Macmillan, 1983).

Preminger, Alex and T. V. F. Brogan, eds, *The New Princeton Encyclopedia of Poetry and Poetics* (Princeton: Princeton UP, 1993).

Ruoff, James E., *Crowell's Handbook of Elizabethan and Stuart Literature* (New York: Thomas Y. Crowell, 1975).

Traversi, Derek A., ed., *Renaissance Drama*, Great Writers Library (London: Macmillan, 1980).

Wynne-Davies, Marion, ed., *The Renaissance: A Guide to English Renaissance Literature: 1500 to 1660* (London: Bloomsbury, 1994).

Anthologies

General

Abrams, M. H. and others, eds, *The Norton Anthology of English Literature*, 6th edn, vol. 1 (New York and London: W W Norton, 1993).

Ashton, John, ed., *Humour, Wit and Satire of the Seventeenth Century* (New York: Dover, 1968) [reprint of original 1883 edn].

Aughterson, Kate, ed., *The English Renaissance: An Anthology of Sources and Documents* (London: Routledge, 1998).

Baker, Herschel, ed., *The Later Renaissance in England: Nondramatic Verse and Prose, 1600–1660* (Boston: Houghton Mifflin, 1975).

Black, Joseph and others, eds, *The Broadview Anthology of English Literature, Volume 2: The Renaissance and the Early Seventeenth Century* (Peterborough, ON: Broadview Press, 2006).

Campbell, Gordon, ed., *Macmillan Anthologies of English Literature: The Renaissance, 1550–1660* (Basingstoke: Palgrave Macmillan, 1989).

Evans, G. Blakemore, ed., *Elizabethan-Jacobean Drama: A New Mermaid Background Book* (London: A & C Black, 1989).

Hodgson-Wright, Stephanie, ed., *Women's Writing of the Early Modern Period, 1588–1688: An Anthology* (Edinburgh: Edinburgh University Press, 2002).

Payne, Michael and John Hunter, eds, *Renaissance Literature: An Anthology* (Oxford: Blackwell, 2003).

Salzman, Paul, ed., *Early Modern Women's Writing: An Anthology, 1560–1700* (Oxford: OUP, 2000).

Poetry

Braden, Gordon, ed., *Sixteenth-Century Poetry: An Annotated Anthology* (Oxford: Blackwell, 2005).

Burrow, Colin and Christopher Ricks, eds, *Metaphysical Poetry* (London: Penguin, 2006).

Clarke, D., ed., *Renaissance Women Poets: Isabella Whitney, Mary Sidney and Aemilia Lanyer* (London: Penguin, 2001).

Clayton, Thomas, ed., *Cavalier Poets* (Oxford: OUP, 1978).

Cummings, Robert, ed., *Seventeenth-Century Poetry: An Annotated Anthology* (Oxford: Blackwell, 2000).

Evans, Maurice, ed., *Elizabethan Sonnets*, Everyman's Library (London: J M Dent, 1977).

Fowler, Alastair, ed., *The New Oxford Book of Seventeenth-Century Verse* (Oxford: OUP, 1991).

Fowler, Alastair, ed., *The Country House Poem: A Cabinet of Seventeenth-Century Estate Poems and Related Items* (Edinburgh: Edinburgh UP, 1994).

Gardner, Helen, ed., *The Metaphysical Poets* (Harmondsworth: Penguin, 1957).

Grierson, Herbert, ed., *Metaphysical Lyrics and Poems of the Seventeenth Century: Donne to Butler* (Oxford: OUP, 1921).

Jones, Emrys, ed., *The New Oxford Book of Sixteenth Century Verse* (Oxford: OUP, 1991).

Norbrook, David and H. R. Woudhuysen, eds, *The Penguin Book of Renaissance Verse*, 2nd edn (London: Penguin, 1993).

Wu, Duncan, ed., *Renaissance Poetry* (Oxford: Blackwell, 2002).

Prose

Nugent, Elizabeth, ed., *The Thought and Culture of the English Renaissance. An Anthology of Tudor Prose, 1481–1555* (Cambridge: CUP, 1956).

Salgādo, Gāmini, ed., *Cony-Catchers and Bawdy Baskets: An Anthology of Elizabethan Low Life* (Harmondsworth: Penguin, 1972).

Vickers, Brian, ed., *English Renaissance Literary Criticism* (Oxford: OUP, 1999).

Drama

Barker, Simon and Hilary Hinds, eds, *Routledge Anthology of Renaissance Drama* (London: Routledge, 2002).

Bevington, David and others, eds, *English Renaissance Drama: A Norton Anthology* (London: W W Norton, 2002).

Cerasano, Susan P. and Marion Wynne-Davies, eds, *Renaissance Drama by Women: Texts and Documents* (London: Routledge, 1995).

Kinney, Arthur, ed., *Renaissance Drama: An Anthology of Plays and Entertainments*, 2nd edn (Oxford: Blackwell, 2004).

Knowles, James, ed., *The Roaring Girl and Other City Comedies* (Oxford: OUP, 2001).

Lindley, David, ed., *Court Masques: Jacobean and Caroline Entertainments, 1605–1640* (Oxford: Clarendon, 1995).

Primary Texts (in modern editions)

Andrewes, Lancelot, *Selected Sermons and Lectures*, ed. Peter McCullough (Oxford: OUP, 2005).

Ascham, Roger, *English Works of Roger Ascham*, ed. William Aldis Wright (London: CUP, 1970).

Bacon, Francis, *The Advancement of Learning*, ed. Michael Kiernan (Oxford: Clarendon, 2000); *The New Organon*, ed. Lisa Jardine and Michael Silverthorne (Cambridge: CUP, 2000); *Essays* , ed. John Pitcher (Harmondsworth: Penguin, 1985).

Barnfield, Richard, *The Complete Poems*, ed. George Klawitter (Selinsgrove: Susquehanna University Press, 1990).

Bible: *The Geneva Bible: The Bible of the Protestant Reformation. 1560 Edition* (Hendrickson Publishers, Inc., 2007); *The Wycliffe New Testament 1388*, ed. W. R. Cooper (London: British Library, 2002).

Book of Common Prayer 1662 Version, intro. Diarmaid MacCulloch (London: Everyman's Library, 1999); *The First and Second Prayer Books of King Edward VI* (London: J M Dent, 1910).

Browne, Thomas, *Selected Writings*, ed. Sir Geoffrey Keynes (London: Faber, 1968) [includes *Religio Medici*].

Browne, William, *Britannia's Pastorals [1613]–1616*, Scolar Press Facsimile (Menston: Scolar Press, 1969).

Bruno, Giordano: in Singer, Dorothea Waley, *Giordano Bruno. His Life and Thought. With Annotated Translation of His Work On the Infinite Universe and Worlds* (New York: Henry Schuman, 1950).

Burton, Robert, *The Anatomy of Melancholy* (New York: New York Review of Books, 2001).

Calvin, Jean, *Insitutes of the Christian Religion. 1536 edition*, trans. Ford Lewis Battles (London: Collins, 1986).

Carew, Thomas: in *Cavalier Poets*, ed. Thomas Clayton (Oxford: OUP, 1978), 155–216.

Cary, Elizabeth, *The Tragedy of Mariam, the Fair Queen of Jewry*, ed. Barry Weller and Margaret W. Ferguson (Berkeley: University of California Press, 1994).

Castiglione, Baldassare, *The Book of the Courtier*, ed. Daniel Javitch, trans. Charles S Singleton (New York and London: W W Norton, 2002); trans. Thomas Hoby [Tudor translation] (London: Phoenix, 1994).

Chapman, George, *Plays and Poems* (London: Penguin, 1998).

____, *Bussy D'Ambois*, ed. N. S. Brooke, Revels Plays (Manchester: Manchester UP, 1999).

Cicero, Marcus Tullius, *On the Ideal Orator*, trans. James M. May and Jakob Wisse (Oxford: OUP, 2001).

Clarendon (Edward Hyde), *Selections from The History of the Rebellion and the Life by Himself*, ed. G. Huehns (Oxford: OUP, 1978).

Cleveland, John, *The Poems*, ed. Brian Morris and Eleanor Whittington (Oxford: Clarendon, 1967).

Copernicus, Nicolaus, *On the Revolutions of the Heavenly Spheres*, trans. Edward Rosen (London: Johns Hopkins UP, 1992).

Cowley, Abraham, *Selected Poems of Abraham Cowley, Edmund Waller and John Oldham*, ed. Julia Griffin (London: Penguin, 1998).

Crashaw, Richard, *The Poems*, ed. L. C. Martin (Oxford: Clarendon, 1927).

Daniel, Samuel, *Selected Poems of Campion, Daniel and Ralegh*, ed. R. Levao (London: Penguin, 2002).

Davies, John, *The Poems*, ed. Robert Krueger and Ruby Nemser (Oxford: Clarendon, 1975).

Dekker, Thomas, *Dramatic Works*, ed. F. T. Bowers (Cambridge: CUP, 1953–1961).

____, *Selected Prose Writings* (London: Arnold, 1967).

____, *Eastward Ho!* See Drama Anthologies above (Knowles).

Dekker, Thomas, William Rowley and John Ford, *The Witch of Edmonton*, ed. Peter Corbin and Douglas Sedge (Manchester: Manchester UP, 1999).

Donne, John, *Selected Prose*, ed. Helen Gardner and Timothy Healy (Oxford: Clarendon, 1967).

____, *Devotions upon Emergent Occasions*, ed. Anthony Raspa (Oxford: OUP, 1987).

____, *The Complete English Poems*, ed. C. A. Patrides, revised edn (London: Everyman's Library, 1991).

Douglas, Gavin. See Virgil.

Drayton, Michael, *Selected Poems*, ed. Vivien Thomas (Manchester: Carcanet New Press, 1977).

____, *Idea: Elizabethan Sonnets*, ed. Maurice Evans, Everyman's Library (London: J M Dent, 1977), 87–113.

Du Bartas, Guillaume, *The Divine Weeks and Works*, trans. Joshua Sylvester (1621), ed. Susan Snyder (Oxford: Clarendon, 1979).

Earle, John, *Microcosmography*, ed. Harold Osborne (London: University Tutorial Press, 1933).

Elizabeth I, *Collected Works*, ed. Leah S. Marcus and others (Chicago: University of Chicago Press, 2000).

Elyot, Thomas, *The Book Named the Governor*, ed. S. E. Lehmberg, 2nd edn (London: J M Dent, 1962).

____, *The Defence of Good Women*, in *The Feminist Controversy of the Renaissance: Facsimile Reproductions* (Delmar, NY: Scholars' Facsimiles and Reprints, 1980).

____, *Literary and Educational Writings 2: De Copia; De Rationae Studii*, ed. Craig R. Thompson, Collected Works of Erasmus, 24 (Toronto; London: University of Toronto Press, 1978). [English translations].

____, *Praise of Folly*, trans. Betty Radice, 2nd edn (London: Penguin, 1993).

Erasmus, Desiderius, *The Education of a Christian Prince*, ed. Lisa Jardine, trans. Neil M. Cheshire and Michael J. Heath, Cambridge Texts in the History of Political Thought (Cambridge: CUP, 1997).

Fletcher, John, *The Island Princess* (London: Nick Hern, 2002).

Galilei, Galileo: in Frova, Andrea and Mariapiera Marenzana, *Thus Spoke Galileo: The Great Scientist's Ideas and Their Relevance to the Present Day* (Oxford: OUP, 2006).

Gascoigne, George, 'A Primer of English Poetry' (1575): in Vickers, Brian, ed., *English Renaissance Literary Criticism* (Oxford: OUP, 1999), 162–171.

____, *Selected Poems, With 'Certayne Notes of Instruction Concerning the Making of Verse or Ryme in English'*, ed. Ronald Binns (London: Zoilus Press, 2000).

Golding, Arthur. See Ovid.

Greville, Fulke, *Poems and Dramas of Fulke Greville*, ed. Geoffrey Bullough, 2 vols (London: Oliver and Boyd, 1939).

____, *The Prose Works of Fulke Greville, Lord Brookes*, ed. John Gouws (Oxford: Clarendon, 1986) [includes *Life of Sidney*].

Grymeston, Elizabeth: Travitsky, Betty S., ed., *Mother's Advice Books*. The Early Modern Englishwoman. Printed Writings, 1500–1640, Series 1, Part 2; vol. 8 (Aldershot: Ashgate, 2001).

Hakluyt, Richard, *Voyages and Discoveries*, ed. Jack Beeching (Harmondsworth: Penguin, 1972).

Harington, John, 'An Apology for Ariosto: Poetry, Epic, Morality' (1591): in Vickers, Brian, ed., *English Renaissance Literary Criticism* (Oxford: OUP, 1999), 302–324.

Hariot, Thomas, *A Briefe and True Report of the New Found Land of Virginia* (Charlottesville: University of Virginia Press, 2007) [facsimile].

Herbert, George, *The Works*, ed. F. E. Hutchinson (Oxford: Clarendon, 1941).

____, *The Temple: Sacred Poems and Private Ejaculations 1633*, Scolar Press Facsimile (Menston: Scolar Press, 1968).

Herrick, Robert: in *Cavalier Poets*, ed. Thomas Clayton (Oxford: OUP, 1978), 3–154.

Hobbes, Thomas, *Leviathan*, ed. Marshall Missner (New York: Pearson Longman, 2008).

Holinshed, *Holinshed's Chronicle as Used in Shakespeare's Plays*, ed. A. Nicoll and J. Nicoll, Everyman's Library (London: J. M. Dent, 1927).

Homer, *The Iliad* and *The Odyssey*, trans. George Chapman (Ware, Hertfordshire: Wordsworth, 2000).

Hooker, Richard, *Books I–V* (Menston: Scolar Press, 1969) [facsimile].

____, *Of the Lawes of Ecclesiasticall Politie: Selections*, ed. A. S. McGrade and Brian Vickers (London: Sidgwick and Jackson, 1975).

Horace, *The Art of Poetry*: in *Classical Literary Criticism*, trans. T. S. Dorsch, ed. Penelope Murray, 2nd edn (London: Penguin, 2000).

Howard, Henry, Earl of Surrey, *Poems*, ed. Emrys Jones (Oxford: Clarendon, 1970).

Hutchinson, Lucy, *Memoirs of the Life of Colonel Hutchinson*, ed. N. H. Keeble, revised ed. (London: J M Dent, 1995).

James I, *Daemonologie* (Amsterdam: Theatrum Orbis Terrarum, 1969).

Jonson, Ben, *The Complete Masques*, ed. Stephen Orgel (New Haven; London: Yale UP, 1975).

____, *The Complete Poems*, ed. George Parfitt (London: Penguin, 1981).

____, *Sejanus: His Fall*, ed. Philip J Ayres (Manchester: Manchester UP, 1990).

____, *The Alchemist*, ed. Elizabeth Cook (London: A & C Black, 1991).

Langland, William, *The Vision of Piers Plowman*, ed. A. V. C. Schmidt (London: J. M. Dent, 1978).

Lanyer, Aemilia: in Clarke, Danielle, ed., *Renaissance Women Poets: Isabella Whitney, Mary Sidney and Aemilia Lanyer* (London: Penguin, 2001).

Lipsius, Justus, *On Constancy*, trans. Sir John Stradling [1594], ed. John Sellars (Bristol: Phoenix Press, 2006).

Longinus, *On the Sublime*, trans. D. A. Russell (Oxford: Clarendon, 1964).

Lovelace, Richard, *Poems*, ed. C. H. Wilkinson (Oxford: Clarendon, 1930).

Lucan, *The Civil War: Pharsalia or Bellum Civile*, trans. Nicholas Rowe (London: Phoenix, 1998).

Lyly, John, *Euphues, The Anatomy of Wit;* and *Euphues and His England*, ed. Leah Scragg (Manchester: MUP, 2003).

Machiavelli, Niccolò, *The Prince*, trans. Peter Bondanella (Oxford: OUP, 2005).

Machyn, Henry, *The Diary of Henry Machyn*, ed. J. G. Nichols (London: Camden Society, 1848).

Malory, Thomas, *Le Morte D'Arthur: The Winchester Manuscript*, ed. Helen Cooper (Oxford: OUP, 1998).

Marlowe, Christopher, *The Complete Poems and Translations*, ed. Stephen Orgel (Harmondsworth: Penguin, 1971).

____, *The Complete Plays*, ed. Frank Romany and Robert Lindsay (London: Penguin, 2003).

____, *Edward II*, ed. Martin Wiggins and Robert Lindsay, New Mermaids (London: A & C Black, 2003).

Marston, John, 'The Metamorphosis of Pygmalion's Image': in Braden, Gordon, ed., *Sixteenth-Century Poetry: An Annotated Anthology* (Oxford: Blackwell, 2005), 552.

The Martin Marprelate Tracts, ed. Joseph Black (Cambridge: CUP, 2008).

Martyr, Peter: in Anglerius, Petrus Martyr, *De Orbe novo decades*, trans. F. A. MacNutt (New York and London: G P Putnam, 1912).

Marvell, Andrew, *Poems*, ed. Nigel Smith (Harlow: Longman, 2006).

Middleton, Thomas and William Rowley, *The Changeling*, ed. Tony Bromham (Basingstoke: Palgrave Macmillan, 1986).

Milton, John, *Complete Shorter Poems*, ed. John Carey (London: Longman, 1968).

____, *Paradise Lost*, ed. Alastair Fowler (London: Longman, 1968).

____, *Political Writings*, ed. Martin Dzelzainis, trans. Claire Gruzelier (Cambridge: CUP, 1991) [Includes *The Tenure of Kings and Magistrates*].

Montaigne, Michel de, *The Essayes of Montaigne: John Florio's Translation*, ed. J. I. M. Stewart, 2 vols (London: Nonesuch Press, 1931).

____, *The Complete Essays*, trans. and ed. M. A. Screech (London: Penguin, 2003).

More, Thomas, *Complete Works*, 15 vols (London and New Haven: Yale UP, 1963– 1997).

____, *A Dialogue of Comfort Against Tribulation*, ed. Frank Manley (New Haven and London: Yale UP, 1977).

____, *The History of King Richard III*, vol. 3, ed. Richard S. Sylvester; *Utopia*, ed. George M. Logan and Robert M. Adams, Cambridge Texts in the History of Political Thought (Cambridge: CUP, 1989).

Nashe, Thomas, *The Unfortunate Traveller*, ed. H. F. B. Brett-Smith, Percy Reprints, 1 (Oxford: Blackwell, 1920).

Ovid, *Metamorphoses*, trans. George Sandys [Tudor trans., facsimile] (New York; London: Garland, 1976).

____, *Metamorphoses*, trans. Arthur Golding [Tudor trans.], ed. Madeleine Foray (London: Penguin, 2002).

____, *Amores*, trans. Tom Bishop (Manchester: Carcanet, 2003)

____, *Metamorphoses*, trans. David Raeburn (London: Penguin, 2004)

Petrarch, *Petrarch's Remedies for Fortune Fair and Foul*, ed. and trans. Conrad H. Rawski (Bloomington: Indiana University Press, 1991).

____, *Selections from the Canzoniere and Other Works*, trans. Mark Musa (Oxford: OUP, 1999).

Pico della Mirandola, Giovanni, *On the Dignity of Man*, trans. C. G. Wallis, 2nd edn (Indianapolis: Hackett Pub, 1998).

Plutarch: *Shakespeare's Plutarch*, trans. Sir Thomas North, ed. T. J. B. Spencer (Harmondsworth: Penguin, 1968).

Purchas, Samuel, *Purchas, His Pilgrimage, or, Relations of the World and the Religions Observed in All Ages* (Montana: Kessinger Publishing, 2003) [facsimile].

Puttenham, George, *The Arte of English Poesie*, ed. G. D. Willcock and A. Walker (Cambridge: CUP, 1970).

Quintilian, *The Orator's Education*, trans. D. A. Russell (Cambridge, MA: Harvard UP, 2001).

Rainolds, John, *Th'Overthrow of Stage-Playes* [1599] (New York: Garland Pub., 1974) [Includes texts by William Gager and Alberico Gentili].

Raleigh, Walter, *The Poems of Sir Walter Ralegh*, ed. Agnes M. C. Latham (London: Constable, 1929).

____, *History of the World*, ed. C. A. Patrides (London: Macmillan, 1971).

Roper, William and Nicholas Harpsfield, *Lives of Saint Thomas More*, ed. E. E. Reynolds, Everyman's Library (London: J M Dent, 1963).

Scot, Reginald, *The Discoverie of Witchcraft* (New York: Dover Publications, 1972).

Seneca, *Dialogues and Letters*, ed. C. D. N. Costa (London: Penguin, 1997).

Shakespeare, William, *The Complete Sonnets and Poems*, ed. Colin Burrow (Oxford: OUP, 2002).

Sidney, Philip, *An Apology for Poetry*, ed. Geoffrey Shepherd, 2nd edn (Manchester: Manchester UP, 1973).

Sidney, Philip, *The Countess of Pembroke's Arcadia*, ed. Maurice Evans (Harmondsworth: Penguin, 1977).

Sidney, Mary and Philip, *The Sidney Psalms*, ed. R. E. Pritchard (Manchester: Carcanet, 1992).

Sidney, Philip, *Defence of Poesie, Astrophil and Stella and Other Writings*, ed. Elizabeth Porges Watson (London: Everyman, 1999).

Smith, Thomas, *De Republica Anglorum 1583* (Menston: Scolar Press, 1970) [facsimile]

The South English Legendary, ed. Charlotte D'Evelyn and Anna J. Mill (Cambridge: D S Brewer, 2004).

Southwell, Robert, *Poems*, eds James H Mcdonald and Nacy Pollard Brown (Oxford: Clarendon: 1967).

Spenser, Edmund, *The Mutabilitie Cantos*, ed. S. P. Zitner (London: Thomas Nelson, 1968).

____, *The Faerie Queene*, ed. A. C. Hamilton (London: Longman, 1977).

____, *A View of the Present State of Ireland*, ed. W. L. Renwick (Oxford: Clarendon, 1970); *Epithalamion*: Payne, Michael and John Hunter, eds, *Renaissance Literature: An Anthology* (Oxford: Blackwell, 2003), 236-243.

____, *The Shorter Poems*, ed. Richard A. McCabe, 2nd edn (London: 2006).

Stow, John, *A Survey of London. Reprinted from the Text of 1603* (Oxford: Clarendon, 1971). [Facsimile]

____, *A Survey of London: Written in the Year 1598*, intro. Antonia Fraser (Stroud: Sutton Publishing, 2005).

Taylor, Jeremy, *Holy Living and Holy Dying*, ed. P. G. Stanwood, 2 vols (Oxford: Clarendon, 1989).

Theocritus, *The Idylls*, trans. Robert Wells (Manchester: Carcanet, 1988).

Tottel's Miscellany 1557 (Menston: Scolar Press, 1970) [facsimile].

Traherne, Thomas, *Selected Writings*, ed. Dick Davis (Manchester: Carcanet New Press, 1980).

Tyndale, William, *New Testament*, ed. David Daniell (New Haven: Yale UP, 1989).

____, trans., *Old Testament*, ed. David Daniell (New Haven: Yale UP, 1992).

____, *The Obedience of a Christian Man*, ed. David Daniell (London: Penguin, 2000).

Vaughan, Henry, *The Complete Poems*, ed. Alan Rudrum (Harmondsworth: Penguin, 1976).

Vergil, Polydore, *The Anglica Historia of Polydore Vergil, AD 1485–1537*, ed. and trans. Denys Hays (London: Royal Historical Society, 1950).

Virgil, *Virgil's Aeneid*, trans. Gavin Douglas, ed. David F. C. Coldwell, 4 vols, Scottish Text Society (Edinburgh and London: 1957–1960, 1964).

_____, *The Aeneid*, trans. David West (London: Penguin, 2003); *The Eclogues*, trans. Guy Lee (Harmondsworth: Penguin, 1984).

Walton, Izaak, *The Compleat Angler. The Lives of Donne, Wotton, Hooker, Herbert & Sanderson, with Love and Truth & Miscellaneous Writings*, ed. Geoffrey Keynes (London: Nonesuch Press, 1929).

Webster, John, *The Duchess of Malfi*, ed. Monica Kendal (Harlow: Longman, 2004).

Whately, William, *A Bride-Bush, or A Wedding Sermon*, The English Experience, 769 (Amsterdam: Theatrum Orbis Terrarum, 1975) [facsimile].

Wilson, Thomas, *Arte of Rhetorique*, ed. Thomas J. Derrick (New York: Garland Publishing, 1982).

Wyatt, Thomas, *The Complete Poems*, ed. R. A. Rebholz (New Haven and London: Yale UP, 1981).

Index

Printed and bound by CPI Group (UK) Ltd, Croydon, CR0 4YY